HISTORY OF CONGREGATIONALISM.

HISTORY OF CONGREGATIONALISM

FROM

ABOUT A. D. 250 TO THE PRESENT TIME

IN CONTINUATION OF THE ACCOUNT OF THE ORIGIN AND EARLIEST HISTORY OF THIS SYSTEM OF CHURCH POLITY CONTAINED IN "A VIEW OF CONGREGATIONALISM"

BY

GEORGE PUNCHARD

SECOND EDITION

REWRITTEN AND GREATLY ENLARGED

VOL. I.

NEW YORK
PUBLISHED BY HURD AND HOUGHTON
BOSTON: E. P. DUTTON AND COMPANY
1865

RIVERSIDE, CAMBRIDGE:
STEREOTYPED AND PRINTED BY
H. O. HOUGHTON AND COMPANY.

PREFACE TO THE SECOND EDITION.

THE first edition of this work was published in 1841, in a single volume, of four hundred pages. Living at that time remote from large libraries, and being much engrossed with the cares of an extensive parish, the author had neither the time nor the facilities for the thorough investigations which the interest and importance of the theme seemed to him to demand. But he did what he could, though, under the constraint of circumstances, not as he would.* The book, perhaps because it had no competitor, was kindly received, and the edition soon exhausted.

Pressing engagements have prevented the earlier accomplishment of the author's cherished purpose to rewrite, enlarge, and improve the work by the use of the more ample materials which for many years have been within his reach; yet, much of

* "Edidi, quæ potui, non ut volui, sed ut me temporis angustiæ coëgerunt." — *Cicero.*

his reading for nearly a quarter of a century has been, almost unconsciously, made tributary to this design.

The original plan of the work — which has been carefully adhered to in this enlarged edition — was, first, to indicate the process by which the polity of the apostolic churches was gradually overgrown, mostly through negligence, by pride, and worldliness, and finally quite crushed down by hierarchism and popery; secondly, to show, that, notwithstanding all this, there have been, in all ages of Christianity, earnest assertors of apostolic principles of church order and government; and, finally, to furnish a summary account of the progress of these principles, from the time of their successful vindication and full recognition, near the close of the sixteenth century, to the present day.

The two volumes now submitted to the public bring down the history to the beginning of the final and triumphant struggle of our English ancestors for religious freedom, about the year 1580, and include the most obscure and difficult portions of the undertaking. Thus far we have the history of Congregational principles and opinions only, not that of the denomination which subsequently was recognized, under the name of Independents, or Congregationalists.

In preparing these volumes the author has been compelled to grope his way alone through dark ages, picking up illustrative facts and hints wherever he could find them in ecclesiastical and profane history. And if, in passing over this hitherto untrodden field, important facts have escaped his notice, and mistakes have been made, it will be no way surprising. He can only say, that he has done his best; and cheerfully and trustingly commit his labors to the Christian denomination which as a child he was taught to respect and love, and which the careful studies of mature years have constrained him to regard as the most truly apostolic in its ecclesiastical polity.

Notwithstanding the suppression of a very considerable amount of material prepared for these volumes, at least one more volume will be required to complete the work according to the original plan.

BOSTON, *June*, 1865.

CONTENTS OF VOLUME I.

INTRODUCTION.

CHAPTER I.

THE NOVATIANS, A. D. 251.

CHAPTER II.

THE DONATISTS, A. D. 311–321.

CHAPTER III.

LUCIFÈRIANS AND ÆRIANS, A. D. 363.

CHAPTER IV.

THE PAULICIANS, A. D. 660

CHAPTER V.

THE WALDENSES AND ALBIGENSES, A. D. 1100.

CHAPTER VI.

GREAT BRITAIN FROM B. C. 55 TO A. D. 1350.

CHAPTER VII.

JOHN WICKLIFFE, THE MODERN DISCOVERER OF THE PRINCIPLES OF CONGREGATIONAL DISSENT, A. D. 1324.

CHAPTER VIII.

ECCLESIASTICAL OPINIONS OF WICKLIFFE.

CHAPTER IX.

THE LOLLARDS. — PERSECUTING EDICTS. — WRITERS AGAINST LOLLARDISM.

CHAPTER X.

THE PERSECUTION OF THE LOLLARDS.

CHAPTER XI.

THE FLAMES OF MARTYRDOM KINDLED.

CHAPTER XII.

TRIAL AND CONDEMNATION OF SIR JOHN OLDCASTLE, "THE GOOD LORD COBHAM."

CHAPTER XIII.

THE PRETENDED LOLLARD INSURRECTION, JANUARY, 1413–14.

CHAPTER XIV.

THE MARTYRDOM OF JOHN CLAYDON. — EXTENSIVE PERSECUTION OF THE LOLLARDS.

History of Congregationalism.

INTRODUCTION.

In the following pages it is proposed to trace the history of Congregationalism from about A. D. 250 to the present time. This history may, therefore, be considered as in some sense a continuation of "*A View of Congregationalism,*" a work already submitted to the consideration of the public, in which the principles, doctrines, practice, and early history, together with some of the supposed advantages of Congregationalism, are briefly detailed. Those who have read that work, need not be told what are the peculiarities of this system of church government: but, as this volume may fall into the hands of some persons who are not acquainted with our denominational peculiarities, it may be desirable to enumerate the leading principles and doctrines of Congregationalism.

The principles may be thus stated:—The Scriptures are an infallible guide to the essentials of church order and discipline.—A christian church is a voluntary association of persons professing repentance for sin and faith in Jesus Christ, united together by a solemn covenant for the worship of God and the celebration of religious ordinances. This company should ordinarily consist of no more than can conveniently and statedly meet together for religious purposes. — To this assembly of professing Christians, united by a covenant, and statedly meeting for church purposes, all executive ecclesiastical, or church power, is intrusted by Jesus Christ, the great Head of the Church.

The most important DOCTRINES of this system are these: — The Scriptures recognize but two orders of permanent church officers, viz. *Elders* (sometimes called pastors, overseers or bishops) and *Deacons*. — There should be an entire ecclesiastical equality among all christian elders, pastors, overseers or bishops. — Councils, consisting of pastors and lay delegates from the churches, have no juridical authority; being simply advisory, or suasory bodies. — Congregational churches, though independent of each other, so far as "their own procedure in worship as well as discipline" is concerned, yet should hold themselves ready to give account to sister churches, of their faith and religious practice.

Such are the prominent outlines of the denomination whose history we are now to consider. Such, we suppose, was the polity of the churches founded by Christ and his apostles, and for more than two hundred years substantially retained by all Christendom. The proof of this, furnished by the Scriptures, the Apostolic Fathers, and the testimony of learned men of different denominations, will be found in the work already alluded to — "*A View of Congregationalism*" — and need not be here recapitulated.

This simple and perfect system of church order, drawn in outline by Christ and filled up in detail by his inspired apostles, was gradually defaced and deformed by the pride and ambition of the clergy, aided by the inattention of the churches to their christian rights and privileges; and, in lieu of it, the complicated and corrupt system of Antichrist was introduced, with its pope and cardinals, its archbishops and bishops, its arch-presbyters and presbyters, its archdeacons and deacons — to say nothing of the sub-deacons, and acolythi, and ostiarii, and lectors, and exorcists, and copiatæ — all of whom were more or less essential to the perfection of that system of church order and worship which was foisted upon the world as alone true and infallible.*

* Some idea of the early corruption of the churches, and of the cumbersome and unscriptural machinery which was introduced into them, may be formed from the account which is given us of the church at Rome about the middle of the third century. Cornelius, bishop of Rome, writing to Fabius, bishop of Antioch, gives the following list of his clergy, etc. "*There are six and forty priests, seven deacons, seven sub-deacons, two and forty acholites* [a sort of waiter to the bishop], *two and fifty exorcists* [persons employed to expel evil spirits], *and readers* [i. e. of the Scriptures in public worship], *with porters.*" All these were subject to one bishop, and were regarded as necessary to a single church of the highest rank and dignity. — *Eusebius' Ecclesiastical History,* bk. VI., ch. 43; or *Milner's Church History,* century III., ch. 9.

Between the order of Christ's house and that of Antichrist's, there is a heaven-wide difference; indeed, there is no resemblance whatever. And the inquiry may very naturally arise: How could a change so entire be wrought in the polity of the churches? Some have urged this question as a capital objection to the belief that Congregationalism was, for substance, the apostolical system of church government. — If it was, say they, how could so great a change have been made? And why were not these encroachments protested against and resisted? *

I expect to show, in the body of this work, that these encroachments were protested against, and resisted even unto blood. In this Introduction, I propose to speak very briefly of the manner in which this change in the polity of the churches was introduced. I am disposed to undertake this, from the conviction that this survey will forcibly illustrate the importance of holding fast the great principles of apostolic church order, while it will prepare the reader for the historical details which may follow in the sequel.

It has already been intimated, that the pride and ambition of the clergy and the carelessness of the people were the main springs in the machinery which overturned the apostolic order and discipline of the christian churches.

This machinery began its operations at a very

* The celebrated Episcopal writer, Stillingfleet, takes this ground, in his *Unreasonableness of Separation.* — See Owen's answer to him.

early period; yea, even before the apostles were in their graves. Paul doubtless anticipated the changes which have since taken place in the order of the churches, when he said to the elders of the church of Ephesus: "I know this, that after my departing shall grievous wolves enter in among you, not sparing the flock." — Acts 20: 29. John experienced the opposition of one of these "wolves," in the person of *Diotrephes;* who so loved "to have the pre-eminence" over the church of which he was pastor, that he rejected even the apostolic authority of John himself. "I wrote unto the church" — or, I would have written, says John to the beloved Gaius — "but Diotrephes, who loveth to have the pre-eminence among them, receiveth us not." — 3 John, 9.* Clement, "the almost apostle," confirms the belief that the apostles anticipated the workings of ambition among the clergy, when he says: "Our apostles knew by our Lord Jesus Christ, that there should contentions arise upon the account of the ministry;" or, "about the name of the bishoprick," † or, Episcopacy itself. These contentions about the episcopal office — or, perhaps, about that presidency among the elders and over the churches, which was early introduced ‡ — was doubtless aggravated, if it was not originated, by the manifest disposition of the members

---

* See *McKnight, in loc.*

† *Clement's Epistle to the Corinthians*, § 44.

‡ See *Mosheim*, cent. I., part II., ch. 2, § 11.

of the churches to attach themselves to favorite preachers. Even in the days of the apostles this leaven began to work. At Corinth, for example, the church-members were strongly inclined to break into parties and arrange themselves under distinct leaders. One said, "I am of Paul; and another, I am of Apollos." Hence arose "envying, and strife, and divisions." — See 1 Cor. 1: 3–7.

Now, if this partisan spirit existed in the churches at so early a period, and if there was a disposition to make even the apostles themselves the heads of factions, we need not be surprised at the apprehensions of those holy men for the future peace and prosperity of the churches; or that, afterwards, this partisan spirit should be taken advantage of by ambitious men, to promote their own selfish ends, regardless of the interests or rights of the churches.

To counteract these workings of the "mystery of iniquity," the apostles did what they could: — by setting in order the churches; by ordaining elders in every church; by giving directions, as Clement tells us they did, "how, when they [the teachers set over them by the apostles] should die, other chosen and approved men should succeed in the ministry;" and also by warnings and admonitions, exhortations and counsels to the churches, to stand fast in the liberty wherewith Christ had made them free.

Notwithstanding all this, the churches began to vary somewhat from the apostolic order before the close of the second century; yea, within the lifetime of some who had been contemporary with the apostles themselves. In the third century very extensive corruptions spread among them. These prepared the way for the establishment of Constantine's hierarchy in the fourth century; which made way for the abounding errors and corruptions of the three succeeding centuries, and the enthronement of the "MAN of SIN" in the eighth century.

Even the very excellencies which distinguished some of the primitive church elders were an occasion of corruption to the churches. This mav seem a paradoxical assertion. It will nevertheless be found susceptible of demonstration, that the virtues of the christian pastors of the first and second centuries were the innocent occasion of corruption to the churches.

To be a christian pastor in those "perilous times" was to take the front rank in danger; for the officers of the churches were the first to be sought after when persecution arose "because of the word." To men who were ready to lay down their lives for the cause of Christ, the churches reasonably supposed that they might safely trust their dearest rights. They would naturally choose to be guided by the opinions, and governed by the wishes of such men. They would be slow to think or speak of their own ecclesiastical rights.* Feel-

* Ecclesiastical history furnishes abundant evidence of the existence of this veneration. For example, the church of Smyrna, in their relation of the martyrdom of their venerable pastor, Polycarp, tells us: "When the fuel was ready, Polycarp, laying aside all his upper garments, and undoing his girdle, tried also to pull off his clothes underneath, *which aforetime he was not wont to do; forasmuch,*

ing that all was safe in the hands of their devoted and venerated pastors, they would readily dismiss all anxious care; and it would be but reasonable to suppose, that ere long it would be forgotten that the churches had any claim to those rights and immunities which they had so long neglected to exercise.

The difficulty and danger of meeting together for the transaction of church business, during the seasons of persecution to which the churches were exposed for more than two hundred years after Christ, would be an additional reason for leaving the man-

---

as always, every one of the Christians that was about him contended who should soonest touch his flesh." — *Apostolical Fathers*, p. 245.

That this veneration for religious teachers was not unknown in the churches at a later period, is obvious from the account given us of the celebrated Martin, bishop of Tours, in the fourth century. "This personage was in the habit of frequenting the palace [of the emperor Maximus], where he was always entertained by the empress, who not only hung upon his lips for instruction, but, in imitation of the penitent in the Gospels, actually bathed his feet with her tears, and wiped them with her hair; and he who had never before sustained the touch of a woman, could not avoid her assiduities. She, unmindful of the state and dignity and splendors of her royal rank, lay prostrate at the feet of Martin; whence she could not be removed until she had obtained permission, first from her husband, and then by his aid from the bishop, to wait upon him at table as his servant, without the assistance of any menial. The blessed man could no longer resist her importunities; and the empress herself made the requisite preparations of couch, and table, and cookery (in temperate style), and water for the hands; and as he sat, stood aloof and motionless, in the manner proper to a slave; with due modesty and humility, mixing and presenting the wine. And when the meal was ended, reverently collected the crumbs, which she deemed of higher worth than the delicacies of a royal banquet." — *Sulpitius' Life of St. Martin*, quoted in "Natural History of Enthusiasm," pp. 189, 190. See also *Milner's Hist. of the Church*, cent. IV., ch. 14.

agement of their affairs more entirely in the hands of their officers than was originally contemplated.

The extra-scriptural authority thus given to their religious teachers, as an evidence of affectionate confidence, and to some extent made necessary by the peculiar circumstances of the churches, was at first, without doubt, faithfully exercised; but, in process of time — and not a very long time either — that authority which had been at first yielded by the churches as *a boon* or from the necessities of the times, was claimed by the clergy as *a right*, and most eagerly, by those most likely to abuse it.

The superiority which the city churches assumed over those in the country, was another step in the progress of deterioration.

The first churches were, for the most part, planted in cities and populous towns. These had elders or bishops placed over them, agreeably to the directions of the apostles. To their ministrations the scattered christians in the country around resorted. But, as these country christians became more numerous, they naturally desired the occasional, or the stated ministrations of the gospel among themselves. Instead, then, of being formed into a separate church, as they should have been, the city church supplied them with one of her elders. Consequently, both he and his rural flock regarded themselves as belonging to the mother church; and naturally paid that deference to her and her teachers which their dependant relation suggested. And, when the city churches came to have *presidents* — who were stated moderators among the elders, and general supervisors of the affairs of the churches — these, of course, exercised a supervision and control over the rural congregations and their elders, as parts of the city churches. In this way Diocesan Episcopacy was gradually and imperceptibly introduced.

This would have been the natural result, in any country, of causes like those just alluded to; but more especially in a country governed like that in which Christianity was first planted. In the Roman empire, the capital cities were looked to as the sources of political power; being the places where the governing officers of the provinces resided, and whence issued the decrees which controlled the provinces.

Another step in the path of declension was the introduction of synods, or general councils, with authority to make laws for the government of the churches.

The earliest appearance of these assemblies was about A. D. 170 or 173. At first, they were composed of the *representatives* of the independent churches, elected for the express purpose of deliberating in behalf, and in the place of those churches. It was not long, however, before these synods assumed the right to act in their own name. These bodies, of course, needed a moderator; and, as they generally assembled in the capital of the province,*

---

* Gibbon tells us: "It was soon established as a custom and as a law, that the bishops of the independent churches should meet in the capital of the province at the stated periods of spring and autumn." — *Decline and Fall,* vol. I., ch. 15.

who so suitable for a moderator as the president of the city church? an officer who began now to be called *bishop*, to distinguish him from his co-equals, the elders. This honor of moderatorship, at first conferred as an act of courtesy, would next be expected as a matter of propriety, and finally be claimed as an official right. In this way the office of Metropolitan, or Diocesan Bishop, was probably introduced into the churches. *

Another way in which these synods corrupted the original order of the churches was by taking to themselves a legislative and juridical authority. It was natural that the churches should pay great deference to the opinions and decisions of these bodies, composed as they usually were of the pastors of an entire province; and it was not at all strange that their decisions should gradually assume the form of *canons*, or rules for the government of the represented churches; for rulers — ecclesiastical as well as civil — will generally assume authority as fast as the people will yield it.

The doctrine that the ministers of the christian churches were the successors of the Jewish priesthood — which, if not *originated* in the second century, was then most successfully inculcated by the clergy — contributed materially to the great work of corrupting the churches.

If the clergy were the successors of the Jewish

---

* See *Mosheim*, cent. II., part II., ch. 2; *Waddington*, pp. 43—45, Harper's Edition; *Gibbon's Decline and Fall*, vol. I., ch. 15, p. 274, Harper's Ed. *Barrow's Works*, vol. VII., p. 302.

priests, why then, of course, a resemblance between the two was to be looked for. The bishops, or presiding elders, were made to answer to the high priests; the presbyters, or elders, to the priests; and the deacons, to the levites. "This idea," says Mosheim, "being once introduced and approved, drew after it other errors;" among which was this, that it gave an *official* elevation and sacredness to the clergy which Christ never authorized.

Another effect of this new doctrine was, to open the way for the exaction of the first fruits and tithes, for the support of the clergy. For, surely, if the christian clergy were successors to the Levitical priesthood, it was but reasonable that they should claim the tithes and first fruits, as means of support. Neither did they stop here; but "argued that, because the bishops, presbyters, and deacons, were respectively the high-priests, priests, and levites of a superior — a more heavenly and spiritual dispensation — they ought to possess more of the unrighteous mammon; that is, more earthly treasures and greater temporal power than did the ministers of the ancient church." "And, what is still more extraordinary, by such wretched reasoning the bulk of mankind were convinced." *

By these several steps the power of the clergy was greatly enhanced, at the expense of the rights and privileges of the churches; and yet, so gradu-

---

* See *Campbell's Lectures on Ecclesiastical History,* lec. x. Also, *Gibbon's Decline and Fall,* vol. I., ch. 15, p. 276.

ally, that those who were most affected by it, were least sensible of the process. There is much truth, doubtless, in what Dr. Owen says on this point: "This declension of the churches from their primitive order and institution is discoverable, rather by measuring the distance between what it left, and what it arrived unto, than by express instances of it. But yet, is it not altogether like unto that of a ship at sea, but rather like unto the way of a serpent on a rock, which leaves some slime in all its turnings and windings, whereby it may be traced?"*

Mr. Waddington very justly remarks: "It is true that the first operations of corruption are slow, and generally imperceptible, so that it is not easy to ascertain the precise moment of its commencement. But a candid inquirer cannot avoid perceiving, that, about the end of the second and the beginning of the third century, some changes had taken place in the ecclesiastical system, which indicated a departure from its primitive purity. * * In closely attending to its history, we observe that it becomes thenceforward the history of men rather than of things; the body of the church is not so much in view, but the acts of its ministers and teachers are continually before us." †

We have now arrived at what Waddington terms — "*The first crisis* in the internal history of the Church." It was in the third century that the

* *Inquiry into the Original, etc., of Evangelical Churches,* vol. xx., complete works, pref. pp. 20, 21.

† *History of the Church,* pp. 49, 50, Harper's Ed.

bishops assumed "the ensigns of temporal dignity —the splendid throne, the sumptuous garments, the parade of external pomp," and the tokens of a "contentious ambition." It was in this century that the addition of the "minor orders" of the ministry — such as sub-deacons, acolythi, readers, exorcists, etc. — gave proof of the growing pride and ambition, as well as indolence of the clergy.*

All these things indicate the corruption, as well as the extension of Christianity. Its influence was indeed perceptibly growing in the empire, though exposed to occasional checks from popular tumults and legalized persecutions. Beyond these limits it was also making progress. And this brings us to notice another, and most powerful cause of the corruption of the churches.

I refer to the admission to the churches of multitudes who were destitute of piety.

---

* *Mosheim*, Century III., part II., ch. 2; *Waddington*, ch. 3. Even *Milner*—who certainly cannot be accused of uncharitableness towards the orthodox and established church—gives a sombre picture of the state of religion near the close of the third century. "If," says he, "Christ's kingdom had been of this world; and, if its strength and beauty were to be measured by secular prosperity, we should here fix the era of its greatness. But, on the contrary, the era of its actual declension must be dated in the pacific part of Diocletian's reign. During this whole century the work of God, in purity and power, had been tending to decay; the connection with philosophers was one of the principal causes; outward peace and secular advantages completed the corruption; ecclesiastical discipline, which had been too strict, [?] was now relaxed exceedingly; bishops and people were in a state of malice; endless quarrels were fomented among contending parties; and ambition and covetousness had, in general, gained the ascendancy in the christian church." —*Milner's Hist. of Ch.* Century III., ch. 17.

When the *ministers* of the churches had become their *governors*, and the ambitious desire of enlarging their dominions and multiplying their subjects had induced these governors to dispense with the apostolic prerequisites for church membership, and to admit whole towns and cities, yea, and entire nations, within the pale of the christian church, upon a profession of their wish to become Christians and to receive baptism;* — when, I say, these things became matters of history, as they did in the third and fourth centuries, it is obvious that the churches could no longer be little, sacred republics. It was no longer possible to manage ecclesiastical matters after the manner of the first century. The world had now overspread the church; and the church, if governed at all, must be governed by worldly policy. And so it was, from about the close of the third century to the sixteenth.

The conversion of Constantine — whether real or nominal I leave others to decide † — was followed, as a matter of course, by a similar conversion of the court and the empire itself. But the cause of corruption, of which I am now speaking, developed itself most fully in connection with the nominal christianization of the barbarians who

* See Dr. Owen — "*The True Nature of a Gospel Church,*" etc. ch. 1, complete works, vol. XX., p. 363.

† The reader will find in *Gibbon* (vol. I., chs. 18 and 20) all that can be said, or, with any color of truth, insinuated, against Constantine, with much that is favorable to him. *Waddington* takes a very just and candid view of the emperor, part II., ch. 6.

conquered and overran the Roman Empire in the fifth and sixth centuries. For, contrary to the usual course of events, these conquerors embraced the religion of the conquered, and entered the church by thousands — yea, I might say, by *nations!* The same is substantially true of the admission of those who had received the christian religion from the hands of missionaries, previous to the overthrow of the empire. These semi-christianized hordes, coming into the church with little knowledge of the principles of the christian religion, and as little acquaintance with its spirit, would add to the numbers and outward glory of the church, but not to her real strength.

Most pertinent and instructive are the words of Dr. Owen upon this subject: "Herein, I say, did the guides of the church certainly miss their rule, and depart from it, in the days of Constantine the Emperor, and afterward under other christian emperors, when whole towns, cities, yea, and nations offered at once to join themselves unto it. Evident it is, that they were not wrought hereunto by the same power, nor induced unto it by the same motives, or led by the same means with those who formerly under persecutions were converted unto the faith of our Lord Jesus Christ. And this quickly manifested itself in the lives and conversations of many, yea, of the most of them. Hence those which were wise, quickly understood, that what the church had got in multitude and number, it had lost in the beauty and glory of its holy profession. Chrysostom in particular complains of it frequently, and in many places cries out, What have I to do with this multitude, a few serious believers are worth more than them all. However, the guides of the church thought meet to receive them with all their multitudes, into their communion, at least so far as to place them under the jurisdiction of such and such episcopal sees; for hereby their own power, authority, dignity, revenues, were enlarged and mightily increased. On this occasion, the ancient primitive way of admitting members into the church being relinquished, the consideration of their personal qualifications, and real conversion to God, omitted, such multitudes being received as could not partake in all acts and duties of communion with those particular churches whereunto they were disposed, and being the most of them unfit to be ruled by the power and influence of the commands of Christ on their minds and consciences, it was impossible but that a great alteration must ensue in the state, order, and rule of the churches, and a great deviation from their original institution."*

Men, converted to Christianity because it was the religion of the court; or because, pressed by their enemies, they hoped to find in Christ a more powerful god than any in whom they had before trusted; or because their pagan monarch, driven to desperation in the day of battle, had vowed to

* *Inquiry*, etc., preface, complete works, vol. xx. p. 21.

be a Christian if he might but conquer; or for some other reason equally remote from what the gospel requires; — such men, it is evident, could know little of the rights of churches; and would care as little.* They, however, within a few cen-

* "The conversion of the Burgundians, early in the fifth century, is thus related, with no improbability. Harassed by the continual incursions of the Huns, and incapable of self-defence, they resolved to place themselves under the protection of some god; and considering that the God of the Romans most powerfully befriended those who served him, they determined, on public deliberation, to believe in Jesus Christ. They therefore went to a city in Gaul and entreated the bishop to baptize them. Immediately after that ceremony they gained a battle against their enemies; and if (as is also asserted) they afterwards lived in peace and innocence, they reaped, in that respect, at least, the natural fruits of their conversion." — *Waddington*, ch. 9, p. 117, note.

"In the year 493 Clovis espoused Clotilda, niece of the king of the Burgundians, a Christian and a catholic. He tolerated the religion of his bride, and showed respect to its professors, especially to St. Remi, archbishop of Rheims; but he steadily refused to abandon his hereditary idols, on the importunity either of the prelate or queen. At length he found himself in a situation of danger; in the heat of an unsuccessful battle, while his Franks were flying before the Alemanni, Clovis is related to have raised his weeping eyes to heaven, and exclaimed, 'Jesus Christ! thou whom Clotilda asserts to be the son of the living God, I implore thy succor. If thou wilt give me the victory, I will believe in thee, and be baptized in thy name.' At that moment the king of the Alemanni was slain; his soldiers immediately fled, and abandoned the field to Clovis. The victor was not unmindful of the God of his adversity. On the conclusion of his expedition he caused himself to be publicly baptized; about three thousand of his soldiers attended him to the holy font with joy and acclamation, and the rest of his subjects followed without any hesitation the faith of their prince. The conversion of Clovis took place in 496; and though it had not the effect of amending the brutal character of the proselyte, it made a great addition to

turies, constituted a majority of those who bore the Christian name.

More than this: such masses of ignorance could not be governed by the rules of Christ's house. They had been accustomed to the arbitrary control of their pagan priests, and they desired no further liberty under their new masters; and if they had desired it, they were manifestly unqualified to use it.

Thus it was, that one error led into another. Thus were the lineaments of the churches of Christ effaced. I speak not of their religious faith. There was, doubtless, much of doctrinal truth retained, and some sincere piety, amidst all the increasing errors of the first seven centuries; yea, there were stars shining in the gathering darkness.—I speak of the polity of the churches. This, as drawn by the hand of Christ and his apostles, was gradually defaced and deformed; and the causes which wrought this deformity were, in part at least, such as have been named.

The wealth and temporal honors conferred upon the clergy—the gifts of princes and the homage of converted nations—had, also, an important agency in corrupting the churches.

---

the physical strength of Christianity." — *Waddington*, ch. 11, p. 116.

The temper of this convert, after his professed conversion, is well exhibited by the following anecdote, related in *Mosheim* (vol. I., p. 315, note 10, Harper's Ed.): "*Clovis* once hearing a pathetic discourse on the sufferings of *Christ*, exclaimed: Si ego ibidem cum Francis meis fuissem, injurias ejus vindicassem. *Had I been there with my Franks, I would have avenged his wrongs.*"

When Christianity became the adopted child of the Roman Emperor, it was natural that he should feel a pride in honoring and elevating her in the eyes of the world. And, as the clergy had now become The Church,* the most obvious way to accomplish the desired end was to heap wealth, honors and privileges upon them. This accordingly was done. "The whole body of the Catholic clergy," says Gibbon, "more numerous perhaps than the legions, was exempted by the emperors from all service, private or public, all municipal offices, and all personal taxes and contributions, which pressed on their fellow citizens with intolerable weight." † The example and command of the Emperor Constantine rendered them the objects of private benevolence and public benefactions.‡

* "From the moment that the interests of the ministers became at all distinguished from the interests of the religion, the corruption of Christianity may be considered to have begun." — *Waddington*, p. 44, note. This period he dates towards the end of the second century.

† *Decline and Fall*, vol. I., ch. 20, p. 429.

‡ *Gibbon* tells us, that the bishop of Carthage was at one time informed by a messenger from Constantine, "That the treasurers of the province are directed to pay into his hands the sum of *three thousand folles*, or *eighteen thousand pounds sterling*, and to obey his further requisitions, for the relief of the churches of Africa, Numidia, and Mauritania." In another sentence the historian informs us, that "An annual income of six hundred pounds sterling may be reasonably assigned to the bishops who were placed at equal distance between riches and poverty; but the standard of their wealth insensibly rose with the dignity and opulence of the cities which they governed." — Chap. 20, p. 430.

The bishops alone, of all the myriads of Roman citizens, enjoyed the privilege of being tried by their peers; and the minor orders were amenable, for all ordinary *civil* offences, to their respective bishops; who, from the time of Constantine, were made judges of *civil*, as well as ecclesiastical causes, in their respective dioceses. Hence arose the "Bishop's Court"; a tribunal which so many of the fathers of New England Congregationalism had most abundant cause to remember.

It is hardly necessary to remark, that the truth of these representations necessarily implies a very considerable change in the order and discipline of the churches — rather, of THE CHURCH, as the "established" religion of the Empire was now called.

This wealth, and these honors, immunities and privileges bestowed upon the clergy, were fuel to their ambition and pride. Instead of satisfying their rapacity, these things acted as incitements to intrigue and unhallowed efforts to increase their wealth and importance.

We have yet, however, deeper shades to throw over this dark picture. In addition to all that the Roman emperors had done to vitiate the order of the churches, by pampering the pride and feeding

---

Mosheim says, that "the vices and faults of the clergy, especially of those who officiated in large and opulent cities, were augmented in proportion to the increase of their wealth, honors, and advantages, derived from the emperors and various other sources; and that this increase was very great, after the time of Constantine, is acknowledged by all." — Cent. IV., part II., ch. 2, § 8.

the ambition of the clergy, there were elements in the community itself which gave peculiar encouragement to clerical usurpations.

The emperor's partiality for the church was, with his subjects, the most powerful of all arguments in favor of a profession of attachment to the new religion. If we may credit the testimony of Gibbon, "in one year twelve thousand men were baptized at Rome, besides a proportionable number of women and children."* The example and smiles of the emperor were a sufficient inducement for all classes in society to think favorably of Christianity — or, at least, to *profess* this opinion — without supposing that bribes were actually offered to all who would become converts.† Men who had been educated amidst the sensuous attractiveness of pagan worship were not displeased to find something of the pageantry of Paganism in their christian worship. The churches were encouraged to erect sumptuous buildings for their accommodation. The costly edifice, with its beams of cedar from Libanus, its roof of glittering brass, enriched with gilding, and its walls and columns and pavement of variegated marble, was an object well suited to attract the Pagan, and to quiet any lingerings of regret in the half-made convert of Christianity.

* Vol. I., ch. 20, p. 425.

† *Gibbon* insinuates, "that a white garment, with twenty pieces of gold, had been promised by the emperor to every convert." In a note, he has the candor to admit that the "evidence is contemptible enough" on which he makes the insinuation.

And when to these superb fixtures were added the splendid ornaments of gold and silver and precious stones, with which the christian altars were made to glisten,* the most fastidious and sensual heathen could scarcely look with lingering, longing eyes upon the temples of the gods, or the gorgeousness of their worship.†

* See *Gibbon's* description of these matters, vol. I., ch. 20.

† *Gibbon* gives a full and interesting account of these innovations: "As the objects of religion were gradually reduced to the standard of the imagination, the rites and ceremonies were introduced that seemed most powerfully to affect the senses of the vulgar. If, in the beginning of the fifth century, Tertullian, or Lactantius, had been suddenly raised from the dead, to assist at the festival of some popular saint, or martyr, they would have gazed with astonishment and indignation on the profane spectacle which had succeeded to the pure and spiritual worship of a Christian congregation. As soon as the doors of the church were thrown open, they must have been offended at the smoke of incense, the perfume of flowers, and the glare of lamps and tapers, which diffused, at noon-day, gaudy, superfluous, and, in their opinion, a sacrilegious light. If they approached the balustrade of the altar, they made their way through the prostrate crowd, consisting, for the most part, of strangers and pilgrims, who resorted to the city on the vigil of the feast; and who already felt the strong intoxication of fanaticism, and perhaps, of wine. Their devout kisses were imprinted on the walls and pavement of the sacred edifice; and their fervent prayers were directed, whatever might be the language of their church, to the bones, the blood, or the ashes of the saints, which were usually concealed, by a linen or silken veil, from the eyes of the vulgar." * * * * "The walls were hung round with symbols of the favors which they had received; eyes, and hands, and feet, of gold and silver; and edifying pictures, which could not long escape the abuse of indiscreet or idolatrous devotion, represented the image, the attributes, and the miracles of the tutelar saint. The same uniform original spirit of superstition might suggest, in the most distant ages and countries, the same method of deceiving the credulity, and of affecting the

It was, unquestionably, to meet the tastes of Pagans — on the plea of winning them over to Christianity — that the rulers of the church introduced many of the ornaments, and elegances, and extravagances, with which, from the days of Constantine, for successive centuries, the beautiful simplicity of apostolic worship has been deformed; not perceiving that by this course they were gradually Paganizing the Church, rather than Christianizing the Pagans.*

In addition to the corrupting influences which wrought within the boundaries of civilized Rome, there were other influences which came from the barbarian nations, who either received the gospel from the hands of missionaries, or, after the overthrow of the empire, were converted to a profession of Christianity under the expectation of finding it a more profitable religion than Paganism.

Some of these barbarians, who had been accus-

senses, of mankind; but it must ingenuously be confessed, that the ministers of the Catholic church imitated the profane model, which they were impatient to destroy. The most respectable bishops had persuaded themselves, that the ignorant rustics would more cheerfully renounce the superstitions of Paganism, if they found some resemblance, some compensation, in the bosom of Christianity. The religion of Constantine achieved, in less than a century, the final conquest of the Roman empire; but the victors themselves were insensibly subdued by the arts of their vanquished rivals." — *Gibbon,* vol. II., ch. 28, p. 198.

* Does not the history of this experiment furnish irresistible evidence of the soundness of the first principle of Congregationalism? and of the danger of all attempts to accommodate the order, discipline, and worship of the church, to any particular form of civil government, or to the tastes and peculiarities of the community in which it exists?

tomed to venerate, and almost deify their priests, and to allow them great secular influence, very naturally transferred much of this veneration to their christian teachers; and it would be strange if this were not heightened by their conviction of the superior power and glory of the new God to whom they had now devoted themselves, and whose servants these ministers were. Credulous and superstitious, as barbarians usually are, accustomed to believe implicitly and to obey unhesitatingly their religious guides, in religious matters, they would expect, and all but *demand*, the same sort of slavery under their new priests. In such circumstances, it would not require a stronger plea to justify the introduction of arbitrary government into the churches, than had sanctioned idolatrous rites in their worship.

Again; the rich among these heathen converts, accustomed to bestow their wealth upon their pagan priests and altars, very naturally inferred, that similar gifts would be equally acceptable to their new teachers, and be no less suitable to their new altars. It is needless to add, that these gifts were not refused. Thus the clergy and their churches were greatly enriched.

These things were abundantly sufficient to corrupt both priests and people, and materially to affect the apostolic order of the churches. But these causes were not alone.

In the eighth century there began to prevail, throughout the western Roman empire, a belief—

encouraged, doubtless, if not originally suggested by the clergy — that the gift of property to churches was a certain passport to the Divine favor; and that wealth thus bestowed, might be lawfully substituted for the severe penances which had previously been inflicted upon religious offenders. These doctrines, so acceptable to the natural heart, were eagerly caught at by the wealthy wicked; and they readily poured out their treasures at the feet of the clergy, in order to purchase the favor of God, or to obtain exemption from severe bodily penance for overt acts of transgression. Others left their estates as legacies to the churches, to purchase peace of conscience upon the bed of death, and to secure an entrance to the rest of heaven.

By such means the bishops and their churches became immensely rich, and, of necessity, corrupt. "The gifts, moreover," says Mosheim, "by which the princes, especially, and the noblemen endeavored to satisfy the priests, and to expiate their past sins, were not merely private possessions, which common citizens might own, and with which the churches and monasteries had often before been endowed; but they were also public property, or such as may properly belong only to princes and nations,—royal domains (*regalia*) as they are called. For the emperors, kings, and princes, transferred to bishops, to churches, and to monasteries, whole provinces, cities, and castles, with all the rights of sovereignty over them. Thus the persons, whose business it was to teach contempt for the world, both by precept and example, unexpectedly became *dukes*, *counts*, *marquises*, *judges*, *legislators*, *sovereign lords;* and they not only administered justice to citizens, but even marched out to war at the head of their own armies. And this was the origin of those great calamities which afterwards afflicted Europe — the lamentable wars and contests about investitures and the regalia." *

It cannot be supposed that this established and pampered church and these stall-fed clergy would exhibit much of the apostolic character.

Father Paul, (Fra Paola Sarpi,) a learned and candid Romanist of the sixteenth century, in his "Treatise of Ecclesiastical Benefices and Revenues," presents a clear and comprehensive view of the progress of church deterioration during the early centuries of Christianity, and attributes this deterioration largely to the accumulation of wealth in the hands of the rulers of the churches. He says, moreover, that even most of the persecutions which the churches suffered, from the death of the Emperor Commodus (A. D. 180–192), arose from this cause. "For, when the princes or their captains of the guards wanted money, they found no shorter expedient for raising it than by seizing the estates of the christian church." †

In another place, speaking of the ease and self indulgence engendered in the clergy by the money

* *Mosheim*, vol. II., bk. III., cent. VIII. part 2, ch. 2.

† *Treatise, &c.*, ch. 3, pp. 7, 8, Westminster Ed., 1736.

intrusted to them by the churches, during the third century, Father Paul says: "But the disorders ended not here; for the bishops, ceasing to make the usual distribution to the poor, reserved them to their own use. Thus enriched with the public spoils of the church, and giving themselves up to all the methods of increasing them — even to usury itself — they quite abandoned the doctrine of Christ." *

After the division of the Roman Empire, and the conquest of Italy by the northern barbarians, the government of the churches, Father Paul says, "took another form: the Eastern church kept still the established usage, of living in common; but in the Western, the bishops, from being supervisors and administrators of the revenues, began to use them as if they were their own; and to assume a sort of absolute power in their disposition. Hence followed great confusions in the application of these estates, to the great detriment of the fabrics, which fell to ruin; and of the poor, who were left destitute and unprovided for." †

Having dwelt with some degree of particularity on the prominent causes of the early corruption of the churches, it may be proper to say distinctly, what I have already repeatedly intimated — that, though in the order and government and worship of the churches, great and gross corruptions had been introduced during the first seven centuries of

* *Treatise*, etc., ch. 4, p. 8.

† *Treatise*, etc., ch. 7, p. 17.

Christian history — yet it must not be presumed, that in religious doctrine the church was utterly unsound and corrupt. The truth was far otherwise. The essential doctrines of the gospel were generally retained by the orthodox part of the church, during the whole period which has passed under review. There were errors and heresies enough abroad in the world, and among professed Christians — as the reader of any ecclesiastical history, particularly Mosheim's, will have occasion to know — yet, the essential truths of religion were so extensively received, that we have reason to believe there were multitudes of truly pious persons within the pale of the church, during even the darkest period of the seven hundred years of which we have been speaking. We have been occupied in tracing the footsteps of error, and declension, and corruption, in the order of the churches, and not the more pleasing marks of sincere piety in their members.*

Further, it must be borne in mind, that we have had the rulers and the great men of the church chiefly before us. These, to be sure, were the men who gave direction to the outward form and character of the church, but these were the men most likely to feel the influence of pride and ambition.

* He who would see the most favorable accounts of the orthodox churchmen, of all ages, must consult "Milner's History of the Church;" a very evangelical work, but, in my humble judgment, much too highly rated, and often very deficient in candor, or judgment, when dissenters of any description are the subject-matter of his history.

To the humbler ministers — the presbyters and deacons of the church — and to individuals among the laity, we must look for the clearest evidences of Christ's spirit. But these, for the most part, are unknown in ecclesiastical history.

We have now very cursorily surveyed some of the more prominent steps of the "Mystery of Iniquity," so far as its traces on the order and discipline of the churches of Christ are visible. These were the stepping-stones on which the "Man of Sin," after a fierce contest with his ambitious rivals, mounted to the throne of universal empire; and, supported by the despotic civil power — the "beast of seven heads and ten horns"* — consummated the work of corruption in the general order of Christ's House.†

---

* See Revelation XVII., and 2 Thess. II.

† The bishop of Rome, favored by his situation in the ancient capital of the empire, and the friendship of Pepin, the powerful French monarch, who made him exarch of Ravenna — a possession which was afterwards confirmed and enlarged by Charlemagne, in consideration of the bishop's services in procuring Charles the title of emperor of the West — out went all his competitors, "remained master of the field, and became SOVEREIGN PONTIFF; thereby obtaining," as Dr. Owen says, "a second conquest of the world."

Owen's "Inquiry into the Original, etc., of Evangelical Churches," presents a learned and condensed view of the declension of the churches from the apostolic order. The entire work is one of great value to the student of this subject.

The exarchate of Ravenna included the territories of Ravenna, Bologna, and Ferrara, and embraced very nearly the same extent of country as is now called "The Roman States," or "The States of the Church." It covered something less than one-third part of Italy.

It is worthy of remark, that the temporal power conferred on the

From the establishment of the temporal power of the Roman Pontiff, about A. D. 755, to the period of the Lutheran Reformation, in the sixteenth century, the Romish hierarchy grew more and more corrupt in its discipline and general character, until the world could no longer bear the grossness of its immoralities and the corruptions of its government. The eyes of men were at length opened; and they beheld a woman sitting upon "a scarlet colored beast, full of names of blasphemy, having seven heads and ten horns. And the woman was arrayed in purple and scarlet color, and decked with gold and precious stones and pearls, having a golden cup in her hand full of abominations and filthiness of her fornications. And upon her forehead a name was written — MYSTERY, BABYLON THE GREAT, THE MOTHER OF HARLOTS AND ABOMINATIONS OF THE EARTH." — Rev. xvii.

Nations, which had been made drunk with "the wine of the wrath of her fornication," awoke from the effects of her enchantments; and they wondered, while they beheld the exact resemblance which the woman upon the scarlet colored beast bore to their own MOTHER CHURCH; and their hearts were turned to hate her.

The translation of the Bible into the languages of Europe and the circulation of it among the common people were important means in promot-

Roman pontiff by Pepin and confirmed by Charlemagne, "has never since been either greatly increased or greatly diminished." — *Waddington's History of the Church*, p. 149.

ing the Reformation. The Scriptures, while they exposed the doctrinal errors and the gross immoralities of Popery, revealed also the primitive model of a christian church. The full discovery of this by the English Puritans was the result of their strict adherence to the grand principle of the Reformation: *That the Scriptures are a sufficient, and the only infallible guide to religious faith and practice.* A rejection of this principle, in its application to church order, has entailed national ecclesiastical establishments upon many Protestant countries, and has marred the beauty and excellence of various systems of church government, the framers of which have adopted the principle — that "Jesus Christ has not himself left any directions for governing the church." *

Though the principle, that the Scriptures are a sufficient guide to the *order*, as well as the faith of the church, was early lost by the christian world at large, and has not yet become generally recognized — still there have never been wanting, even in the darkest ages, some witnesses to this truth. From very early antiquity we are able to trace the footsteps of sects, or denominations of professed christians, who, by the adoption of this principle, or for some other reason, have been led to embrace and maintain some of the distinctive principles, or distinguishing doctrines of Congregationalism.

* I quote the language of Dr. Burton, Prof. of Divinity in Oxford, Eng., as given and indorsed by an American Presbyterian periodical of high standing

In the following pages I propose to notice these different sects, and to present a summary of their history. And it may be well at the outset to apprise the reader, that he must be prepared to find these dissenters from "*The Church*" classed among heretics and schismatics, and often loaded with reproaches. He need not be surprised if he sometimes finds them really defective in some important particulars, and not even deserving so good a name as could be wished. But, when it is remembered that for most that we know of the dissenters of early ages we are indebted to the writings of their enemies, we shall be prepared to receive ill reports with caution, while we estimate more highly the good that may be said of them.

Yet, whether those of whom I shall write deserve an evil or good report, it is manifestly the duty of one who attempts to give the history of Congregationalism, to mention all those sects which, previous to the full development of the Congregational system, embraced any of its distinguishing features; however unlike, in other respects, they may have been to modern Congregationalists.

HISTORY.

CHAPTER I.

ORIGIN AND HISTORY OF THE NOVATIANS, A. D. 251.

THE NOVATIANS were probably the first organized body of dissenters from the Catholic church; certainly the first that attracted much attention. There may have been individuals who dissented from the impurities of the church at an earlier period; and isolated churches, which stood aloof from the Catholic* party: but no very general protest was entered against the growing impurities in church order, until the Novatians appeared, about the middle of the third century.

And even these church reformers seem not to have protested against all the incipient corruptions which began to show themselves in their day. Their attention was chiefly directed toward a great principle relating to church order, involved in the question — What should be the character of members of the churches of Christ?

The cursory view which has been taken of the

* I use the term *Catholic*, in its original sense, as synonymous with *general*, to designate the dominant party.

progress of church corruption will show, that the positive encroachments of the bishops upon the rights of the presbyters and their lay brethren began in this century. And, to give plausibility to these encroachments, some new doctrines respecting the church and the episcopal office were cautiously advanced. But they were so covertly and obscurely brought forward, that they attracted but little attention; and, consequently, occasioned little or no alarm.*

It was toward the middle of this century that Cyprian, the renowned bishop of Carthage, began to advocate the doctrine, that bishops were "the successors of the apostles;" and to draw a line of distinction between bishops and presbyters; and, also, to advance some notions which have been understood to countenance a sort of supremacy in the bishop of Rome.† But, while he claimed for bishops a certain superiority in rank over presbyters, "yet, when urged by necessity, he could give up his pretensions, and submit everything to the judgment and authority of the church."‡ And, while he intimated that the bishop of Rome, as the successor of Peter, held a sort of supremacy (primatum) in the church, he maintained that there should be nothing insolent or arrogant (aliquid insolenter, aut arroganter) in the assumption or exercise of this supremacy. And by "the church," he did not

---

* *Mosheim*, bk. I., century III., part II., ch. 2.

† See notes on the passage just referred to, in *Mosheim's Ecclesiastical History;* also *Gieseler*, Vol. I., § 68.

‡ *Mosheim*. See also *Milner*, particularly cent. III., ch. 9.

mean merely the clergy and officers, or representatives of the christian people, but the whole body of the faithful, including the bishop, presbyters, and all the members in good standing: — "quando ecclesia in episcopo et clero et in omnibus stantibus sit constituta." And that he did not claim for the bishops of Rome any dictatorial supremacy over other bishops, is evident from the style in which he addressed them — as brothers and colleagues (fratres et collegas), and the reproofs which he unhesitatingly administered to them, when he considered them in error, as was the case in regard to both Stephen and Cornelius; bishops of Rome. He seems rather to have countenanced an honorary supremacy in the bishops of Rome over other bishops, more nearly resembling what is allowed the presiding bishop in the Protestant Episcopal church of the United States, than any such supremacy as the Pope now claims and exercises. Neither did he, with all his lofty notions of episcopal dignity, venture to claim lordly power over his church. On the contrary, he distinctly declares (Epist. xxvii.) that the church was, by Divine appointment, constituted superior to the bishop; and that all church business was to be done by the church, under the general direction of the bishop: — "ut ecclesia super episcopos constituatur, et omnis actus ecclesiæ per eosdem præpositos gubernetur." He then proceeds to say, that this was "divina lege fundatum." And in repeated instances, in his epistles to his presbyters and deacons, during his absence from Carthage, Cyprian distinctly acknowledges his obligations to consult the church — the people (plebs, plebe ipsa universa) to obtain their consent in all important matters of church business. Thus, on one occasion, in writing to his presbyters and deacons, in reply to some inquiries which they had made of him, he tells them, that in relation to the matter about which they had written him, he could say nothing while alone; in as much as, from the commencement of his episcopacy, it had been a principle with him to do nothing on his own private judgment, without their advice and the consent of the people. But when, by Divine favor, he should be restored to them, then they all together would attend to the business as their mutual honor required.*

Hence we may infer, that although there were manifest deviations from the scriptural doctrine of the equality of all bishops and presbyters, in the churches of the third century, yet there was not that avowed rejection of the apostolic model, at the time the Novatians appeared, which would have provoked any organized opposition to the usurpations of the clergy. Such opposition could not be

* See *Epistola* v., also xiv. Compare Ep. xiii., Ep. xix., *ad Presb. et Diac.*, Ep. xxviii. Mosheim, in his Commentaries, has collected these, and many other passages from Cyprian's letters, to illustrate the views of the Carthaginian bishop on the rights of the presbyters, deacons, and the people, in respect to church matters; and the whole subject is very ably, and thoroughly, and candidly discussed by him. — See *Historical Commentaries*, vol. ii., pp. 115–128. Such of Mosheim's quotations as I have used, I have compared with the originals, in Du Puis' edition of Cyprian's Works, Paris, 1666.

expected until there were settled and avowed principles or doctrines to be opposed. But even Cyprian, at times the most strenuous and arrogant defender of episcopal power, was far from being fixed and uniform in his ecclesiastical principles and practice. "No man," says Schlegel, "can speak in higher terms of the power of the bishops, than the arrogant Cyprian — that very Cyprian, who, when not fired by any passion, is so condescending toward presbyters, deacons, and the common people."

The historians of the church represent the usurpations of the clergy up to this time, and beyond it even, as of a gradual and insensible character. They were an unobserved, yet powerful undercurrent, which, while presenting scarcely a ripple on the surface, was yet rapidly bearing toward the vortex most of the rights and privileges of the churches. Or, like the way of a ship when leaving port, whose progress is discoverable rather by a view of what it has left, than by any apparent movement.*

These remarks may explain why the earliest organized dissenters from the Catholic church, on the score of church order, presented no distinct remonstrance against the usurpations of the clergy over the rights of the churches.

Mosheim, in his Historical Commentaries on the state of Christianity during the first three hundred and twenty-five years from the Christian Era — regards the controversy between Cyprian, and Fel-

* See preface to Dr. Owen's complete works, vol. xx.

icissimus and his coadjutors, of whom Novatus was perhaps the most efficient — which was contemporaneous with the Novatian controversy — as "the last struggle of expiring liberty in the African church, against episcopal domination. * * * No one," he says, "will approve of every thing done by his [Cyprian's] antagonists; yet, that they contended for the rights of the clergy and people, in opposition to a bishop affecting to have absolute dominion over them, is placed beyond all controversy by the scanty and obscure documents which have come down to us." *

But, to return from this apparent digression, to the circumstances attending the origin of the Novatians. During more than thirty years of the first half of the third century — commencing A. D. 211, and extending toward A. D. 249 — the churches were exempt from general persecution; † and enjoyed, for the most part, the protection, and sometimes the favor of the Roman emperors. Christians

---

* Vol. II., p. 58, 8vo. ed. N. Y., 1852.

† The bishops and ministers of the churches were, for a short time, exposed to persecution, by the edict of the emperor Maximin, A D. 235–237, while the body of the churches were exempted. The laity were, however, constantly liable to the lawless attacks of the populace, excited by the Pagan priests. — *Mosheim*, century III., part II., ch. 11.

Gibbon, who seems disposed to make as light of the persecutions of the Christians by the Pagans, as possible, represents the Christians as enjoying "*a calm of thirty-eight years;*" i. e. from A. D. 211 to 249. He speaks of the sufferings of the Christians under Maximin, as improperly called a persecution, and as "of a very local and temporary nature." — Vol. I., ch. 16.

found their way into places of trust and importance, in the army, in the court, and even in the palace. They dared openly to transact their church business; and were allowed to purchase land, and to erect places for public worship within the imperial city itself. This season of rest was one of outward prosperity, but of inward corruption.*

From this state of repose and corruption, the churches were suddenly aroused, by the accession to the imperial throne, of Decius, A. D. 249. This emperor began the most terrible and extensive persecution which the church of Christ has ever experienced. It extended to all parts of the empire, and involved all classes of christians, exposing them to every species of suffering. "Immense numbers, dismayed not so much by the fear of death as by the dread of the long continued tortures by which the magistrates endeavored to overcome the constancy of christians, professed to renounce Christ; and procured for themselves safety, either by sacrificing (offering incense before the idols), or by certificates purchased with money." † God, in

* A vivid picture of the corrupt state of the church is given by Cyprian in his treatise concerning the lapsed. — See *Milner's History of the Church*, century III., ch. 8. Milner says: "The peace of thirty years had corrupted the whole christian atmosphere." — Chap. 11. Taylor, in his "*Ancient Christianity*," presents us with a most loathsome exhibition of the corruptions of this age — particularly of "the zealous and upright Cyprian's" "*delinquent stew of ecclesiastical virginity, at Carthage.*" — First Proposition.

† *Mosheim.* — A full and interesting account of this persecution, is given in *Milner's History of the Church*, century III., chs. 8–11.

mercy to his church, cut short the career of this monster.* He reigned less than three years.

On the return of peace, the lapsed and apostate christians were found at the doors of the churches, seeking admission. And so numerous were they, that they were emboldened to demand admission to church privileges without undergoing the severe penance usually insisted upon in such cases. Many of the bishops and other clergy were for admitting the lapsed on their own terms; some, however, were of a different mind. Among the latter was Novatian, a presbyter of the church of Rome; a man of extensive learning, unblemished morals, and devoted piety. He had witnessed with disgust the time-serving and unscriptural management of the bishops and their churches, in admitting unworthy members to their communion, and even restoring them to christian fellowship after they had once apostatized from the faith. By a view of the evils attending this course, he was at length brought to take the high ground — that the church should consist of none but the pure in heart and the blameless in life; and to maintain, that if any one in time of persecution fell away from his christian steadfastness, he should be utterly repudiated by the church, and on no condition re-admitted to her

* *Gibbon* says, so oppressive to the christians was the government of Decius, that their former condition, ever since the time of Domitian [A. D. 96], was represented as a state of perfect freedom and security, if compared with the rigorous treatment which they experienced under the short reign of Decius, whom Lactantius calls an "*execrable animal.*" *Gibbon*, vol. I., ch. 16, § 4, and note 121.

fellowship. He did not deny the lapsed the hope of final salvation — he even urged them to repentance, that they might be saved; but he denied them re-admission to the bosom of the christian church; maintaining, that "the church should be a society of innocent persons, who, from their entrance into it, had defiled themselves with no sin of any considerable magnitude."

Now, whether or not we can fully justify the ground taken by Novatian, we certainly must admit, that the oscillating course of multitudes who professed the Christian name in those days — now worshipping "Christ as God," in christian congregations, and now sacrificing before the altars of Paganism, to the gods of the heathen, and denying the Lord that bought them, and anon returning to their profession of Christianity — we must, I say, admit that such conduct was anything but reputable, or commendatory to the cause of Christ. And before we condemn the doctrine of Novatian, we must place ourselves fully in his circumstances, and consider the vast importance of the general principle for which he contended.

The principle on which he denied admission to the church of Christ to all but the pure in heart and the blameless in life, is, beyond question, the same on which the apostolic churches were originally gathered. This, too, is one of the fundamental principles of the Congregational system. Indeed, it lies at the very foundation of the whole system. It is hopeless to think of maintaining the

Congregational polity where this principle is disregarded.

The talents and piety of Novatian, and the arguments which he drew from the Scriptures and the character of the apostolic churches, soon gathered around him many friends and followers.

About A. D. 251, Novatian and his followers separated themselves from the church of Rome, and, indeed, from the entire Catholic community; "not for a reason of faith" — for they agreed in doctrinal belief with the great body of the church — but on the ground that the Catholic church had corrupted herself by the admission of unworthy members, and was no longer a body of "innocent persons;" and that her congregations were no longer entitled to the name of christian churches.

"Novatian maintained, that one of the essential marks of a true church being purity and holiness, every church which, neglecting the right exercise of church discipline, tolerated in its bosom, or readmitted to its communion, such persons as by gross sins have broken their baptismal vow, ceased by that very act to be a true christian church, and forfeited all the rights and privileges of such a church."*

Eulogius, bishop of Alexandria, complains, that the Novatians at Alexandria did not pay due rev-

* *Neander's General History of the Christian Religion and Church,* vol. I., p. 246. A general account of the Novatian controversy is given by Neander in his first volume, pages 237–248. *Mosheim,* in his Historical Commentaries, goes pretty fully into the entire controversy, vol. II., pp. 45–73.

erence to the martyrs, nor allow that there was any virtue in their relics.* Another evidence, in our judgment, of their good sense and just apprehension of the teachings of God's word.

Another peculiarity of the Novatians, according to several ecclesiastical authorities, was the rejection from their communion of persons who had been twice married — digamists. Bingham speaks of this repeatedly, as unquestionably a tenet of the Novatians.† Lardner also mentions several ancient writers who assert this (vol. VI., 218); but Socrates tells us that there was a diversity of practice on this subject (lib. v., c. 22); and Lardner thinks that it was not a doctrine of Novatian, but was added afterwards.

So agreeable to the convictions of multitudes were the doctrines of Novatian, that, besides the church which was organized by him in Rome, another sprang up in Carthage, by the side of the "arrogant Cyprian;" and within the third century the schism had spread into Gaul. And there were churches in Nice, Nicomedia, in Phrygia, in Scythia, three in Constantinople, and probably in numerous other places all over the empire, before the close of the fourth century. The vast extent of this sect, says Dr. Lardner, is manifest from the names of the authors who have mentioned them, or written against them, and from the several

* *Lardner's Credibility of the Gospel History*, vol. III., p. 219.

† *Christian Antiquities*, vol. VI., pp. 377–379, 587–589; VII., 213.

parts of the Roman empire in which they were found.*

The following is Mr. Robinson's account of the rise, progress, and character of the Novatians:

"It was in the third century, when the first system of discipline [the apostolic] was going a great pace over from the people into the second, the sacerdotal system, that a great separation took place at Rome, and multitudes bore a noble testimony against the prevailing corruption. At Rome these dissenters were called Novatians, from Novatus, one of the chief managers of the affair. They called themselves Puritans, or, as the Greeks translated the word, Cathari; and they intended by the name to signify the fact, that they separated from the rest because their morals were impure. It was precisely such a case as that of the Donatists in Africa. There was no dispute about doctrines: but the whole was summed up in one word, virtue. It is very remarkable, that, though both sides allowed they agreed in doctrine, and the great party allowed the Novatians were christians, yet the Novatians thought the want of virtue had unchurched those who called themselves Catholic, and therefore they disowned their competency to administer christian institutes, and if any went from the Catholics to join them, as great numbers did, they rebaptized every one. It is a shame for Protestants to put these people into lists of heretics, and troub-

* *Cred. Gosp. Hist.*, vol. III., p. 228.

lers of the church.* Mosheim says: 'This sect cannot be charged with having corrupted the doctrine of Christianity by their opinions. They considered the christian church as a society where virtue and innocence reigned universally, and none of whose members, from their entrance into it, had defiled themselves with any enormous crime; and of consequence, they looked upon every society, which re-admitted heinous offenders to communion, as unworthy of the title of a true christian church. It was from hence also that they assumed the title of Cathari, i. e. the pure, and what showed a still more extravagant degree of arrogance, they obliged such as came over to them from the general body of Christians, to be baptized a second time, as a necessary preparation for entering into their society.' A people sound in doctrine, virtuous in their manners, so sound and so virtuous that their most implacable enemies allow both: for what crime then have so many pens blackened them over, and held them up to the world as schismatics, to be execrated by all good men? Mosheim says, 'Their crime was, that by the unreasonable severity of their discipline, they gave occasion to the most deplorable divisions, and made an unhappy rent in the church.' It is surprising to see to what lengths a party spirit hath been carried, and what adepts some men are in the science of heresiography. One

* Henckel de hæresi Novatiana. Ittigius de hæresibus. — *Mosheim's Ecclesiastical History,* century III., ch. V. Divisions and Heresies.

doctor of the Lutheran church hath given a comment on heresy and schism, and hath inserted catalogue-wise no less than six hundred and thirty-two sorts of heretics, heresiarchs, and schismatics, diversified as the birds of heaven, and agreeing in only one single point: the crime of not continuing in what is called the church.* If it be inquired, what was the state of this church, which it was a crime to quit? the same Mosheim says, 'The most respectable writers of that age have put it out of the power of an historian to spread a veil over the enormities of ecclesiastical rulers. By a train of vices they were sunk in luxury and voluptuousness, puffed up with vanity, arrogance, and ambition, possessed with a spirit of contention and discord, and addicted to many other vices. The bishop assumed a princely authority, was exalted above his equals, and had a throne surrounded with ministers. Presbyters followed their example, neglected their duties, and abandoned themselves to the indolence and delicacy of an effeminate and luxurious life. Deacons imitated their superiors, and the effects of a corrupt ambition were spread through every rank of the sacred order.' This is the church, which, it is said, the Novatians troubled in the third century.

"The history of Novatian is long, and, like that of all others in his condition, beclouded with fables and slander. The character of the man ought no

* M. Pauli Stockmanni Elucidarius hæres. Schismatum. cum epist. Alberti in commendationem opusculi. Lipsiæ, 1693.

more to be taken from Cyprian, than his ought from the Pagans, who, by punning on his name called him Coprian, or the scavenger.* The case in brief was this.† Novatian was an elder in the church at Rome. He was a man of extensive learning, and held the same doctrine as the church did, and published several treatises in defence of what he believed. His address was eloquent and insinuating, and his morals were irreproachable. He saw with extreme pain the intolerable depravity of the church. Christians within the space of a very few years were caressed by one emperor, and persecuted by another. In seasons of prosperity many rushed into the church for base purposes. In times of adversity they denied the faith, and ran back to idolatry again. When the squall was over, away they came again to the church, with all their vices, to deprave others by their examples. The bishops, fond of proselytes, encouraged all this, and transferred the attention of christians from the old confederacy for virtue, to vain shows at Easter, and other Jewish ceremonies, adulterated too with Paganism. On the death of bishop Fabian, Cornelius, a brother elder, and a vehement partizan for taking in the multitude, was put in

* Labbei Concil. Sever. Binii notæ in vit. Fabiani Papæ. Cyprianus rhetor ab ethnicis per contemptum Coprianus, id est, stercorarius, nominatus.

† Cypriani epist. XLIX., etc. Cornelii papæ vita. Ejusdem epist. Concil. Carthag. in causa lapsorum. An. 254. Epist. Synod. Afric. De lapsis. Epiphanii Hæres. lix. Cathari. Philastrii De hæres. ch XXXIV. Euseb. Hist. Eccles. lib. VI., ch. 43.

nomination. Novatian opposed him: but as Cornelius carried his election, and he saw no prospect of reformation, but on the contrary a tide of immorality pouring into the church, he withdrew, and a great many with him. Cornelius, irritated by Cyprian, who was just in the same condition through the remonstrances of virtuous men at Carthage, and who was exasperated beyond measure with one of his elders, named Novatus, who had quitted Carthage, and had gone to Rome to espouse the cause of Novatian, called a council, and got a sentence of excommunication passed against Novatian. In the end, Novatian formed a church, and was elected bishop. Great numbers followed his example, and all over the empire Puritan churches were constituted, and flourished through the succeeding two hundred years. Afterward, when penal laws obliged them to lurk in corners, and worship God in private, they were distinguished by a variety of names, and a succession of them continued till the reformation.

"They say, Novatian was the first anti-pope: and yet there was at that time no pope, in the modern sense of the word. They call Novatian the author of the heresy of Puritanism; and yet they know Tertullian had quitted the church near fifty years before, for the same reason; and Privatus,* who was an old man in the time of Novatian, had,

* Milner mentions Privatus only to call him "an impostor." It would have been more satisfactory had he given us his reasons for so calling him.

with several more, repeatedly remonstrated against the alterations taking place; and, as they could get no redress, had dissented and formed separate congregations. They tax Novatian with being parent of an innumerable multitude of congregations of Puritans all over the empire; and yet, he had no other influence over any, than what his good example gave him. People saw everywhere the same cause of complaint, and groaned for relief; and when one man made a stand for virtue, the crisis had arrived; people saw the propriety of the cure, and applied the same means to their own relief. They blame this man and all these churches for the severity of their discipline: yet this severe moral discipline was the only coercion of the primitive churches, and it was the exercise of this that rendered civil coercion unnecessary. Some exclaimed: It is a barbarous discipline to refuse to re-admit people into christian communion because they have lapsed into idolatry or vice. Others, finding the inconvenience of such a lax discipline, required a repentance of five, ten, or fifteen years: but the Novatians said, if you be a virtuous believer, and will accede to our confederacy against sin, you may be admitted among us by baptism, or if any Catholic has baptized you before, by re-baptism: but, mark this, if you violate the contract by lapsing into idolatry or vice, we shall separate you from our community, and, do what you will, we shall never re-admit you. God forbid we should injure either your person, your property, or your character, or even judge of the truth of your repentance, and your future state: but you can never be re-admitted to our community, without our giving up the best and only coercive guardian we have of the purity of our morals. Whether these people reasoned justly or not, as virtue was their object, they challenge respect, and he must be a weak man indeed who is frighted out of it because Saint Cyprian, the most intolerant of all saints, says, they were the children of the devil." *

Gibbon tells us, that about the middle of the fourth century, a large district of Paphlagonia, a province in the northern part of Asia Minor, on the Euxine Sea, was almost entirely inhabited by these sectaries, the Novatians.†

Socrates, the ancient ecclesiastical historian, born about A. D. 380, gives the following account of the rise and progress of the Novatians, and the reasons therefor:

"About this time the Novatians inhabiting Phrygia changed the day for celebrating the Feast of Easter. How this happened I shall state, after first explaining the reason of the strict discipline which is maintained in their church, even to the present day, in the provinces of Phrygia and Paphlagonia. Novatus,‡ a presbyter of the Roman

* *Ecc. Researches,* by R. Robinson, Camb. Eng., 1792, 4to., pp. 124–128.

† *Decline and Fall,* vol. I., p. 467.

‡ The Greeks usually term him Novatus, but his right name was Novatian.

Church, separated from it, because Cornelius the bishop received into communion believers who had sacrificed during the persecution which the emperor Decius had raised against the church. Having seceded on this account, on being afterwards elevated to the episcopacy by such prelates as entertained similar sentiments, he wrote to all the churches insisting that they should not admit to the sacred mysteries those who had sacrificed; but, exhorting them to repentance, leave the pardoning of their offence to God, who has the power to forgive all sin. These letters made different impressions on the parties in the various provinces to whom they were addressed, according to their several dispositions and judgments. The exclusion of those who, after baptism, had committed any deadly sin * from participation in the mysteries, appeared to some a cruel and merciless course: but others thought it just and necessary for the maintenance of discipline, and the promotion of greater devotedness of life. In the midst of the agitation of this important question, letters arrived from Cornelius the bishop, promising indulgence to delinquents after baptism. On these two persons writing thus contrary to one another, and each confirming his own procedure by the testimony of the Divine word, as it usually happens, every one identified himself with that view which favored his previous habits and inclinations. Those who had pleasure in sin, encouraged by the license thus granted them,

* *Εἰς θάνατον ἁμαρτίαν* "a sin unto death."—See 1 John v. 16, 17.

took occasion from it to revel in every species of criminality. The Phrygians however appear to be more temperate than other nations, and are seldom guilty of swearing. The Scythians and Thracians are naturally of a very irritable disposition: while the inhabitants of the East are addicted to sensual pleasures. But the Paphlagonians and Phrygians are prone to neither of these vices; nor are the sports of the circus nor theatrical exhibitions in much estimation among them even to the present day. And this will account, as I conceive, for these people, as well as others of a similar temperament and habit in the West, so readily assenting to the letters then written by Novatus. Fornication and adultery are regarded among the Paphlagonians and Phrygians as the grossest enormities; and it is well known that there is no race of men on the face of the earth who more rigidly govern their passions in this respect. Yet, although for the sake of stricter discipline Novatus became a separatist, he made no change in the time of keeping Easter, but invariably observed the practice that obtained in the Western churches, of celebrating this feast after the equinox, according to the usage which had of old been delivered to them when first they embraced Christianity. He himself indeed afterwards suffered martyrdom in the reign of Valerian, during the persecution which was then raised against the Christians. But those in Phrygia who from his name are termed Novatians, about this period changed the day of celebrating Easter, being averse to communion with other christians even on this occasion. This was effected by means of a few obscure bishops of that sect convening a synod at the village of Pazum, which is situated near the sources of the river Sangarius; for there they framed a canon appointing its observance on the same day as that on which the Jews annually keep the feast of Unleavened Bread. I obtained my information on this point from an aged man who was the son of a presbyter, and had been present with his father at this synod. But both Agelius, bishop of the Novatians at Constantinople, and Maximus of Nice, were absent, as also the bishops of Nicomedia and Cotuœum, although the ecclesiastical affairs of that sect were for the most part under the control of these prelates. How their church soon after was divided into two parties in consequence of this synod, shall be related in its proper course." *

Such representations of "a heretical sect," by an impartial historian like Socrates, are sufficient praise, and outweigh and give the lie to the bitter denunciations of Cornelius of Rome and Cyprian of Carthage, both of whom, though contemporary, were the prejudiced and bitter enemies of both Novatus and Novatian.†

---

* *Ecc. Hist. of Socrates*, bk. v., ch. 28.

† *Cornelius* is very abusive in his treatment of Novatus: accuses him of "precipitate ambition," of "artifice and duplicity," of "perjuries and falsehoods," of being a "dissocial and savage character," and much else that is bad. — See *Eusebius' Ecc. Hist.* bk. vi., ch. 43.

Cyprian accuses Novatus of great fondness for novelties; of un-

I use the terms, Novatus *and* Novatian. The reader should be apprised that there were two associated leaders in the "Novatian schism," of very similar names, who are often confounded together, though unlike in character — Novatus and Novatian, or Novatianus. The former was a Carthaginian presbyter, an active, energetic, resolute, and perhaps managing man; who, after a protracted quarrel with Cyprian, his bishop, left Carthage and went to Rome, and there became an efficient associate with Novatian, the Roman reformer, in his efforts to resist the progress of episcopal domination and church corruption. His character, though manifestly maligned by the violent bishop of Carthage, and by Cornelius bishop of Rome, whose letters are our chief sources of information respecting Novatus, was yet possibly less unexceptionable than that of Novatian, from whom the Novatian dissenters derived their name.

Mosheim, while he admits that Novatus might have been "contentious, prone to innovation, and also factious," says that the good Cyprian could sometimes discover faults where there were none, and was too virulent against those whom he regarded as hostile to his reputation and dignity; and adds: "To express my own opinion, I cannot

---

bounded avarice and rapacity, pride and arrogance; of being an enemy to the episcopacy; a man condemned by the voice of all the clergy as a perfidious heretic; an enemy to peace; an instigator of dissensions; a thief, a robber, and a perpetrator of sacrilege; a parricide, and even of committing a violent and dangerous assault on his pregnant wife. — *Cyprian's* XLIXth *Epistle* abounds in such charges

look upon Novatus as so black a character as Cyprian represents him; because, he neither sought nor obtained for himself any great advantages throughout this long and vehement contest." And, as it respects the crimes charged upon Novatus by Cyprian, it is observable, that Novatus was never convicted of them; nor were these charges ever, in any form, substantiated against him. "It is therefore," adds the historian, "no rash conjecture, to suppose that the truth of those enormous imputations could not be substantiated. Felicissimus, the friend of Novatus, Cyprian condemned and excommunicated: and why should he spare Novatus, if he knew him to be guilty of such enormities?" *

Lardner, however, insists that the name of the Roman presbyter was Novatus, the same as that of the Carthaginian presbyter. He says: "Cornelius was chosen bishop of Rome in June, 251. Soon after, *Novatus*, presbyter in the same church, got himself ordained bishop of Rome." †

In another place, Lardner speaks of "Novatus *or* Novatian." He also speaks of the Carthaginian Novatus as a much less important person-

* *Commentaries*, vol. II., pp. 48, 49; *Neander*, vol. I., p. 241.

† *Complete Works*, vol. III., p. 66, Lond., 1788. "Got himself ordained." The implication contained in this phraseology is not sustained by any proofs; and is contradicted by other authorities, which represent Novatian as in a manner forced to accept the office of a bishop; his philosophical habits and all his tastes, as well as his whole character, being in opposition to any such forth-putting of himself as Lardner's words would imply.

age than the Roman Novatus. He treats Cyprian's charges against him as declamation; and says some of them had no better foundation than suspicion and conjecture.*

A single sentence in one of Cyprian's epistles, in which he speaks of Novatian, furnishes, perhaps, a key to the bishop's readiness to believe all evil of a separatist from *the* church:—"whoever and whatever (he says) one may be, he is not a christian who is not in the church of Christ.†"

Ecclesiastical writers agree in representing Novatian as strictly orthodox in his religious doctrines; and the sect, as remarkably strict in its discipline and pure in its morals. Milner, who mourns over the broken unity of the church—broken, for the

* Vol. III., p. 222. Lardner devotes an entire chapter, and a long one, to Novatus and Novatianism, vol. III., pp. 206–254. His account is quite full and impartial. In two long notes (vol. III., pp. 248–252 and 363–367) he considers the question, whether Novatus or Novatian was the true name of the Roman presbyter, the father of Novatianism, and comes to the conclusion, that *Novatus* was his name. In this, however, he is contradicted by Mosheim and Neander, not to mention other authorities. Neander says, that the man who properly was the moving soul of the Novatians, and to whose influence, doubtless, it was owing that they broke entirely from the Catholics, was Novatus, a Carthaginian presbyter, who had been a leader among the disaffected in Cyprian's church in Carthage.—Vol. I., p. 241. Lardner's opinion is, nevertheless, very ably maintained, and I am far from being satisfied that he has not the best of the argument; though the current of authorities is against him.

† "Quod vero ad Novatiani personam pertinet, pater carissime, desiderasti tibi scribi quam hæresin introduxisset, scias nos primo in loco non curiosos esse debere quid ille doceat, cum foris doceat. Quisquis ille est, et qualiscunque est, Christianus non est, qui in Christi ecclesia non est."—*Epistola* LII.

first time, by these "schismatics," and who "can by no means justify the separation of Novatian" —is yet constrained to admit, that these were the most respectable of all the dissenting churches, and that they "preserved for a considerable time, a strictness and purity of discipline and manners;" and "that they held no opinions contrary to the faith of the gospel." *

Neander selects Irenæus and Novatian as representatives of a class of men who exhibited "a sober and chaste practical bent of the christian mind, springing immediately from Christianity, and which inclined the soul to elevate itself to God by the heart, rather than by speculation and fancy." †

Mosheim, after speaking of the rapid progress and long continuance of the Novatian sect, through Christendom, says: "For this, its good fortune, it was indebted to the gravity and probity of the teachers who presided over it, and to the severity of its discipline, which tolerated no base characters, none guilty of the grosser sins." And again, he says: "The authors of most of the schisms among Christians have been charged, justly or unjustly, with many crimes and faults; but this Novatian was not only accused of no criminal act, but was commended, even by those who viewed him as warring against the interests of the church,

* *Church History*, century III., ch. 9.

† *Neander's General History of the Christian Religion and Church*, vol. I., p. 560, Torrey's translation.

— by Cyprian, Jerom and others — on account of his eloquence, his learning, and his philosophy."*

Lardner, after enumerating a number of distinguished Novatian bishops and others, who flourished at different times and in divers countries, adds: "From the several instances that have been mentioned, it may be inferred, that this people had among them not a few men of polite learning and fine accomplishments."

Du Pin, the celebrated French ecclesiastical historian, gives the following glowing description of Novatian: "This author had abundance of wit, knowledge, and eloquence; his style is pure, clean and polite; his expressions choice, his thoughts natural, and his way of reasoning just. He is full of citations of texts of scripture that are always to the purpose; and, besides, there is a great deal of order and method in those treatises of his we now have; and he never speaks but with a world of candor and moderation." †

Mr. Waddington's account of the Novatians is worth transcribing, not because it adds anything of importance to what has already been adduced, but as the testimony of a candid Episcopalian. It is as follows: "Novatian, a presbyter of Rome, was a man of great talents and learning, and of a character so austere, that he was unwilling, under any circumstances of contrition, to re-admit those who

---

* *Commentaries,* vol. II., p. 60.

‡ *History of Ecclesiastical Writers,* vol. I., p. 146. Quarto Ed. Lond., 1693.

had been once separated from the communion of the church. * * He considered the christian church as a society where virtue and innocence reigned universally, and refused any longer to acknowledge, as members of it, those who had once degenerated into unrighteousness. This endeavor to revive the spotless moral purity of the primitive faith, was found inconsistent with the corruptions even of that early age: it was regarded with suspicion by the leading prelates, as a vain and visionary scheme; and those rigid principles which had characterized and sanctified the church in the first century, were abandoned to the profession of schismatic sectaries in the third." *

The Novatianists were repeatedly condemned by Church and State; but still they increased. And if, as Milner tells us, "purity of principle and inflexibility of discipline were their favorite objects," † no good man can do otherwise than rejoice in their prosperity, even though it did break the ecclesiastical unity of the church.

For several centuries we are able to discover distinct traces of this earliest organized sect of dissenters; and, alas, that these traces should sometimes be the blood of their martyrs! Novatian himself was put to death in the persecution under Valerian. ‡

Socrates says, that Cyril, who succeeded Theophilus at Alexandria in 412, "exercised a kind of

* *History of the Church*, p. 79, Harper's Ed.

† *Century* III., ch. 11.

‡ *Socrates*, bk. IV., ch. 28.

princely authority and government, for he immediately shut up the churches of the Novatians, and took away their sacred vessels and ornaments; and as for their bishop, Theopemptus, he deprived him of all he had." He further says, that Anastasius, who succeeded Innocent (A. D. 401–417), was the first pope that persecuted the Novatians at Rome, taking away from them their churches. Celestinus (who succeeded Boniface, who succeeded Zosimus) about A. D. 422–432, deprived the Novatians of Rome of their churches, and forced their bishop, Rusticula, to hold his meetings secretly in private houses. Until that time, he says, the Novatians had flourished mightily at Rome, having a great number of churches and large congregations. "But envy attacked them also, as soon as the Roman episcopate, like that of Alexandria, extended itself beyond the limits of ecclesiastical jurisdiction, and degenerated into its present state of secular domination. From thenceforth the Roman bishops would not suffer even those who perfectly agreed with them in matters of faith, and whose purity of doctrine they extolled, to enjoy the privilege of assembling in peace, but stripped them of all they possessed." *

About the middle of the fourth century a war of conversion or extermination was waged upon such of them as dwelt in the region of Paphlagonia. Macedonius, the Arian bishop of Constantinople, supported by the emperor Constantius, resolved

* *Ecc. Hist.* bk. VII., ch. 11.

either to convert or extirpate them. Socrates gives the following account of this war: "Hearing that there was a great number of the Novatian sect in the province of Paphlagonia, and especially at Mantinium, and perceiving that such a numerous body could not be driven from their homes by ecclesiastics alone, he caused, by the emperor's permission, four companies of soldiers to be sent into Paphlagonia, that, through dread of the military, they might receive the Arian opinion. But those who inhabited Mantinium, animated to desperation by zeal for their religion, armed themselves with long reap-hooks, hatchets, and whatever weapon came to hand, and went forth to meet the troops; on which a conflict ensuing, many indeed of the Paphlagonians were slain, but nearly all the soldiers were destroyed."*

From some historians we should infer, that the persecuting efforts of "*The Church*" extinguished the sect of Novatianists before the close of the fifth century. Others, however, and among them Mr. Robinson, tell us that they continued, under various names, down to the time of the Lutheran Reformation.†

* *Socrates*, bk. II., ch. 38. The entire chapter is devoted to this Arian persecution. *Gibbon* gives some account of this persecution, vol I., ch. 21, p. 467.

† *Jones' History Christian Church*, vol. I., pp. 312, 313. *Milner* gives a pretty full account of the Novatians, in connection with the life of his admired Cyprian, their violent enemy. — See particularly the 9th, 10th, and 11th chapters of the third century. The reader may collect nearly the whole truth from Milner, and yet, he will

Lardner says, that though there were Novatians in some places at the latter end of the sixth century, or afterwards, yet it is probable that they

---

hardly fail to be amused by the efforts of that good man to prevent his antipathy to dissenters from running away with his conscience. He seems to write like a man in a strait betwixt two. He can by no means approve of Novatian's schism; yet he must admit that the church from which he separated had become very corrupt. His followers were certainly, says Milner, *schismatics;* and yet, they certainly were very *respectable* and *virtuous,* and enjoyed the presence of God's Spirit. "The author" "would by no means be understood to encroach upon the right of private judgment. * * * It is the right of ACTING according to this right of opinion that is contested," etc.

It might well be answered: Of what value is "the right of private judgment," if one can have no liberty to follow that judgment in action? always supposing that his actions do not interfere with the rights of other men.

"Can it be right," asks this pious historian, "for a small number of individuals to dissent — and that on no better ground than their own fancy and humor? * * Such however was the first origin of the Novatian schism." — *Cent.* III., ch. 10. One might retort upon this advocate of Diocesan Episcopacy, who is "convinced that the Almighty has not limited his creatures to any particular and strictly defined modes of church government" — by asking, Can it be right to require a small number of individuals, contrary to their private judgment, to conform to "the fancy and humor" of a larger number? If *any one's* fancy and humor should be consulted, why not one's own? Why should I be required to conform to a hierarchy, many of whose rites and ceremonies, if not its entire order, have no better foundation than "fancy and humor?"

It is, however, very obvious, that the true ground of dissent in the case of Novatian was something widely different from "fancy or humor." It was *principle* — deep, religious principle — which constrained him to separate from the impure, and increasingly and hopelessly impure church of his day. It is the same that has removed thousands of the best of men from the inclosures of the Church of England in later times; the same which, I verily believe, declined after the middle of the fifth century, if not sooner.*

Of what has now been said of Novatianism, this is the sum: A learned and pious presbyter of the church at Rome, about the middle of the third century, alarmed at the progress of corruption in the churches, occasioned chiefly by a disregard of the apostolic example, in admitting the unworthy to the fellowship of the churches, after pleading in vain for a reformation in this respect, separated himself from the church at Rome, and formed another church on this distinctive and fundamental principle — *The church of Christ should consist of none but the truly pious; and if any forfeit this character by an open denial of the faith* (or, as he termed it, "a sin unto death") *they should be rejected, and never more received into the church.* This principle found advocates in all parts of the Roman empire, and was adopted and practised on by multitudes of the most virtuous and excellent persons. Churches were formed all over the empire, and probably continued to exist, under various names, until the dawn of the Reformation.

---

will ultimately reduce all the anti-scriptural hierarchies of Christendom to the simple model of the apostolic churches.

Socrates has given many historical particulars and anecdotes illustrative of the Novatians. So favorable are his notices of Novatian and his followers, that his translator deemed it necessary to defend him from this "*slander.*" *Sozomon*, another ancient ecclesiastical historian, has been suspected of partiality to Novatianism; but, as *Gibbon* thinks, without sufficient reason.

* Vol. III., p. 231.

This sect, though it may have developed but a single principle of the denomination whose history I am attempting to write, deserves the first place among the restorers of "the old paths;" and may with propriety be regarded as the vanguard of that army of church reformers, of which Congregationalists are the rearward.

CHAPTER II.

THE RISE AND HISTORY OF THE DONATISTS, A. D. 311.

THE Donatists, Milner calls "the second class of dissenters." Like the Novatians, they agreed with the Catholic party in their doctrinal belief, but dissented on the ground of church order. The Donatists believed that the church had so corrupted herself that she was no longer the spouse of Christ; — "that immorality had unchurched the Catholics, and sunk them into a mere worldly corporation." They therefore separated entirely from them; and would neither commune with the Catholics, nor receive them to their churches, until they had been re-baptized.

Neander, in speaking of the Donatist schism, says: "The most important and influential church division which we have to mention in this [second] period is the Donatist, which had its seat in North Africa. This schism may be compared in many respects with that of Novatian, in the preceding period. In this, too, we see the conflict, for example, of Separatism with Catholicism; and it is therefore important, in so far as it tended to settle and establish the notion of the visible, outward unity of the church, and of the objective element in the things of religion and of the church. That which distinguishes the present case is, the reaction, proceeding out of the essence of the christian church, and called forth in this instance by a peculiar occasion — against the confounding of the ecclesiastical and political elements; on which occasion, for the first time, the ideas which Christianity, as opposed to the Pagan religion of the State, had first made men distinctly conscious of, became an object of contention within the church itself — the ideas concerning universal, inalienable human rights; concerning liberty of conscience; concerning the rights of free religious conviction." *

The Donatist controversy, then, according to Neander, originated in the practical expansion and development, within the church itself, of that essential element of Christianity which recognizes, as the inalienable right of every man, the right to form his own religious creed, and to act out freely the deliberate convictions of his own conscience, without regard to any mere human authority.

The Donatists appear in church history, as a distinct and powerful body of dissenters, early in the fourth century, A. D. 311–321. It is very difficult, however, to do them full historical justice; for, though in the course of the fourth and fifth centuries many volumes were written by Catholic and

---

* *General History of Christian Religion and Church,* vol. II., p. 182.

Donatist bishops, and others, on the points at issue between them, yet, unfortunately—though very naturally, considering who finally triumphed in the controversy—next to nothing of the Donatists' writings remain; while the letters, and tracts, and larger works of their adversaries have been carefully preserved and handed down to posterity. Augustine alone, who was one of the chief controversial opponents of the Donatists, wrote at least forty-five different works—letters, tracts, and treatises—"*adversus*" aut "*contra Donatistas.*" The mere index in Augustine's works to what relates to the Donatists fills about two columns, folio.* From his representations, and those of Optatus, a kindred spirit of an earlier date, ecclesiastical historians have derived most of their knowledge of the Donatists. But who does not know that the representations of opponents in an excited controversy are utterly unreliable? However honest a man may be, it is extremely difficult for him to represent truly and exactly the opinions of one whom he regards as in dangerous error. When, therefore, we find Augustine, bishop of Hippo, denouncing Donatism as "*diabolicam separationem,*"

* *Dupin*, in his New History of Ecclesiastical Writers, devotes 82 quarto pages to St. Augustine, and these are chiefly occupied with an analysis of this saint's voluminous writings. Any one who will take the pains to examine this analysis, will see that the Donatists were an ever present topic with Augustine; were as pricks in his eyes and thorns in his side to vex him; they were the Mordecai in his gate, who refused to do him reverence.

we must make due allowance for the heated state of the good father's mind, and believe that a separation which the Catholics were so extremely anxious to close by a hearty union with themselves, could not, after all, have been so very diabolical in its character.

The account given of the origin of the Donatists, though not altogether satisfactory, is substantially as follows: In the year A. D. 311, Mensurius, bishop of Carthage, dying, three rival candidates appeared for the vacant episcopal chair. Cæcilian, the arch-deacon of the church, was the successful aspirant. With a degree of haste and irregularity which threw suspicion on the movement, a few of the neighboring bishops proceeded to consecrate the bishop elect. Against this procedure, Botrus and Celesius, the rival candidates, and their friends, strenuously protested. They asserted that the ordination of Cæcilian was null and void: 1st, Because the bishops of Numidia, a neighboring province attached to the See of Carthage, had not been consulted, or called to take part in the ordination of the new *primate;** which was a violation of established usage, if not of ecclesiastical law. 2dly, Because one or more of the consecrating bishops was a *Traditor*, i. e. one who, to avoid persecution, had delivered the sacred books to the

* This appears to have been the title given to the bishop of Carthage; who was virtually the *archbishop*, patriarch, or pope of Africa.

heathen magistrates, to be burned. This, they asserted, was true of the principal bishop concerned in the consecration of Cæcilian. 3dly, They charged Cæcilian with having been hard-hearted towards the witnesses for Christ, or martyrs, during the persecution of Diocletian, even forbidding food to be carried to them while in prison.

The Numidian bishops, to the number of seventy, having assembled at Carthage, undertook to investigate the affair. But Cæcilian and his party refused to appear before them; asserting that the Numidians had been prejudiced by the representations, and bribed by the gold of the other party. This council, "with the approbation of a considerable part of the clergy and people of Carthage," set aside the ordination of Cæcilian, and consecrated Majorinus, one of the deacons, or readers of the church, bishop of Carthage.

Thus began the schism of the Donatists, so called probably from Donatus, the name of two of their principal bishops.*

---

* *Mosheim*, vol. I., century IV., part II., ch. 5; *Neander*, vol. II., pp. 182–188; *Lardner's Credibility of the Gospel History*, vol. IV., p. 95; *Fleury*, vol. II., p. 668. *Fleury*, in his *Ecclesiastical History* (vol. II., p. 668), says the Numidians were quartered in the city among those, exclusively, who were opposed to Cæcilian; and that Lucilla, a wealthy lady who was personally inimical to Cæcilian, had furnished not less than £2000, to bribe and buy up the Numidian bishops. Whatever we may think about the probability of this latter story, it certainly furnishes a hint respecting the reputed morality of the African church, in the fourth century. For further hints, see Taylor's *Ancient Christianity*. This learned writer, in his

From Carthage, Donatism extended into all parts of Africa, and even into Spain and Italy. In Rome itself there was a considerable congregation of these "schismatics." That they were not in very good repute there, however, is evident from the fact, that although there were more than forty churches (houses for public worship) in the city, the Donatists could not obtain the use of any one of them; and were therefore compelled to assemble in a cave, in a mountain, beyond the city walls; and hence were called *Montenses*, or Montagnards, i. e.

---

refutation of Oxford divinity, has, as it seems to a humble believer in "the crude assumptions" of modern Congregationalism — completely undermined the foundation of his own admired Church of England.

Fleury treats very fully of the Donatist schism. And he seems to have been regarded by several authors who have spoken of this schism, as authority. Milner follows him very closely; Gibbon's account gives evidence of his familiarity with the French Romanist's relation; so does Waddington's. Fleury, though a Papist, and sufficiently attached to *the* church, and abundantly credulous when the honor of his saints is concerned, is yet apparently a dispassionate and honest historian.

Lardner's account of the Donatists is very much briefer than of the Novatians; Neander, however, goes much more fully into the whole controversy, devoting thirty-five octavo pages to the subject; and though not particularly friendly to the Donatists, he furnishes a fuller and more satisfactory exposition of the controversy than any writer to whom I have had access, except perhaps Fleury. The chief original authorities are Augustine, bishop of Hippo, and Optatus, bishop of Milevi, in Numidia, whose works may be found in all the editions of the Fathers; and some few Donatist works, added to Dupin's edition of the Fathers.

Dupin gives quite a full analysis of Optatus' work against Parmenianus, a Donatist bishop. — *Ecc. Writers*, vol. II., pp. 87–97.

mountaineers.* That they occupied this cave for a considerable time, is obvious from the circumstance that *six* Donatist bishops, in succession, presided over this church of Montagnards.

In Africa the schism became so extensive and alarming, that in the year 313 the emperor Constantine was induced to adopt measures to stop its progress. He appointed commissioners to examine the controversy. This court decided against the Donatists, so far as their charges against Cæcilian were concerned. This decision might, perhaps, have been anticipated, from the character of the judges, who were bishops of that party from which the Donatists had openly separated, as an immoral and corrupt community.

The year following (A. D. 314) another court was held upon the affairs of the Donatists, by Aelian, the pro-consul for Africa. His decision was also unfavorable to the separatists. Another and larger body of Catholic bishops was called together the same year at Arles, to consider these troublesome matters. Their decision was likewise adverse to the interests of the Donatists. Against the decisions of these several courts of "High Commissions,"† the condemned party raised many

* *Fleury*, vol. III., bk. x., pp. 76, 77; bk. XII., p. 396. *Optatus*, who wrote against the Donatists as early as A. D. 370, adduces this very circumstance as an argument against their pretensions of being the church of Christ. — *Optatus*, bk. II., (b) p. 364 of vol. II. of Bigne's edition of the Fathers; *Dupin*, vol. II., pp. 90, 91.

† Fleury calls these bodies "*Councils;*" but Schlegel, in his note to Mosheim's account, says: "They were not properly *councils*, but

exceptions; and from his Commissioners, appealed to the emperor Constantine himself. After some hesitation, Constantine resolved to hear the parties at Milan, and give judgment in his own person upon these vexed questions. This he did in the year A. D. 316. His decision, like all that had preceded, was adverse to the Donatists.

These "obstinate schismatics" were no better satisfied with the judgment of the emperor, than they had been with his High Commissioners. They averred that Constantine himself had given a partial decision; that he had been prejudiced against their rights by the misrepresentations of his favorite bishops. But, "as their cause was examined with attention, perhaps, it was determined with justice. Perhaps their complaint was not without foundation, that the credulity of the Emperor had been abused by the insidious arts of his favorite Osius." *

If Fleury's account of the matter be received, we certainly need not wonder at the dissatisfaction of the Donatists. He tells us, that the emperor, so far from considering his own judgment in the case as superior to that of the bishops who had already examined the controversy, declared, that "he himself ought to be judged by them; and that he regarded their judgment as that of God himself." And Fleury adds: "He did it, then, only to

rather *courts*, held by special judges, appointed by the emperor; or, to speak in the language of modern times, *High Commissions*."

* *Gibbon.*—Bishop Osius, or Hosius, was a favorite with the emperor, and a friend of Cæcilian.

yield to the importunity of the Donatists, for to close their mouths forever; and to leave no means untried of pacifying the church." *

This solemn hearing of the parties before the emperor was, then, no better than an ecclesiastical *ruse*, "to close the mouths of the Donatists forever." The great man had no thought, it would seem, of correcting the errors of his ecclesiastical commissioners — if any they had committed; he was too modest even to think himself capable of such a task. And Fleury certainly assigns a very sufficient reason for this modesty, when he says: "The emperor did not yet well understand the laws" [i. e. as I suppose, the principles on which the church should be organized and governed], "not being baptized, nor even a catechumen." †

If such be a correct view of the matter, we cannot be surprised that the Donatists were no better satisfied with the decision of Constantine, than with that of his ecclesiastical commissioners; for it was, in point of fact, nothing but a pre-determined confirmation and sanction of their doings; the emperor consenting to go through the formalities of a public hearing, on the ground "that the Donatists, obstinate as they were, would not sub-

---

* *Ecc. Hist.*, bk. x., p. 56. Augustine represents Constantine's object in hearing the Donatists in person, to be, — *to oblige them to yield.* — *Dupin*, vol. II., p. 12.

† *Fleury*, bk. x. According to *Eusebius*, Constantine was not baptized until a few days before his death, during his last illness. *Gibbon* comments with severity on the indulgence shown to Constantine by the church. — Vol. I., ch. 20.

mit themselves to the judgment of others;"*— that is, of any one but the emperor himself.

It is quite apparent, from the whole account of Constantine's connection with this controversy, that he had by some means been bitterly prejudiced against the Donatists. For, the very first laws which he promulgated, after obtaining the sovereignty of Africa, made an invidious distinction between the Catholics and the Donatists. While bestowing on the Catholics various privileges, he expressly excluded the Donatists from any share in them, and indulged himself in the use of opprobrious epithets towards them. And subsequently he manifested his displeasure towards them by the most violent expressions, and treated them with great injustice and cruelty.†

Constantine, indignant at the failure of all his efforts to silence and reclaim the Donatists, ordered their temples to be taken from them in Africa, some of their bishops to be banished and others to be put to death. These efforts were continued for about four years, i. e. to A. D. 321; when, finding that violence did but beget violence — that the "schismatics" were determined to resist even

---

* *Fleury*, bk. x.

† *Neander*, vol. II., pp. 189, 190; *Lardner*, vol. IV., pp. 162, 163, 179.

The importance of the Donatist controversy, and the degree of interest which was felt in it by Constantine, may be judged of by the fact, that in the list of letters written by the emperor on various topics (thirty-four in number), not less than nine relate to the Donatists. — See *Dupin*, vol. II., pp. 15, 16.

unto blood — he was induced to repeal the penal laws against them, and to give liberty of conscience to the Africans, to follow either party as they chose. The immediate effect of this decree was to increase the number of the Donatists; so that they shortly outnumbered, in some places, the Catholics.* This of course alarmed the clergy of the court. Constantine being now dead, his son Constans, to whom the government of the African provinces had been assigned, was induced to send from his court two legates, Paul and Mercurius, authorized to heal the "deplorable schism." They were furnished with money and arms; the former, as the Catholics said, to be distributed among the poor churches; the latter, as a protection against the *Circumcelliones.*† The Donatists, however, suspected that other uses were to be found for these things; and facts seem to have justified their suspicions. It was not long before these imperial legates commenced an exterminating or converting war upon the African schismatics. Conversion, banishment, or death, were the alternatives placed before the poor Donatists. A few embraced the

* *Robinson's History of Baptism,* p. 197.

† This was the name given to bands of African peasants who, exasperated by the cruelties inflicted on the Donatists, undertook to defend them by fire and sword. If we may believe the Catholic writers, these "vagrants" committed the most wanton cruelties. *Fleury* tells us of their putting lime and vinegar into the eyes of some of the Catholics. He says they spared neither the aged nor infants. He is careful, however, not to detail the cruelties of the Catholics, which provoked these acts of retaliation. — Vol. v., bk XXIII.

former; but most of them accepted one or other of the latter alternatives. This bloody persecution continued thirteen years, i. e. from A. D. 348 to A. D. 361.

The accession of Julian to the imperial throne (A. D. 361) stopped this persecution, restored the banished Donatists to their country, and secured to them their churches and their religious rights. The explanation of this is, that the Donatists, being opposed to the union of Church and State, and it being the policy of Julian to sever the union which the Catholics had brought about between their Church and the Roman State, he very naturally favored this large and important body of men, who sympathized in this general purpose of his administration. Julian's reign was, however, short. His successor, Gratian, resumed the policy of Constans. He commanded the temples of the Donatists to be taken from them, and their assemblies to be broken up. But the strength of the Donatists was now so great (A. D. 377) that the emperor dared not press the execution of these persecuting edicts, from fear of a civil war.

At the close of this century the number of Donatist bishops in Africa was estimated at 400.* The Catholic bishops, alarmed by the increase of the Donatists, sent deputies to the emperor Honorius (A. D. 404) to urge the execution of the imperial edicts against "the schismatics" and their defend-

* *Mosheim.*

ers, the Circumcelliones. This request was graciously answered, by the imposition of fines upon the common people, and the sentence of banishment upon all the bishops and teachers who refused to return to the bosom of the Catholic church.

The next year (A. D. 405) messengers were sent from the same body — the council of Carthage — to render thanks to Honorius for the destruction of the Donatists.* The triumphing of the bishops was, however, short; for, within about two years they thought it necessary to send another embassy to the emperor, to stir him up to new violence against the Donatists. These efforts not succeeding, the church party, led on by the celebrated Augustine, bishop of Hippo, dispatched another commission to the imperial court, A. D. 410 or 411. By these persevering efforts, the Catholics at length obtained the appointment of an *Imperial Commissioner*, Marcellinus, to visit Africa, "with power to bring this long and pernicious controversy to a conclusion."†

In obedience to the imperial orders, the contending parties assembled at Carthage. The Donatist bishops, Fleury says, entered the city in procession, to the number of 270, drawing all eyes towards them; but the Catholics entered without pomp, in

---

* *Fleury*, bk. XXII., p. 280.

† *Mosheim*, century V., part II., ch. 5; *Gieseler's Ecc. Hist.*, vol. I., p. 420.

number about 286.* The imperial legate announced to the parties the rules by which the conference, or rather the *trial*, was to be governed.† Difficulties arose at the very outset. The Donatists had had sufficient experience of High Commissions to expect no favor from such quarters. They could not but remember that the men who had solicited this commission were their determined enemies; and that the man who had appointed this Commissioner was the same who, but the year before, had forbidden them to assemble in public for religious worship, on pain of proscription and death.‡ They remembered how their fathers were treated at the bar of Constantine: and when they heard Marcellinus declare his inferiority to the bishops, in language very similar to that which Constantine had used — "that he ought to be judged himself by the bishops" § — they could not well avoid intimating their lack of confidence in the pageantry before them, and their conviction that they had been summoned, rather to a *trial* than to a conference.

The result justified the suspicions of the Donatists. They were formally condemned; a scale of fines was established, graduated according to their wealth; forfeiture of goods was to follow; corporal punishment was to be inflicted on slaves and peas-

* Vol. v., bk. xxii.

† For the particulars, see *Fleury*, who devotes no inconsiderable part of his 22d Book to this important trial. See also *Neander's* account of the matter, vol. ii., pp. 200–217.

‡ *Fleury*, vol. v., bk. xxii., p. 319. § *Fleury*, ut supra, p. 330.

ants; the clergy were to be banished beyond the limits of Africa; death itself was to be inflicted upon the more determined and obstinate; and all their churches were transferred to the Catholics.

This persecution appears to have been conducted with great violence. The party in power seem to have resolved on the utter extirpation of the Donatists. Many of them preferred death, even, to a union with such "sinners" and "pagans" as the Catholics were considered. Multitudes fled the country. Others, driven to despair, cast themselves from precipices and perished, suicides. So common was this self-immolation among the Circumcelliones, that Fleury says, it was their "*common play*."* But men are not much given to this kind of "play" until driven to desperation. If such was the "common play" of the Donatist party, we may easily infer what was the "common play" of the Catholics.

Augustine acted a conspicuous part in exciting and defending these persecuting movements. He maintained, that, though it was better to *draw* than to *drive* the "schismatics" into the truth, yet it was better to *drive* them than to have them perish in error. He justified violence by the example of Paul's conversion; who was knocked down and made blind, etc., that he might be driven from his errors. He employed the parable of the supper, in Luke 14: 16–24, to justify the Catholics in going out into "the highways and hedges" and

* Vol. v., bk. XXIII., p. 469.

compelling men to come in.* Gibbon tells us, Augustine insisted, that it was better for the Donatists to burn on earth than in hell.† Optatus argues, that the Donatists did justly suffer those mischiefs, because they broke the unity of the church; that the persecution which they endured was an evil that was necessary for procuring the

---

* *Fleury,* ut sup. pp. 471–2.

† *Gibbon* gives a summary, but somewhat particular account of this persecution, in vol. I., ch. 21, and vol. II., ch. 33. *Milner* puts the conduct of Augustine towards the Donatists in the most favorable light he is able. He extenuates and apologizes as far as his conscience would allow. He tells all the good he knew of the bishop of Hippo — and that was not a little. Yet he admits: "His conduct towards the Donatists bids the fairest for reprehension; but he acted sincerely. You differ with him in judgment, but it is impossible for you to blame his temper and spirit, if you read him candidly. He carefully checks his people for calumniating the Donatists, and is constantly employed in moderating and healing." — Cent. v., chs. 6 and 10.

This is Milner's story; others represent the "saint" as the master spirit of the persecution. Mr. Robinson is extremely violent in his denunciation of Augustine. He says: "When the Donatists reproached him with making martyrs of their bishops and elders, as Marculus, Maximian, Isaac, and others, and told him God would require an account of their blood at the day of judgment, he answered: 'I, I know nothing about your martyrs. Martyrs, martyrs to the devil! They were not martyrs; it is the *cause,* not the *suffering,* that makes a martyr. There is no such thing as a martyr out of the church [i. e. the Catholic church]. Besides, it was owing to their obstinacy; they killed themselves; and now you blame the magistrate.' " — *Hist. of Baptism,* p. 199. Optatus took the same view of the matter; insisting that those who suffered in this persecution were not martyrs, since they had not charity, without which none could be crowned. This was not a persecution of the church, but only a just punishment of some persons who were refractory to the church.

good of peace and union; that this proceeding against them was authorized by the example of Moses, who put to death 3000 men for worshipping the golden calf; of Phineas, who killed two persons for violating the law of God in committing adultery; and of Elias, who put to death 450 false prophets.*

If such were the tender mercies of the Catholic bishops towards the Donatists, what must have been the cruelties of the common soldiery, who were "the Church's instruments" for procuring "peace and union?"

This violent persecution continued fifteen or sixteen years — from A. D. 411 to 427 — and greatly weakened the Donatist party. Geneseric, the king of the Vandals, who invaded and conquered Africa in the year 427, showed himself the protector and friend of these persecuted dissenters.† Under his reign they revived, and flourished again; but they seem never to have recovered fully from the blow inflicted by the long and cruel persecution which they had endured.

They continued to exist as a distinct body, amidst the various revolutions in the country, for more than a century and a half. The last notice of them is found near the close of the sixth cen-

* *Optatus*, bk. III., Bigne, vol. II., pp. 380, 381; or *Dupin's Hist. Ecc.*, vol. II., p. 92.

† *Gibbon* ascribes the success of Geneseric to the persecution, and consequent co-operation with the Vandals, of the Donatists. — Vol. II., ch. 33. *Milner* rejects this intimation with considerable warmth. — Cent. VI., ch. 6, note.

tury, when their increasing efforts to rise and propagate their peculiar tenets were met by the vigorous opposition of Gregory the Great; which, we are led to believe, was so far successful as to drive the Donatists "into corners," if not absolutely to destroy them.*

The view which has now been taken of the history of this "second class of dissenters," will justify, I think, the assertion, that the cause usually assigned for the rise of the Donatists is scarcely adequate to the effects developed in their history.

The simple question, whether Cæcilian or Majorinus should be bishop of Carthage, seems insufficient to account for the immediate formation of a distinct class of religionists throughout Africa. It is true, "a little fire" will kindle "a great matter;" but it requires some time for the process to be effected. Donatism seems to have sprung up almost at once, in its full proportions, and armed with principles so strong that neither flattery nor bribery could overcome them; and which defied even the pains and penalties of confiscation of goods, corporal punishment, banishment, or death itself.

The repeated condemnation of the Donatists by

* *Mosheim,* century VI., part II., ch. 5. This was the same Gregory who abhorred human learning in the clergy; who defended the use of images in the churches; who flattered Phocas the usurper and murderer; who was an enthusiastic promoter of monkery, and the honor of his see. — *Mosheim,* vol. I., *passim,* particularly p. 399, note 29. Also, *Jones' History of the Christian Church,* vol. I., pp 375–387.

the Roman emperors, and their legates and high commissioners, has been regarded as *prima facie* evidence against the sect. But a consideration of the fact, that the very enemies of the Donatists admitted their soundness in the faith, and earnestly desired their union with the Catholic church;* that there was a fair proportion of learned and pious men among their clergy, and of "truly humble and godly persons" among the laity;† affords presumptive evidence that this schism had for its foundation something better than mere caprice and prejudice; that it must have lain upon some broad and important principle. Nothing else could have prevented its early and total overthrow.

The violent enmity of the professedly christian Roman emperors and their favorite bishops towards this persecuted sect is, perhaps, sufficiently account-

* Augustine, during the trial at Carthage, A. D. 411, declared the readiness of the African bishops to receive the Donatists to their churches, and their bishops to their Catholic sees. —*Fleury*, bk. XXII.

† *Milner*, century V., ch. 6, professes his belief, that "there were many such [among the Donatists] in Africa." It is not, to be sure, very obvious how this assertion can be reconciled with another, by this historian (cent. IV., ch. 2), where he says: "With the Donatists there does not appear to have been any degree of real spirituality." But it is not my business to reconcile Milner with himself. I marvel that some of his admirers have not attempted it.

The anxiety of the Catholics to bring the Donatists into 'The Church,' and their readiness to admit the "schismatic" bishops to catholic seats, is sufficient evidence of the correctness of Mosheim's assertion: "That the Donatists were sound in doctrine, their adversaries admit; nor were their lives censurable, if we except the enormities of the Circumcelliones, which were detested by the greatest part of the Donatists." — Cent. IV., part II., ch. 8.

ed for by two, oft-repeated inquiries of the Donatists, when urged to unite with the "established church": — "QUID EST IMPERATORI CUM ECCLESIA?" — *What business has the emperor to meddle with the church?* "QUID CHRISTIANIS CUM REGIBUS, AUT, QUID EPISCOPIS CUM PALATIO?" — *What have Christians to do with kings, or what have bishops to do with the court?** These few words throw a flood of light on the principles of the Donatists. They show us, that they were opposed to the unholy alliance of Church and State, which was consummated in their day; that they had no fellowship with the pomp and pride and courtly manners of the Catholic bishops, and the consequent corruptions of the laity — Quid Christianis cum regibus? and prepare us to believe Mr. Robinson, when he says: "The Donatists thought the church ought to be kept separate from the world, a religious society voluntarily congregated together for pious purposes, and for no other. With this view they admitted none without a personal profession of faith and holiness, and them they baptized; or, if they had belonged to the great corrupt party, rebaptized. They urged for all this, the New Testament. The Catholics, of whom Austin [Augustine] was the head, taxed them with denying, in effect, if not in express words, the Old Testament, and particularly such prophesies as spoke of the

---

* The Catholic reply to these questions was: — "Non Respublica est in Ecclesia, sed Ecclesia in Republica est, i. e. in Imperio Romano." — *Optatus*, bk. III., vol. II., p. 376.

accession of kings and Gentiles and nations to the Church of Christ. 'Is it not foretold,' said Austin, 'that "*To me every knee shall bow?*"' The Catholics, then, were for a national church, for the sake of splendor; *the Donatists for a Congregational church, for the sake of purity of faith and manners.**

It is worth one's while who would investigate this matter thoroughly, to compare bishop Optatus' mode of treating the Donatists, with that of the English churchmen's treatment of the Independents. Optatus calls the Donatists "schismatics and heretics," "impious children," who had forsaken the Catholic church, their mother, "being cut off from the church, had become rebels and enemies;" he charges divers crimes, and even sacrilege on the Donatists: such as—throwing the eucharist to the dogs; throwing a bottle of "holy oil" out of the window; of driving away the bishops; abusing men, women, and children; even murdering two deacons at the foot of the altar:—in fine, of violating everything that was most sacred. In subsequent pages of this history may be found specimens of the abusive misrepresentations by the court clergy, of the early Congregationalists. Could we get at the truth in respect to the Novatians and Donatists, as we can in respect to the early Congregationalists, we might, and probably should find, that the Dissenters and Separatists of the third century were as much maligned and misrepresented by the dominant church party of that

---

* *Robinson's Hist. of Baptism*, pp. 197–200.

period, as were the Independents or Congregationalists of the sixteenth century.*

The Catholics called the Separatists after the name of some leading man among them, as a reproach, that men might infer that these Separatists did not derive their principles from Christ, but from a mere man. Thus, we have Novatians, Donatists, and in later days, Brownists, as nick-names for conscientious dissenters from the Established Church. A Donatist writer, Cresconius, quoted by Augustine, declared that Donatus was not the author and founder of a church which had no previous existence, but was only one of the bishops of the ancient church derived from Christ.

---

* When the Separatists first appeared in England, the Church-and-State party denounced them as DONATISTS. In 1590 appeared "*A short Treatise against the Donatists of England, whom we call 'Brownists,'*" etc. And in the following year, "*A Plain Declaration that our Brownists be full Donatists; by comparing them together, from point to point, out of the writings of Augustine;*" both by "George Giffard, Minister of God's Holy Word in Maldon."—*Hanbury's Memorials*, vol. I., p. 49.

Milman, in his History of Christianity (Harper's Edition, pp. 291–296), gives a general, but by no means a fair account of the Donatist schism. He attributes the rise of the Donatists entirely to the controversy which sprung up in the African church about Traditores. He also adopts the Catholic representations of the Circumcelliones. He speaks of them as half-savage, licentious fanatics. He believes the story of their loving and seeking martyrdom, and even being guilty of self-murder, when they could not obtain the coveted boon, death, from their enemies. But he has the candor to admit, that such excesses as he ascribes to the Donatists and the Circumcelliones rarely "burst out into dangerous excesses to society, unless goaded and maddened by persecution."

CHAPTER III.

LUCIFERIANS AND ÆRIANS, ABOUT A. D. 363.

HE alone who attempts to investigate the origin of the early schisms in the Christian Church can be fully sensible of the difficulty of the task. The account given us of the commencement of the Luciferian schism is nearly as unsatisfactory as that of the Donatist; indeed, the two are not very dissimilar. "Lucifer," says Mosheim, "bishop of Cagliari in Sardinia,* a man of decision, sternness, and vigor, * * first separated from Eusebius of Vercelli, in the year 363, because the latter was displeased that the former had consecrated Paulinus bishop of the church of Antioch; and he afterwards separated himself from the communion of the whole church, because it had decreed that absolution might be granted to those bishops who, under Constantius, had deserted to the Arians." †

According to this account, which agrees substantially with Socrates' (bk. III., chap. VII; bk. V., chap. V) and Milner's (cent. IV., chap. IX), the schism

* Cagliari was the metropolis of Sardinia and the neighboring isles. — *Fleury*.

† Vol. I., bk. XI., cent. IV., part II., ch. 3.

orginated in a personal quarrel between two orthodox bishops; and was irreconcilably widened by the decree of the council of Alexandria, which ordained, that "the Arian bishops, and still more, those who had only held communion with such bishops, might, after acceeding to the Nicene creed [which was the standard of ancient orthodoxy], be received into the church, and remain in their offices."*

Socrates represents Lucifer as particularly vexed at this decree, because, though not present himself at the council, he had sent his deacon,* authorized to act in his name, and had bound himself to observe the decision of the council. Whether this was true or not, it is very certain that the dissatisfied bishop did not long observe the commandments of men, which were contrary to the convictions of his conscience. If bound while in the church, to observe the decrees of the council, which spoke in the name of the church, he soon relieved himself of all obligation, by separating himself entirely from this corrupt body, and establishing a church upon principles more agreeable to his convictions of truth.

The materials for a sketch of this denomination of christian dissenters are very few. Of Lucifer, the founder of it, the general voice of historians is very favorable. "No man," says Milner, "ever exceeded Lucifer in courage and hardiness of spirit."

* *Schlegel's* note to Mosheim's account.

† *Fleury* says *two* deacons, and gives their names, bk. xv., p. 58.

* * "Lucifer was consistent throughout."* In another place he speaks of his "magnanimous constancy" and "sincere spirit of piety" in defending the Nicene faith."† Again, speaking of the different classes of dissenters who had appeared within the first four centuries, he says: "A fourth appears, the Luciferians, who, if they imbibed the spirit of Lucifer, must have been firm and sincere in the love of the truth." And further on, he says: "The spirit of the gospel probably prevailed most among the Luciferians." He afterwards draws a picture of those times (the middle of the fourth century), and contrasts it with later days. "Damascus, orthodox, and violent in the support of orthodoxy, without humility and piety, is as strong a contrast to the primitive bishops, as Sharpe, archbishop of St. Andrews in the time of Charles II., is to our first reformers. *The persecuted Luciferians may seem to resemble the Puritans of the same period;* while such men as Eusebius of Vercellæ, and Hilary of Poictiers, may be likened to archbishop Leighton."‡ This is certainly high praise, coming as it does from such a man as Mr. Milner.

---

* *Cent.* IV., ch. 9. † *Cent.* IV., ch. 4.

‡ *Cent.* IV., ch. 12. Damascus obtained the bishopric of Rome, A. D. 366, after "a bloody warfare" with a rival candidate, "in which there was fighting, burning of buildings, and many lives lost." —*Mosheim,* Cent. IV., bk. II., part II., ch. 2.

Sharpe, during the protectorate of Cromwell, was a Scotch Presbyterian, and a professor in St. Andrews University. He was sent as commissioner to support the cause of Presbyterianism, first to London, and afterwards to the island of Breda, to treat with Charles II. about his restoration. On the restoration of Charles, Sharpe

Fleury tells us that Lucifer's contempt for the world, his love for the Holy Scriptures, the purity of his life, his constancy in the faith, had, previous to his schism, rendered him illustrious in the church.* He was the pope's legate at the council of Milan; which is a sufficient proof of his rank in the church.

After his separation from the Catholics, the same author informs us, that he was accused of nothing but his inflexible obstinacy — they did not accuse him of any error in faith.†

Dr. Lardner (vol IV., pp. 371–374) furnishes the following particulars of Lucifer: —

"Lucifer, bishop of Cagliari, or Carali (as the ancients always write it), in Sardinia, well known in his time, and a sufferer with Eusebius in the reign of Constantius, has a place in Jerome's catalogue of Ecclesiastical Writers. He seems to have been removed [in the course of his banishment] several times; Faustinus and Marcellinus say four times. The last place of his banishment was Thebais, where he was with Eusebius

---

abandoned his old friends, and became the advocate of prelacy; for which he was rewarded by the gift of the archbishopric of St. Andrews. His perfidy made him odious to the Presbyterians. His cruelty to the Covenanters, and his supposed agency in the persecution of those who dissented from the Church of England, have loaded his name with infamy. Repeated attempts were made upon his life; and he finally perished by the hands of nine assassins, who dragged him from his coach and stabbed him in twenty-two places. — *Hume's Hist. Eng.*, vol. IV., pp. 181, 227, 305, 343; *Edinburgh Encyclopœdia*, Art. Sharpe.

* Vol. III., bk. XIII., p. 414.

† Book XV., p. 69.

at the time of the death of Constantius. He is supposed to have died in 370. Athanasius, for a while at least, had a great regard for him, and he wrote to him two letters. In the first of which he desires him to send his writings: and by his order they were translated out of Latin into Greek. Faustinus and Marcellinus express themselves as if they had been translated by Athanasius himself. Lucifer was always a man of a vehement temper, as appears from his books, written in the time of Constantius, and during his banishment. And after his liberty, in the time of Julian, contrary to the sentiment of the Catholic bishops in general, he went into a rigid principle, refusing, though it had been determined in a synod at Alexandria in 362, to receive those bishops who in the reign of Constantius had in any measure complied with the Arians; or to communicate with those who received them upon the acknowledgment of their fault. Jerome at once represents his principle, and speaks tenderly of Lucifer himself; as does also Sulpicius Severus.

"Lucifer and his followers, as it seems, were willing to receive the laity who came over from the Arians, upon renouncing their error; but they would not consent that bishops who had complied with the Arians should be received as such. They might, upon returning to the Catholics, be received as laymen, but they were not any more to officiate in the church. This occasioned a schism; which, however, never spread very far. Rufinus speaks of it as very small, and Theodoret as extinct in his time. And yet, in the year 384, or thereabout, they obtained a rescript from Theodosius, to secure them from persecution, since they made no innovations in the faith. However, they were for some time in several parts of the world; and the authors of the aforesaid request complain particularly that at Rome, where they had a bishop named Aurelius, pope Damasus disturbed their assemblies, and did all he could to hinder their worship, whether by day or by night.

"Lucifer's writings consist very much of passages of the Old and the New Testament, cited one after another, which he quotes with marks of the greatest respect. Particularly, he has largely quoted the book of the Acts; he has likewise largely quoted the epistle to the Hebrews, the second epistle to John, and the epistle of Jude.

"Faustinus and Marcellinus, in their request to the emperors Valentinian, Theodosius, and Arcadius, say, that one thing for which Lucifer was eminent was the study of the Sacred Scriptures: that Athanasius commended his writings for the many passages therein collected out of the prophetical, evangelical, and apostolical scriptures. They continually speak with the highest veneration for the writings of the prophets, evangelists, and apostles; and they blame those who teach or practice any thing contrary to their authority. The epistle to the Hebrews is quoted here very respectfully. Finally, they complain that they were called

Luciferians. They say, that Christ is their master, and his doctrine they follow: they ought therefore to be called by no other than the sacred name of Christians, as they hold nothing but what Christ taught by his apostles."

Dupin (Ecc. Hist., vol. IV., pp. 79, 80) thus notices Lucifer: —

"Lucifer, bishop of Calaris, the metropolitan city of the Isle of Sardinia, was deputed with Hilary and Pancratius, by pope Liberius, to the emperor Constantius, after the fall of Vincentius of Capua. He came to the council of Milan, held in the year 354, where he defended Athanasius and his cause with great courage. The emperor being provoked by his firmness, sent him into banishment, where he was detained till the reign of Julian; but they forced him many times to change his habitation: for, at first, he was banished to Germanicia, a city of Syria, whereof Eudoxus was bishop; afterwards to Eleutheroplis in Palestine, where he was extremely tormented by Eutychus, bishop of that city. At the death of Constantius, he was found banished in Thebais, and he suffered also a fourth banishment, the place whereof is not known. It was at the time when he was in Palestine, towards the year 356, that he wrote his books. They are all against Constantius, in behalf of St. Athanasius and his defenders. The two first have no other title, but, 'The Books in behalf of St. Athanasius against Constantius.' The third is entitled, 'Of Apostate Kings.' The fourth bears this title, 'That we must not Assemble with Heretics.' And the fifth, 'That we must not Pardon those that Offend against God.' All these books are written with so much heat and boldness, that Lucifer must needs have a soul fully prepared to suffer martyrdom, when he wrote them, as is observed by St. Jerom. But that which is most surprising is, that he was not contented with publishing of them, but also sent a copy of them to Constantius, and caused them to be presented to him in his own name. The emperor being astonished at his boldness, gave this copy to Florentius, grand-master of his palace, to send it to Lucifer, that he might declare whether the book was his or no. Lucifer confessed it openly, and acknowledged that it was by his order that it was presented to the emperor. He had charged one named Bonosus, to report this at court, and now made answer to Florentius, who had written to him, that he was ready to suffer death with joy. It was probably upon this occasion, and at this time, that he added his last book, entitled, 'That we should die for the Son of God.' St. Athanasius understanding that Lucifer had undertaken his defence with so much courage, sent a deacon to him named Eutychus, to carry a letter in his name, wherein, after he had testified the obligation that he had laid upon the church, he prays him to send him a copy of his works; which having received, he sent him a very obliging letter of thanks, and translated them into Greek. We have now those letters of St. Athanasius, the letter of Florentius, and the answer of Lucifer, at the end of the works of this bishop of Calaris; and what we have said of the rest of his life is taken out of St. Jerom, and a petition presented to the emperors Theodosius and Valentinian, by Marcellinus and Faustinus, two Luciferian priests.

"After the death of Constantius, Lucifer obtained his liberty, as well as the other bishops that were banished for the faith. He came to Antioch, and found the church of that city in division. For after that Eustathius had been forced to leave it, many Catholics did always separate from those bishops that some would have set over them. They were not willing to acknowledge Meletius, who was then bishop of Antioch, though they had nothing to reprehend in his faith. These Catholics were then governed only by priests, and they were called Eustathians. Lucifer, a severe man, and a rigorous defender of discipline, being come to Antioch, was persuaded that Meletius was ordained by Arian bishops, or such as were suspected of Arianism and had communicated with them, and therefore could not be a lawful bishop; whereupon he joined himself to the Eustathians, and ordained Paulinus, a priest, to be their bishop. This ordination, which still heightened the division of the church of Antioch, was disapproved by Eusebius of Vercellæ, who was sent to Antioch in the name of the Synod of Alexandria. He condemned the conduct of Lucifer, and retired into the West, having no more hope of restoring peace to the church of Antioch; Lucifer, on the contrary, to maintain what he had done, resolved to have no more conversation or correspondence with any of the bishops who had received into their communion those that had formerly signed the Arian creeds. He withdraws therefore into his own island, and separates from the communion of almost all the bishops of the world. He died in this resolution, and left some followers called Luciferians, who spread themselves over all the world."

Mr. Robinson gives the following brief account of this sect: "There was a party nearer to Augustine than the Donatists, who were called Luciferians, from Lucifer; * * a man of eminent piety and goodness. He and his followers held the doctrine of the Trinity; they re-baptized nobody; and their lives were exemplary: but they held separate assemblies, and would not hold communion with Austin's [Augustine's] worldly church. *They were a sort of Trinitarian Independents.* The Donatists were Trinitarian Anabaptists. * * Austin held all in like execration, for all stood in the way of that hierarchy which this Carthaginian genius was endeavoring to set up. While each bishop tyrannized over his own congregation, all was easy; but when one in the chair had begun to treat the bench as the bench had treated the people, the bench rebelled against the chairman, and made the people free for the sake of being free themselves."*

* *History of Baptism*, p. 200.

The cause here assigned for the rise of both the Luciferians and Donatists is certainly reasonable. The tyranny of the principal bishops over their inferiors, and the arbitrary and oppressive canons of the provincial councils, which assumed the right to make laws for the government of all the churches within their limits — would naturally excite the inquiry in the minds of the oppressed: "By what authority doest thou these things? and who gave thee this authority?" This vein of thought once struck, and the Scriptures taken as a guide, would unavoidably result in the discovery of the great principles on which modern Congregationalists have built their system of church order.*

The Luciferians seem not to have been very

* The history of schism in the Methodist Episcopal church, which occurred about 1840, furnishes an illustration of the above remarks. One of the leaders in that schism, Rev. George Storrs, "defined his position," by stating his utter abhorrence of Episcopacy, and his cordial reception of Congregationalism, or Independency. Now, what brought him and his friends to that position? The historian of the M. E. church would without doubt say: The difficulty they experienced, in that church, in carrying out their favorite measures for the abolition of slavery. A person unacquainted with the whole affair, would very naturally ask: — What connection is there between the cause assigned and the effect manifested? It is only by knowing the whole history of the difficulties, that we can answer this question. And even then, we shall be unable to perceive any connection between the cause, abstractly considered, and the effect practically developed. The whole story may be briefly thus told: Mr. Storrs and his clerical friends were easy under Methodist Episcopacy — though it deprives the people, as such, of their scriptural rights in the government of the church — until they began to feel the power of the bishops and of the General Conference in controlling their own movements as abolitionists. The bishops presiding in the

numerous. The schism was confined chiefly to Sardinia and Spain. There were, however, assemblies of Luciferians in Rome, as early as A. D. 367–374, notwithstanding they were forbidden to come within a hundred miles of the city. They were not only subject to trial and condemnation by the Catholic bishops, but were forbidden to appeal to the emperor for any revision of Catholic decisions. Under this law, Damascus, bishop of Rome, caused several Luciferian priests and laymen to be arrested and exiled. One of these priests was accused of holding a conventicle in a private house in the night time. All the efforts of their persecutor could not prevent Aurelius and his successor Ephesius, Luciferian bishops, from remaining in the city until the time of their deaths.*

It was the fortune of the Luciferians to live amidst the fires of the Arian controversy. And, having little sympathy with either the Arians or the Orthodox, in their struggle for supremacy in the empire, they suffered persecution from both parties: in which respect they resembled the Separatists — the strictest portion of the English Puritans, and the immediate ancestors of the Congre-

---

Yearly Conferences refused to put their anti-slavery motions; and the General Conferences passed decrees prohibiting "any travelling preacher from engaging in any agency for any object not approved by the General Conference." These things led the aggrieved brethren to inquire — "By what authority doest thou these things? and who gave thee this authority?" The result of this inquiry may be found in the "American Wesleyan Observer" for Aug. 13, 1840.

* *Fleury*, bk. XV. and XVI., *passim*.

gationalists — as well as in their views of christian doctrine and practice, and the independency of their churches.

THE ÆRIANS.

Nearly contemporary with Lucifer (A. D. 363) appeared Ærius. He was a native of Pontus, a province of Asia Minor. Fleury represents him to have been an Ascetic. He was the intimate friend and fellow monk of Eustathius, who was afterwards raised to the bishopric of Sebaste, a city in the northern part of ancient Cappadocia. This elevation of his companion is said to have excited the jealousy and ambition of Ærius. Eustathius did what he could to appease him; he ordained him presbyter, and gave him the chaplaincy of a hospital, or a house for the entertainment of strangers; but nothing would satisfy him. Caresses and menaces were equally ineffectual. Ærius at length broke away from his friend and the Catholic church, and began to preach doctrines which neither Eustathius nor the church could at all approve. Such, for substance, is Fleury's account of the rise of Ærianism.*

Lardner's account of the Ærians (vol. IV., pp. 306–308) is brief, but quite comprehensive. It is as follows: —

"Ærius, of Pontus, or Lesser Armenia, was liv-

---

* Vol. IV., bk. XIX.

ing when Epiphanius wrote in 376. He was a thorough Arian; but the principles by which he was distinguished were such as these: He denied the difference between a bishop and a presbyter, saying, they are one order, office, and dignity. He was likewise of opinion, that no offerings ought to be made for the dead: forasmuch as such things tended to make men think that the practice of piety is not necessary; and that, if near the period of life they could by presents or legacies, or some how or other, procure friends to pray for them after their death, they might escape the just punishment of their sins. They likewise denied the obligation of set fasts and feasts. The keeping of Easter, they said, was unnecessary: for *Christ our passover had been sacrificed for us*, 1 Cor. 5: 7. To keep Easter [or passover] now, was *to give heed to Jewish fables*, Tit. 1: 14, and 1 Tim. 1: 4. Set fasts, too, they said, were Jewish ordinances. If I have a mind to fast, I will take the time that best suits me. Not but that they would sometimes fast on the fourth day of the week, as others do: however, they said, they did it not as bound thereto, but only of their free will: which last particular is sufficient to show, that what Epiphanius also says of their choosing to fast on the Lord's day is a calumny, and an unrighteous aggravation of their principle.

"These then were the sentiments of this people: this is the institution of Ærius and his followers. But how came they to differ so much from the rest of the world — from most of the Arians, as well as the Homousians? A necessary inquiry: for all heresy is supposed to spring from some evil root. Well, what was it? Let us attend. It is said, that Ærius was a friend of Eustathius, a man of Arian principles, too; and that when Eustathius was made bishop of Sebaste in Lesser Armenia, about the year 355, Ærius was much concerned that he was not bishop likewise. Eustathius endeavored to oblige him. He ordained Ærius presbyter, and appointed him governor of the hospital in the city: but Ærius was still uneasy, and therefore set up a new discipline: a story that does not seem to me to have the appearance of probability: nor are his principles so unreasonable, but that, without being under the bias of any prejudice, he might think them founded in scripture.

"These people, as we learn from Epiphanius, met with great difficulties. Ærius and his followers were excluded from churches, and cities, and villages; and being obliged to wander abroad, they suffered great hardships, especially in the winter and cold weather.

"From Augustine's manner of speaking, we may be apt to think that he knew of some such people at the time of writing his book of heresies in the year 428.

"Tillemont considers these people as Calvinists. For certain, they went much upon the Presbyterian plan; and they may induce us to think, that in most times there have been some who opposed growing superstition in the church, and asserted the freedom of the gospel; but being generally opposed, and with much violence, they could not increase to any great number, and in time they were reduced to nothing. We formerly saw another like instance in the people of Neocæsarea, disciples of Gregory, generally called Thaumaturgus."

Gieseler, in his Text-Book of Church History (vol. I., pp. 455, 456, Harper's edition), speaking of the attempts at reformation in the fourth and fifth centuries, says: "The new tendencies of christian life could not slide in unnoticed, especially as it is certain that the Catholic church was frequently reproached with them by the elder christian parties. Nor were the morally dangerous aspects of these tendencies entirely overlooked by the more acute; though they were too often exculpated on the ground of pious intentions. The men who looked into the ecclesiastical and religious errors of the time more profoundly, and attacked them publicly, were declared heretics by the offended hierarchy; and their voice soon died away, without being able to give another direction to the incipient development of ecclesiastical life. To these latter belonged Ærius, presbyter in Sebaste, and friend of bishop Eustathius (about A. D. 360)." * * He adds in a note, after quoting Epiphanus' account of Ærius' heresies: "The Protestants were frequently accused of the heresy of Ærius." And well they might be, for, after the same way which the Catholic church has for many centuries called "heresy," have the modern Protestants, as did the Ærians, worshipped God; believing all things which are written in the law and in the prophets (Acts 24: 5, 14), and nothing else, as obligatory on their consciences.

From a comparison of several accounts of this sect, I suppose the truth to be very nearly as follows: Ærius, like many others of his day, disgusted with the pride and tyranny of the bishops, may have remonstrated with his friend Eustathius for taking a bishopric, or for following in the beaten track of episcopal usurpations. Eustathius, with the hope of stilling his reprover, ordained him a presbyter, and made him his private chaplain. Finding that these favors did not remove the objections of Ærius, he next resorted to threats. But neither excommunication nor any other ecclesiastical punishment had sufficient terrors to stop the mouth of the dissenter. Finding his remonstrances with his friend fruitless, and his efforts at reform in the church unavailing, Ærius at length decided, as Novatian and Donatus and Lucifer had before him, to abandon a communion in which so much error and corruption were allowed. Having resigned his station in the hospital of Sebaste, he at once avowed himself the advocate of a simple and primitive organization and worship of the church. (1.) He maintained, first of all, that, by Divine appointment, there was no difference between bishops and presbyters; (2.) That prayers for the dead were wrong; and (3.) That the feasts and fasts observed by the church on set days were Jewish, rather than Christian observances.

The actual language of Ærius, in speaking on these points, as quoted by Epiphanius, in his work on heresies, is as follows: "(1.) What is a bishop to a presbyter? This differs from that in no respect; for there is one rank, one honor, and one authority. (2.) What is the Passover which is observed by us? There is no necessity for observing this passover; for Christ is our passover. — 1 Cor. 5: 7. (3.) Why do you invoke the names of the dead? But if in reality the prayer of the living benefits the dead, then indeed piety and good works are unnecessary; one has only to secure friends to pray for him, that he may not suffer in another world. (4.) Neither should fasting be made imperative; for this is Jewish, and under the yoke of bondage. For, if I really wish to fast, on whatever day I may choose, I fast, according to the liberty which Christ has given his disciples." *

* The original Greek of Epiphanius, of which the above is a somewhat close translation, is as follows:

"(1.) Τί ἐστιν ἐπίσκοπος πρὸς πρεσβύτερον; οὐδὲν διαλλάττει ὄυτος τούτου· μία γάρ ἐστι τάξις, καὶ μία τιμὴ καὶ ἓν ἀξιώμα. (2.) Τί ἐστι τὸ πάσχα, ὅπερ παρ' ὑμῖν ἐπιτελεῖται;—οὐ χρὴ τὸ πάσχα ἐπιτελεῖν· τὸ γὰρ πάσχα ὑμῶν ἐτύθη Χριστός. (3.) Τίνι τῷ λόγῳ μετὰ θάνατον ὀναμάζετε ὀνόματα τεθνεώτων;—εἰ δὲ ὅλως εὐχὴ τῶν ἐνταῦθα τοὺς ἐκεῖσε ὤνησεν, ἄρα γοῦν μηδεὶς εὐσεβείτω, μηδὲ ἀγαθοποιείτω, ἀλλὰ κτησάσθω φίλους τινάς,— καὶ εὐχέσθωσαν περὶ αὐτοῦ, ἵνα μή τι ἐκεῖ πάθῃ. (4.) Οὔτε νηστεία ἔσται τεταγμένη· ταῦτα γὰρ 'Ιουδαϊκά ἐστι, καὶ ὑπὸ ζυγὸν δουλείας.—εἰ γὰρ ὅλως βούλομαι νηστεύειν, οἵαν δ' ἂν αἱρήσομαι ἡμέραν ἀπ' ἐμαυτοῦ νηστεύω διὰ τὴν ἐλευθερίαν."—*Epiphanius Contra Octoginta Hæreses*, 75; *Gieseler*, vol. I., p. 456, Harper's ed.

Epiphanius, it will be seen, has numbered the heretical sentiments of Ærius up to four. But these "heretical" views are such as Protestants pretty generally embrace as Bible doctrines. Ærius, who was a diligent student of the Bible, found these doctrines there; and so will every one who takes the Scriptures for his only infallible guide. The truth of these doctrines—so directly opposed to the teachings and practice of the church of that day—he supported by appeals to the Scriptures. Such were the outlines of Ærius' system of church reform.

"He seems," says Mosheim, "to have aimed to reduce religion to its primitive simplicity." And it is a proof that there were some remains of primitive feeling among the people, that his doctrine respecting the equality of bishops and presbyters "was very pleasing to many, who were disgusted with the pride and arrogance of the bishops of that age."

This advocate of "primitive simplicity" in the order of the church, in opposition to the usurpations of the bishops; and of the same simplicity in the worship of the church, in opposition to the growing errors and superstitions and idolatries of the people, found "a great multitude" to follow him. Armenia, Pontus, and Cappadocia were rent by the schism.

The Catholic doctors attempted by their writings to refute the "heresies" of this reformer. Among them, Epiphanius, bishop of Salamina in Cyprus, took the lead. According to Fleury, he "refuted the heresy principally by an appeal *to tradition* and the *consent of all the churches;*"* an example which the advocates of Diocesan Episcopacy, and the oppugners of the Congregational doctrine — that bishops and presbyters are, *jure divino*, of the same rank — have wisely followed, from the days of "St. Epiphanius" to the present time. Such arguments were then, as they are now, lightly esteemed by those who look to the Scriptures as their guide. The Catholics, not content with denouncing, and in their judgment refuting the heresy, resorted to more pungent, if not more convincing arguments. "They drove the Ærians, everywhere, from the churches, from the cities, and the villages." But this, it seems, did not quench their zeal for the truth; for, "they assembled in the woods, in caverns, in the open country, even sometimes when covered with snow."†

Thus, these advocates for church reform resembled the primitive Christians in their *sufferings*, as well as in their *doctrines;* and shared the fate of all who had preceded them as church reformers.

Whether Ærius was "*entirely* Arian," as Fleury asserts; or "*semi*-Arian," as Mosheim says; or entirely sound and orthodox in the faith; — it is evident that he was a man of talents and learning and eloquence; and, what is better than all, a man who

* Vol. IV., bk. XIX., pp. 672, 673; *Dupin*, vol. II., p. 235.
† *Fleury*, ut supra.

regarded the Scriptures as a sufficient, and the only infallible guide to the order and worship of the church, as well as the religious faith of Christians. This appears from the very doctrines which he professed, as well as from his appeals to the Scriptures in defence of these doctrines.*

Instead of being branded as a heretic, Ærius ought to be regarded as one of those, who, in an age of great degeneracy, when the church had grievously departed from "the right way," and was "bent to backsliding" yet more and more — stood in the ways, and asked for the old paths (Jer. 6: 16) wherein Christ and his apostles had walked; and having found them, proclaimed the good news to others.

Had this warning voice been heeded, the flood of corruption which was beginning to overflow the church would have been stayed; the pride, ambition and usurpations of the bishops would have been checked; the superstitious and idolatrous worship of the dead would have been prevented; and the entire order and worship of the church would have been brought back to that "primitive simplicity," which was the beauty and the glory of the apostolic churches.

The accusation, that "Ærius was anxious to be a bishop," and because Eustathius outran him in the race of ambition, therefore conceived "a furious jealousy against his friend"† — carries with it

* *Schlegel's* Note to *Mosheim*, cent. IV., bk. II., part II., ch. 3.

† *Fleury*, ut supra; *Schlegel*, in *Mosheim*.

its own refutation. Had Ærius wished to become a bishop, he certainly was in the highway to that honor before he separated from the church. The confidential friend and private chaplain of a bishop — who so likely to be promoted to the next vacant see in the neighborhood? Under such circumstances, would Ærius have broken friendship with the bishop of Sebaste, had he wished to rise in the church? He would have been far more likely to have played the sycophant — the humble servant to his friend, the bishop.

Schlegel tells us, that Ærius accused his bishop and his friend "of avarice and misappropriation of the funds for the poor;" an accusation far more likely to be true, than that which has been laid at the presbyter's door; for avarice and dishonesty were sins in which the bishops of that age very freely indulged. The discovery of such propensities in the bishop of Sebaste would have furnished a much more satisfactory ground for the breach between the two friends, than that which Fleury assigns. Be this as it may, one thing is certain: Ærius embraced one of the leading doctrines of modern Congregationalism, viz: — *that, jure divino, there is no difference between bishops and presbyters;* and acted upon the fundamental principle of this system, viz: — *that the Scriptures are a sufficient guide to church order, as well as religious faith.* He therefore deserves a place in the History of Congregationalism.

CHAPTER IV.

THE HISTORY OF THE PAULICIANS, A. D. 660.

The Paulicians were dissenters from the corruptions of the Greek and Romish churches of the seventh century. Their history is involved in much obscurity, and contradictory accounts are given of their religious tenets. They are often confounded with other sects — as indeed were many of the ancient dissenters; and sentiments are ascribed to them which they, without doubt, abhorred. These things are to be attributed to the ignorance and prejudice of their enemies, to whom we are almost exclusively indebted for our knowledge of this interesting sect of Christians.

The original authorities for the early history and peculiarities of the Paulicians are Photius and Petrus Siculus, or Peter of Sicily. These authors were contemporaries of each other, but neither of them were contemporaneous with the early Paulicians, and personally knew nothing of them for some two hundred years after their rise. Photius was a learned bishop or patriarch of Constantinople; made so, according to Dupin, on Christmas day, A. D. 858. Peter of Sicily was an envoy, sent by the Emperor Basil, to Tibrica, in Armenia, A. D. 870, to treat with the Paulicians for an exchange of prisoners. These two authors appear to agree substantially. Which wrote first, however, is not ascertained. But both of them were Catholics, and strongly prejudiced against the Paulicians, whose history and peculiarities they profess to give.

In the persecutions which these dissenters from Rome endured, the same policy was adopted as was pursued at a later date by the same unalterable church in her persecution of the Waldenses: all the manuscripts and books of the persecuted, which could be found, were ruthlessly destroyed; so that they might not be able to tell their own story, in their own way, to posterity. This leaves us dependent on what the enemies of the Paulicians chose to relate of them. But all that has been written about the Paulicians has been pretty carefully examined by different parties, who, for different purposes, have written about these interesting and important dissenters from Rome. Among the moderns, Gibbon, in his Decline and Fall of the Roman Empire, has gone quite fully into the story of the Paulicians, and given an intelligible, interesting, and candid account of them. Mosheim and Neander have also given considerable attention to the Paulicians; Geiseler's account is brief; Robert Robinson furnishes some details respecting the Italian Paulicians, or Paterines as they were called in Italy, which are of particular interest; Bossuet, in his Variations of Protestantism, goes quite fully, but not fairly, into Paulicianism; Fleury, Jones, Milner, and Waddington, all notice the Paulicians; Blair's History of the Waldenses also contains many facts respecting these dissenting Christians. All the writers which have been mentioned, together with Reinerius and others have been examined in the preparation of the following chapter; and from them all, I have drawn out such an account of the Paulicians as seems to me, on the whole, to be most agreeable to the truth.

About the year of our Lord 660, there lived in Mananalis, an obscure village near the city of Samosata, not far from the borders of Armenia and Syria,* a humble man named Constantine, probably a Gnostic, of a Marcionite sect. This man, acting in the spirit of the apostle's directions, though perhaps ignorant of the letter, on a certain occasion received to his house a travelling stranger. The stranger proved to be a christian deacon, returning from Syria, whither he had been carried captive by the victorious Mohammedans, who were then extending their conquests over the empire of the East. Having enjoyed the hospitality of Constantine for a considerable time (ἡμέρας ὀυκ ὀλίγας), the traveller gave him, in return, a Greek New Testament. It may have been all he had to give; or he

* According to Photius and Peter Siculus, Constantine was a native of Armenia; but Samosata, or Samiscat, lies on the Euphrates, between 36 and 38 degrees north latitude, and the same parallels of west longitude, and within the limits of ancient Syria. The south-eastern corner of Armenia approaches near to Syria.

may have discovered from the conversation of his host, that no remuneration would be so highly valued as the sacred writings.*

In an age like that which we are now contemplating — when it was scarcely a reproach to a bishop to subscribe the acts of an ecclesiastical council by the hand of another, because he could not write himself — a copy of the New Testament was indeed a treasure; and the disposition and ability to read it were alike honorable to the heart and the head of any one. This honor Constantine merits; for he immediately began to study with diligence the sacred writings. This study begat in him, as it has in thousands of others, a reverential regard for the sacred volume, which soon became, as Gibbon says, "the measure of his studies, and the rule of his faith." † Adopting this measure and following this rule, he and his disciples were brought to embrace opinions entirely at variance with the doctrines of the church of their day.

(1.) In the first place, they insisted that the New Testament should be diligently read by all the people; in opposition to the opinion of the dominant

* *Photius, Contra Manichæos*, lib. I., § 16, says, the deacon gave Constantine two books; one containing the holy Evangelists, and the other the Epistles of the great apostle Paul. Peter's epistles they seem to have repudiated, because he denied his Lord; justifying themselves by the words of Christ: "Whosoever shall deny me before men, him will I also deny," etc. — Matt. 10 : 33. *Sic. p.* 30.

† *Gibbon.* All the quotations from Gibbon, under this head, will be found in vol. IV., ch. 54, of his Decline and Fall of the Roman Empire, Harper's edition. *Photius,* lib. I., § 16; *Sic.* 13, 30.

church, which taught that the priests alone should be trusted with the sacred treasure. * (2.) Not finding in the New Testament the three distinct orders of the clergy — bishops, priests, and deacons — which the Catholic Church recognized, the Paulicians rejected that dogma of the church. (3.) Their ordinary religious teachers appear to have been called Pastors and Teachers (ποιμένας και διδασκάλους); † but they had also what were called "Apostles and Prophets," (ἀποστόλους καὶ προφήτας), titles given to leading and particularly influential men, who travelled among the churches in different countries, preaching the gospel and propagating the Paulician faith; such as Constantine or Sylvanus, Simeon or Titus, and others.‡ The persons who accompanied and assisted these chief men in their missionary labors, were called συνεκδῆμοι — *Fellow Travellers.* Besides these, they had in their churches what they called *Notaries* (νοταρίοι), who probably assisted the pastors, and were transcribers of the sacred records, which were held in great reverence by the Paulicians, and the diligent reading of which was enjoined on all. These teachers and helpers were distinguished from the laity by no peculiarity of dress, manner of living, or any thing else designed to indicate a difference between them and the mass of the people. (4.) A single congregation of believers, assembled for religious conference

† *Photius*, lib. I., § 21, pp. 114, 11[illegible]. **S*[illegible]*ul s* [illegible], 44.

‡ *Photius* enumerates seven of these leading spirits. — Lib. I., § 4. pp. 12, 13.

and discussion, was regarded by them as a true church, καθολικὴν ἐκκλησίαν. (5.) Their mode of worshipping God was simple and primitive, consisting chiefly of prayer and religious conference; and hence, instead of calling their places of worship *churches*, they called them *proseuchas* — (προσευχὰς) — *places of prayer;* a title probably suggested by Acts 16: 13, 16. (6.) Their teachers and assistants were elected to office, as were the officers of the apostolic churches, by the votes of the churches;*

---

* Thus, according to Photius (lib. I., § 3), Constantine himself was constituted an apostle and prophet of these primitive reformers, by the popular vote of the church. After stating (lib. I., § 2,) that the Paulicians derived their origin and name from two sons, Paul and John, of a certain Syrian woman, of Samosata, Callinece by name (a story not credited by the best informed ecclesiastical historians), he goes on to say: After the lapse of some time, the assembly [church — συνέδριον — see lib. I., § 9] of these apostates chose *by hand-vote* [χειροτονοῦσι, the same word used by the evangelist in describing the election of church officers by the apostolic churches, Acts 14: 23, 24; 15: 22–29; 2 Cor. 8: 19, etc. — see View of Congregationalism, pp. 55–58, third edition] another teacher, whose surname was Constantine, but which he changed to that of Sylvanus.

Now, if in this way they constituted their chiefs — their apostles and prophets — it is reasonable to presume that their other, and indeed all their ecclesiastical officers were constituted in the same way; particularly, as they had abundant apostolic authority for such a course, and that the leading design of the Paulicians was to follow exactly apostolic example.

This outline of Paulician views of church polity has been drawn primarily from Photius. To save trouble, the several references to Photius are here given together, in the order in which they are required by the text: *Photius, Contra Manichæos,* lib. I., § 20, 9, 9 and 18, 25, 3. See also, *Mosheim,* vol. II., p. 103, Harper's ed.; *Gibbon,* vol. IV., ch. 54; *Neander,* vol. III., pp. 245, 251, 263–265; *Gieseler,* vol. II., p. 209. *Siculus,* 11—53.

and it is probable that all their church business was done substantially in the same popular way — in accordance with the voice of the majority of the brethren.

In addition to these distinctive views, relating generally to church polity, the Paulicians entertained other views, equally adverse to the prevalent hierarchal opinions of their time: as, concerning the folly and sin of worshipping the Virgin Mary; or looking to the mediation of saints and angels for favor with God; or of idolizing the work of the sculptor or painter; the worthlessness of all *relics*, whether bones or ashes; the impiety of all worship of the cross, a piece of mere wood; and the absurdity of regarding the eucharistic wine and bread as any thing but "the gifts of nature and the symbols of grace," the *emblems* of the body and the blood of Christ.*

That all these important truths were at once discovered and proclaimed by the father of the Paulicians, I do not assert; but, that these were the distinguishing peculiarities of this sect is perfectly apparent from the accounts given us by their very enemies. And if so, the taunt of the Romanists — that the Protestants can find no better predecessors

---

* Peter Siculus says, they were so spiteful against Mary, as not to allow her a place even among the good and virtuous. *p.* 1[illegible]. Photius tells us (lib. I., § 7) that they were opposed to the worship of the cross — the worship of a mere bit of wood, as they called it — the sign of a curse, according to Gal. 3 : 13 — "cursed is every one that hangeth on a tree."

than the Paulicians—will scarcely be regarded as a reproach.*

It is true, that those who hated and persecuted these lovers and followers of "primitive simplicity" in the order and worship of the church, charge them with numerous and detestable errors; just as the ancient heathen did the primitive disciples of Christ. The Paulicians are represented as denying God to have been the Creator of this lower and visible world; as believing that matter was eternal; and that light and darkness were the originals, or "two first principles of all things," over each of which an independent Lord had reigned eternally. They are accused of rejecting the Old Testament Scriptures entirely; and disregarding the sacrament of the Lord's supper; and, in various other particulars, of following the vagaries of Manes: in short, they are charged with being *Manichæans*. † This charge they indignantly repelled. "They sincerely condemned the memory and opinions of the Mani-

---

* Bossuet, in his Historie des Variations des Eglises Protestantes, after retailing all the slander which his Catholic predecessors had furnished him with against the Paulicians, thus concludes: "Whence comes it, then, that Protestants undertake the defence of these wicked men (*scelerats*, wretches)? The cause of it is but too clear. It is the desire of giving themselves predecessors. They find their predecessors only among such as reject the worship of the cross, the invocation of the saints, and oblations of the dead. They are vexed at not finding the commencement of their reform, except in the Manichæans. Inasmuch as these growl against the Pope and the Roman church, the Reform is well disposed in their favor."—*Book* XI., § 70.

† *Siculus*, 42; *Hallam*, *M. A.* 503.

chæan sect, and complained of the injustice which impressed that invidious name on the simple votaries of St. Paul and of Christ." *

---

* *Photius* tells us, that the Manichæans of his day freely anathematized Manes, though they greatly reverenced Constantine, and considered him and his successors as equal to the apostles of Christ. — Lib. I., § 15.

Gibbon. Manes or Manichæus was a Persian magus, who embraced Christianity in the fifth century. He was, for his time, learned in the arts and sciences; a man of genius, eloquence, and exuberant imagination; grave in aspect, and simple and innocent in his life. He became the father of a numerous progeny, who were troublers of the church for many ages. His great object seems to have been, to reconcile Christianity and the Persian mythology. For this purpose he is said to have given out, that Christ left his system but imperfectly revealed, and that he (Manes) was the *Paraclete* or Comforter, who was to complete the work. By the aid of his genius and imagination he wrought out of the christian system and that of the magi, one that suited his taste better than either. Some of his notions are alluded to in the text. For a more particular account, see *Mosheim*, book I., cent. III., pt. II., ch. 5. This sect, or branches of it, were the bane and curse of the church for ages; and it seems to have been a favorite device of the churchmen of different periods, to doom the troublesome sectaries of their day, by giving them the odious title of *Manichæans.* They acted upon a well-established principle of Lynch law, that "a bad name will hang a dog." According to *Fleury* (bk. XLV., pp. 463, 464), the Paulicians were called "vagabonds" and "country dogs."

Bossuet unhesitatingly, and continually, calls the Paulicians *Manichæans;* and never intimates, so far as I have noticed, that there was any question about this relationship, or that the Paulicians ever objected to the allegation that they were Manichæans. — See *Variations of Protestantism*, bk. XI., *passim.*

Mosheim, in speaking of Bossuet's account of the Paulicians, says. "The moderns, who treat of the Paulicians, as Peter Boyle, Wolf, and others, seem to have derived their information chiefly from Bossuet, Hist. des Variations, etc. But this writer certainly did not go

That the Paulicians were not Manichæans, is evident from their own solemn denial of the charge, and from the very tenets which their enemies ascribe to them. The Manichæans rejected the Old Testament and a large part of the New, as fabulous and false; and maintained that even what remained was interpolated and somewhat corrupted; and they substituted another gospel for the writings of the four Evangelists. In opposition to all this, the Paulicians cordially received and highly reverenced the Gospels, and the Acts of the Apostles, and all the other books of the New Testament, with, perhaps, the exception of the two epistles of Peter; and Milner regards it as very improbable that they made even this exception. As it respects the Old Testament Scriptures, it is obvious that one cannot easily receive and reverence the New Testament and yet reject and deny the authority of the Old; since Christ and his apostles are continually referring to and quoting the "Law and the Prophets." Gibbon, while he admits the truth of this charge against the followers of

---

to the sources, and being influenced by party zeal, he was willing to make mistakes." — Vol. II., p. 102, note 5.

Gieseler (vol. II., pp. 209–212, Edinb. ed.) gives the original text of Photius and Peter Siculus, in their representations of this sect. *Mosheim* (bk. III., cent. IX., pt. II., ch. 5) contains references to the original authorities, but not the text of those authors.

A beautiful edition of *Photius*, in Greek and Latin, was published by I. C. Wolf, Hamburg, 1722, in his "Anecdota Græca, Sacra et Profana," a very nice copy of which may be found in Harvard College Library.

Constantine, says: "Their utmost diligence must have been employed to dissolve the connection between the Old and New Testament." Mr. Jones' solution of this difficulty is probably a true one He says: "The advocates of popery, to support their usurpations and innovations in the kingdom of Christ, were driven to the Old Testament for authority, adducing the kingdom of David for their example. And when their adversaries rebutted the argument, insisting that the parallel did not hold, for that the kingdom of Christ, which is not of this world, is a very different state of things from the kingdom of David, their opponents accused them of giving up the Divine authority of the Old Testament."* The rejection of the ordinance of the Lord's Supper, with which they are charged, may be accounted for in the same way. They rejected the dogma of the church, that after consecration the eucharistic bread and wine became the real body and actual blood of Jesus Christ. Their candid adversaries immediately charged them with a contempt for the ordinance itself.

Milner, a man no one will accuse of partiality towards sectaries, gives no credit to the charges of

---

* *History of the Christian Church,* vol. I., pp. 423, 424, 5th ed. Would such a misrepresentation be more strange than one which is found in the Encyclopædia Americana, which gives, as a description of the English Congregationalists or Independents, that they "now differ from other Protestant sects in rejecting any formula of faith, requiring only a belief in the Gospel; and *their pastors are not ordained?*" — See, also, *A. Fuller's Works,* vol. II., p. 644.

Manichæism and heresy, which have been so plentifully heaped upon this interesting sect of dissenters. He speaks of them as originating "from a heavenly influence, teaching and converting them;" and as being the recipients of "one of those extraordinary effusions of the Divine Spirit, by which the knowledge of Christ and the practice of godliness is kept alive in the world." *

Mosheim says: "These Paulicians are by the Greeks called Manichæans; but, as Photius himself states, they declared their abhorrence of Manes and of his doctrine: and it is certain that they were not *genuine* Manichæans, although they might hold some doctrines bearing a resemblance to those of that sect. There were not among them, as among the Manichæans, bishops, presbyters, and deacons; they had no order of clergymen, distinguished from laymen by their mode of living, their dress, and other things; nor had they councils, or any similar institutions," etc.†

Neander (vol. III., pp. 244, 245) says: "As it regards Manichæism, the truth is, that in this period there was a universal inclination to call everything of a dualistic tendency Manichæism [i. e.

---

* *Church Hist.*, cent. IX., ch. 2.

† Book III., cent. IX., pt. II., ch. 5, § 5. Mosheim quotes, in support of his positions, *Photius*, contra Manichæos, lib. I., pp. 17, 56, 65; *Peter Siculus*, Hist. Manich., p. 43; Photius, pp. 31, 32; Peter Siculus, p. 43. And yet, in spite of the testimony of these their own original witnesses, Bossuet and his favorite authors persist in denouncing the Paulicians as complete Manichæans.

every tendency to recognize two contending agencies or principles in the universe, one good the other evil, was pronounced Manichæism]; while no one seemed correctly to understand the distinctive marks which separated the Gnostic from the Manichæan tenets. We find nothing at all, however, in the doctrines of the Paulicians, which would lead us to presume that they were an offshoot from Manichæism: on the other hand, we find much which contradicts such a supposition."

* * * * * * * *

"We may confidently reckon it among the characteristics of the Paulicians, that they knew of no higher distinction than to be, in the true sense of the word, christians; that they reckoned no loftier position than that of χριστιανός or χριστοπολίτης [a christian, or a christian citizen — Photius, lib. I., 6]; and hence, too, nothing higher than the complete and pure knowledge of truths belonging to this position. To separate these from all debasing mixtures, and to give them universal spread, was their highest aim. The Scriptures were prized by them at a vastly higher rate than they could be, according to the principles of Manichæism; and it is certain, that when they sought to attach themselves so closely to the sacred Scriptures, they did so, not in the way of accommodation to the universal christian principle — not barely as a means to procure readier access for their tenets to the minds of other christians; but it is evident, even from the manner in which their teachers write to the members of the sect, and from the order and denominations of their ecclesiastical officers, that they designed and strove to derive their doctrines from the New Testament; and particularly from the writings of the Apostle Paul."

Mr. Robinson, in his Ecclesiastical Researches, furnishes sundry interesting details respecting this branch of the primitive church. He speaks of them generally under the title of Paterines, though he says they had numerous other names, e. g. Manichæans, Gazari, Josephists, Arnoldites, Passagines, Bulgarians, or Bougares. The name Paterine — which was a generic term, like that of Methodist, in England, to denote the more devout and strict sort of christians — was a term of reproach, applied to the Paulicians in Italy at a somewhat later period than that now under consideration. In a notice of the Church of Italy, Mr. Robinson thus speaks of the Paterines, who, he says, there is the highest reason to believe had always been in Italy: —

"Protestants observe, very truly, that during the darkest ages of the Catholic church, there were many of the community who opposed the reigning errors and vices of the times. There were several in Italy, as Paulinus of Aquileia, who opposed, along with a council at Frankfort, the worship of images: Angilbert, archbishop of Milan, who resisted the supremacy of Rome, and Roboald, Anselm, and other bishops of Lombardy, who declared they would sooner agree to have their noses slit up to their eyes, than submit to such an indignity: Claude, bishop of Turin, who imbibed his religious principles at Urgel in Spain, under Felix, and who sowed, as it were, the seeds of the reformation in his diocese: Fluentius, bishop of Florence: Arnold of Brescia, who was burnt at Rome in the year eleven hundred fifty-five: Jeronimo Savonarola, who was burnt at Florence: and many more. * * * * * *

"During the kingdoms of the Goths and Lombards the Unitarian Baptists, or as the Catholics called them Anabaptists, had their share of churches and baptisteries, and held no communion with either Rome, Milan, Aquileia, Ravenna, or any other hierarchy. Chapels and oratories were annexed to baptismal churches, and went along with them. After the ruin of these kingdoms, laws were issued by the emperors to deprive the laity and the Unitarians of baptismal churches, and to secure them to the Catholic clergy. It was not very easy to effect this; however, time did effect it. Then dissidents under various names worshipped either in their own houses, or in places hired for the purpose; which places, it should seem, were tenanted by one of the brethren. Their public religion consisted of nothing but social prayer, reading and reasoning on the gospel, baptism once, and the Lord's supper as often as was convenient; and this was practicable in any place where two or three could assemble together. Italy was full of such Christians; and, omitting many names by which they were called, and which are local and indescriptive, there are three, which describe them in different points of light, and the union of the three is probably their true character. They were called Manicheans: this regarded their speculations. They were called Paterines: this described their condition in life. They were called Gazari: this regarded their morals. They were moreover denominated heretics: for their whole religion implied the belief of some political principles which were accounted heresy by popes, prelates, viscontis, and tyrants of every name, and which they avowed when they were interrogated. It may be proper to take a brief view of each.

"As there are no histories of these dissidents written by themselves, and as all the accounts of them come from their persecutors, who detested them with a mortal hatred, so the inference which is drawn by all Protestants, and by many modern Catholics, is very fair, that it is credible their names were unjustly aspersed, their characters blackened, and their opinions grossly misrepresented. Clear as noon it is, they well understood civil and religious liberty, and practised the duties of it. They are reproached with diversity of sentiment, but this was no crime in their societies, for virtue more than faith seems to have been the bond of their union. Their history defies every effort to class them, after the modern fashion, in speculative divisions; and it is certain they allowed of a variety of modes of speculation, and were held together by ties of a far superior kind, principles of freedom and virtue, in which they all had a general interest. * * * * * * *

"Much hath been written on the etymology of the word PATERINE: but as the Italians themselves are not agreed on the derivation, it is not likely foreigners should be able to determine it. In Milan, where it was first used, it answered to the English words vulgar, illiterate, low-bred; and these religionists were called so, because they were chiefly of the lower order of people, mechanics, artificers, manufacturers, and others who lived of their honest labors. GAZARI is a corruption of Cathari, Puritans: and it is remarkable that in the examinations of these people, they are not taxed with any immoralities, but were condemned for speculations, or rather for virtuous rules of action, which all in power accounted heresies. They said: a christian church ought to consist of only good people: a church had no power to frame any constitutions: it was not right to take oaths: it was not lawful to kill mankind: a man ought not to be delivered up to officers of justice to be converted: the benefits of society belonged alike to all the members of it: faith alone could not save a man: the church ought not to persecute any, even the wicked: the church cannot excommunicate: the law of Moses was no rule to Christians: there was no need of priests, especially wicked ones: the sacraments, and orders, and ceremonies of the church of Rome were futile, expensive, oppressive, and wicked: with many more such positions, all inimical to the hierarchy. In these reasons and rules of action they all agreed, but in doctrinal speculations they widely differed." *

The particularity with which I have described the origin and peculiarities of the Paulicians will be appreciated as we proceed in their history.

Constantine having discovered, as he believed, the true light, was anxious to communicate the same to others. He accordingly began to preach "primitive Christianity" in the regions of Pontus and Cappadocia; regions doubly dear to this preacher of righteousness because once the field of Paul's labors, the favorite apostle of the rising sect, and after whom they probably called themselves *Paulicians.* The strength of his principles, the reasonableness and scriptural nature of his doctrines, his arguments and eloquence, soon collected around him numerous disciples. These were gathered into churches, six of which, out of respect to the memory of their favorite apostle, were named after those churches to which his epistles were originally addressed.†

The Paulician teachers, aiming to restore the simplicity and beauty of the primitive order and worship of the church, and taking the New Testament for their unerring guide, refused to be called "Rabbi;" claiming only the modest title of *Fel-*

---

* *Eccl. Researches,* by Robert Robinson, pp. 404–408, quarto. ed. Camb. Eng.

† *Photius,* lib. I., § 5., pp. 14, 15.

low Pilgrims, or *Fellow Travellers*. And by a conceit, pardonable, if not justifiable, they dropped their own names and assumed those of the fellow-laborers of the apostles. Constantine was called Sylvanus; another distinguished teacher was called Sergius; others were named Titus, Timothy, Tychicus, etc. "The austerity of their lives, their zeal or knowledge," gave them great influence with the people. Success attended their labors, and the new sect spread itself rapidly over Asia Minor.*

After seven-and-twenty years of labor and success, the founder of this sect took up his abode near Colonia, on the river Lycus, in the northern part of ancient Pontus. While there, complaint was made to the emperor Constantine Pogonatus of the "presumptuous heretic." Pogonatus ordered a commissioner, Simeon by name, to proceed to Colonia and investigate the matter. Armed with legal and military authority, the commissioner investigated the case sufficiently to be satisfied that Constantine was a dangerous man to "*the* Church," if not to the State; and consequently condemned him to be stoned to death. In order to aggravate the sufferings of the teacher, and to punish the temerity of his disciples, the commissioner placed the venerable Sylvanus before a company of his own followers, who were commanded, "as the price of their pardon and the proof of their repentance, to massacre their spiritual father." But a single Judas was found among them all. One Justus

* *Photius*, lib. I., § 3, 4.—*Gibbon*; *Siculus*, 32

alone preferred his own safety to his teacher's life, and was canonized by the Catholics as "a new David, who boldly overthrew the giant of heresy;" while he was execrated by the Paulicians, as a new Judas, who basely betrayed his innocent master. Their leader dead, the disciples were scattered like sheep without a shepherd. The laws of "the divine and orthodox emperors" against the Manichæans and Montanists, were turned against these advocates of primitive Christianity. Capital punishment was inflicted upon them; their books, wherever found, were burned; and death and confiscation of goods were the doom of all who harbored and concealed them.*

The effects of this persecution were as usual in such cases: if some were frightened into apostasy, others were made more stable and bold in the faith. "From the blood and ashes of the first victims, a succession of teachers and congregations repeatedly arose." It was found more easy to kill the bodies, than to quench the invincible spirit of the Paulicians. For one hundred and fifty years they endured whatever malice and power could inflict. Like the bush at Horeb, they were enveloped in flames but were not consumed. Primitive truth made them like primitive Christians: they were neither afraid nor unwilling to die in defence of their faith.

* *Gibbon.* This very commissioner afterwards became a Paulician missionary; counting the reproach of Christ greater riches than the honors of the empire. *Siculus*, 32, 33.— Gibbon, vol. IV., p. 30, and note 14. *Photius*, lib. I., pp. 66–74, 125–127.

But to be more particular: The murder of Sylvanus and the dispersion of his disciples seem to have quieted, for a season, the fears of the churchmen. But in the succeeding reign of Justinian II., (A.D. 685–711*) they were again complained of, and "their principal leader was burned alive."† Blood was a luxury to Justinian II., "and he vainly hoped to extinguish in a single conflagration the name and memory of the Paulicians."‡ But, it is the memory of the wicked that shall rot; and the seed of evil-doers that shall be cut off. Other leaders appeared. One Paul and his two sons spread the "heresy" in Cappadocia, Phrygia, and Pisidia; being driven from place to place by persecution. "Leo III., the Isaurian§ (A. D. 716–41), harassed them in various ways, and labored to extirpate the sect."‖ But all such efforts were in vain. After enduring nearly a century and a half of persecu-

* Justinian II. was the son of Constantine IV., surnamed, or nicknamed, Pogonatus—from πώγων-ωνος (pogonos), the beard—from the circumstance of his beard beginning to show itself about the time of his elevation to the throne. His reign began in 685; he was dethroned, and mutilated, and banished by Leontius, one of his generals; who, in his turn, was dethroned, mutilated, and imprisoned by Apsimarius Tiberius. After an exile of about ten years, Justinian found means to regain his throne, and rioted in the luxury of tormenting and destroying his enemies for several years. He fell by an assassin, about 711, unlamented, as he had lived unbeloved.

† *Schlegel*, in Mosheim, bk. III., pt. II., ch. 5. ‡ *Gibbon*.

§ So named from a mountainous region of country lying between Cilicia and Phrygia, which was his birth-place. From the family of a grazier he ascended to the throne of the Greek Empire.

‖ *Mosheim*, ut supra. *Photius*, lib. I., § 18, p. 77. *Sic.* 35.

tion, the Paulicians enjoyed a little respite under the reign of Nicephorus Logotheta (A. D. 802–811); who, though an usurper, and stained with crimes of almost every hue, relaxed the penal laws in favor of this sect, and gave them free toleration.*

This reprieve was but short. For Michael I., Curopalates, and Leo IV., the Armenian, the immediate successors of Nicephorus (A. D. 811–820), ordered the Paulicians to be searched out through all the provinces of the Eastern Empire. *Return to the Church, or die!* were the only alternatives presented to the conscientious dissenter.†

This merciless persecution opens a new era in the history of the Paulicians. Hitherto they had labored, and suffered, and died for their faith, and had not, as a body, returned evil for evil, by resisting their persecutors. Like the apostles, their teachers when persecuted in one place had fled to another; and thus had spread their principles over nearly the whole of Asia Minor; and when seized by the emissaries of power and condemned to death, these good men had yielded up their lives without a murmur. But during the progress of this ten years persecution by Michael and Leo, when death or something worse was everywhere urged upon these primitive confessors, many of them felt

* It is a noticeable fact, that during the reign of Heathenism the Christians generally suffered the *least* under the worst emperors, and *most* under the best. This may be accounted for by the indifference of these infamous men to all religion; or their desire to secure the support of a growing sect. *Siculus*, 52.

† *Photius*, lib. I., § 18, 24.

that patience had had its perfect work. Forgetting, in the desperation of their circumstances, the milder precepts of the gospel, some of the sufferers seized their arms, like the Hussites of a later period, and rose in rebellion against the tyranny by which they were trodden under foot. The governor of Pontus and the bishop of Neo-Caesarea, who were charged with the execution of the imperial edicts, were the first to feel the fury of desperate men. Blood once shed by them, a bold and organized resistance, or the endurance of an indiscriminate slaughter was all that was left to them. They chose the former Some of them retreated to the recesses of the neighboring mountains,* and there maintained their independence and their faith. Others, retiring within the territories of the Saracens, purchased liberty of conscience and the sweets of revenge by uniting with the enemies of the empire. The efforts of their persecutors gradually ceased, as did also the resistance of the persecuted. Before the expiration of twenty years from the death of Leo, the Paulicians had returned in considerable numbers to their habitations within the Grecian territories ; and, so far as appears, with the intention of resuming their former inoffensive and christian deportment. They were not, however, suffered to remain long unmolested.

* The Taurus mountains, in different ranges and under various names, intersect Asia from West to East, almost from the Ægean Sea to the Caspian. A long range of them is found not far from Neo-Caesarea, between the Euphrates and the Black Sea.

Theodora, the regent of the empire during the minority of her son Michael III. (841–855), and sainted by the Greek church as the restorer of image worship, "decreed that the Paulicians should be either exterminated by fire and sword, or brought back to the Greek church."* Such a decree was in keeping with the character of its author; and the execution of it was in no way unworthy of her saintship. Her officers and soldiers, commissioned to do this work of blood, discharged their trust in a most cruel manner. These dogs of war explored the cities and villages, and even the mountains of Asia Minor, in pursuit of their victims. And so successful were they, that they confiscated the property and destroyed the lives of about *one hundred thousand* Paulicians! The miserable remnant of this unfortunate people took refuge from christian (!) persecution, among the followers of the false prophet. Hospitably received by the Mohammedans, the fugitives formed an alliance with those implacable enemies of the empire, and chose for their leader Carbeas, a valiant soldier, once a commander under one of the generals of the East, and the son of a Paulician martyr. The mountains of Taurus became a second time the home of the persecuted disciples of Constantine. Here they fortified a city and supplied it with provisions and munitions of war, as their dernier resort. Tibrica, or Tephrice, became the metropolis of the Paulician

---

* *Mosheim*, vol. II., p. 102; *Gibbon*.

mountaineers.* From this stronghold they made incursions into the surrounding provinces. For more than thirty years, or till near the close of the ninth century, this warfare was carried on with various success and great severity. Immense numbers perished on either side. So formidable did these enemies at length become, that several provinces of the empire were actually ruined by them; and the emperor, Michael III., marching to the rescue of his subjects, was defeated and compelled to flee before the heretics whom his mother had condemned to the flames. Another emperor, Basil, was obliged to send an envoy to the mountain metropolis, to treat with his rebellious subjects, as with a sovereign people.†

On the death of Carbeas, Chrysocheir became the leader of the Paulician bands. In alliance with the Moslems, he boldly penetrated into the heart of Asia; the troops of the frontier, and of the palace even, were repeatedly overthrown; the edicts of persecution were answered by the capture of Nice and Nicomedia, of Ancyra and Ephesus.‡ Basil

---

* The precise situation of this city I cannot ascertain. Gibbon says, it was between Siwas and Trebizond; but these are very far apart, according to the best authorities to which I have access. It was, probably, not far from the intersection of the 40th parallels of north latitude and east longitude from Greenwich, that this stronghold among the mountains of the Taurus was erected. *Sc.* 53.

† This envoy was Petrus Siculus, who has given a particular account of the Paulicians; though Gibbon represents him as sufficiently prejudiced against these dissenters from the hierarchy.

‡ *Photius*, lib. I., § 26, 27; *Gibbon*. *Sic.* 52.

trembled upon his throne, and humbly sued for peace. But, flushed with victory, and beginning now to lust for empire, Chrysocheir spurned the royal donative of gold, and silver, and silk garments; demanding, as the only price of peace, the abdication of the throne of the Eastern Empire. The tables were now completely turned. The question was no longer, shall the followers of Constantine be tolerated? but, Shall the emperor of Constantinople retain the throne of his ancestors? Basil felt that it must be victory or death; and rousing himself and his troops for the contest, he marched upon the haughty sectaries. God made him the instrument by which the degenerate Paulicians were taught, that he who taketh the sword shall perish by the sword. The army of Chrysocheir was routed; and though, for a time, in the stronghold of Tibrica, his followers defied the efforts of the emperor's troops, the city ultimately fell before his victorious arms; and the haughty leader of the Paulicians was surprised and slain, and Basil had the desire of his heart, in being permitted to shoot three arrows into the lifeless head of his enemy. His followers who escaped with life, sued for mercy, or fled to the borders of the empire. This defeat was a death blow to the growing power of the Paulicians; but their independence and their faith they still maintained.

As early as the middle of the eighth century, some of these "heretics" had found their way from the banks of the Euphrates and the mountains of

Armenia to the capital of the empire. It may have been in the ranks of the Isaurian bands, which Constantine V. raised in his paternal mountains, to deliver his capital from the usurpations of the image worshippers.*

From Constantinople they spread themselves into Thrace. From thence they found their way to the Bulgarians, a people living along the Danube, who had then recently been converted to Christianity. This was a favorable soil for the primitive doctrines of the Paulicians ; and here, as in Thrace, their doctrines took deep root, and for eight or nine centuries, if not longer, continued to live and thrive.* From Bulgaria, the Paulicians migrated into Italy, France, and Slavonia ; and thence spread into other parts of Europe.†

Bossuet, in his History of the Variations of the Protestant Churches (book xi., § 13, 14), says of the Paulicians, or Manichæans (as he is pleased to call

---

* Constantine was the sworn enemy of images; and proceeded as roughly in the overthrow of them, as Theodora afterwards did in the re-establishment of them. In his absence from Constantinople, the lovers of images raised a rebellion, seized the capital, and overturned the government. Constantine immediately retired to Isauria, the home of his ancestors ; and having raised an army of hardy and faithful soldiers, marched to Constantinople and regained his throne. In this army, the Paulicians would have been very likely to enlist, as they were most inveterate haters of images.

* *Mosheim* says, that "there certainly were some there in the seventeenth century." But, they were probably degenerate plants from a good stock. — Vol. ii., p. 103, *n.*

† *Mosheim*, cent. x., pt. ii., ch. 5 ; *Bossuet's Variations*, etc., bk. xi., § 16.

them) of Armenia: "This so hidden a sect, so abominable, so full of seduction, of superstition, and hypocrisy, notwithstanding imperial laws which condemned its followers to death, yet maintained and diffused itself. The emperor Anastasius, and the empress Theodora, wife to Justinian, had given it countenance. The followers thereof are to be seen under the children of Heraclius, that is, in the seventh age, in Armenia, a province bordering on Persia, the birthplace of this detestable superstition, and formerly subject to the empire. They were there settled, or confirmed, by one named Paul, from whom the name of Paulicians was given them in the East, by one named Constantine, and, finally, by one named Sergius. They arrived to such great power in that country, either by the weakness of the government, or the protection of the Saracens, or even by the favor of the emperor Nicephoras, much wedded to this sect, that at length, being persecuted by the empress Theodora, the wife of Basil, they were able to build cities, and take up arms against their sovereigns.

"These wars were long and bloody under the reign of Basil the Macedonian, to wit, at the close of the ninth century. Peter of Sicily was sent by his emperor to Tibrica in Armenia, which Cedrenus calls Tephrica, a stronghold of these heretics, to treat about the exchange of prisoners. During this time, he became thoroughly acquainted with the Paulicians, and dedicated a book concerning their errors to the archbishop of Bulgaria, for reasons hereafter specified."

In a subsequent section (§ 16), the same author thus speaks of the extension of the Paulicians into other parts of Europe:

"A great desire of enlarging their sect was always remarked amongst them. Peter of Sicily discovered, whilst ambassador at Tibrica, that it was resolved in the council of the Paulicians to send preachers of their sect into Bulgaria, in order to seduce those new converts. Thrace, bordering on this province, had been infected with this heresy long before. So there was but too much reason to fear the worst for the Bulgarians, should the Paulicians, the most cunning of the Manichæan sect, attempt to seduce them; and it was this which induced Peter of Sicily to inscribe the above-mentioned book to their archbishop, to secure them against such dangerous heretics. In spite of all his pains, it is certain the Manichæan heresy took deep root in Bulgaria, and thence soon after spread itself over the other parts of Europe; whence came, as we shall see, the name of Bulgarians, given to the followers of this heresy."

This "abominable heresy," Bossuet says (§ 18), was brought by an Italian woman into France about A. D. 1017; and that two canons of Orleans, one called Stephen or Heribert, the other Lisoius, "both men of reputation, were first inveigled." He adds: "there was great difficulty in discovering their secret." "At the same time,"

Bossuet says (§ 21), "the same heresy is discovered in Aquitaine and Toulouse."

In the tenth century the European Paulicians were considerably strengthened by emigrations from their native regions and by proselytes in Europe. They possessed the city of Philippopolis, at the head of navigation on the Merise, or Hebrus, and held "the keys of Thrace." A line of their villages and castles extended thence, along through Macedonia and Epirus, towards the Adriatic. They were a brave and warlike people, and their voluntary bands were distinguished in the armies of the empire. These facts illustrate their numbers and importance. Notwithstanding this, they were liable to occasional abuse, if not to persecution, from the government and the church.

During the eleventh century they experienced much suffering from the reigning powers. Still they retained their principles and importance.

It is a question which the bishop of Meaux does not answer, how "this *so hidden* a sect, *so abominable*," whose "secret" there was so much difficulty in discovering, could yet spread itself so rapidly through the cities and even entire provinces of France and other countries, and draw into it men of acknowledged reputation in the church — such as the canons of Orleans; and of eminence in the State, as was Simeon, the commissioner of Constantine Pogonatus; who, after having visited Pontus and tried and condemned the poor Paulicians to death for their "abominable heresy," at length became a convert to their faith, and, renouncing his honors and wealth, a Paulician missionary and a martyr to their sentiments.

According to Vignier * many people were taken and burnt for this heresy in Orleans, France, in the presence of king Robert, and many were executed elsewhere, as in Toulouse and in Italy. And of the Orleans martyrs, Bossuet says, "they went to the stake with joy, in hopes of a miraculous delivery, so strangely were they possessed with a spirit of seduction:" — the spirit of the ancient martyrs, rather.

"In process of time," says Bossuet (bk. XI., § 26), "the evil grew more apparent, principally in Languedoc and Toulouse, for this city was like the metropolis of the sect, 'whence the heresy, extending itself,' as speaks the Canon of Alexander III., in the Council of Tours, 'like a cancer, into the neighboring countries, infected Gascony and the other provinces.' As the source of the evil, as I may say, there took its rise, there also the remedy was first applied. The Pope Callixtus II., held a council at Toulouse, where were condemned the heretics that 'rejected the sacrament of our Lord's body and blood, infant baptism, the priesthood, and all ecclesiastical orders, with lawful marriage.' The same canon was repeated in the general Council of Lateran under Innocent II."

One of the emperors of this century, Alexius

* In *Bossuet's Variations*, etc., bk. XI., § 20, 23.

Comnenus, adopted a new method of subduing the obstinacy of these heretics. He went in person to their principal city, and spent whole days in disputing with these schismatics. "Not a few," we are told, "gave up to this august disputant and his associates." We shall cease to wonder at this, when we learn, that the arguments of the emperor and his suit were supported by the promise of "rich presents, honors, privileges, lands and houses" to those who should be convinced, and retract their errors and return to the bosom of the church; while to the obstinate, perpetual imprisonment was threatened.

As early as the middle of the eleventh century the Paulicians were numerous in Lombardy and Isubria, and especially in Milan; and strolling bands of them were to be found in France, Germany, and other countries, "who by their appearance of sanctity captivated no small number of the common people." Their missionaries and teachers seem to have found their way into almost every part of Europe, and made converts wherever they went. In Italy they were called Paterini, and Cathari or Gazari (καθαροί) i. e. the pure, or puritans. In France they were called Albigenses. Among other names given them, was that of *Separates*, a name which we shall hear frequently in the progress of this history.*

* *Mosheim*, cent. XI., bk. III., pt. II., ch. 5; *Bossuet*, bk. XI., § 7, 13, 21, 22, 25, 55, etc.

Mr. Robinson gives the following summary account of the condition and sentiments of the Paterines, between the tenth and thirteenth centuries:

"From the tenth to the thirteenth century the Italian Dissidents continued to multiply and increase.* Several reasons may be assigned for this. The excessive wickedness of the court of Rome and the Italian prelates was better known in Italy than in other countries.† There was no legal power in Italy in those times to put Dissidents to death. There were many Greeks from Bulgaria and Philippopolis, who came to settle in Italy about the time that the emperor Alexias Comnenas disturbed the Philippopolitans, and burnt Basil the Bogomilan. There was a zealous Bohemian female, named Guillelmina, who settled at Milan, and who taught and baptized with great success.‡ Errors the most gross are laid to her charge, but they scent strongly of fable. Popular preachers in the church, such as Arnold of Brescia, and Claude of Turin, increased the number of dissenters, for their dis-

---

* *Murat. Antiq. Ital.* tom v. diss. 60. Post annum a Christo nato millesimum serpere in Italia cœpere Manicheismi semina, etc.

† *Reineri contra Waldens.* ch. 6. Ecclesiam Romanam dicunt meretricem. Unde Domino papæ, et omnibus episcopis, sacerdotibus et clericis catholicis contradicunt dicentes, se ecclesiam Dei, et illos mundi seductores.

‡ *Murat.* ut sup. E Bohemia Mediolanum se contulit perditissima hæc femina. Processus inscribitur contra Guilielmam Bohemam, vulgo Guilielminam, ejusque sectam. Baptizavit mulieres in nomine patris, et filii, ac sui. Virgo decora valde, pariterque facunda.

ciples went further than their masters. The adjacency of France and Spain, too, contributed to their increase, for both abounded with Christians of their sort. Their churches were divided into sixteen compartments, such as the English Baptists would call associations.* Each of these was subdivided into parts, which would here be called churches, or congregations. In Milan there was a street called Pararia, where it is supposed they met for divine worship. At Modena they assembled at some water-mills. They had houses at Ferrara, Brescia, Viterbo, Verona, Vicenza; and several in Rimini, Romandiola, and other places.† One of

---

* *Reineri*, ch. 6. Sunt autem XVI. omnes ecclesiæ catharorum. Illi autem de Concorezzo sunt fere per totam Lombardiam, et sunt bene mille quingenti, vel etiam plures. Albanenses morantur Veronæ, et in pluribus civitatibus Lombardiæ, et sunt numero fere quingenti utriusque sexus.

† *Examen Testium contra Armannum Punzilupum Hæreticum Ferrariensem*, ab anno 1270 usque ad annum 1288. *Murat. Not.* Ex hoc complurium testium examine colligimus, Catharorum, Patarenorum, seu Manichæorum hæresim sæculo Christi tertio decimo virus suum nedum late in civitate Ferrariensi effudisse, sed et pestifera contagione sua Mantuanam, Veronensem, Bergomensem, Vicentinam urbes, ac Sermionis oppidum infecisse, atque per Romandiolam radices protendisse, et Arimini præsertim domicilium sibi quæsivisse.

Ch. 6. Magister Johannes juratus dicit. Quod semel invenit Punzilupum in Contrata Sancti Pauli, et dixit ei dictus Punzilupus, quod veniebat de Arimino, et quod erant in Arimino multæ domus Paterenorum. Et quum ipse testis quæreret ab eo, quomodo cognosceret dictas domos, respondit ei: Ego bene cognosco eas, quia habent aliqua signa, per quæ cognosco eas. Et quum ipse testis diceret: Indicate illa: ipse Punzilupus dixit: Hoc ego nolo facere.

Ottonis IV. Edictum contra Patarenos sive Gazaros. Statuimus

the principal churches was that of Concorezzo, in the Milanese, and the members of churches in this association were more than fifteen hundred. The houses where they met seem to have been hired by the people, and tenanted by one of the brethren; there were several in each city, and each was distinguished by a mark known only by themselves. They had three, some say four, sorts of officers: the first were teachers, called bishops. John de Casalolto was the resident teacher at Mantua; Albert and Bonaventura Belasmagra, at Verona; Lorenzo or Lawrence, at Sermione.* The second are called quæstors, and by some, elder and younger sons: here they would be named teaching elders or deacons. The third were messengers, that is, men employed in travelling to administer to the relief and comfort of the poor and persecuted. In times of persecution they met in small companies of eight, twenty, thirty, or as it happened, but never

---

quod eorum domus, in quibus steterint, vel in antea recepti fuerint, vel se congregaverint, destruantur, et ulterius non liceat alicui eas reædificare.

Francisci Pippini Chron. ab an. 1176 ad an. 1314, lib. II. ch. 38, De legibus contra hæreticos. Fredericus II. nonnullas contra hæreticos severissimas condidit leges. Quod domus Paterenorum, sive ubi docuerint, vel ubi aliis manus imposuerint, destruantur, nullo umquam tempore reparandæ.

* *Examen Testium.* ut sup. Videas, Johannem de Casalolto circiter an. 1258 Mantuæ agentem episcopum Hæreticorum sectæ de Bagnolo: et circiter an. 1267 in urbe veronensi Albertum episcopum sectæ de Bagnolo: in Sermione vero degentem an. 1273. Laurentium episcopum: circiter an. 1268. Bonaventura Belasmagra. Episcopus Veronæ morabatur.

in large assemblies, for fear of consequences. The different associations held different doctrines, but they were all united in opinion against the whole of popery, and in perfect agreement among themselves on the great leading points above mentioned.* They received members by imposition of hands, and some practised the washing of feet.

"The Paterines were decent in their deportment, modest in their dress and discourse, and their morals were irreproachable. In their conversation there was no levity, no scurrility, no detraction, no falsehood, no swearing. Their dress was neither fine nor mean. They were chaste and temperate, never frequenting taverns or places of public amusement. They were not given to anger, and other violent passions. They were not eager to accumulate wealth, but were content with a plain plenty of the necessaries of life. They avoided commerce, because they thought it would expose them to the temptation of collusion, falsehood, and oaths; and they chose to live by labor or handicraft. They were always employed in spare hours either in giving or receiving instruction.† Their bishops and

---

* *Reineri*. ch. 6. Nulla ecclesia Catharorum concordat in omnibus cum Catharis ecclesiæ de Concorezzo. Ecclesia Franciæ concordat cum Bagnolensibus. Illi vero de Marchia, Tervisina, Tuscia, et Valle Spoletana concordant cum Bagnolensibus in pluribus, quam cum Albanensibus. Item omnes ecclesiæ Catharorum recipiunt se invicem, licet diversas habeant opiniones, et contrarias. Et Concorezenses, qui se damnant ad invicem, sicut supra dictum est.

† *Reineri*. ch. 7. Quomodo sectæ agnoscantur. Hæretici cognoscuntur per mores et verba. In verbis præcisis et modestis. Cavent etiam

officers were mechanics, weavers, shoemakers, and others, who maintained themselves by their industry. In vain, to avoid the fury of the clergy, they sometimes took a cross and walked in procession with their neighbors; their speech, and even their looks betrayed them.

"About the year one thousand and forty the Paterines had become very numerous and conspicuous at Milan, which was their principal residence, and here they flourished at least two hundred years.* They had no connection with the church, for they rejected not only Jerom of Syria, Augustine of Africa, and Gregory of Rome, but Ambrose of Milan, and they considered them and all other pretended fathers as corrupters of Christianity. They particularly condemned pope Sylvester as the antichrist, the son of perdition, mentioned by

---

a scurrilitate, et detractatione, et verborum levitate, et mendacio et juramento. In moribus compositi et modesti: superbiam in vestibus non habent, quia nec preciosis, nec multum abjectis utuntur. Casti etiam sunt. Temperati etiam sunt in cibo et potu. Ad tabernas non eunt, nec ad choreas, nec ad alias vanitates. Ab ira se cohibent. Divitias non multiplicant, sed necessariis sunt contenti. Negotiationes non habent propter mendacia, et juramenta, et fraudes vitandas, sed tantum vivunt de labore, ut opifices. Semper operantur, discunt vel docent, et ideo parum orant. Doctores etiam ipsorum sunt sutores et textores. Ad ecclesiam ficte vadunt, etc.

* *Sicardi Episcopi Cremonensi Chronicon* ad an. 1213. Anno MXL. Heinricus regnavit xvii annos cujus temporibus in papatu sederunt Leo, Victor, Stephanus cujus tempore Pathera Mediolani exorta est.

Romualdi II. Archiepiscopi Salernitani Chronicon. Anno MLIII. Quibus temporibus Paterea, id est Patareanorum secta apud Mediolanum exorta est.

Paul, as sitting in the temple of God as God. They called the cross the abomination of desolation standing in the holy place, and they said that it was the mark of the beast. Nor had they any share in the State, for they took no oaths and bore no arms.* The State did not trouble them, but the clergy preached, prayed, and published books against them with unabating zeal. About the year eleven hundred seventy-six, Galdin de Sala, archbishop of Milan, an old infirm man, as he was preaching against them with great eagerness, dropped down in a fit, and expired as soon as he had received extreme unction.† About fourteen years after, one Bonacursi, who pretended he had been one of these Paterines, made a public renunciation of his opinions, and embraced the Catholic faith, and filled Milan with fables, as all renegades do. This good Christian published, that cities, suburbs, towns, and castles, were full of these false prophets; that this was the time to suppress them; and that the prophet Jeremiah had directed the Milanese what to do, when he said: 'Cursed be he that keepeth back his sword from blood.' He says, the Paterines affirmed the devil wrote the old testa-

---

* *Bonacursi* vita hæreticorum. Manifestatio hæresis Catharorum. Doctores autem damnant omnes; videlicet Ambrosium, Gregorium, Augustinum, Hieronymum, et alios universaliter damnant. Beatum Sylvestrem dicunt Antichristum. Crucem dicunt characterem bestiæ. Credunt etiam quod omnis qui jurat damnabitur.

† *Ughelli Ital.* sac. tom. IV. Archiep. Mediolanensis. Arch. LXXXVII.

ment.* He should have said, he expounded it, for this was their meaning. Bonacursi was the Sacheverell of Lombardy.

"In twelve hundred and ten they had become so numerous, and so odious (for Paterine was become a common name for all sorts of persons ill-affected to the church) that Ugo, Uguccio, or Hugh, the old bishop of Ferrara, obtained an edict of the emperor Otho IV. for the supression of them; but this extended only to the city of Ferrara. Five years after, pope Innocent III. held a council at the Lateran, and denounced anathemas against heretics of all descriptions, and against the lords and their bailiffs, who suffered them to reside on their estates. The canons complain of the Greeks for rebaptizing the Catholics, and declare that baptism was efficacious to little ones as well as adults.† In this council the Milanese were censured for sheltering the Paterines.‡ To the honor of the Italian bishops be it said, they were not in general of the

---

* *D'Acherii Spicileg.* tom. I., p. 208. De Catharis monitum. *Bonacursus* adversus Hæreticos, qui Cathari vocantur. Quis tam parvi sensus est, qui non apertissime intelligat istud esse tempus, de quo prophetiæ prædictæ loquuntur? nonne jam civitates, suburbia, villas et castella hujusmodi pseudoprophetis plena esse videmus?

† *Concil. Lateranens.* IV., ch. 4. Baptizatos etiam a Latinis, et ipsi Græci rebaptizare ausu temerario præsumebant: et adhuc, sicut accepimus, quidam agere hoc non verentur, ch. 1. Sacramentum baptismi tam parvulis quam adultis proficit ad salutem.

‡ *Richardi de S. Germano* chronicon. Marchio Montis-Ferrati opponens quod non deberent Mediolanenses audiri, quia eorum civitas Paterenos fovebat.

bloody disposition of the court of Rome, and the bishop of Ferrara. Romuald II. archbishop of Salerno, who was contemporary with Galdin of Milan, observes, that pope Leo IX. was the first bishop of Rome who personally made use of the temporal sword. He adds: 'Leo was a saint, and acted with a good intent, but he was not executing his own office; for the Lord Jesus had not commanded his disciples, or the successors of the apostles, to intermeddle with secular affairs and like princes to make use of the material sword, but he had commanded them to instruct people in sound doctrine, and to confirm it by giving mankind a good example of living.'* The Roman policy, however, prevailed, and in twelve hundred and twenty pope Honorius III. procured an edict of Frederick II. the day of his coronation, and this extended over all the imperial cities.† Thirteen years after a stone was placed in a square at Milan, with an inscription on it to the honor of Oldrad, the governor of the city, for doing his duty by burning the

---

* *Romualdi Chron.* An. M.LIII.

† *Murat* ut. sup. Anno Christi 1220, atque eo ipso die, quo imperialem coronam ex manibus Honorii III. Romæ suscepit, promulgavit in ipsa basilica principis apostolorum celebre alterum edictum, gravissimas pænas complectens adversus hæreticos, eorumque fautores, quod in corpore juris civilis adhuc legitur. Inter cetera inquit; Gazaros, Patarenos, Leonistas, Speronistas, Arnaldistas, circumcisos, et omnes hæreticos utriusque sexus, quocunque nomine censeantur, perpetua damnamus infamia, diffidamus atque bannimus.

Gazari.* The bloody office, however, was generally performed by inquisitors, who made it the sole business of life (to use the language of Jesus Christ) TO STEAL, TO KILL, AND TO DESTROY."†

The light of the Inquisitorial fires enables us to trace this interesting sect of dissenters, from the eleventh century down to the dawn of the Lutheran Reformation. And though as a body they had doubtless greatly degenerated in principles and morals, yet the rack and the stake bear record, that even during the darkest ages, many of the disciples of Constantine were not unworthy of the name of *Paulicians*. Scattered in every clime, mingled with people of every name — Greeks, Romans, Saracens, and Barbarians — and the objects of hatred and persecution for a thousand years, it would be strange indeed had they retained perfectly the principles and doctrines of their venerable founder. Still, they stand out on the page of history among the most interesting bodies of dissenters from the usurpations, and corruptions, and tyranny of the Greek and Romish churches. And, as their founder, by the light of sacred truth, discovered and proclaimed several of the leading tenets of Congregationalism, the Paulicians deserve a prominent place among

---

* Mediolani in mercatorum platea adhuc visitur lapis positus Oldrado Prætori urbis anno 1233, inter cujus laudes hæc recensetur:

QUI SOLIUM STRUXIT: CATHAROS, UT DEBUIT, UXIT.

Ita ibi scriptum pro ussit.

† John x. 10.

the ecclesiastical ancestors of the denomination of christians to whose history these pages are devoted.*

---

* *Mosheim* says : " Perhaps there still are Paulicians, or Paulians as some call them, remaining in Thrace and Bulgaria. There certainly were some there in the seventeenth century, and they resided at Nicopolis, according to *Urb. Cerri.* Etat present de l'Eglise Romaine, p. 72."

In *The Missionary Herald* for September, 1857, there is an interesting account of a recent exploration of European Turkey, made by the Rev. Henry Jones of the Turkish Missionary Aid Society, and the Rev. Dr. Hamlin of the American Board. In describing their visit to Philippopolis, it is said :

" The travelers found here, to their surprise, a remnant of that interesting Paulician sect, which arose among the Armenians in the seventh century, and whose missionary zeal, aided by the dispersions of persecution and exile, produced such wonderful results among the Bulgarians. * * * Centuries of darkness and persecution have passed over them, and dispersed them into various parts of Europe; but they still live, still call themselves Paulicians here, in their ancient head-quarters, but unfortunately have lost their light and love, and taken refuge from Greek oppression under the shadow of Rome." * * * * *

" Dr. Hamlin thus presents the results of inquiries and observations, during this interesting and important tour : ' The field, a part of which we have surveyed, is peculiarly accessible and compact. It is a population earnestly calling for the word of God. No unevangelized people ever purchased the Bible with such eagerness as the Bulgarians. Much of the preparatory work is already done. The Bible for the Bulgarians is mostly translated, and is waiting Mr. Riggs's return. The Bible Society is ready for active and efficient measures to circulate it as soon as printed. The Bulgarian population have such a desire for schools, for the cultivation of their own language, and for freedom from Greek despotism, that they will be disposed to receive the assistance which otherwise they might reject.' "

CHAPTER V.

THE WALDENSES AND ALBIGENSES, ABOUT A. D. 1100.

No ancient sects, if sects they may be called, have excited more interest and received more attention than the Waldenses and Albigenses. And yet, several important points in their history are far from being satisfactorily settled. The very heading of this chapter suggests some of them. — Are the Waldenses and Albigenses the same sect under different names? or are they independent branches of the primitive church? Did they rise in the twelfth century? or were they of a much earlier origin?

Mr. Gilly maintains, "that the Italian Waldenses, the Albigenses, the Subalpins of Dauphine and Provence, and the Pyrenean Waldenses, were all independent of each other, and remains or branches of the primitive churches in those parts."* The Catholic bishop, Bossuet, in his "Variations des Eglises Protestantes," argues — and Mr. Waddington thinks successfully — that the Albigenses held many opinions which are condemned by all Protestants. Respecting the Vaudois, or Waldenses, Waddington says, "Bossuet shows the

* *Memoirs of Felix Neff,* Introduction.

great uncertainty, perhaps the entire vanity, of their claims to a separate descent from the ante-Nicene Church." *

Bossuet tries to prove that the Albigenses were Manichæans, as he does that the Paulicians were, who are regarded by Mosheim as the true ancestors of the French Albigenses, the latter being but another name for the former. †

It is not unlikely that there were among the numerous dissenters of the twelfth and thirteenth centuries many individuals, and even some associated bodies, who held some Manichæan notions. These persons, though not harmonizing with the Albigenses on several points of faith, would so sympathize with them on others — and particularly with their opposition to the hierarchial and anti-scriptural claims of the church of Rome — that they would be very likely to associate and co-operate together, and thus be easily confounded together by their violent and prejudiced enemies. But the charge of Manichæism against either the true Paulicians or Albigenses is equally groundless.‡ The gist of Bossuet's argument against the claims of the Vaudois or Waldenses, to very high, if not apostolic origin, is, that the early Fathers knew nothing of them. He says: "A man must have lost his wits, to persuade himself that, ever since

* *Hist. of the Church*, pp. 552, 553.

† Bk. III., cent. XI., pt. II., ch. 5.

‡ See the preceding chapter of this work on the Paulicians. See the *Confessions of the Waldenses*.

St. Sylvester's time — that is, about the year 320 — there was a sect among Christians which the Fathers knew nothing of." *

The answer to this is, first, that if the early Fathers really knew nothing of the Vaudois or Waldenses, this would only prove that the end which those Christians had in view in hiding themselves among the mountains was fully attained; that thus they entirely escaped from the observation and persecution of the hierarchies of Greece and Rome. But, secondly, it seems quite apparent that the early Fathers did know, have described, and did persecute unto death, the Vaudois, though under other names. The reader of ecclesiastical history must be satisfied that substantially the same sort of dissenters from Rome and Greece were called by different names, in different countries, and in different parts of the same country. So that, if Mr. Waddington was convinced by the arguments of the Bishop of Meaux on the points alluded to, he must have been rather easily satisfied. The subsequent pages of this chapter will, it is believed, illustrate the force of these remarks.

Milner seems to have regarded the Albigenses as a branch of the Waldenses, and the proper founder of them, "Claudius of Turin, the Christian hero of the *ninth* century." † Mosheim — on most topics in ecclesiastical history a standard authority — attributes the origin of the Waldenses to the

---

* Bk. XI., § 5.

† Cent. XIII., chaps. 1, 3.

labors of Peter Waldo, or Waldus, or Valdo, in the *twelfth* century; and declares, that "those who assign a different origin to the Waldensians * * have no authorities for their opinions, and are refuted by all the historians." He admits, however, that "long before these times [i. e. the twelfth century] there had been resident in the valleys of Piedmont persons who rejected the prevailing opinions of the Romish church, and who agreed in many things with the Waldensians."* The Albigenses he treats as a branch of the great Paulician family; and supposes that the name given to them in France was derived from the circumstance that they were first condemned by a council which sat at Albi, or Albigea, a town of Aquitain, or Aquitania, the name anciently given to the southwestern part of France.† Gibbon takes substantially the same view of the Albigois; he speaks of them as identical with the Paulicians.‡ Gieseler agrees substantially with Mosheim about the origin of the Waldenses, so called; and regards the Albigenses as belonging to the family of the Cathari, who entertained sundry Manichæan notions.§ Mr.

---

* Book III., cent. XI., pt. II., ch. 5; Cent. XII., pt. II., ch. 5.

† The name Albigenses seems to have been at one period a common title given to heretics of all descriptions in France. Gieseler says (*Ecc. Hist.*, vol. III., p. 394, note 7, and p. 447, note 12) that "the names Bulgari and Albigenses first came into general use in the thirteenth century."

‡ *Decline and Fall*, vol. IV., chap. 54.

§ *Ecc. Hist.*, vol. III., pp. 411–413, 419 note 14, 447 note 12.

Jones, in his valuable history of the Waldenses, while he shows conclusively, as it seems to me, their very high antiquity, treats the Albigois or Albigenses, as but another name for the Waldenses. Adam Blair, in his learned history of the Waldenses (2 vols. 8vo., Edinb., 1833), maintains with great ability, and fortifies his position with an immense number of quotations from ancient authorities, friends and foes — that the Waldenses themselves, their friends, and their adversaries, have been convinced of their existence since the age in which the apostles lived; that the lamp which shone in the valleys of the Alps during the darkness of the middle ages, was lighted by the hand of the first preachers of Christianity; and that the Waldenses, the Vaudois, the Albigenses, Petrobrusians, Henericans, and Paulicians, were all substantially the same.* He insists, too, that the Waldenses were thus called, not after Peter Waldo, but that they were known by this name at least half a century before Waldo appeared on the stage. In proof he quotes "The Noble Lesson," so called, a Waldensian document dated about A. D. 1100, and preserved in manuscript, in which the religious

* Vol. I., pp. 1–17, 168, 191–193, 200, 216, 217, 224, 228, 232, 236, 247. "The Albigenses," he says, "held the same sentiments as the Waldenses; yet they did not come from the valleys of Piedmont, but belonged to France" (p. 228). In another place (vol. I., p. 236) he says: "The Waldenses, Albigenses, and Paulicians were now [in the twelfth century] so intermixed that we find the distinction of these from one another difficult; and indeed it is in a great measure unnecessary."

views of these primitive Christians are summarily presented in verse, like the Troubadour's poems.*

Arnaud, a Waldensian writer of the seventeenth century, claims for his church an apostolic origin. "The Vaudois," he says, "are in fact descended from those refugees in Italy, who, after St. Paul had there preached the gospel, abandoned their beautiful country, and fled, like the woman mentioned in the Apocalypse, to these wild mountains, where they have to this day handed down the gospel, from father to son, in the same purity and simplicity as it was preached by St. Paul." †

"The Noble Lesson," which, doubtless, was written as early as the twelfth century, claims for the Waldenses not only great purity of faith, but great antiquity, even a direct apostolic descent. Only a few passages can be given from this noble compendium of christian doctrines and duty.

"O Brethren, give ear to a Noble Lesson.
We ought always to watch and pray,
For we see this world to be near a conclusion.
We ought to strive to do good works,
For we see the end of this world to approach.
A thousand and one hundred years are fully accomplished
Since it was written thus, that 'it is the last time.'
* * * * * * *
Now, after the apostles, were certain teachers,
Who taught the way of Jesus Christ our Saviour;
And these are found even at this present day;

---

* Vol. I., pp. 3, 209–211; and Appendix No. 1, where the entire document may be found. *Gieseler* places the date of this document at the close of the twelfth century, (vol. III., p. 418, note 12); but his reason for so doing is by no means conclusive.

† *Glorious Recovery,* Preface; — Blair's *Hist. Wald.*, vol. I., p. 7.

But they are known to very few,
Who have a great desire to teach the way of Jesus Christ,
But they are so persecuted that they are able to do but little,
So much are the false Christians blinded with error,
And more than the rest, they that are pastors;
For they persecute and hate those who are better than themselves;
And let those live quietly who are false deceivers.
But by this we may know that they are not good pastors;
For they love not the sheep but only for the fleeces.
The Scripture saith, and it is evident,
That if any man love those that are good, he must needs love God and Jesus Christ.
Such an one will neither curse, swear, nor lie;
He will neither commit adultery, nor kill; he will neither defraud his neighbor,
Nor avenge himself on his enemies.
Now, such an one is termed a *Waldensian*, and worthy to be punished;
And they find occasion, by lies and deceit,
To take from him that which he has gotten by his just labor.

* * * * * * *

For I dare say, and it is very true,
That all the popes which have been from Sylvester to this present,
And all cardinals, bishops, abbots, and the like,
Have no power to absolve or pardon
Any creature so much as one mortal sin.
It is God alone who pardons, and no other.
But this ought they to do who are pastors:
They ought to preach to the people, and pray with them,
And feed them often with divine doctrine,
And chastise the sinner with discipline.*

If the date of this manuscript is correctly given by the Waldenses; or rather, if the reckoning, "*one thousand and one hundred years,*" to the time when

---

* *Blair,* vol. I., pp. 473–484, gives the entire poem, making nearly five hundred lines.

the apostle John uttered the words quoted, ("It is the last time," 1 John, 2: 18,) be correct—then was the name "Waldensian" given to these christian dissenters long before Waldo appeared in the world. And for their pastors, it is quite evident that the Waldenses claimed an apostolic origin and descent.

In the early part of the twelfth century (1115–46), we are told, a sect similar to the Petrobrusians and Henericans appeared in the Rhine provinces, and diffused itself rapidly and very extensively, in connection with other dissenting sects. They are described by one authority as denying transubstantiation, and the saving efficacy of infant baptism, and many other things too bad to mention:—"et alia perplura, quæ memoriæ tradere nefas duxi." * Another Catholic authority, Evervin, or Evervinus, provost at Stanfield, diocese of Cologne, about A. D. 1146, describes, in an epistle to St. Bernard, certain heretics who had appeared in his diocese. † Among other things, he says that some of these people who, after disputing with the church dignitaries for some time, were seized by the populace, against the will of the church authorities—"nobis tamen invitis"—and burned to death, sustained the torment of fire not only with patience but even with joy: a thing most wonderful in the eyes of Evervin; and he begs his reverend father Bernard

* *Gesta Trevirorum*, in Gieseler, vol. III., p. 396.

† *S. Bernardi Opera Omnia*, vol. I., pp. 3054–3059. Paris, 1839.

to explain to him how these Devil's limbs (Diaboli membris) could manifest such a degree of fortitude in suffering for their heresies as is scarcely to be found even among the most eminently religious of the Christian faith.* He describes their heresies to consist in claiming that among them only was the church, for they alone followed the footsteps of Christ and were faithful imitators of the apostolic life; their rejection of milk, in any form, as food; the daily administration of the supper at their own tables, after the example of Christ and the apostles; the pretence that they could baptize with the Holy Spirit and fire, which baptism was accompanied with the imposition of hands; the claim that any of the elect among them had power to administer baptism and the Lord's Supper; a disregard of Catholic baptism; and a denial of marriage; — probably a denial of the *sacrament* of marriage. There is certainly nothing very anti-Christian and alarming in these tenets: nothing surely worthy of bonds, imprisonment, and death.

Evervin also describes to St. Bernard another class of "heretics," who had appeared in "terra nostra," who denied that the body of Christ was made on the altar, because all the priests of the church

* Hic Sancte Pater, vellem, si presens essem, habere responsionem tuam, unde istis Diaboli membris tanta fortitudo in sua hæresi, quanta vix etiam invenitur in valde religiosis in fide Christi.—*Bernardi Opera*, vol. I., p. 3056, B.; *Gieseler*, vol. III., p. 396 note 11, Edinb. edition.

were not consecrated; * * * * and thus make void the priesthood of the church, and condemn the sacraments, except baptism alone, and this only when administered to adults. * * All marriages they call fornication, except such as are contracted between virgins, male and female. In the intercessions of saints they have no confidence. Fasts, and other afflictions which are submitted to for sins, are of no avail to the just or to sinners. Other church observances, which Christ, and the apostles learning from him, had not established, they call superstitions. The fire of purgatory after death they do not believe in; but that souls, immediately on leaving the body, pass either into eternal rest or punishment, agreeably to what Solomon says, Ecclesiastes 11: 3—"In whatever place the tree falleth there it remaineth." And thus they render null the prayers of the faithful, or their oblations for the dead.

Evervin is also careful to tell St. Bernard, that certain apostates from this sect who had returned to the Catholic church, informed him that these "heretics" were very numerous, and were scattered almost all over the earth, and had among them many even of the former clergy and monks of the church. And those of this sect who had been burned, he tells Bernard, declared in their defence, that *this heresy had remained concealed to their day, from the time of the martyrs*, and had been preserved in Greece and in other countries.*

---

* Noveritis etiam, Domine, quod redeuntes ad Ecclesiam nobis

The great Bernard seems to have entered heartily into the business of denouncing these dissenters. Yet he is compelled to admit, that in their every-day life they were an industrious, honest, blameless people; and that even their professions of Christianity generally were unexceptionable, for he says: "If you ask them of their faith, nothing can be more Christian; if you observe their conversation, nothing can be more blameless; and what they speak, they prove by deeds." *

It would certainly not be unreasonable for men and women of whom their bitterest enemies were constrained to admit such things, to think they might be allowed to live in the world, even though they did reject Romanism.

Now, whoever these "heretics" were, and whatever were their precise tenets, it is quite evident that their general rejection of Romish pretensions, their reliance on the simple teachings of Christ and the example of the apostles and primitive martyrs, affiliated them with the good people who were afterwards known generally as Albigenses and Waldenses.

---

dixerunt, illos habere maximam multitudinem fere ubique terrarum sparsam, et habere eos plures ex nostris clericis et monachis. Illi vero, qui combusti sunt, dixerunt nobis in defensione sua, hanc hæresim usque ad hæc tempora occultam fuisse a temporibus martyrum, et permansisse in Græcia et quibusdam aliis terris." —*Evervin. Epist. ad Bernardum,* in vol. I., p. 3059; *Gieseler,* vol. III., pp. 397–398; *Blair,* vol. I., pp. 237–243; *Jones,* vol. I., pp. 479–483.

* *S. Bernard's* (65 and 66) *Sermons on the Canticles,* Opera, vol. I., 3063; Gieseler, III., 398; *Jones,* I., 483; *Blair,* I. 242, 243.

Reinerius Sachonus, an apostate Waldensian preacher, who became an Inquisitor, and wrote against the Waldenses about A. D. 1254, ascribes to them very high antiquity. Speaking of them under the title of *Leonists*, he says: "Among all these sects [which he numbers up to seventy], which still are, or have been, there is not one more pernicious to the church [popery] than that of the Leonists; and this on three accounts. The first is, because it is of longer duration; for some say that it has endured from the time of Sylvester [bishop of Rome A. D. 335]: others, from the time of the apostles. The second, because it is more general; for there is almost no country in which this sect may not be found. The third, because, when all other sects, by their blasphemies against God, produce horror in the hearers, this, namely, of the Leonists, has a great appearance of piety, because they live justly before men, and believe all things rightly concerning God, and all the articles which are contained in the creed — *in symbolo.* Only they will blaspheme the Roman church and clergy, which many of the laity are but too ready to believe.*"

---

* *Max. B. V. P.* . XXV., 26 4 (. *Gieseler*, III., 467; *Blair*, I., 14; *Neander*, IV., 611.

This Inquisitor's name is spelled in a great variety of ways, and not always in the same way by the same author: thus in *Mosheim* the same man is called Reinerius Sachonus, Rainerius Sachonus, Raynerius, Rainerius Saccho, Rayner. *Neander* generally calls him Rainerio Sacchoni and Rainer. *Blair* calls him Reinerus Sacchon. *Gieseler* quotes the passage above translated, as from *Pseudo*-Rainerius, whom he treats, however, as good authority.

From these quotations from unexceptionable Catholic authorities, it is quite evident that there were in the Rhine provinces, early in the twelfth century (1115–1146), persons who held sentiments quite opposed to the hierarchal notions of that day, and akin certainly to, if not identical in essential points with those subsequently ascribed to the Albigenses and Waldenses; and furthermore, that these "heretics" claimed to be very numerous all over the world, and to have existed from the time of the primitive martyrs.

To the controverted points respecting the Albigenses and Waldenses already mentioned, may be added others, as — Were they anciently what they now are? Did they maintain or reject infant baptism? And, what is more to our present purpose — were they, in the order of their churches, Episcopalians, Presbyterians, or Independents? Mr. Waddington says: "They maintained and imitated the Divine institution of the three orders in the priesthood." * Dr. Miller, in his "Letters to Presbyterians," asserts that they were *anti*-episcopal, and substantially Presbyterian in their church government. Adam Blair, a Scotch Presbyterian, † makes the following statement relative to the ecclesiastical system of the Waldenses, which is perhaps as near the truth as any which has been noticed:

---

* *Hist. of the Church*, p. 291.

† *Hist. Waldenses*, I., 340.

"Though the doctrine of church-government does not lie so near the foundation of our hopes as the principles of the atonement, and such points, yet we ought to adopt that form of government which is nearest the Scripture pattern. No form of ecclesiastical government in Britain seems exactly the same as that of the ancient Waldenses. Viewing them as having a constant moderator, Episcopalians think him like a bishop. But in regard to episcopal consecration, Mr. Acland, an Episcopalian, informs us that 'this ornament of our church establishment, so justly cherished by us, is unquestionably no longer preserved among the Vaudois.' Viewing them as having a synod, and having a consistory or session in each congregation, they are Presbyterians; yet with this difference, that in our country, synods and presbyteries have a new moderator every year, and the lay-elders are sent by the session in each congregation, or by some court, while the Waldensian congregations meet and appoint an elder. The visits of the moderator to the different congregations, as appointed by the court, have nothing in them inconsistent with presbytery. Mr. Gilly admits that the present Vaudois are nearer Presbyterians than they are to any form of church government, only not so rigid. In this last particular, and in the congregation appointing the synod elder, their government is more popular than our presbyterianism, and verges nearer to the Independents, though not quite the same."

Amidst this conflict of opinions, a person will

find strong inducements to act the part of an eclectic, and choose from all parties what seems most probable; or, Manichæan-like, attempt a reconciliation of these conflicting statements. And, if one should even venture an independent opinion, when the rabbins so disagree, he could hardly be chargeable with presumption.

The latter course, after examining all the authorities upon this subject within my reach — and they are more numerous than upon any topic on which I have yet touched — I have ventured to adopt; though not to the exclusion of the other two courses suggested above. The view which on the whole is most satisfactory to my own mind, is substantially this: The Waldenses or Vaudois, and the Albigenses or Albigois, who were discovered in the twelfth century among the valleys of the Alps and Pyrenees, were not so much independent branches of the apostolic church, as the collected remnants of several sects, which had been persecuted unto death, in different ages, by the Greek and Romish churches. Many of these "sectaries" would wander from country to country, seeking rest; and wherever they could find an asylum from intolerance and persecution, there would they stop; that would become their pilgrim-home. Such a resting-place being discovered by one or more of these christian wanderers, others would be informed immediately of the safe retreat, and thither resort. Thus their numbers would be increased. The places most likely to furnish rest to these sufferers for conscience sake, would be retired and mountainous sections of country — the least known and the least accessible to the busy world. Here they might live, and multiply, and extend their faith, for a long period, without exciting much interest or notice from the great men of the Church or the State. It deserves notice, that in just such places the Waldenses and Albigenses of the twelfth and thirteenth centuries were chiefly found. Such countries were Savoy and Piedmont (*Pie di monte* — foot of the mountain), now known as Sardinia, so famed for "heretics." These territories were embosomed in the lofty Alps; diversified with hill and dale, and divided by deep-cut valleys, which, though opening into fruitful slopes, were fortified by the God of the hills, and rendered well nigh inaccessible to any but practised feet. In these valleys, and along the foot of these towering mountains and up their verdant sides, multitudes of devout persons were discovered by the vigilance of the Romish persecutors of the twelfth and thirteenth centuries. The same general description will answer for the countries of Dauphine and Provence, for the French and Spanish sides of the Pyrenees, and for Bohemia — all of which places were noted in the annals of the Inquisition for harboring heretics from the Romish faith.

To some of these secluded spots a few of the devout dissenters of very early times may have found their way, and there commenced settlements. Thither may have fled, first of all, some of the earliest of all dissenters, the followers of Novatian; with these, some remnants of the Donatists may afterwards have found a home; the Luciferians, and Ærians, and Paulicians, and other sufferers may have followed, in smaller or larger numbers, at different periods. The very impulse which would direct the steps of one of these sects to a land of toleration, or to the protection of the mountains, would lead them *all* thither. I mean not, of course, to the same country, or the same mountains; but to such as were nearest to them. Those first established in their mountain homes would welcome the persecuted of all sects who should flee to them from Catholic violence. These bleeding remnants of different bodies, though disagreeing somewhat in other respects, would all agree in their hearty hatred of the corrupt hierarchies which had driven them from the home of their fathers and the land of their nativity.

These persecuted Christians, drawn together by common sympathy at different periods of time, and from different sections of country, and with religious sentiments varying in some particulars, would unavoidably modify each other's peculiar tenets; and by mutual compromise would meet on common ground in respect to the circumstantials of their religious belief. These little communities, scattered among the mountains or wherever security from persecution might draw them, would thus present to a stranger points of strong resemblance, which would secure for them a common name.

At the same time, there would be in reality considerable dissimilarity between them, produced by the preponderance of numbers or influence in favor of certain distinctive peculiarities, in given cases, which would be discovered only by a familiar acquaintance with the several dissenting bodies. Thus, when certain persons were discovered by the Inquisitors who agreed in leading points — such as their supreme regard for the Scriptures, their abhorrence of the idolatry and tyranny of the hierarchy, their love for the simple, experimental truths of gospel, which their fathers and themselves had learned from the Bible through the operations of the Divine Spirit upon their hearts; when, I say, persons were found agreeing with each other in their opposition to Romanism on these points, — their persecutors would naturally conclude that they were all one and the same sect, however remotely situated from each other; and consequently, they would describe them as the same sect, with some points of variance. In this way we may account for the different descriptions of the Albigenses and Waldenses given to us by their persecutors. Congregations called by these names, being discovered in different sections of country, may have differed from each other in several minor points; yea, they may have been, in reality, the remains of different sects; and yet they were so much alike as easily to be confounded together. By this theory we may account for all the different faces which these dissenters from Romanism are said to have presented to their inquisitorial visitors and murderers.

Some of these sufferers of the twelfth and thirteenth centuries are accused of Manichæan errors. So were the Paulicians of a much earlier date. These latter, we know, fled to the mountains of Asia for protection: and when they migrated to Europe, as early as the ninth century, their stronghold for some time was around the eastern extremity of that range of mountains which proved the resting-place of multitudes of persecuted Christians in later times. This range begins near the western borders of the Black sea, runs across Turkey in Europe, towards the Gulf of Venice, and along the entire length of the gulf, through Austria, to the borders of Switzerland; and, forming the boundary line between that country and Italy, and between the latter and France, it then turns towards the southeast, and runs the whole length of Italy, towards the shores of the Mediterranean sea. From the point where these mountains turn southeastward, towards the centre of Italy, the distance is not great to another range, which runs down through France, in a southwest direction, towards Spain; and, forming the boundary between the two kingdoms, runs along near the northern borders of Spain, towards the Atlantic, on the west. These were the high places *in* which, or *near* which most of the Waldenses and Albigenses were ultimately found.

Now, we may reasonably suppose, that among

some of these mountain recesses, many of the persecuted Paulicians found a safe retreat, and mingling with other sufferers for conscience sake, imparted a Paulician character to the little communities in which they lived; for, wherever their numbers and influence were in the ascendancy, their peculiar tenets would of course stand forth prominently. In another Alpine recess, the disciples of Claude of Turin may have predominated; they, perhaps, would be more inclined to maintain the Episcopal order, which they had associated with the excellencies of their godly bishop of Turin. Among a third company of these christian refugees, the disciples of Berengarius may have been most numerous and influential; these, following the opinion of their admired master, with the rejection of the doctrine of the real presence of the identical body of Christ in the sacramental elements, rejected also the doctrine of infant baptism. Their opinions prevailing, would give a distinctive character to the little community in which they lived. The sects to which reference has now been made, appeared and spread, and were persecuted, before the close of the twelfth century, when the powers of hell were stirred up to destroy the followers of Waldo and the Albigenses. In this way, then, I am able to reconcile much of the conflicting testimony respecting these interesting Christians, whose history and peculiarities we are presently to consider.

I have most unexpectedly run into a long digression from the main business of these pages — the exhibition of the history of Congregational sentiments upon Church order and government; but I hope it will not be considered a useless one.

The reader of ecclesiastical history cannot fail to remark, that from the rise of the Paulicians in the seventh century, to the commencement of the persecutions against the Waldenses and Albigenses in the twelfth century, there was a continual succession of dissenters from the hierarchies of Greece and Rome. Many of those dissenters were devout persons, who professed a reverential regard for the word of God, and who kept themselves from the prevailing impurities of the times in which they lived. They were variously styled — Paulicians, Cathari, Puritani, Paterini, Publicani, Bulgarians, Josephists, Petrobrusians, Henricians, Leonists, and more lately, Waldenses and Albigenses. These names were derived from their habits — as Cathari, from Καϑαροι, (katharoi) *pure ones;* or from their residences — as Bulgarians, from Bulgaria, where they were supposed to have originated; or from distinguished leaders among them — as Henricians, from Henry; Petrobrusians, from Peter de Bruys, etc. etc.

I do not suppose that all these were but one sect, or that they perfectly agreed in sentiment; still, they were all dissenters from the hierarchies of their day, and many of them, if not most of them, maintained tenets which entitle them to honorable notice in these pages. But, as the materials for a sketch of these sects are very imperfect, I select the Waldenses and Albigenses, as embodying the prominent peculiarities of most of those who dissented from the dominant church in the twelfth and thirteenth centuries.*

They are accused of "a contempt of ecclesiastical power;" or, in plain English, they denied the right of the pope and the bishops to lord it over God's heritage. "They declare themselves to be the apostles' successors, to have apostolic authority, and the keys of binding and loosing.— They hold that none of the ordinances of the church, which have been introduced since Christ's ascension, ought to be observed, as being of no value.— The feasts, fasts, orders, blessings, offices of the church, and the like, they utterly reject.— They say, the bishops,

---

* The reader may find a condensed, but yet very complete historical summary of these dissenters, in the first volume of Adam Blair's History of the Waldenses, pp. 1–293. William Jones, in his History of the Christian Church, vol. I., also furnishes quite an extended and connected account of these early dissenters from Rome. Robert Robinson's Ecclesiastical Researches are also chiefly devoted to the same general subject.

Reinerius Saccho, the Inquisitor, who was undoubtedly familiar with the opinions of the Waldenses, accuses them of "*mixing the erroneous doctrines of the heretics of old with their own inventions.*" Indeed, the term *Waldensian* came to signify a determined dissenter from Rome, and an unflinching opposer of all the unscriptural doctrines and anti-Christian practices of the church of Rome. And, according to Bossuet (bk. XI., § 46), the term *Vaudois* had much the same significancy in the eleventh and twelfth centuries and downward to the Lutheran Reformation.

clergy, and other religious orders are no better than the Scribes and Pharisees, and other persecutors of the apostles." *

In addition to the above peculiarities, Reinerius accuses them of rejecting the Old Testament, "that they may not be overthrown by it; pretending that upon the introduction of the gospel dispensation all old things were to be laid aside." Yet he reckons among the means which had increased these heretics, the translation by them of the Old and New Testaments into the vernacular tongue of the country; and says he had seen an illiterate peasant who could repeat the whole book of Job, and several others who had committed to memory the entire New Testament. And he further says, that it was the boast of the Waldensians, that a man or woman could rarely be found among them who could not repeat the whole of the New Testament in the vernacular language. He also says of these persecuted Christians: "They are orderly and modest in their manners; their dress is neither expensive nor mean; they eschew oaths, falsehood, and fraud; they engage in no sort of traffic: they live on what they earn by the labor of their hands from day to day. They are also chaste. They are never found hanging about wine-shops; they attend no balls, nor other

* I quote the words of R. Saccho, who, after having been connected in different ways with the Waldenses for seventeen years, apostatized, and became an Inquisitor, and a bitter persecutor of these good men. *Max. B. V. P.* xxv, 268, D. E.

vanities. They govern their passions; they are always at work."* Such is the testimony of this Inquisitor, to the peculiarities of these devout people, known by various local names, who dwelt in and around the Alps and Pyrenees about the middle of the thirteenth century. I have omitted the larger part of his charges, because they have no relation to the subject in hand; but I may say in a word, that Reinerius charges upon these dissenters very little that any Protestant would object to as a part of his own creed.†

The account given us by another Inquisitor — who says, "he had exact knowledge of the Waldenses" — of a branch of this family which appeared in Bohemia in the fourteenth century, will afford some further light upon their ecclesiastical peculiarities. He tells us, that they maintained that our obedience is due unto God alone, and not to prelates; which they found on Acts 4: 9; that none in the church ought to be greater than their brethren, according to Matt. 20: 25; that no man ought to kneel to a priest, because the angel said to John (Rev. 19: 10) "See thou do it not;" that tithes ought not to be given to the priests, because there was no use of them in the primitive church; they reject all the titles of prelates, as

* *Neander*, IV., pp. 611, 612. *Max. B. V. P.* XXV, 272, H. 273 C.

† For the entire account, see *Allix's Remarks upon the Churches of Piedmont*, pp. 188–191; or *Jones's Hist. of the Christ. Church*, vol. II., pp. 21–27. *Max. B. V. P.* 262.

pope, bishop, etc.; they condemn all ecclesiastical offices, and the privileges and immunities of the church, and all persons and things belonging to it, such as councils and synods, parochial rights, etc.; they hold the sacrament of different orders of the clergy to be of no use—every good layman being a priest, and the apostles themselves being all laymen; that the priestly vestments, altar, ornaments, pall, corporals, chalices, patins, and other vessels, are of no efficacy;* that the holidays of saints are to be rejected; and that there is no merit in observing the fasts instituted by the church. Whatsoever was preached without Scripture proof, they accounted no better than fables. They despised the decretals, and sayings and expositions of holy men, and cleaved only to the text of Scripture; they never read the liturgy; they contemned all approved ecclesiastical customs which they did not read of in the gospel; such as the observation of Candlemas, Palm-Sunday, etc.†

This is the testimony of an enemy; and yet, it is by no means discreditable to those of whom he speaks. His testimony agrees, in nearly every particular with that of Reinerius, upon the points already referred to. It is, however, worthy of remark, that this last inquisitor clearly refutes the

---

* A *Pall* was the consecrated mantle of an archbishop, sent from Rome. A *Corporal* was the sacred cloth used to cover the elements, etc., of the eucharist. A *Chalice* was a sacramental vessel. A *Patin* was the plate which contained the consecrated bread.

† *Jones' Hist. Waldenses*, vol. II., pp. 31–38.

charge of his brother inquisitor, respecting their rejection of the Old Testament. He mentions several opinions which he says they sustained *by quotations from the Old Testament.* This shows conclusively that the Bohemian Waldenses did not reject that portion of God's word. Indeed, this author tells us: "*They can say a great part of the Old and New Testaments by heart.*"

A Catholic bishop of the fifteenth century, who lived in the immediate neighborhood of the Waldenses of Piedmont — *Seisselius*, of Turin — bears almost precisely the same testimony to the peculiarities of the Christians of those valleys, as that which we have just heard respecting the Boheмeian Waldenses. He says distinctly: "They receive only what is written in the Old and New Testaments." *

Thus do their very enemies testify to the Protestant and Congregational principles and doctrines of the persecuted Waldenses.

In addition to the testimony of the enemies of the Waldenses, we have two or three of their ancient Confessions of Faith, which have been preserved for centuries by these mountain Christians. One of these — which is believed to have been written as early as A. D. 1120, and which is given by Perrin, book I., chap. XII., and by Leger, part I., chap. XVII., from ancient manuscripts, and may be found entire in Blair's History of the Waldenses, vol. I., pp. 503–505 — reads thus:

---

* *Jones*, vol. II., pp. 38–45.

"*A Confession of Faith of the Waldenses and Albigenses, A. D.* 1120.

"I. We believe and firmly hold all that is contained in the twelve articles of the Creed which is called the Apostles', holding to be heresy every thing which differs and does not agree with the said twelve Articles. II. We believe in one God, the Father, Son, and Holy Ghost. III. We acknowledge for Holy Canonical Scriptures, the books of the Holy Bible, namely [here follows an enumeration of all the books of the Old and New Testaments.] IV. The books above said, teach thus, that there is one God, almighty, all wise, and all good, who has made all things by his goodness. For he formed Adam according to his own image and similitude, but by the envy of the devil, and the disobedience of the said Adam, sin entered into the world, and we are made sinners in Adam, and by Adam. V. That Christ was promised to our fathers who received the law, that thus by the law knowing their sins, unrighteousness, and their insufficiency, they might desire the coming of Christ to satisfy for their sins, and accomplish the law by himself. VI. That Christ was born at the time appointed by God his father, that is to say, at a time when all iniquity abounded, and not for good works only, for all were sinners; but to the end that, being faithful, he might cause (fè) grace and mercy to us. VII. That Christ is our life, and peace, and righteousness, and pastor, and advocate, and sacrifice, and priest, who died for the salvation of all those that believe, and rose for our justification. VIII. We, in like manner, firmly hold, that there is no other Mediator and Advocate with God the Father, but only Jesus Christ: but that the Virgin Mary is holy, humble, and full of grace: and we believe the same thing of all the other saints, that they in heaven hope the resurrection of their bodies at the judgment. IX. We also believe, that after this life, there are only two places, the one for the saved, which is called by name paradise, and the other for the damned, which we call hell, altogether denying purgatory, which is a dream of antichrist, and invented against the truth. X. We have always believed all the inventions of men to be an unspeakable abomination before God, such as the feasts, and the vigils of the saints, and the water which they call blessed, abstinence from flesh on certain days, and the like things, and principally the masses. XI. We abominate all human traditions as being antichristian, by which we are troubled, and which are prejudicial to the liberty of the Spirit. XII. We believe that the sacraments are signs or visible forms of holy things, holding it to be good that the faithful do from time to time use these signs or visible forms, if it can be done. But we do, notwithstanding, believe and hold, that the foresaid faithful can be saved, when they have not place nor means to use them. XIII. We do not acknowledge any other sacrament but baptism and the eucharist.

XIV. We owe honor to the secular power in subjection, in obedience, in promptitude, and in tribute."

To this exposition of doctrine may be added an article or two from what is termed "The Ancient Discipline of the Evangelical Churches of the Valleys of Piedmont," which may be found entire in Blair, vol. I., pp. 533–540.

"*Art. II. — Concerning Pastors.*

"All those who are to be received as pastors among us, while they remain with their relations they entreat us to receive them into the ministry, as likewise that they would be pleased to pray God that they may be made worthy of so great a charge; but the said petitioners present such supplications to give a proof of their humility. We also appoint them their lessons, and set them to get by heart all the chapters of St. Matthew and St. John, with all the Epistles called canonical, and a good part of the writings of Solomon, David, and the prophets. And afterwards, having good testimonials, they are, by the imposition of hands, admitted to the office of preaching. He that is last received ought to do nothing without the license of him that was received before him; and in like manner the former ought to do nothing without the license of his associate, to the end that all things among us may be done in good order. Our food and clothing are administered to us, and given gratuitously, and by way of alms by the good people whom we instruct. Among the other powers which God has given to his Servants, he hath given them authority to elect the Leaders who govern the people, and to constitute the Elders in their charges, according to the diversity of the work in the unity of Christ: which is proved by the saying of the Apostle in the Epistle to Titus, in chap. 1: 'For this cause left I thee in Crete, that thou shouldst set in order the things that are wanting, and ordain elders in every city, as I had appointed thee.' When any of us, the aforesaid pastors, fall into any gross sin, he is both excommunicated and prohibited from preaching."

"*Art. IV.—Concerning Elders, the Collections and Councils.*

"Rulers and elders are chosen out of the people, according to the diversity of the work, in the unity of Christ. And the Apostle proveth it to Titus, chap. 1: 'For this cause left I thee in Crete, that thou shouldest set in order the things that are wanting, and ordain elders in every city, as I had appointed thee.' The money which is given us by the people, is by us carried to the foresaid general council, and there delivered publicly in the presence of all; and afterwards the same is taken and distributed by our stewards, part of the money being given to such as are sent upon journeys for occasion, and part of it given to the poor. We that are pastors assemble once a year, to treat of our affairs in a general council."

The Magdeburg Centuriators give an abridged, condensed statement of the Waldensian faith, said to be drawn from an old manuscript, as follows:

"In articles of faith, the Holy Scriptures are the highest authority, and for that reason should be the standard of judging; so that whatever does not agree with the word of God, is deservedly to be rejected and avoided. — The decrees of fathers and councils are [only] so far to be approved as they agree with the word of God. — The reading and knowledge of the Holy Scriptures are free to and necessary for all men — the laity as well as the clergy; and moreover, the writings of the prophets and apostles are to be read, rather than the comments of men. — The sacraments of the church of Christ are two, baptism and the Lord's supper; and in the latter, Christ has instituted the receiving in both kinds, both for priests and people. — Masses are impious; and it is madness to say masses for the dead. — Purgatory is the invention of men; for the believing go into eternal life, the unbelieving into eternal damnation. — The invoking and worshipping of dead saints is idolatry. — The church of Rome is the Whore of Babylon. — The pope and bishops are not to be obeyed, because they are the wolves of the church of Christ. — The pope has not the primacy over all the churches of Christ; neither hath he the power of both swords. — That is the church of Christ, which hears the pure word of Christ, and observes the sacraments instituted by him, in whatsoever place it exists. — Vows of celibacy are the inventions of men, and productive of uncleanness — *sodomam nutrientia.* — So many orders [of the clergy] are so many marks of the beast. — Monkery is a fetid carcase — *cadaver fœtidum.* — So many superstitious dedications of temples, commemorations of the dead, benedictions of creatures, pilgrimages, so many forced fastings, so many superfluous festivals, those perpetual bellowings — *boatus hominum indoctorum,* [alluding to the practice of chanting] and the observations of various other ceremonies, manifestly obstructing the teaching and learning of the word, are *diabolical inventions.* — The marriage of priests is both lawful and necessary.*"

Such appears to have been the faith of the Waldenses in the twelfth century. I have given the Centuriator's abridgment entire, because it contains the substance of other Waldensian creeds which have come down to us, and presents a correct view of these Alpine Christians.

These sentiments — if we may believe one who had apostatized from the faith and become its bitter persecutor, Reinerius Saccho — were embraced by vast multitudes of persons before the middle of the thirteenth century; for he says, "There is scarcely a country to be found in which this heresy is not planted." These doctrines were propagated with great assiduity by all who embraced them. Reinerius tells us, that one method adopted by them

---

* *Centuriators,* cent. XII., pp. 548–549. Basil ed., 1624.

was, to travel up and down the country as pedlers of jewelry and trinkets, needle-work and handkerchiefs. Having gained access to a family and disposed of some of their wares, they would tell the inmates of more valuable matters; they would then repeat portions of the Word of God, and inform the listening family that by this "He communicates his mind to men, and inflames their hearts with love to him."

That the faith and works of the Waldenses did not materially deteriorate with the progress of time appears from the account given by *Vignaux*, near the close of the sixteenth century. He was pastor of a Waldensian church in Piedmont for forty years, and wrote a treatise concerning their morals and faith, in which he says:

"We live in peace and harmony one with another, have intercourse and dealings chiefly among ourselves, having never mingled ourselves with the members of the church of Rome by marrying our sons to their daughters, nor our daughters to their sons. Yet they are so pleased with our manners and customs, that Catholics, both lords and others, would rather have men and maid servants from among us, than from those of their own religion; and they actually come from distant parts to seek nurses among us for their little children, finding, as they say, more fidelity among our people than their own." He then gives a summary of their doctrinal principles, for the sake of which they have been persecuted; such as—"that the Holy

Scriptures contain all things necessary to our salvation, and that we are called to believe only what they teach, without any regard to the authority of man.— That nothing else ought to be received by us except what God hath commanded.— That there is only one mediator between God and man, and consequently that it is wrong to invoke the saints. That baptism and the Lord's supper are the only standing ordinances in the church of Christ.— That all masses are damnable, and ought to be abolished.— That all human traditions are to be rejected. That the saying and recital of the office, fasts confined to particular days, superfluous holy-days, differences of meats, so many degrees and orders of priests, monks, and nuns, so many benedictions and consecrations of creatures, vows, pilgrimages, and the whole vast and confused mass of ceremonies, formerly invented, ought to be abolished. They deny the supremacy of the pope, and more especially the power that he has usurped over the civil government, and admit of no other degrees than bishops and deacons. They contend that the See of Rome is the true Babylon — that the marriage of the clergy is lawful, and that the true church of Christ consists of those who hear the word of God and believe it." *

Not to weary the reader with further particulars respecting the Waldenses and Albigenses, this is the sum of what we have learned: Between the

---

* *Perrin's History,* b. I., ch. VI.; in *Jones,* vol. II., pp. 84, 85.

ninth and thirteenth centuries there appeared in different parts of Europe numerous bodies of dissenters from the Catholic hierarchy, who, though known by various names, and differing in minor particulars, yet agreed generally on the following points: 1. That the Scriptures of the Old and New Testaments are an infallible and sufficient guide to Christian faith and practice; and that men are under no obligations to believe or practise, as a religious duty, any thing not enjoined in the Scriptures. 2. That these teach that the church of Christ should consist of such only as hear and obey the truth. 3. That Christ has given his church no authority to make laws for the government of his people; but simply requires them to administer such as He has given in his Word. 4. That the whole hierarchal system of church government, then existing in the world, was anti-Christian; since the Scriptures nowhere recognize the different orders of the clergy, or the right of the pope, and his bishops, and priests, and other officers, to rule over the people of God. 5. They seem to have recognized no other church officers but bishops, or elders, and deacons.* 6. These appear to have

---

* Mr. Waddington's assertion — that the Waldenses recognized three orders in their clergy — has been referred to, page 165. Upon the theory that the Waldensian churches of the twelfth and thirteenth centuries were in part composed of the scattered remnants of divers dissenters, it would not be strange if some among those called Waldenses by the Catholics, held to the three orders of the clergy. But certain it is, that the standard confessions of the Waldenses in the twelfth and subsequent centuries, and their own writers at a

been elected by the brethren; and the bishops, at least, ordained by the imposition of the hands of others in office. 7. Their churches were composed of persons "previously confessing and declaring [their] faith and change of life."

These were the prominent principles and doctrines of the Waldenses and Albigenses in relation to the order, and government, and worship of their churches; and which seem to authorize an enrolment of their names among the ecclesiastical ancestors of modern Congregationalists. These sentiments, connected with a faith and morality

---

subsequent period, convey a very different impression of the belief of these persecuted Christians. See *ante*, pages 178–186. Their enemies generally represent the early Waldenses as indulging in contempt for the clergy, and accuse them of saying that a good layman was quite as competent to perform ministerial duties as a clergyman. Thus Reinerius Saccho accuses them of saying, that the sacrament of rank in the clergy is a nullity, and that every good layman may perform the duties of a priest, since the apostles were laymen:—"Item sacramentum ordinis dicunt nihil esse. Item dicunt, quod omnis laicus bonus sit sacerdos, sicut Apostoli laici erant."—*Max. B.V.P.* XXV, 265, G. This was said in the thirteenth century; and in the sixteenth century, an aged Waldensian pastor, in giving a summary of the faith of the Waldenses, said: "They admit of no other degrees than bishops and deacons." See Vignaux's testimony, *ante* p. 186. Dr. Clarke, in his *Martyrology*, says, that among the opinions for which the Waldenses were "so declaimed against and cruelly persecuted by the Romanists, were these: That there is no difference between a bishop and a minister,—that it is not the dignity, but deserts, of a presbyter, that makes him a better man."—Chap. 22, folio ed. Dr. Miller thinks there is evidence of their having the office of *ruling elder* among them. This, however, would not necessarily affect the assertion in the text.

eminently pure and scriptural, spread over almost all parts of the continent of Europe,* and found their way even into England;† preparing the ground, if not sowing the seed for the harvest of later days.

It was not to be expected that these scriptural Christians should escape the hand of persecution. The story of their sufferings has been so often told, and may be so easily known to all who have access to even a good Sabbath School Library, that I need not dwell upon particulars. The decrees of councils, the efforts of bishops, the bulls of popes,‡ the rack and fires of the Inquisition, the armies of the crusaders, cheered on with the war cry—"*Persecute them with a strong hand!*"§—swept hundreds

---

* "Cesarius saith: That this heresy so increased, that in a short time it infected—*usque ad mille civitates*—a thousand cities."—Clarke, p. 37.

† Clarke tells us that, "Anno Christi, 1160, some of them came into England, and at Oxford were punished in the most barbarous and cruel manner."—*Martyrology*, folio, p. 36.

‡ Pope Alexander III. (A. D. 1160–1163) doomed these unfortunate Christians to utter extirpation: "Giving them over to Satan; interdicting them all communion and society with others; * * * confiscating their goods, disinheriting their heirs; ordering their houses to be razed to the ground, and their lands to be given to others; * * commanding kings, princes, magistrates, councils, and people, to make an exact inquisition, to shut the gates, to ring the toll-bell; to arm themselves, to apprehend, kill, or use any other violence to them; giving their accusers a third part of their estates; condemning all favorers to the same punishment."—*Clarke's Martyrology*, chap. 22.

§ The words of Pope Innocent III. in his exhortation to the crusaders against the Albigenses.

of thousands of these excellent people, and their defenders, from the plains and valleys of Europe, and filled the very caves of the mountains with their lifeless bodies. "Yet, notwithstanding all the cruelties used against them, their enemies could never prevail, to a total extirpation of them; but they still lay hid like sparkles under the ashes, desiring and longing to see that, which now, through God's grace, their posterity do enjoy, viz.: The liberty to call upon God in purity of conscience, without being enforced to any superstition and idolatry. And so instructing their children in the service of God, the Lord was pleased to preserve a church amongst them, in the midst of the Romish corruptions, as a diamond in a dunghill, as wheat amongst chaff, as gold in the fire; till it pleased God to disperse the gospel in a more general and public way, by the ministry of Luther, and his associates and fellow-laborers in the Lord: at which time, these Albigenses received with greediness the doctrine of the gospel, and so became more eminent in their profession of piety than they were formerly." *

---

* *Clark's Martyrology*, chap 25. *Sismondi's Hist. of the Crusades against the Albigenses in the Thirteenth Century*, is a brief but very comprehensive story of the terrible cruelties perpetrated by the church of Rome on these primitive Christians. A translation of this work from the French was published by H. Hooker, Phil. 1848. A valuable and interesting work was published in London in 1827, and dedicated to the bishop of Llandaff, entitled, *Authentic Details of the Valdenses*, etc., etc. 8vo., 464 pp. It contains Bresse's Hist. of the Vaudois, abridged; Arnaud's Glorious Return; Original Letters, etc., etc.

CHAPTER VI.

HISTORICAL VIEW OF GREAT BRITAIN, FROM B. C. 55 TO ABOUT A. D. 1350.

BRITAIN is a name dear to every Congregationalist. It was upon the soil of Britain that the principles which he loves were first fully restored to the Church of Christ, after an oblivion of a thousand years. It was in this island, regarded by the ancients as "the ends of the earth," that those great and good men arose, who shone as lights in the world, and became the guides of inquiring thousands, to the simple and apostolic doctrines respecting the faith, and order, and worship of the Christian Church.

As Great Britain is to be the field of our investigation for a considerable time, and as our whole denominational history is intimately associated with the church history of Britain, it will not be deemed an inappropriate introduction to this field, to present a brief outline of her religious history, from the invasion of Julius Cæsar to the days of John Wickliffe.

The most ancient names of this island were *Briton*, *Albion*, or *Albin*. According to Ordericus Vitalis, "it was named *England*, after their native country, by the Angles, who came into Britain from the isle of Angle, in which the metropolis of Saxony is situated, and under Hengist, their principal chief, conquered or exterminated the Britons, now called the Welch."* Its very early history contains so much that is fabulous, that it is difficult to distinguish between truth and falsehood. Hume rejects "all traditions, or rather tales, concerning the more early history of Britain," and begins his history with the invasion of Julius Cæsar, B. C. 55–56. Lingard does the same. Sharon Turner, on the contrary, makes considerable use of the ancient traditions, preserved in the Welsh Triads particularly, in confirmation of historical intimations collected from various other sources; and Milton seems to have regarded these ancient fables and traditions as containing "footsteps and reliques" worth noticing.

It seems most probable, that the island was known to the Phœnicians, those ancient navigators, some centuries before the Roman invasion; and also to the Carthaginians and the Greeks;† and the earliest inhabitants of the British Islands are believed to have come from the Kimmerian and Keltic stock, through Gaul or France.‡

---

* *Hist. England and Normandy*, bk. x., ch. 15. This honest and laborious old monkish historian was born in England, A. D. 1075; at the age of ten years he entered an abbey in Normandy, where he studied and wrote until he was sixty-seven years old; having left his monastery only three or four times, and then chiefly to collect materials for his history. He died about A. D. 1143.

† *Hist. of the Anglo Saxons*, vol. I., b. I.

‡ *Hist. Anglo Sax.*, vol. I., chaps. 3 and 4, and vol. I., ch. 2; *Bede's Ecc. Hist.*, chap. 1.

About the years 54–56 before Christ, Julius Cæsar, having overrun Gaul with his victorious legions, turned his eyes towards the neighboring island of Briton. Influenced, probably, more by love of conquest than anything else, he effected a landing on the island, and made some attempts towards conquering the ferocious inhabitants. But so determined was their resistance, that the Roman conqueror seems at first to have done little else than to establish a temporary and precarious footing upon their shores; and finally but half conquered the barbarous people. The complete conquest of Briton was not accomplished until more than a century and a third after the first attempt of Cæsar, by the celebrated Cneius Julius Agricola, A. D. 84; and this, according to Gibbon, after a war of about forty years.*

The inhabitants of this island, when visited by the Romans, appear to have consisted of two races; the Belgic, inhabiting the south-eastern part, and the Celtic, who had been driven into the interior. The former of these had made so much progress toward civilization as to have become, to some extent, an agricultural people. The latter were more fierce, barbarous, and ferocious; dwelling in temporary huts in the woods, clad in skins, if covered at all, and depending chiefly upon their flocks and the wild game of the forests for their living.

---

* *Decline and Fall,* vol. I., ch. 1; *Hume's England,* vol. I., ch. 1; *Lingard's Hist. Eng.*, vol. I., ch. 1.

They were broken up into numerous independent tribes, without any common bond of union among themselves, except what their common faith furnished.*

Their religion was of the most despotic character. Their priests, who were called Druids, not only superintended the offering of sacrifices — which, on great occasions, were sometimes human — but engrossed the entire business of instructing the youth; were the physicians of the island; the chief arbiters in disputes between States, as well as individuals; no public business could be transacted without their authority; they claimed judicial power, in criminal as well as civil cases; were exempt from the burdens of war and taxation; in a word, were the sovereigns of the Britons. To enforce their decrees, the druids had the power to excommunicate any offender from public worship; to debar him from any intercourse with his fellow-citizens in any of the affairs of life; to refuse him protection from violence of any kind; and thus to render life an insupportable burden: or, they could absolve one from all guilt, and thus free him from all punishment. At the head of these mighty priests was an *Arch-Druid*, who was *their* sovereign, and ruled them as absolutely as they ruled the nation.

Their worship was in the open air; and usually,

* Sharon Turner enumerates forty-five distinct tribes, which were spread over what is now Great Britain, when the Roman invasion began. — *Hist. Anglo Saxons*, vol. I., ch. 5.

if not uniformly, under the shade of the oak; which they are said to have worshipped as the symbol of the Supreme Being himself, or the place of his special residence. From these circumstances, the priests and their worship are supposed, by some antiquaries, to have derived their name — *Druids* and *Druidism* — from δρῦς (*druse*) an oak. They are supposed to have believed in the immortality of the soul, and its transmigration after death. They used no books in their instructions. All their religious and scientific knowledge; all that they taught of history, or of the deeds of their ancestors, was oral, and much of it in verse. These verses their pupils were required to commit to memory, but were forbidden to write down.

The better to accomplish their purposes, the druids carried their pupils into distant and desolate regions, and there instructed them, from day to day, in lonely caves. Their course of instruction seems not to have been finished until twenty-four thousand verses, containing divers kinds of knowledge, were committed to memory. Cæsar says, Druidism began in Britain, and was thence extended into Gaul.

Never were a people so completely controlled and enslaved by their religious rites and religious teachers, as were the ancient Britons. After the conquest of the island, the Romans finding it impossible to govern the people while their religious superstitions were tolerated, were compelled, contrary to their usual policy, to abolish Druidism by penal statutes.*

It was among this people that Roman colonies were settled, and Roman laws, manners, customs, and learning, were introduced; and, above all, that religion which ultimately became the faith of the Romans.

The precise time when Christianity was introduced into this island is uncertain. It is equally doubtful by whom. It seems quite probable that it entered from Gaul, and not later than the third century. It may have been received at an earlier period, even from apostolic lips. Bede tells rather a confused and unreliable story about one Lucius, King of the Britons, sending a letter to Eleutherus, "a holy man who presided over the Roman church, A. D. 156, entreating that he might be made a Christian." This request, the venerable historian says, he soon obtained; and adds, that "the Britons preserved the faith which they had received, uncorrupted and entire, in peace and tranquility, until the time of the Emperor Diocletian," A. D. 286, when a terrible persecution raged against the Christians for about ten years. This persecution, we are told, "at length reached Britain, and many persons, with the constancy of martyrs, died in the confession of their faith." Bede gives a particular account of the sufferings and death of St. Alban,

---

* *Hist. Anglo Saxons*, vol. I., ch. 5; *Hume*. vol. I., ch. 1; *Lingard*, vol. I., ch. 1.

one of the most distinguished of these martyrs, who suffered A. D. 305.* It is also well established that there were three British bishops at the council of Arles, in the year 314; an indication, certainly, that Christianity had made considerable progress in the island at that time.

The Romans, after being masters of Briton for above three centuries, were obliged to abandon this province to the care of its own inhabitants, somewhere about the middle of the fifth century.† In the mean time, considerable progress in civilization had been made. Nearly one hundred cities and towns had arisen; and the arts and learning of the Romans had made very considerable progress among these provincials.‡ Intermarriages

---

* *Bede's Ecc. Hist.*, bk. I., chaps. 4, 5, 6, 7.

† *Hume* says, A. D. 448; the *Edinburgh Encyc.*, 421; *Gibbon*, about 409. *Bede* says, "The Roman ceased to rule in Britain about 470 years after Caius Julius Cæsar entered the island;" or about A. D. 410.—*Ecc. Hist.* bk I., c. 11. *Sharon Turner* adopts Bede's date as probably the correct one for the termination of the Roman power in Britain.—*Hist. Anglo Sax.*, vol. I., bk. II., ch. 7. *Whitaker*, a standard authority on antiquarian questions, says the Romans finally deserted the island of Britain, A. D. 446, 501 years after their first descent on the island, and 403 years after their first settlement in the country.—*Hist. Manchester* (Eng.), quarto ed., vol. I., p. 461.

‡ *Gibbon* says: "Ninety-two considerable towns had arisen; * * and among them thirty-three were distinguished above the rest by their superior privileges and importance."—Vol. II., p. 279. See also *Sharon Turner*, Hist. vol. I., bk. II., ch. 8., p. 189.

Sharon Turner (vol. I., bk. II., ch. 8) presents an interesting picture of Britain when the Romans abandoned the island. "Its towns were no longer barracadoed forests; nor its houses wood cabins

had softened the *hauteur* of the conquerors and the prejudice of the conquered. Christianity, too, had exerted some influence in reforming the manners, if not in changing the hearts of the Britons. Gibbon supposes that when the Roman emperor ceased to exercise sovereignty over the island, "the British church might be composed of thirty or forty bishops, with an adequate proportion of the inferior clergy."* And from the circumstance that they were rather distinguished for their poverty than their wealth, we may infer that they retained a respectable character for christian activity and piety.†

Such, substantially, appears to have been the state of Briton when the weakness and approach-

---

covered with straw; nor its inhabitants savages, naked, with painted bodies, or clothed with skins. It had been for above three centuries the seat of Roman civilization and luxury. Roman Emperors had been born [as Constantine the Great], and others had reigned in it. The natives had been ambitious to obtain, and hence had not only built houses, temples, courts, and market-places in their towns, but had adorned them with porticoes, galleries, baths, and saloons, and with mosaic pavements, and emulated every Roman improvement. They had distinguished themselves as legal advocates and orators, and for their study of the Roman poets. Their cities had been made images of Rome itself, and the natives had become Romans. * * * Britain, at the time of the Saxon invasion, had become a wealthy, civilized, and luxurious country" — comparatively so. — Pp. 195–197.

* Vol. II., ch. 31, p. 280. See also *Bingham's Ecc. Antiquities*, vol. I., bk. IX., ch. 6, p. 394.

† Of three British bishops who attended the council of Rimini, A. D. 356, it is said: "tam pauperes fuisse ut nihil haberent," i. e. they were so poor that they had absolutely nothing. — See *Gibbon*.

ing dissolution of the Roman empire compelled the imperial government to withdraw the legions, which had heretofore been the principal defence of the island.

Immediately on the final removal of the Roman legions from Briton, the Scots and Picts — the native inhabitants of Ireland and Scotland — broke in upon the Britons, as Gildas says, "like hungry wolves into a sheep-fold;" and, as Bede says, "like men mowing ripe corn, bore down all before them."* The northern walls, erected and fortified by the Roman generals for the protection of the provincial islanders, presented but a feeble barrier to the inroads of these fierce barbarians. They desolated with fire and sword considerable portions of the island; they took possession of the frontier towns, and finally overran the country. The inhabitants were massacred, driven out, or conquered. After a season of oppression, the Britons rose upon their conquerors, cut in pieces great numbers of them, and drove back the remainder into Scotland. A short season of peace and prosperity followed; and, if we may credit Gildas, of "corruption of manners among all ranks," not excepting the clergy themselves. The good monk complains bitterly, that those "who should have reclaimed the laity by their example, proved the ringleaders in every vice; being addicted

---

* *Ecc. Hist.*, bk. I., ch. 12.

to drunkenness, contention envy," etc.* The false security which this state of things implies, was soon broken up by the return of the Scots and Picts in greater numbers than at first; and the evils which they inflicted on this unhappy people were proportionally terrible.

While suffering the ravages of these barbarians, the miserable Britons sought an alliance with the *Saxons*. This seems to have been the common name of several tribes of Northmen, who inhabited the northern parts of Germany, along the Baltic Sea and the eastern shores of the North Sea. Their inhospitable climate, the barrenness of the soil, and their maritime situation, had enticed them into the roving habits and lawless lives of free-booters. They were the pirates of Europe. In their light boats, framed of wicker and covered with hides, they coasted along the shores of the sea, plundering the coasts, or ascending rivers and creeks, as the hope of gain directed. In this way they acquired a predatory acquaintance with ancient Gaul, and ultimately found their way across the narrow strait which separated Gaul from Briton.

It was, probably, the experience of the hardihood and bravery of the Saxons, in their piratical attacks upon the island coast, which led the suffering Britons to propose an alliance with them, in order

---

* Bede adopts this representation of Gildas as characteristic of the times. — *Bede's Ecc. Hist.*, bk. I., ch. 14.

to expel the barbarous Scots and Picts. The Saxon leaders readily accepted the proposed alliance. They furnished a band of warriors, who, united with the British forces, readily drove the northern tribes to their native fastnesses.*

Scarcely, however, had the unsuspecting Britons time to rejoice over the success of their alliance, when they began to find, to their amazement, that they had introduced a more formidable enemy than had just been driven from the island. The Saxon chiefs, perceiving the weakness and unwarlike character of their allies, the fruitful nature of their soil, and the wealth of the island, immediately set their hearts upon the conquest of the country. Establishing themselves upon the small and fertile island of Thanet, on the south-western coast of Briton, they sent to their German friends an account of the country, and communicated their purpose of conquest. The hardy, piratical fishermen of the North Sea and the Baltic eagerly embraced the opportunity of changing their abode and improving their condition. Under various pretences, successive thousands of Saxons were introduced to the adjacent islands and to the mainland of Briton. Finding at length their numbers sufficient, the Saxon leaders sought occasion to quarrel with the Britons; threw off the mask of friendship, and,

* *Bede* says (bk. I., ch. 15): "The nation of the Angles, or Saxons, being invited by the aforesaid king (Vortigern, ch. 14), arrived in Britain in three long ships, and had a place assigned them to reside in, by the same king, in the eastern part of the island." * *

forming an alliance with the very men whom they had been commissioned to drive out of the country (the Scots and Picts), commenced a war of conquest or extermination against the unfortunate islanders. Vast multitudes of them were slaughtered; their towns and cities were sacked and burned; and large tracts of country were made desolate. Some of the inhabitants fled across the strait to Holland; some to Gaul; others took refuge in the woods and mountains of the interior.

The Britons were at length roused by the desperation of their circumstances, and fought heroically for their native land.* Rivers of blood enriched the devoted soil. Various successes attended conflicting armies; yet the invaders, constantly augmented by swarms from their northern hives, gradually encroached upon the miserable islanders, until the whole of Briton became the prey of the Saxon spoilers. Thus, after a most terrible and desolating contest of nearly one hundred and fifty years (i. e., from about A. D. 450 to A. D. 600),

* Bede gives us to understand that the successes of the Britons against their oppressors were mainly owing to the interposition of "the holy bishops," whose assistance being implored, hastened to the aid of the Britons, and "inspired so much courage into these fearful people that one would have thought they had been joined by a mighty army." And he narrates one instance of wonderful success, in which the Britons, fresh from a religious festival, and "still wet with the baptismal water," are said to have gained a great victory, much as Gideon did his — by standing still and shouting "Hallelujah!" three times over. — *Bede's Ecc. Hist.*, bk. I., chs. 16 and 20.

the Saxon heptarchy, of seven kingdoms, was established on the territory which is now known as England.* The original inhabitants were almost totally extirpated. A few of the most daring and successful resistants were driven back, fighting, into the mountains of Cornwall and Wales; hence the terms Wales and Welchmen, which, in the Saxon tongue denote a strange country, or a stranger. Among the mountains of Wales, the ancient Britons maintained their independence for more than six centuries.

The Saxon invasion and conquest swept away from the island all traces of former civilization and Christianity, and covered this land, a second time, with the darkness of the harshest Paganism. Woden, or Odin, was the supreme god of the Saxons; from whom several of the heptarchy princes were supposed to have descended. He was a god of war, and slaughtered thousands at a blow. In his palace of Valhalla, he received to supreme felicity the souls of those who fell in battle, bravely fighting. Their days were there all spent in employments most congenial to their tastes — in mimic hunting matches or imaginary combats. Their nights were devoted to feasting upon delicious viands, served by virgins of surpassing beauty and never-fading charms; and in regaling themselves

---

* *Sharon Turner* calls the government of Briton an *octarchy*, of eight kingdoms. — Bk. III., ch. 5.

with mead, drunk from the skulls of their slaughtered enemies.*

A conquest made by the worshippers of such a god, and the expectants of such pleasures, and under the immediate direction of men who claimed affinity to Woden himself, must, of necessity, have been destructive of everything civilizing or humanizing.

Gregory the Great was the father of the Anglo-Saxon † church, about A. D. 596. The same Gregory who destroyed the monuments of ancient Roman greatness, lest the visitors of Rome should give more attention to them than to the pursuits of religion; and who is infamous among the lovers of classical literature, for having burned numerous ancient manuscripts, among which were several of Livy's, lest the clergy should be more instructed in the polished productions of pagan Rome, than in the monkish learning of papal Rome. The same who encouraged the use of pictures and images in the churches, as needful helps to the instruction and edification of the ignorant populace, though he condemned the *worship* of them. Such was the fountain-head from which flowed the Christianity of the Saxon church. Not that Gregory himself went to Briton; though he would gladly have done so had his duties as pope of Rome

---

* *Lond. Encyc.*, art. Mythology; *Hume*, I., ch. 1; *Russell's Mod. Europe*, let. XI.; *Hist. Anglo Saxons*, bk. II., Appendix, ch. 3.

† This title is sometimes given to the conquerors of Briton, because the *Angles* were a leading tribe among the Saxon conquerors.

allowed him. He, however, was the great patron and promoter of the mission to these reputed barbarians. Augustine, commonly called St. Austin, the chosen leader of the forty monks who were sent on this embassy of proselytism, seems to have been a worthy representative of his sovereign lord the pope. Jortin calls him "a sanctified ruffian."* Whether or not he deserves so harsh an appellation, certain it is that the religion introduced by Austin was little better than that which it superseded. By the order of the pope, Austin established public worship in the heathen temples, after purifying them with "holy water;" and encouraged the people on festive occasions to gather around these temples, to build their booths, and slaughter their cattle, and feast and carouse, as they had been accustomed to do under the reign of Woden.

This, and much else of the same general character, his saintship allowed, on the very convenient plea of adapting the forms of worship and the order of the church to the peculiarities of the people among whom they were to be established. And it will not be easy, I apprehend, for the modern advocates of this very convenient doctrine of accommodation, to show wherein Gregory or his vicegerent, Austin, acted inconsistently. If we may depart from the apostolic model in order to accommodate the prejudices of *one* class of people

* See Jortin's remarks, quoted by Waddington, p. 134, note.

or to adapt the church to *one* form of civil government, why may we not be equally accommodating to *all?* And who shall say: Thus far shalt thou go, but no further! The truth is — and good men will yet, it is believed, come to see it — there is no stopping place, if we go beyond the Law and the Testimony. If the apostolic churches are not our patterns, we have none. And if we have none, every people may consult their own taste and fancy in church architecture.

With a knowledge of Gregory's principles and Austin's policy, we need not wonder that eight years sufficed to spread Christianity, such as it was, over the kingdom of Kent, the eldest of the heptarchy kingdoms. This event was hastened, doubtless, by the circumstance that Ethelbert, the king of Kent, had married Bertha, a christian princess, daughter of the king of Paris; who, for eighteen years previous to the arrival of Austin, had supported a private chaplain and maintained christian worship at the court. The kingdom of Northumberland followed the example of Kent; twelve thousand persons, we are told, were baptized in a single day. Before the close of the seventh century (about A. D. 686), Christianity had become the religion of the seven kingdoms of the Anglo-Saxons.

The character of the converts may be estimated by the ease with which they were made, the means employed, and by the readiness with which these converts threw off their Christianity and returned to Paganism, and put it on again, at the bidding of their king. A single story shall suffice for an illustration of this whole matter: Eadbald, the son and successor of Ethelbert, the first christian monarch of Kent, conceiving a violent passion for his mother-in-law, renounced the christian religion, because it forbade such incestuous marriages, and, with most of his subjects, returned to the worship of Woden. In this posture of affairs, there was little to encourage the bishops to remain in the kingdom; and two actually left. Laurentius, the primate, was upon the point of giving up all further attempts to Christianize the kingdom, when a happy expedient was suggested to his mind. He appeared one morning before Eadbald, and throwing off his priestly robes, presented his lacerated body to the astonished king. The monarch immediately demanded who had dared thus to abuse so venerable a person. Laurentius informed him that no earthly hands had thus wounded him; but that St. Peter had appeared to him in a vision, and after severely reprimanding him for his intended desertion of the sheep of Christ, had inflicted the blows which he saw, as a punishment for his unfaithfulness. The apostate monarch could resist no longer; he immediately divorced his wife and returned to the church. His subjects, as in duty bound, followed his example; and thus the christian religion (!) was firmly established in the eldest of the heptarchy kingdoms.*

* *Mosheim*, bk. II., cent. VI., pt. I., ch. 1; pt. II., ch. 2, § 9; cent. VII., pt. I., ch. 1; *Hume*, vol. I., ch. 1; *Lingard*, vol. I., ch. 2, A.

Christianity propagated among pagans by men and means like those just described, could be little else than a change of superstitions. The history of Anglo-Saxon Christianity, from the arrival of Bertha and her chaplain in 579, to the end of the heptarchy in 827, a period of 248 years, is a confirmation of this reasonable supposition.* It would be too much to assert, that there was no intelligent piety in the land; but it is perfectly apparent from the history of those times, that Christianity had little else than a name to live while it was dead. Flowing to the Saxons from the corrupt fountain-head of papal usurpation, it must have been the waters of death, rather than of life, to the ignorant islanders. The church history of the heptarchy is a loathsome story of papal imposition on

---

D. 589–670. *Bede*, bk. I., chaps. 23–34, gives a somewhat particular account of the establishment of Romanism in Briton; see also bk. II., ch. 15. *Sharon Turner*, bk. III., ch. 6, furnishes a summary of the same, in which he speaks kindly words of Pope Gregory, for the deep interest which he felt and manifested for the conversion of Briton. See also *Anglo-Saxon Chronicle*, A. D. 596, 601, 616, 626, 627, 637, *passim.*

* Even "the venerable" Bede's Ecclesiastical History of Briton, so much lauded, abounds in illustrations of these remarks. Take, for example, the following headings of chapters: "Cuthbert, being an anchorite, by his prayers obtained a spring in a dry soil, and had a crop from seed sown by himself out of season."—Bk. IV., ch. 28. "Of one that was cured of a palsy, at the tomb of St. Cuthbert."—Ch. 31. "Of one that was cured of a distemper in his eye, at the relics of St. Cuthbert."—Ch. 32. In bk. V. we find a succession of like miracles recorded in successive chapters: The sea calmed—A dumb man cured—A sick maiden healed—An earl's wife cured with holy water, etc., etc.

the one hand, and of ignorant and superstitious devotion on the other hand. Many of the putrescent abominations of Rome were incorporated into the Saxon church. Reverence for their sovereign lord, the pope, was the first article of the Saxon creed; a devout regard for all that wore the sacerdotal habit, stood next in order; the worship of saints and reliques was held to be scarcely less important than the worship of God himself; the payment of "Peter's pence," would purchase pardon for a thousand sins; a pilgrimage to Rome, the establishment of a monastery, or the gift of property to the church, would cover the most flagitious crimes. The hoary-headed villain could wash his hands in innocency, quiet the upbraidings of conscience and smooth his path to hell, by making over to the church the profits of his villainy and spending his last days within the hallowed walls of a monastery.

This was substantially the state of English Christianity up to the time of the Danish invasion, A. D. 787–851. Confusion, war, pillage, flames, and blood, attended the successive incursions of the Danish freebooters. The persevering energy and the bravery of Alfred, finally expelled these fierce invaders, or converted them into obedient subjects; and his wisdom restored peace and prosperity to England, after more than half a century of confusion and suffering, A. D. 893–901.*

* *The Anglo-Saxon Chronicle*, under date of A. D. 787, says: "This year * * * first came three ships of Northmen, out of Hære-

Alfred is celebrated in English history for his martial valor, for the excellence of the laws and regulations which he established, for his encouragement of learning, and, finally, for his pious regard for the interests of religion. That there was a call for his fostering care of learning and piety, is but too obvious, from the complaint of Alfred himself, who, in speaking of the churchmen at the time of his accession to the throne of England, said: "Very few were they on this side the Humber (the most improved part of England) who could understand their daily prayers in English, or translate any letter from the Latin. I think there were not many beyond the Humber; they were so few, that indeed I cannot recollect *one single instance* on the south of the Thames, when I took the kingdom."*

Half a century had scarcely elapsed from the death of Alfred, before the notorious Dunstan, ycleped *saint*, issued from his narrow den, to delude the ignorant with his miracles, and to curse the land with his machinations. Having failed as a

---

tha-land [Denmark]. * * * These were the first ships of Danishmen which sought the land of the English nation."—*Hist. Anglo-Sax.*, bk. IV., ch. 3: "In 787 the fierce visitors [the Northmen] first appeared in England." * * * "In 851 they first ventured to winter in the isle of Thanet. This was a new era in their habits." Chaps. 4–11, of bk. IV., and the whole of bk. V., Hist. Ang. Sax., are devoted to Alfred's history and his successful struggle with the Northmen. *Hume*, vol. I., ch. 2; *Lingard*, vol. I., ch. 4.

* *Alfred's Preface to Wise's Asser.*, in Hist. Anglo-Saxons, vol. II., bk. V., ch. 1.

courtier, he turned *fakir*. He built him a cell, so low that he could not stand erect in it, and of dimensions so contracted that he had not room to stretch himself. Here he spent his time in devotion and manual labor. But even here — if we may believe his monkish biographers — his saintship was not exempt from company. The devil often visited him and sorely troubled him. At length, coming one day under the form of a beautiful woman, and thrusting his head into the cell of the saint, Dunstan, detecting the fraud, and exasperated beyond further forbearance, seized a pair of red hot pincers — made ready perhaps for the occasion — and caught the fair devil by the nose, and thus held him in durance vile, while the neighborhood resounded with his bellowings.

This veritable piece of tragi-comic history being industriously circulated and unhesitatingly believed, established Dunstan's character as a saint. His reputation soon introduced him to the court of Edmund and the rich abbey of Glastonbury. In the succeeding reign of Edred (A. D. 946), he became the prime minister of England, the confidential adviser of the king and the keeper of his conscience. This arrangement facilitated Dunstan's plan for enslaving the kingdom to the sovereign pontiff. For this purpose he introduced into the island a new order of monks, the Benedictines, the very body-guard of the pope. These monks having bound themselves to a life of celibacy, were loud in their denunciations of the regular clergy.

The old clergy of the kingdom being married men, were bound to the State by a tie not less strong than that which held them in obedience to the Head of the Church. The ambitious designs of the popes could not well be attained without an order of men entirely separate from an interest in the State. In the Benedictines this class of men was found; and it was the policy of the Roman pontiff to employ these men in making the church independent of the throne; in making the sceptre subservient to the crosier. That Dunstan and his monks did much to accomplish this purpose, is but too apparent from the insolent abuse which Edwy, or Edwin, and his beautiful queen suffered at their hands.

This prince, the successor of the superstitious Edred, venturing to marry a princess more nearly allied to him by birth than the canon law allowed, incurred the wrath of his chaste ecclesiastics. On the day of his coronation feast, Edwy, having retired from the noisy revellings of his barons, to the apartment of his queen and her mother, was rudely broken in upon by Dunstan and another priest. Upbraiding the king for his retirement, and abusing the queen and her mother for their share in the king's conduct, Dunstan tore him from his affrighted bride, and dragged him back into the banquet of the nobles.

The king, though afraid to resist the imperious saint at the time, soon after attempted to revenge this insult, by calling Dunstan to account for his administration of the treasury under the previous reign. The haughty minister refusing to give account of his stewardship, was banished the realm. But the saint ultimately proved too strong for the king. The kingdom was filled with praises of the banished one and murmurs against his persecutor. And when the public mind was ripe, the infamous Odo ordered the queen to be seized; and having branded her beautiful face with a hot iron, carried her away captive to Ireland. Edwy, finding it vain to resist, at length submitted to a divorce. In the meantime Elgiva, being healed of her wounds, and regarding herself still as the wife of the king, found means to escape from her exile, and was fleeing to her husband, when Odo, being apprised of her movements, intercepted her and doomed her to death. She was hamstringed; and expired a few days after, at Glocester, in the most acute torments. This, however, was not the end of the tragedy. The people were stirred up by the ecclesiastics to rebel against their sovereign. Edwy was driven from his throne and excommunicated from the church, and at length died, the object of clerical hatred and persecution. Dunstan was recalled in triumph, loaded with wealth and honors while he lived, and canonized at death.*

---

* *Hist. Anglo-Saxons*, bk. VI., ch. 5, is devoted to the tragic story of Edwy and Elgiva, in connection with Dunstan and his coöperators. Dunstan's life is continued through the two succeeding chapters, the 6th and 7th, of the same book. Turner's view of Dunstan, and of his treatment of Edwy and his queen, is substantially the same

I have given the story of Dunstan and Edwy as a fair illustration of the state of religion, as a national establishment, in England, to the end of the tenth century. And, indeed, with slight additions, it will answer well for the reflector of the English church for another half century.

The Norman Conquest (A. D. 1066), which was sanctified by pope Alexander II., greatly aided by

---

as that taken by Hume, *Hist. Eng.*, vol. I., ch. 2, A. D. 955, and given in the text above. It is proper, however, to apprise the reader that there is not an entire agreement between ancient or modern historians on this subject. Lingard, the celebrated Catholic historian of England (vol. I., ch. 5), gives quite a different version of this story. He represents Edwy as a passionate, licentious young man; and his retirement from the coronation feast to have been by appointment with a favorite female, whose distinguishing virtue was not chastity. In short, he gives his readers to understand that the king forsook his nobles to meet a prostitute. But, if Edwy had married his second or third cousin, as Elgiva is said to have been, contrary to the church canons and the advice of his clergy, his lawful wife might, and probably would have been denounced by the monkish historians as his mistress, and as a prostitute; and this is probably the explanation of the discrepancies between some ancient, as well as some modern authorities. — See Hume, vol. I., note B, at the end of the volume; and S. Turner, *ut supra*. *The Anglo-Saxon Chronicle*, A. D. 958, contains this record: "In this year archbishop Odo separated king Edwy and Elfgiva, *because they were too near related.*" *Roger of Wendover*, A. D. 955, says: "A certain light woman, who was nevertheless of lofty birth, inveigled him [Eadwy] by her infamous familiarity into marrying either herself or her grown-up daughter." And this person he afterwards calls "the harlot, whose name was Algiva." Under date of A. D. 958, Roger records: "In the same year St. Odo, archbishop of Canterbury, separated king Eadwy and Algiva from each other, either for the cause of consanguinity, or for their adulterous intercourse."

the church dignitaries of Normandy, who contributed ships, arms, and men to the Conqueror,* and facilitated by the clergy of England — many of whom were Frenchmen or Normans, introduced by the policy of Dunstan and his coadjutors — was the instrument in the pope's hands of breaking down the spirit of English ecclesiastical independence, which had so long been struggling with the papal hydra; and before the close of the eleventh century, England was hardly second to France or Italy in devoted attachment to the see of Rome.

It is true that the Conqueror controlled this growing superstition by the might of his power and the strength of his genius, as he did everything else, so as to make it subserve his own interests. Still the evil grew apace during his reign, and proved too strong for some of his successors.†

* *Ordericus Vitalis*, bk. III., ch. 11. The whole number of "ships" — generally small vessels, probably — furnished by the clergy, is set down at seven hundred and eighty-two. See note to O. V., Bohn's ed., vol. I., p. 464; *Hume*, vol. I., chaps. 3, 4.

† *Turner's Hist. Eng.* (Middle Ages), vol. I., ch. 4, p. 131, Lond. 1830; *Gieseler's Ecc. Hist.*, vol. III., period III., div. 3., ch. 1, pp. 1–27, Edinb. ed.; *Mosheim*, bk. III., cent. XI., pt. 2, ch. 2.

Ordericus Vitalis, a contemporary of William the Conqueror, supplies numerous details of his "pious care" for the church. At his request, we are told, three special legates, two of them cardinal canons, were sent from Rome, to crown the king at Winchester; and that these Romans he detained at court a year, "listening to and honoring them as if they were the angels of God." He was, too, according to Vitalis, the great patron of abbeys and religious establishments. He built many monasteries, and repaired the dilapidated churches. But it is quite evident that the Conqueror used

Towards the close of this century the right of election to church preferments, and investiture in the same, was denied to laymen; and a fierce contest began between the English monarch and his clergy, and their sovereign head, upon this question. This, and other matters involving the question of the pope's supremacy over kings and princes, as well as over all laymen, continued to distract the kingdom, and all Christendom indeed, for a long time. Henry I. found it for his interest to flatter the clergy, and not to break with the pope; and yet, he was exceedingly reluctant to yield any of the ancient prerogatives of the crown. The contest was carried on during the greater part of his reign; which ended A. D. 1135. And, though neither party gained a complete victory, yet it was evident on the whole, that the pope and his party made progress towards sovereignty.*

---

the church as an essential handmaid to help him along in subjugating and governing the State. — See *The Ecc. Hist. of England and Normandy,* by Ordericus Vitalis, bk. IV., chaps. 6, 8. The account given by this ancient historian of the Norman Conqueror is quite full, and apparently very candid. The history of his reign will be found scattered along through the first two volumes of Vitalis's Ecc. Hist., commencing bk. III., ch. 11, and ending with an account of William's miserable death and brutal burial, bk. VII., chaps. 14–16.

The contest between William Rufus and Archbishop Anselm, continued in different forms for some time, illustrates the ambitious designs and the growing power of the clergy. — See *Turner's Hist. Eng.* during the Middle Ages, vol. I., ch. 5.

* *Mosheim,* ut sup., and bk. III., cent. XII., pt. 2, ch. 2; *Neander,* vol. IV., sec. II.

Under the disastrous reign of the usurper Stephen, the successor of Henry I., and during the civil wars which occurred in this reign,* the clergy being indispensable to the success of either party, had opportunity to advance yet further towards an entire independence of the crown. And appeals to the pope to settle ecclesiastical controversies, which had not before been tolerated by English monarchs, becoming common during these troublous times, gave his holiness greater power in that kingdom than he had ever before possessed.

The last half of the twelfth century witnessed a spectacle "such as had never before been exhibited to the world;"† two crowned heads, Henry II. of England and Lewis of France, on foot, each with his hand upon the rein of the pope's horse, conducting his holiness into the castle of Torci. Such were the honors paid to the *Man of Sin* in that age.

Henry II., nevertheless, was not a man to submit, even to the pope, longer than he perceived it

---

* *The Anglo-Saxon Chronicle* (A. D. 1137) says: "In this king's time was all discord, and evil-doing, and robbing. * * Then was corn dear, and flesh, and cheese, and butter, for there was none in the land, — wretched men starved with hunger. * * Never was there more misery, and never acted heathens worse than these." See also *S. Turner's Hist. Eng.*, vol. I., ch. 7.

† Cardinal Baronius, in *Hume*, vol. I., ch. 8. Hume's account of the struggle between the civil and ecclesiastical despotism of these times is quite full and reasonably fair. He devotes his 8th and 9th chapters chiefly to this topic.

for his interest. Having by the mediation of the pontiff relieved himself from the danger of a war with Lewis, he immediately turned his attention to the state of ecclesiastical affairs in his kingdom. Perceiving, as Hume says, that "the usurpations of the clergy had mounted to such a height that the contest between the *regale* and the *pontificale* was really arrived at a crisis in England," and that it had become necessary to determine "whether the king or the priests (particularly the archbishop of Canterbury) should be sovereign of the kingdom" — Henry resolved to curb the ambition of the clergy, and to bring the church, as well as the realm, entirely under his control. And he was doubtless the man to do this, if arbitrary power could accomplish the object. For this purpose he raised to the see of Canterbury his favorite, confidential friend and chancellor, Thomas á Becket; a man who well understood the king's plans, and who heretofore had been entirely subservient to the monarch's wishes. Becket possessed capacity and learning, lofty ambition and unshrinking firmness, and soon showed himself capable of playing the saint as perfectly as he had previously done the courtier. The dainty chancellor, whose equipage and style of living had been the admiration of the kingdom, suddenly became another Dunstan. Instead of the narrow cell, lower than a man could stand in, and shorter than a man could stretch himself in, Becket resorted to a hair shirt, worn next his skin, which he changed so seldom that it became extremely filthy and was filled with vermin. And, instead of wounding the devil's nose with red-hot pincers, he lacerated his own back with frequent flagellations. By his austerities and affected humility he soon became a saint of the highest grade.

In the meantime the archbishop, so far from coöperating with the king in his efforts to curb the clergy, set himself in direct opposition to his master. Henry, as may be supposed, was exasperated to the highest degree to find his chosen instrument of church reform turned against him. And in his wrath he resolved to humble, if not to destroy the prelate. Becket, perceiving his intention, fled in disguise, and took shelter under the wing of the pope. Alexander treated him with distinguished favor; and soon made Henry feel the strength of the pope's long arm. Though the king struggled manfully to shake off the grasp, he was compelled at length to yield. And so low was the imperious monarch of England reduced, that he condescended to hold the stirrup of the victorious Becket while he mounted his horse. Though afterwards the peace between the king and his archbishop was broken, and the arrogance of Becket and the violence of Henry caused the prelate's death, yet the triumph of the church was finally complete, and the humbled monarch was glad to make his peace with Rome by doing penance at Becket's grave. He was required to go barefoot to the tomb of the martyr, and after kneeling and praying for some time upon the grave, and submitting to be scourged by the monks, he was compelled to pass the day and night without refreshment, kneeling upon the naked stone.

The story of Becket may serve to illustrate the relative position of Church and State in England, up to the close of the twelfth century.* It was reserved, however, for king John, one of the most cruel, odious, contemptible creatures that ever filled the English throne, and pope Innocent III., to complete the work of British degradation.

John began his career by putting out of the way his innocent nephew Arthur, duke of Brittany.†

* *Roger of Wendover*, A. D. 1158–1174, abounds in notices of this famous controversy between the king and the archbishop; in fact, his chronicle for about sixteen years is almost entirely devoted to this matter. *Turner's Hist. Eng.*, vol. I., ch. 8, presents a very fair, full, and comprehensive view of the life and death of this extraordinary man. *Lingard's* account of the controversy between Henry and Becket is very full and fair.—*Hist. Eng.*, vol. II., ch. 5.

† The contemporaneous tale was, that John stabbed Arthur with his own hand, severed his head, and threw his body into the sea.—See *Guillermus Brito.*, in Turner, vol. I., ch. 12., p. 406. *Roger of Wendover* (A. D. 1202) says, that John, "troubled" at the ill-advised reply of Arthur to his attempt to separate the young prince from the French king, "gave orders that Arthur should be sent to Rouen, to be imprisoned in the new tower there, and kept closely guarded; but shortly afterwards the said Arthur suddenly disappeared." * * * "In this same year [continues the Chronicle] king John came to England and was crowned at Canterbury. * * * On his arrival there an opinion about the death of Arthur gained ground throughout the French kingdom and the continent in general, by which it seemed that John was suspected by all of having slain him with his own hands; for which reason many turned their

John's next step was to apply to the pope to preserve him from the destructive consequences of a war with Philip of France, which his murderous cruelty towards Arthur had excited. Encouraged by the pusillanimity of John, Innocent took occasion, from an appeal soon after made to him to decide between the conflicting claims of two persons who had been elected to the archbishopric of Canterbury, to establish the right of the papal throne to appoint whom it would to this high office, the second in the kingdom; a usurpation upon the rights of the crown which no pope had ever before attempted. John by this act was inflamed to the highest pitch of resentment, and vented his spite upon such of the clergy in his kingdom as countenanced the proceedings of the pope. The pope warned the refractory monarch; gently reminding him of the story of Thomas á Becket. But finding that John was not inclined to submit, Innocent laid the kingdom under an interdict. By this, most of the outward rites of religious worship were suspended; the altars were stripped of their ornaments; the *reliques* and images of saints were laid upon the ground and carefully covered up; the bells were removed from the steeples of the churches; the dead were buried without religious rites, in common ground, or thrown like cattle into ditches; marriages were celebrated in the grave-

affections from the king from that time forward wherever they dared, and entertained the deepest enmity against him." —*Flowers of History*, vol. II., pp. 205, 206.

yards; meat was denied to all classes; entertainments and pleasures of all kinds were forbidden; men were prohibited to pay even a decent regard to their persons — their beards were to go unshorn and their apparel unchanged; the ordinary salutations of friends, even, were condemned. These were some of the terrific consequences of an interdict from the "Vicar of God."

John raved and swore at this act of papal impudence. But this did not improve his situation. All the resistance he could make was of no avail. Excommunication followed the interdict. The king now began to quail. It was not, however, until the sovereign pontiff had uttered another thunder, by which John was deposed from his throne and his subjects absolved from their allegiance to him, and a powerful French army was prepared to carry out the plans of His Holiness, that the English monarch was completely subdued and tamed. He was now ready to make his peace with Rome on any terms. In token of his penitence, and as an evidence of his entire submission to his sovereign lord the pope, John was required to resign his kingdom to St. Peter and St. Paul, to St. Innocent III. and all his holy successors, and abjectly to agree to hold his dominions as a feudatory of Rome. The legate and representative of the pope was the person to whom this surrender was made. Having made this submission of all his rights, and honors, and titles, John was next required to do homage to the legate, for the privilege of holding his crown and administering the government of the kingdom. This he did under the following humiliating circumstances: Unarmed, the monarch entered the room where Pandolfo, or Pandulph, the legate, sat upon a throne; and throwing himself upon his knees, placed his joined hands between those of the legate, and swore fealty to the pope in the following words: "I John, by the grace of God, king of England, and lord of Ireland, for the expiation of my sins, and out of my own free will, with the advice and consent of my barons, do give unto the church of Rome, and to pope Innocent III. and his successors, the kingdoms of England and Ireland, together with all the rights belonging to them; and will hold them of the pope, as his vassal. I will be faithful to God, to the church of Rome, to the pope my lord, and to his successors lawfully elected; and I bind myself to pay him a tribute of one thousand marks of silver yearly; to wit, seven hundred for the kingdom of England, and three hundred for Ireland."

Roger of Wendover gives a detailed account of this memorable contest between the king of England and the pope of Rome. It lasted five years, and was fought out by John with a measure of brutal courage which is quite surprising, considering the character of the king and the peculiarities of the times. The pope seems to have made little or no headway against the king until he succeeded in stirring up a powerful army of crusaders against him. This, coupled with the apprehended disloyalty of some of his own nobles, and the indefinite dread of the prophecy of Peter the hermit — who had proclaimed that John would not be a king on the next ascension-day, nor afterwards, for on that day the crown of England would be transferred to another — these things induced the king to yield at last to the solicitations of his own barons and the pope's agents, and make his peace with Rome; — a peace nearly or quite as much desired by Innocent as by John; for, what John told Innocent in a saucy letter, written to His Holiness during the controversy, was doubtless true: that "more abundant profits accrued to them [the pope and the court of Rome] from his kingdom of England, than from all other countries on this side of the Alps." And in confirmation of this, we read, that after John had submitted to the pope's legate, he "Pandulph, crossed the sea into France, taking with him these aforesaid charters [by which John submitted and did homage to the pope, etc., etc.], *and also eight thousand pounds stirling money.*" *

It was during the reign of this same John, and under the patronage of this same "rough, cruel, avaricious, and arrogant" Innocent III., and during the memorable controversy between John and the

* See *Roger of Wendover's Flowers of History,* A. D. 1205–1214, vol. II., pp. 215–271, Bohn's Ant. Lib. edition; *Turner's Hist. Eng.,* Middle Ages, vol. I., ch. 12; *Hume,* vol. I., ch. 11; *Russell's Mod. Europe,* vol. I., pt. I., let. 31; *Lingard,* vol. III., ch. 1.

pope, that the crusade against the Albigenses was preached and practiced. Simon de Montfort, the incarnate fiend, who was the pope's favorite agent in that horrible persecution, was an English nobleman, the Earl of Leicester. And John himself, though thoroughly depraved and unprincipled — as ready to become the vassal of the Mohammedan emperor as of the pope, — was a willing persecutor of the "heretics" of Gascony, ordering his seneschal "to extirpate them entirely."*

The reign of Henry III. was as memorable for papal tyranny and extortion as was that of John his immediate predecessor. It was the longest and one of the most grievous reigns that England ever experienced. The kingdom was filled with foreign monks, chiefly Italians, who possessed themselves of the richest benefices in the land; the income of which, at one time during this reign, was estimated at sixty thousand marks† — a sum greater than the income of the crown itself. Pluralities and non-residences were notoriously common. Mansel, the king's chaplain, is computed to have held, at once, *seven hundred* ecclesiastical livings. The policy of the pope during this reign evidently

---

* *Mosheim,* vol. II., p. 296, Harper's ed.; also pp. 348–350; *Roger of Wendover,* vol. II., pp. 278–286; *Turner,* vol. I., pp. 427–429, 441–446.

† A mark was thirteen shillings and four pence, or about three dollars and twenty cents; which would make the sum equal to forty thousand pounds, or nearly two hundred thousand dollars; which, considering the value of money in those days, was an enormous sum.

was, to reap a golden harvest from the usurpations of the preceding reigns. And Henry, though variable in his tone, seemed disposed to encourage, rather than to repress these exactions. The legate of the pope is said to have carried out of the kingdom, at one time, more money than he left in it. "He exacted the revenues of all vacant benefices; the *twentieth* of all ecclesiastical revenues without exception; the *third* of such as exceeded a hundred marks a year, and the *half* of such as were possessed by non-residents. He claimed the goods of all intestate clergymen; he pretended a title to inherit all money gotten by usury; he levied benevolences upon the people; and when the king, contrary to his usual practice, prohibited these exactions, he threatened to pronounce against him the same censures which he had emitted against the emperor Frederic;" who had been excommunicated and deposed, and had died under his troubles. In addition to all these impositions, Innocent exercised the right of setting aside any elections or appointments to ecclesiastical offices. Three archbishops were successively set aside by him; and it was not until one was elected of his own nomination, that he would confirm the election.

Matthew Paris' English History is filled with illustrations of the impudent rapacity of the Roman court during the epoch now under review. He has one chapter (A. D. 1241) entitled "The Roman Court likened to a Harlot;" which, being quite short, I will copy out for the entertainment of the reader, as follows:

"About this time, either with the permission or by the instrumentality of Pope Gregory, the insatiable cupidity of the Roman court grew to such an extent, confounding right with wrong, that, laying aside all modesty, like a common, brazen-faced strumpet, exposed for hire to every one, it considered usury as but a trivial offence, and simony as no crime at all; so that it infected other neighboring States, and even the purity of England, by its contagion. Although the examples of this which offer themselves abound, I have thought proper briefly to relate one, in order to show how justly, although tardy, the anger of God was kindled against the said court.

"Pope Gregory, wishing to aid one of his special partisans, sent letters into England, which pressed heavily upon some of the churches. At this time, an apostolic message, accompanied by mixed entreaties and threats, was sent to the abbat and conventual assembly of Peterborough, ordering them to give to the pope an annual revenue to the value of at least a hundred marks for each church, the patronage of which belonged to them; and if it were worth twice as much, it would please him well. He, the pope, would then grant that church to them to be held from him on an annual farm, on condition that they would each year pay him a hundred marks for it, and all the residue they might convert to their own uses. And in order that he might the more easily incline the aforesaid abbat and monks to agree to this arrangement (or, rather, pernicious compact, simony, and secret fraud), as if it were necessary for their welfare, his holiness wrote to some clerks from his side the Alps, who held good benefices in England, ordering them, by the power granted to them, effectually to advise the said abbat and monks to consent to this; and, if necessary, to compel them to it."—Vol. i., p. 332.

This honest old chronicler says of the pope's legate, Otto, whose arrival in England in 1237 he announces (p. 54), and whose oppressive proceedings he very frequently mentions during the three succeeding years: "On the day after the Epiphany (A. D. 1241), the legate, after receiving an embrace and kisses from the king, took ship at Dover, and, laying aside the insignia of his legateship, turned his back on England, leaving no one except the king, and those whom he had fattened on the property of the kingdom, to lament his departure. And at that time (as was truly stated) there was not left in England so much money (with the exception of the vessels and ornaments of the holy churches) as he, the said legate, had extorted from the kingdom. He had, moreover, given away at his own will, or at that of the pope, prebends, churches, and more than three hundred rich revenues, owing to which the kingdom was like a vineyard exposed to every passer-by, and which the wild boar of the woods had laid waste, and languished in a miserable state of desolation. He left the church of Canterbury, which was the most noble of all the English churches, in a state of inquietude and languishing in widowhood, as well as many other cathedral and conventual churches destitute of all comfort and consolation. And he had not strengthened any of the weaker parts of the country, as was proved by clear evidence, because he was sent, not to protect the sheep which were lost, but to gather in the harvest of money which he had found."*

Paris tells us, that in the year 1246, "assuming boldness from past successes in trampling on and impoverishing the wretched English, the pope now imperiously and more imperiously than usual, demanded that all beneficed persons in England, who resided in their benefices, should give a third of their property to him, the pope; and those non-resident, a half, with the addition of many most severe conditions," etc.—Vol. II., p. 191. Against this "unreasonable exaction of the pope," the clergy earnestly protested, and among other things said, that in order to meet these demands "it would be necessary annually to collect from the revenues of

---

* *English History*, vol. I., p. 319. See also Matt. Paris, A. D. 1244–50, *passim*, particularly "The Letter from the community of England on the Extortions of the Roman Court," vol. II., pp., 73–77 and 108–109; and the king's speech to his parliament, about Mid-Lent, 1246; and sundry letters addressed to the pope by the king, the community of England, the abbots, etc., etc., in reference to the grievances endured, and the injuries inflicted on them by the court of Rome.—*Vol.* II., pp. 141, 148–157; also, pp. 203–206.

the clerks [the clergy] the sum of *eighty thousand marks* [$256,000], which sum the whole kingdom of England would scarcely be able to pay; how much less, then, can the clerks, whose property consists only in the profits,"* etc., etc.

---

* *M. Paris*, vol. II., A. D. 1246, p. 194. *Hume*, vol. I., ch. 12, gives a vivid but truthful picture of Roman rapacity and venality during the reign of Henry III. *Lingard's* account is scarcely less severe, vol. III., ch. 2, particularly pp. 103–114; see also *Turner's* comprehensive summary of the state of affairs during this long and oppressive reign, vol. I., ch. 13, particularly pp. 441–446; also *Collier, Ecc. Hist.* vol. II., p. 501. *Roger of Wendover* devotes more than a fifth part of his entire work, to the reign of Henry III; and his records of particular events and transactions during this reign fully sustain the general denunciations of modern historians. See particularly, pp. 403–404, 429–432, 446, 459, 461–462, 466–479, 485, 508, 528–530, 539, 542–546, 551–552, 562, 567 — Bohn's edition.

Having quoted so frequently Matthew Paris's English History, in exposing the avarice and venality of the court of Rome, it is perhaps only common fairness to add, that the Romanist historian, Dr. John Lingard, denounces Matthew as "the most querulous" of those clerical writers of the reign of Henry III., "who have labored to interest in their favor the feelings of posterity by the description, probably the exaggerated, of their wrongs." And he characterises Matthew's work as "a romance rather than a history." — *Hist. Eng.*, vol. III., pp. 159–160. But, when we consider that the old monk of St. Albans is quoted by the most reliable English historians, as unexceptionable authority for contemporaneous events, that Dr. Lingard is emphatically the *Romish* historian of England, and that Matt. Paris presents a most appalling picture of Roman cupidity and corruption during his own times, it is not remarkable that John should not like Matthew. Bishop Nicolson, no mean authority in bibliography, says of Matt. Paris's History: "The whole book manifests a great deal of candor and exactness in its author, who furnishes us with so particular a relation of the brave repulses given by many of our princes to the usurping power of the Roman see, that it is a wonder how such an heretical history came to survive thus long." He calls him "One of the most renowned historians

Papal tyranny reached its highest pitch during this and the succeeding reign. The miserable people, ground to the dust by the high-handed robberies of the king and the pope, began at length to show signs that patience had had its perfect work; and that there were bounds beyond which even their "sovereign Lord God the Pope" and his Italian banditti could not safely go. Hoodwinked and priest-ridden, as the English had long been, they began, towards the close of this long and oppressive reign, to exhibit some indications that common sense had not entirely abandoned the nation. False decretals and new orders of monks were imported to allay the threatening storm. But the almighty potency of the enchantments of *The Mother of Harlots* was broken. The eyes of the nation began to behold things in their true light.

Henry's successor, Edward I., was a vigorous prince; by no means disposed to yield to the

---

of this kingdom." —*Nicolson's English, Scotch, and Irish Libraries*, quarto, p. 51.

Matthew Paris was a monk of St. Albans Abbey, England; and though perhaps born, or at least educated in Paris — whence his name — was a thorough Englishman at heart, and the historiographer of his convent. His whole life seems to have been devoted to the study of history; and the most important part of his *Historia Major*, and that from which I have quoted most freely, relates to events with which he was contemporary, and for which he is an original authority. The *London Encyclopædia* says: Matthew Paris was "one of the best English historians, from William the Conqueror to the latter end of the reign of Henry III. * * He was a man of extraordinary knowledge for the thirteenth century; and of an excellent moral character; and, as an historian, of strict integrity."

usurpations of the clergy or the pope. He paid the tribute money promised by John, with great reluctance; and though the oppressions of Rome long continued a burden heavy to be borne, and the kingdom was bound in the chains of ignorance and superstition for successive ages yet to come, still it was during the reign of the third Henry and the first Edward that some rays of light began to break upon benighted England—sufficient to show something of the true character of his pretended holiness of Rome; and his power over England began now to wane.

The bare-footed and poverty-pleading Dominicans and Franciscans, who first appeared in England about 1221–1234, raised, for a season, the drooping credit of Rome. These mendicant monks, by their pretensions to piety, by their austerities, and indefatigable labors in travelling through the land, and preaching, and visiting the sick and dying, secured to their orders immense wealth, and finally engrossed nearly all of the clerical influence of the kingdom. These friars being now the favorite troops of the pope, made good for a time his possession of the kingdom, which the ignorance, and indolence, and corruptions of the old clergy, and the rapacity of the papal court itself, had of late considerably weakened. At length, however, the audacity and success of these sanctified harpies aroused the bishops and the secular and established clergy, and the war which broke out between them helped to prepare the way for the emancipation of the kingdom from papal chains.*

It was about the middle of this century that Grosseteste, or Greathead, as he is sometimes called, died. He was bishop of Lincoln; and is celebrated by Matthew Paris, as "the open reprover both of my lord the pope and of the king, and the censurer of the prelates, the corrector of monks, the director of priests, the instructor of the clergy, the supporter of scholars, the preacher to the laity, the punisher of incontinence, the diligent investigator of various writings;" and lastly, "as the scourge of lazy and selfish Romans, whom he heartily despised:" or, as Clarke has it, as "a mall to the Romanists, and a contemner of their doings."

This good man's labors and protests against papal extortion and corruption were of little avail. He lived too soon. The time had not yet come for one to chase a thousand, or for two to put ten thousand to flight. He was honored with an excommunication from the pope, as a reward for

---

* *Milner's Church History*, cent. XIII., ch. 5; *Mosheim*, bk. III., cent. XIII., pt. 2, ch. 2, secs. 18–40. *Roger of Wendover* mentions the appointment of the Minorites, by the pope, "to preach the cross throughout all the world," vol. II., p. 606; and *Matthew Paris* (A. D. 1235) has a chapter on "The Insolence of the Minorite Brethren." — *English History*, vol. I. pp. 5–6, Bohn's edition. See also, A. D. 1236, pp. 37–38, and A. D. 1247, vol. II., pp. 207–211, 218, 221–223, etc., etc. *Archbishop Usher* says: "The orders of the Friars Minorites came into England [during the reign of Henry III.] to suppress the Waldensian heresy." — *Jones's Hist. Chh.*, vol. II., p. 163.

the fidelity with which he had labored to correct ecclesiastical abuses. He nevertheless continued in his bishopric to the day of his death, regardless of the thunder of the Vatican. "He departed this world, which he never loved," A. D. 1253, to the great joy of Innocent IV., who exclaimed, on hearing the intelligence, "I rejoice, and let every true son of the Roman church rejoice with me, that my great enemy is removed."*

But the "Man of Sin" was not to be so easily rid of reprovers. Other, and more successful laborers, if not more worthy men, were soon to appear in the same field in which Grosseteste had toiled and died. The learned, humble, and pious Bradwardine, confessor to Edward III., and afterwards archbishop of Canterbury; and the intrepid Irish prelate, Fitzralph, whose vigorous opposition to the mendicant imposters of his day and the tyranny

---

* Milner devotes an entire chapter to this honest and godly old bishop. — *Hist. Chh.*, cent. XIII., ch. 7. Jones also gives an interesting account of Grosseteste, or Greathead, as he calls him. — *Hist. Christ. Chh.*, vol. II., pp. 164–171. Lingard honors his learning and boldness and honest piety; but says "no man ever professed a more profound veneration for the successors of St. Peter, or entertained more exalted notions of their prerogatives." He ignores the Pope's excommunication of Grosseteste, and Innocent's fiendish exclamation on hearing of the bishop's death. — *Hist. Eng.*, vol. III., ch. 2, pp. 177–180. Collier gives entirely satisfactory reasons for believing that Grosseteste died excommunicated. He refers particularly to the fact that the pope wished to have the body of the bishop taken up, after it had been buried, and thrown out of consecrated ground. — *Ecc. Hist. Brit.*, vol. II., p. 509, London, 8vo. — See also *Fox's Acts and Monuments*, vol. I., bk. 4, pp. 365–68.

of Rome embittered his life with persecution and terminated it in painful exile — deserve to be mentioned among "the mighty men" of the fourteenth century. But he who "sat in the seat, chief among the captains" of the Lord's hosts in this century, is yet to be named.*

We are now drawing near to a memorable epoch in the history of the English church — yea, of Christendom itself: an epoch, for the better understanding and appreciation of which this whole survey of English church history has been undertaken. It was in the course of this century that the STAR OF THE REFORMATION arose in the English horizon; a star of heavenly radiance, whose light, while it shot terror into "the Seat of the Beast," cheered the hearts of multitudes who were waiting for the "Consolation of Israel," by guiding the footsteps of wise men to the source of all truth.

JOHN WICKLIFFE was born early in the four-

---

* *Milner*, cent. XIV., ch. 1, notices Fitzralph, or Fitzraf, as he calls him. Prof. Le Bas, in his "Life of Wicklif," Introduction, gives some account of Fitzralph, Grosseteste, and Bradwardine, and many other topics introduced in these pages. Dr. Robert Vaughan, professor in the London University, devotes half of the first volume of his admirable life of Wycliffe to topics kindred to those which have been considered in the preceding pages of this work. His section "On the Ecclesiastical Establishment and the state of Society in England, previous to the age of Wycliffe," is a learned and valuable historical summary. — *Life and Opinions of John De Wycliffe*, D. D., 2 vols., 8vo., pp. 436 and 460, London, 1828.

teenth century. The two following chapters will be devoted to an exhibition of the life and sentiments of this great and good man; and thus will be resumed, after this long digression, the proper history of Congregationalism.

CHAPTER VII.

JOHN WICKLIFFE.

JOHN WICKLIFFE, "honored of God to be the first preacher of a general reformation to all Europe," as Milton says; and "the modern discoverer of the doctrines of Congregational dissent," as a more modern writer styles him,* deserves a prominent place in the History of Congregationalism.

The name of this reformer is spelt in almost every conceivable way, as, Wiclif, Wicliff, Wyclif, Wycliff, Wycliffe, Wycclyff, Wickleif, Wickliff, Wickliffe, etc. Neither the time nor the place of his nativity is certainly known; though he was probably born about 1324, near Richmond, in Yorkshire, England; † and of his youthful history nothing is known. It is said, indeed, that he was early devoted to the Church, and was entered at

* *London and Westminster Review*, No. 1, 1837.

† Lewis, one of Wickliffe's earliest biographers, says, that "he was born, very probably, about the year 1324." Leland in his *Itinerary*, says: "They say John Wiclif, hæreticus, was born at Spreswell, [Hipswell] a poore village, a good myle from Richmont."—Vol. v., p. 114, of folio edition. Vaughan, one of his latest biographers, says, "he was born at the small village of Wycliffe, about six miles from Richmond. Compare Shirley's Introduction to "*Fasciculi Zizaniorum*," pp. x.–xii.; and *Whitaker's Richmondshire*, vol. i., pp. 20, 197, 198, and vol. ii., pp. 41, 42.

Queen's College, Oxford, in 1340, when he was about seventeen years old; and that he afterwards removed to Merton College, for the sake of better opportunities of study. But, we really know nothing of his connection with Oxford until about 1361, when we find him master, or warden, of Balliol College. In 1363–5, 1374–5, and in 1380, he was also residing in rooms in Queen's College. During a part of this time he read lectures on divinity. This he was authorized to do by his degree of Doctor of Divinity, which was conferred on him by Oxford University, probably sometime between 1361 and 1372.* He is often spoken of as a *Professor* of Oxford; and a papal bull styles him "Professor of the Sacred Page;" but, in the modern sense of the term, Wickliffe was never a Professor. He was simply a Lecturer on Divinity.

But, wherever he may have spent his early years, it is quite evident that they were devoted to close study; so that one of his bitterest enemies, Knighton, a contemporary, declared him to be "second to no one in philosophy, and in scholastic accomplishments altogether incomparable." He was also familiar with civil and ecclesiastical law, and with the municipal laws and customs of his own country.

---

* Bishop Bale, and Wickliffe's biographers generally, place the doctorate under 1372; but Mr. Shirley, whose special mission it seems to be, to correct the errors of previous writers on Wickliffe, thinks the doctorate must have been given to him sometime between 1361 and 1366, probably in 1363. See *Fasciculi*, Intr. xv.—xviii.

His varied, extensive, and accurate knowledge enabled him to stand without a rival in the public disputations, which were then in high repute; and procured for him the highest reputation in the university, and in the kingdom generally. This reputation for logical acuteness and scholastic learning gave his peculiar theological opinions great influence. These were formed chiefly by a diligent study of the sacred Scriptures. In the knowledge of these Wickliffe excelled all his contemporaries, and earned from them the enviable title of *The Evangelical Doctor*, or *Gospel Doctor*. But in his devotion to the inspired volume he did not neglect the fathers of the church: Augustine, Jerome, Basil, and Gregory, appear to have been his favorite authors among the primitive writers; and Groseteste and Fitzralph among the moderns.*

It is impossible for us in this age of scriptural intelligence duly to estimate the strength of mind, the depth of principle, and the intrepidity of the man, who, in the fourteenth century, could break away from Duns Scotus, Peter Lombard, Aristotle, and "Mother Church," and form his theological opinions from the word of God, aided by the lights of the fourth century. A writer of the twelfth century, quoted by Prof. Le Bas, tells us, that in his day—and it was not materially otherwise in Wick-

---

* *Vaughan*, vol. I., p. 234; *Le Bas*, p. 102; *Milner*, cent. XIV., ch. 3; *Fox*, bks. IV. and V., particularly vol. I., p. 484, folio edition, 1684; *Collier*, vol. III., p. 189; *Fasciculi*, Intr. pp XII., XXXIX.

liffe's — those teachers who appealed to the Scriptures for authority were "not only rejected as philosophers, but unwillingly endured as clergymen; nay, were scarcely acknowledged to be *men.* They became objects of derision, and were termed *The bullocks of Abraham*, or the *Asses of Balaam.*" Fox, the martyrologist, thus describes the church and the world, at the time of Wickliffe's appearance: "This is without all doubt, that when the world was in a most desperate and vile state, and lamentable darkness and ignorance of God's truth overshadowed the whole earth, this man [Wickliffe] stepped out like a valiant champion. Scripture learning and divinity was known but to a few, and that in the schools only, and there also it was almost all turned into sophistry. Instead of the Epistles of Peter and Paul, men occupied their time in studying Aquinas, and Scotus, and Lombard, the Master of Sentences. The world, leaving and forsaking God's spiritual word and doctrine, was altogether led and blinded with outward ceremonies and human traditions. In these was all the hope of obtaining salvation fully fixed, so that scarcely anything else was taught in the churches." *

In the midst of this gross darkness, and in defiance of all this contempt for God's word, John Wickliffe became a diligent student of the Bible, and a constant expounder of its sacred contents.

---

* *Acts and Monuments,* bk. v., A. D. 1370–1389.

Some three hundred of his manuscript homilies, or expository discourses, are still preserved in the British Museum, and in the libraries of Cambridge and Dublin, and in other collections.

This intimate acquaintance with the truth of God opened the eyes of the faithful student, to the falsehoods of men. He began to see the inconsistencies, absurdities and iniquities of those who were the spiritual guides of the people. And what he saw, he dared to speak; and what he spake, was not in doubtful terms. His first publication is assigned to the year A. D. 1356, when he was in his thirty-second year. The nation at that time had been suffering for several years under a grievous plague: probably more than one hundred thousand of his countrymen had fallen before the destroyer, and "men's hearts were failing them for fear, and for looking after those things which [had come] on the earth." The devout, and perhaps somewhat excited mind of Wickliffe regarded this awful pestilence as the servant of an angry God, sent forth to chastise the nation for its sins, and to announce the commencement of "the last age" and the speedy approach of the end of the world. Under these impressions, he published a tract, bearing the title: "*De Ultima Ætate Ecclesiæ*," Concerning the Last Age of the Church.* In this work he boldly inveighs against the worldliness, the ra-

* Some of Wickliffe's biographers assign this publication an earlier date—when he was about twenty-five years old. I follow *Vaughan*, vol. I., p. 241. *Shirley* denies that Wickliffe wrote this tract.—*Fasciculi*, Intr. p. XIII.

pacity, the sensuality, the simony, and the utter degeneracy of the clergy; and denounces them as blind guides, who, instead of leading the people by precept and example into the ways of truth and holiness, had plunged with them into the abyss of sin and crime. Thus the Reformer fairly launched forth among the stormy elements, whose buffetings he was destined long to endure.

About four years after this publication (1360), Wickliffe was found in the front rank of opposition to the Mendicants.* Allusion has already been made to the introduction of these pretended poverty-loving beggars. Under pretence of zeal for "Holy Church," they spread themselves thickly over the kingdom, and engrossed nearly all of the clerical duties of the nation. Travelling continually as they did, and numerous as they were, they gained access to all classes of society, in every section of the country. They were the companions and confessors of the rich, and the preachers and directors of the poor. Ever ready to confess all who came to them, and ignorant, as they neces-

* The title of *Mendicants* is given to the numerous orders in the Romish church, who, under pretence of renouncing the world and all earthly acquisitions, were licensed by the pope to roam over the world and make proselytes to Antichrist, and subsist upon the gifts of the people, without having, like the regular clergy, any fixed revenues for their support. In this account of Wickliffe's contest with the Mendicants I have but followed the current of the history of the times. Mr. Shirley, however, says, these "are facts only by courtesy and repetition." He thinks that another contemporary John Wickliffe, or Whyteclyve, of Mayfield, was the real antagonist, at this time, of the Mendicants.—*Fasciculi,* Intr., XIII., and Appendix, 513–38.

sarily were, of the character of those who applied for absolution, these Mendicants virtually encouraged every species of iniquity. The wicked would say to each other, according to Matt. Paris: "Let us follow our own pleasure. Some one of the preaching brothers will soon travel this way; one whom we never saw before, and never shall see again; so that, when we have had our will, we can confess without trouble or annoyance." Bishop Fitzralph makes the following statement of the doings of the Mendicants in Ireland: "I have in my diocese of Armagh, about two thousand persons who stand condemned by the censures of the church denounced every year against murderers, thieves, and such like malefactors; of all which number, scarcely fourteen have applied to me or to my clergy for absolution. Yet they all receive the sacraments as others do, because they are absolved, or pretend to be absolved, by friars."*

Not content with this absorption of the duties of the regular clergy, and this encouragement of crime, these voracious animals laid hold of every civil office within their reach. They even entered the Court in the character of counsellors, and chamberlains, and treasurers, and negotiators of marriages. By their numerous arts and efforts — by

* *Fox's Acts and Monuments*, bk. v., where may be found the "conclusions" of Armachanus (Fitzralph) against "the begging friars." See also, *Vaughan's Life of Wycliffe*, vol. I., p. 254; and Fox's account of monks and monkery, ancient and mediæval, bk. III., A. D. 928–965, and bk. IV., A. D. 1220.

lying, and begging, and confessing, by frightening the ignorant and flattering the rich — "within the four-and-twenty years of their establishment in England," Matthew Paris says, "these friars piled up their mansions to a royal altitude."*

A man of Wickliffe's character could not contemplate these movements without indignation. But that which brought him more immediately

---

* Matthew of Westminster tells us, that the Franciscans once offered the pope forty thousand ducats in gold (about $100,000) to sanction the violation of their rule respecting property. His Holiness quietly took the offered bribe, and then sent the honest monks his order, *not* to violate the rule of St. Francis. — *Vaughan*, II., 255.

Fox (bk. IV., A. D. 1220) preserves a caustic little "Treatise of Geoffrey Chaucer's, intitled 'Jack Upland,'" against the friars. Jack, "a simple ploughman," proposes sundry significant questions to the friars, for his own private satisfaction: *e. g.* — "Why make ye so costly houses to dwell in, sith [since] Christ did not so?" — "Why say ye not the Gospel in houses of bed-ridden men, as ye do in rich men's, that mow [might] go to the church and hear the Gospel?" — "Why covet ye shrifts [confessions] and burying of other men's parishens [parishioners], and none other sacrament that falleth to Christian folk?" — "Why covet you not to bury poor folk among you, sith that they bin most holy, as ye saine that ye been for your poverty?"

Notwithstanding the overwhelming evidence furnished by all contemporaneous history, of the deceitful, avaricious, corrupt, and iniquitous character of the monkery of Wickliffe's day, and the manifest fact, that the vital interests of true religion were ruthlessly sacrificed by the monks, Dr. Lingard speaks of Wickliffe's controversy "with the different orders of friars" as "a fierce, but ridiculous controversy;" and launches forth into a panegyric on the "zeal, piety, and learning" of the friars, by which they "had deservedly earned the esteem of the public." — *Hist. Eng.*, vol. IV., ch. 2, p. 157. If they "had deservedly earned" anything, it was the detestation of all good men. Even Sir Thomas Moore satirized the monks.

into conflict with these "Black Friars,"* was their encroachment on the University of Oxford. The first monastery of the Dominicans was erected near this ancient seat of learning, and at first enjoyed the countenance and encouragement of its professors. It was not long, however, before the university had reason to deplore the influence of the friars. Their acquaintance with all classes in society, in all parts of the kingdom; their pretensions to piety; their influence and wealth, enabled them to draw away from the university, to their monasteries, vast numbers of young men. Many parents, unwilling to have their sons enter on a life of mendicancy, "were more willing," as Fitzralph tells us, "to make them '*erthe tilyers*' [earth tillers], and *have* them, than to send them to the universitie, and *lose* them." The operation of these causes, in a few years reduced the number of students in Oxford from *thirty* thousand to *six* thousand.

It was not to be expected that the university would tamely submit to such encroachments upon its prerogatives. Aided by the bishops and the regular clergy, her professors had for some time been at war with the mendicant army, when, in 1360, Wickliffe entered the lists. His earnest, bold, and effective opposition to these depredators secured the gratitude of the learned and the esteem of the

* This appellation they bore from the circumstance that their dress was black. When they first settled in London, a tract of land was given them by the city, which lies along the Thames and still bears the name of *Blackfriars*.

virtuous generally; and, it is not unlikely, procured for him the wardenship of Balliol College, Oxford, where we find him as early as April, 1361. How long he had been there, or how long he remained, we cannot exactly tell; but probably not long. In May, 1361, Wickliffe was instituted to the rectory of Fylingham, in Lincolnshire.* In November, 1368, he exchanged this living, for that of Ludgershall, in Buckinghampshire; and in April, 1374, he exchanged this, for the living of Lutterworth, in Leicestershire, which he retained to the day of his death.

His biographers generally describe him as warden, or master, of Canterbury Hall, about the year 1365; and one of his contemporaries, and many of his modern enemies, ascribe to his violent removal from that post of honor, by Archbishop Langham, in March, 1367 — an act confirmed by Urban V., in May, 1370 — Wickliffe's subsequent opposition to the Pope and his clergy generally. But, there is good reason to doubt whether *our* John Wickliffe was ever warden of Canterbury Hall; and, if he was, the fact that he kept up his attacks on the ambition, tyranny, and avarice of the rulers of the church, and the idleness, debauchery, and hypocrisy of the Monks, during the pendency of this Canterbury-Hall question, sufficiently refutes this old monkish slander.†

---

* *Fasciculi,* Introduction, pp. XIV. and XV., notes 4 and 5.

† See *Fasciculi,* pp. 517-18, 513-28.

The year 1366, when the kingdom was threatened with another war with France, before it had recovered from the losses and exhaustion consequent on previous wars, was chosen by the Pope, then much in the interest of France, as the time to demand the arrears of the tribute money guaranteed by King John, in 1213, to save himself and the kingdom from an interdict and excommunication. In May, 1366, Parliament assembled to consider this claim, and soon gave the Pope such an answer as set the matter at rest forever.

The minions of Romanism, of course, denounced this decision of the King and Parliament; and one of them, a monk, challenged Wickliffe, who was then a royal chaplain, to defend his prince and the parliament, in the schools of the university. Wickliffe immediately accepted this challenge, and stepped boldly forward in defence of his country's independence.

About this time the Reformer sent forth a plain and familiar exposition of the Ten Commandments. The necessity for such a work may be estimated by what he tells us in his preface:—that it was no uncommon thing for men "to call God, Master, forty, three-score, or four-score years, and yet remain ignorant of his Ten Commandments." This publication was followed by several small tracts, entitled "The Poor Catiff," or instruction for the poor; written in English, as the author declares, for the purpose of "teaching simple men and women the way to heaven."* These humble labors of the learned professor furnish a beautiful commentary on his religious character, and are in perfect keeping with the enviable title which he long enjoyed, of *The Evangelical Doctor*.

In the year 1374, Wickliffe was called from the university into public life. He was sent by parliament on an embassy to the pope, to obtain the redress of certain ecclesiastical grievances under which the kingdom was then suffering.†

In the chapter preceding this, a brief sketch has been given of some of the prominent abuses to which the English nation was for a long time subjected; by which the wealth of the kingdom was absorbed by the clergy — mendicant and regular — or drained off by the pope. These abuses had continued, despite of complaints, and protests, and temporary resistance. There had long been gather-

---

* These tracts, with some other selections from Wickliffe's practical writings, have been published by the London Religious Tract Society. Dr. Vaughan gives an analysis of this treatise on the Ten Commandments, with extracts from the work, illustrative of its spirit. —*Life of Wycliffe*, vol. I., pp. 303–314.

† See an account of these grievances, and of the abortive embassy of Wickliffe and his associates to the pope, then at Avignon, in *Vaughan*, vol. I., ch. 4. A summary of the complaints against the papal court, urged by the several parliaments of Edward III., may be found in *Fox*, bk. v., A.D. 1376. This summary the martyrologist thus quaintly concludes: "Whereby it may appear, that it was not for nothing that the Italians and other foreigners used to call Englishmen —*good asses;* for they bear all burdens that were laid upon them."

ing in the breasts of the people, a spirit of opposition to the tyranny of Rome. This with difficulty had been kept under, by the united power of the throne and the clergy. England had now (in 1374) been ruled for more than forty years by one of her most accomplished and popular monarchs. Edward III., though guilty of many arbitrary acts of government, had the wisdom, or the policy, to consult the opinions and wishes of his subjects more than any one of his predecessors. He was a hero and a conqueror; and, as such, had acquired great applause and influence in that semi-barbarous age. His numerous warlike expeditions compelled him to call frequently for supplies from his parliaments; and his good sense, or his necessities, induced him to yield more to their pleasure, in granting privileges, and immunities, and protections to the people, than had been common previous to his time. The authority of the Great Charter was so often confirmed during his reign, that it became immovably fixed as a limitation of the royal power. The king was made to feel that there was a power *under* the throne, if not above it, whose heavings were not to be despised nor disregarded with impunity. The people, for whose benefit all government, civil and ecclesiastical, should be administered, but who had hitherto been least regarded in its administration; who had been trampled upon by their princes and nobles, and worst of all by their clergy, began now to rear their heads and raise their indignant voices.

With such teachers as John Wickliffe and his disciples, the English people were likely to understand something of their ecclesiastical rights, and to assert them with more courage and success than ever before. The people moved parliament, and the parliament moved the king — himself nowise unfavorably disposed — to inquire into the ecclesiastical abuses by which the pope and his creatures were eating out the vitals of the kingdom. The result of this inquiry was the discovery, that more than one half of the landed property of the kingdom was in the hands of a corrupt and indolent clergy; that many of the most lucrative benefices were in the possession of foreigners, and some of them but boys, who knew not the language of the country, nor had even so much as set foot on English soil; that the pope's collector and receiver of Peter's pence, who kept "an house in London, with clerks and officers thereunto belonging, transported yearly to the pope twenty thousand marks, and most commonly more;" that other foreign dignitaries, holding ecclesiastical benefices in the kingdom, though residing at Rome, received yearly an equal, or greater sum (twenty thousand marks) for their sinecures; and finally, "that the tax paid to the pope of Rome for ecclesiastical dignities, [did] amount to *five-fold* as much as the tax of all the profits, as appertained to the king, by the year, of his whole realm."*

* *Fox*, bk. v., A. D. 1376; *Vaughan*, vol. I., ch. 4, particularly pp. 332–335; *Cotton's Abridg.*, in Henry, vol VIII., p. 65.

Such were some of the results of the inquiry set on foot by the parliament, into the ecclesiastical abuses of that age. Wickliffe was one of the commissioners chosen by parliament to lay these complaints before the court of Rome.

The conference with the pope was appointed at Bruges, a large city of Austria. Thither the English commissioners repaired. They soon found, however, that they had brought their wares to a glutted market. Ecclesiastical abuses were things little regarded by the Roman traders. It was like carrying coals to New Castle, to carry their budget of complaints to Bruges. The mission was, nevertheless, attended with one advantage — it forced wide open the eyes of the Reformer; he no longer saw "men as trees walking;" but he beheld, as with open vision, the full grown *Man of Sin*, the Antichrist of the latter days. On his return to England, Wickliffe openly denounced "His Holiness," as "*the most cursed of clippers and purse kervers*" (*purse cutters*); and made the kingdom ring with his descriptions of papal impostures and papal corruptions.

These bold and violent attacks upon the sovereign pontiff and his dissolute clergy were neither unnoticed nor unheeded at Rome. The storm of hierarchal wrath had long been gathering; and its thunders at length began to mutter over the Reformer's head. King Edward was now aged and infirm, and nigh unto death; and Richard II., his grandson and successor, was a minor. The hierarchy, probably, deemed this a favorable time to attack the obnoxious heretic. Accordingly, in 1377, Wickliffe was cited to appear before the convocation of the clergy, to answer to the charge of heresy. It was a moment of peril to the Reformer. His judges were his enemies; and without some better protection than their sense of justice would afford, the days of the good man's usefulness, and perhaps of his life, would have been quickly numbered. At this critical juncture God raised up for his servant a powerful friend and protector, in the person of the duke of Lancaster, commonly known as John of Gaunt, so called from the place of his birth. He was the third son of Edward III., and uncle to Richard II., and was principal regent of the kingdom during the minority. Henry Percy, earl marshal of England, also befriended Wickliffe. These noblemen bade him be of good cheer; and, for his encouragement and protection, attended him in person to the house of convocation. Immediately on the entrance of the party, a quarrel commenced between the high-blooded Percy and the bishop of London; which, from words had well-nigh come to blows. This personal quarrel between my lord clerical and my lord secular so disturbed the proceedings of the convocation, that it soon broke up in confusion, and its victim escaped untouched.

During the same year (1377), parliament called on Wickliffe to give his judgment on the question: —" Whether the kingdom of England, on an eminent necessity of its own defence, might lawfully detain the treasure of the kingdom, that it might not be carried out of the land; although the lord pope required it, on pain of censures, and by virtue of the obedience due to him." This question, so illustrative of the exorbitance of the pope and of the rising spirit of the nation, Wickliffe answered boldly in the affirmative.*

These repeated good offices for his country, though they rendered the Reformer eminently popular in England, were treasuring up wrath for him in Rome. Before the close of the year 1377, the thunders of the Church were again pealing over his head. No less than four bulls were let loose by the Pope against "the audacious innovator." In these instruments "His Holiness" laments and denounces "the pernicious heresy" and the "detestable insanity" which had induced "John Wickliffe, rector of the church of Lutterworth and professor of the Sacred Page (it were well if he were not a master of errors) to spread abroad opinions utterly subversive of the church;" and ordered *secret* inquiry to be made into the matters charged against him, and if found true, the heretic to be immediately seized, and imprisoned, and detained "until further directions should be received." Three of these papal bulls were addressed to the archbishop of Canterbury and the bishop of London, who cordially reciprocated the *dolors* of His Holiness,

---

* *Vaughan*, vol. I., pp. 343–47; *Fasciculi*, 258–71.

and eagerly desired to glut their malice upon the impudent reformer. But the fourth bull, addressed to the University of Oxford, met with a very cold reception. A fifth bull, or rather letter, was addressed to the king of England, soliciting his aid in suppressing the doctrines of Wickliffe; which are described as opposed to the existence of the church, and to all the forms of civil authority.*

The zeal of the primate soon prepared another inquisitorial court to try the heretic; and Wickliffe was summoned to Lambeth chapel, to give account of himself to the ecclesiastical powers. The Londoners, who were now "deeply infected by the heresy of Wickliffe"—and who, Walsingham affirms, were nearly all Lollards — getting wind of what was going on, surrounded the chapel of the archbishop and gave such demonstrations of interest in the defender of the people's rights, as materially to disturb the equanimity of the papal conclave. To add to their discomfiture, in the midst of their deliberations a messenger arrived from the court, positively forbidding them to proceed to any definite sentence against Wickliffe. Thus, a second time, was the prey delivered from the jaws of the devourer.

These threatening dangers and narrow escapes rather inflamed, than cooled the ardor of the Re-

---

* *Vaughan,* vol. I., ch. 5, partic. pp. 352–356. The bulls and the epistle to the king may be found in the Appendix to *Vaughan,* vol. I., pp. 417–426. Also, *Wilkins' Concil.* Vol. III., pp. 116-118.

former. He boldly advocated a thorough reform of the church; and declared his willingness to suffer, and die if necessary, in order to promote this desirable end.

The death of pope Gregory XI., which occurred the next year, 1378, and the notorious papal schism occasioned by the election of two popes as successors to Gregory, saved Wickliffe for some time from further molestation. Their Holinesses were too much occupied in forging and fulminating thunderbolts against each other, to pay much attention to the English heretic. This interval of rest from persecution was diligently employed by Wickliffe in writing and circulating tracts and books, in which the corruptions of the clergy and the antichristian character of popery were unsparingly exhibited. But the great work of Wickliffe during these years of rest from papal persecution (1379–1381), and that which did more than all his other labors to promote the truth, and to open the eyes of the nation to the antichristian character of the entire hierarchy, and which has handed down to posterity the name of this great man in the brightest halo of glory, was the translation of the entire Bible into the vernacular language of the country.

The enemies of the great Reformer, ancient and modern, very unwillingly admit this; and labor to deprive him of this great honor, or to depreciate the advantages of this great labor of christian love. Thus Dr. Lingard (Hist. Eng., vol. IV., ch. 3, p. 196), asserts, that "several versions of the sacred writings were even then extant" — i. e. at the time Wickliffe made his new translation. He admits, however, that "they were confined to libraries, or only in the hands of persons who aspired to superior sanctity." And to sustain his assertion, he quotes Sir Thomas More's Dialogues (III., 14). But Sir Thomas — who was not born until about a hundred years after Wickliffe's death — is by no means unexceptionable authority. His object in making the assertion, however honest he may have been in his belief of its truth, was precisely the same as that of Lingard in repeating the assertion, viz: to screen the Romish church from the scandal and the crime of withholding God's Word from the people. But this they fail, signally, to do; for Knighton, a Romish historian who was contemporary with Wickliffe, and who doubtless expresses the current opinion of the churchmen of his time, inveighs bitterly against this rash and presumptuous measure of the great Reformer, in unveiling the mysteries of God's Word to the eyes of the vulgar multitude. He says:

"Christ delivered his gospel to the clergy and doctors of the church, that they might administer to the laity and to weaker persons, according to the state of the times and the wants of men. But this Master John Wycliffe translated it out of Latin into English, and thus laid it more open to the laity and to women who could read, than it had formerly been to the most learned of the clergy, even to those of them who had the best understanding. And in this way the gospel pearl is cast abroad, and trodden under foot of swine, and that which was before precious to both clergy and laity, is rendered, as it were, the common jest of both. The jewel of the church is turned into the sport of the people, and what was hitherto the principal gift of the clergy and divines, is made forever common to the laity."*

This question of priority is ably discussed and satisfactorily settled in the Preface to the noble edition of Wickliffe's Bible, published from the University press of Oxford, England. The learned editors of that edition, avow their conversion to the belief of Wickliffe's claim to priority over all others, as a translator of the entire Bible into the

* *De Eventibus*, col. 2,644. To the same effect is the decision of an English council in 1408, with the Archbishop Arundel at its head: "The translation of the text of Holy Scriptures out of one tongue into another is a dangerous thing, as St. Jerome testifies, because it is not easy to make the verse in all respects the same. Therefore we enact and ordain, that no one henceforth do, by his own authority, translate any text of Holy Scripture into the English tongue, or any other, by way of book or treatise; nor let any such book or treatise now lately composed in the time of John Wycliffe aforesaid, or since, or hereafter to be composed, be read in whole or in part, in public or in private, under pain of the greater excommunication." — *Wilkin's Concilia*, III., 317. The spirit of this enactment was evidently that of the majority of the clergy in the age of Wickliffe. He describes them as affirming it to be "heresy to speak of the Holy Scriptures in English;" but this is said to be a condemnation of "the Holy Ghost, who first gave the Scriptures in tongues to the apostles of Christ, as it is written, to speak the word in all languages that were ordained of God under heaven." — *Wicket*. See Vaughan's *Life of Wycliffe*, vol. II., p. 44; *Wycliffe's Bible*, Preface, p. VI., Oxford, 1850.

vernacular of the English nation. This was not their belief when they began their investigations. Influenced by the confident assertions of such men as More, and James, and Usher, they supposed that earlier translations than Wickliffe's had been made. But this opinion they were compelled to abandon after careful original investigation.

In reference to Sir Thomas More's assertion, quoted by Lingard and others, the editors of the Oxford edition of Wickliffe's Bible say: "Sir Thomas More, in his Dialogues, anxious to save the Romish party from the scandal of withholding the Word of God from the laity, maintains, that long before the days of Wycliffe, the whole Bible had been translated into the English tongue; and vouches for himself having seen copies of the kind. "Thomas James, though he had the opportunity of examining several manuscripts of the Wycliffe version, describes one of them, as a Bible in the English tongue, long before the coming of Wycliffe. From him Archbishop Usher adopted the error, assigning the translation to the year 1290. Wharton, in his Auctarium to the archbishop's work, which was posthumous and unfinished, truly determines the respective characters and dates of the two versions, *rightly giving the elder to Wycliffe.*"

They further say, as the result of careful investigations, that "the versions [Wickliffe's] now for the first time printed in an entire form," under their supervision, "may be regarded as the earliest in the English language which embrace any considerable portion of the Holy Scriptures;"—and "that it [Wickliffe's Bible] is the earliest translation of the whole Bible in the English language, *admits of no reasonable doubt.*"*

John Wickliffe undoubtedly, then, deserves the honor of having given to his country the first complete translation of the Scriptures in the English language. With great personal labor, and by the aid of learned assistants, he wrote out an entire English version of the Sacred Word. Copies of this were multiplied by transcribers — for there was no printing in those days; and the "poor priests,"

---

* *Preface to Wycliffe's Bible*, pp. 1, 6, 21, *etc.* Copies of this noble monument of Wickliffe's piety, learning, and sagacity, may be found in our City Library and in the Athenæum, in four quarto volumes. The work was edited by Rev. Josiah Forshall, F. R. S., *etc.;* and Sir Frederic Madden, K. H., F. R. S., *etc.*, Keeper of the MSS. in the British Museum. It was published in 1850.

The question of Wickliffe's claim of having given the first version of the whole Bible in the English language to the people, is ably discussed and satisfactorily settled by Vaughan, *Life of Wycliffe*, vol. II., ch. 2, and by Le Bas, *Life of Wiclif*, ch. 6.

The impossibility of answering, satisfactorily, the question: "Where are those copies of the whole Bible in the vernacular tongue of England, of which Sir Thomas More and others after him speak?" — is, under the circumstances of the case, almost a conclusive refutation of their position. For, if copies of Wickliffe's Bible have survived — when it was so much for the interest of the dominant hierarchy to destroy them — and in spite of the systematic efforts to destroy all his writings — surely some copies of those Bibles, so carefully kept in libraries or in the hands of "persons of superior sanctity," of which More and Lingard speak, could scarcely have failed to reach us; especially, when it was so needful for the defence of the Roman church, to be able to show that she had been willing to give the Scriptures to the people.

as Wickliffe's preaching disciples were called, scattered them over the kingdom. To the Scriptures the Reformer appealed for the truth of his doctrines; and men were everywhere urged to search the Scriptures and "see if these things were so."

The minions of the hierarchy were in the terrors of death when they saw this light streaming through the land. They hated the light, because their deeds were evil; and they would not come to it, lest their deeds should be reproved. Wickliffe was denounced as a sacrilegious wretch, who had presumed to rend the veil from the holy of holies, and expose the secrets of God's honor to the unhallowed gaze of the profane multitude. For centuries the reading of the Bible, by the common people, had been prohibited. A needless exercise of papal impiety, to be sure, when the Sacred Treasure was locked up in a language unknown to the mass of the people, and when the scarcity and cost of a single copy was such as to defy the ability of nine hundred and ninety-nine men in a thousand to procure the prohibited book.* Still, the prohibition was a fair exhibition of papal principles; and should not be forgotten by the friends of the Bible.

* Some notion may be formed of the difficulty of getting a copy of the Bible before Wickliffe's translation appeared, from the fact, that, although his versions were multiplied beyond any previous precedent, and scattered over every part of the kingdom — yet a copy of his New Testament alone, cost from thirty to forty pounds, or from one hundred and thirty-three to one hundred and seventy-seven dollars, Federal money. — See *London Encyclopædia*, Art. Scriptures.

But while the clergy declaimed against the impious version, the "poor priests" multiplied and scattered "the seed of the word;" and the poor people, so long doomed to endure "a famine of the word of God," devoured the bread with great avidity: and, like the honey tasted by Jonathan in the wood, it enlightened the eyes of all who partook of it. It enabled them to see, not only the corrupt and antichristian character of the entire system of popery, to which they had so long been dupes and willing slaves; but it taught them also the corruption of their own natures, and their need of the washing of regeneration. It became to the people of England, what it did to the children of Israel, when in the days of Josiah "the Book of the Law" was discovered among the rubbish of the temple, and was brought out and "read in their ears"—the means of an extensive revival of pure religion in the nation.

Wickliffe, profiting by the example of the Man of Sin, reared up numerous preachers of his doctrines, and sent them forth as the mendicant orders had at first gone—or rather as Christ's disciples first went forth—with their staves in their hands and the sacred word in their bosoms, preaching everywhere that men should repent and turn from their vanities, to the worship of the only living and true God, and to the exercise of faith in the only Savior of man and intercessor with God, Jesus Christ the Righteous. And so wonderfully successful were these preachers, that Knighton, a contemporary, tells us, that above one half of the inhabitants of the kingdom in a short time became Lollards, or Wickliffites.

Though this may be an exaggerated statement, yet there can be no doubt of the very great success of Wickliffe's plans for enlightening the common people in respect to true religion. Even Lingard admits, that Wickliffe's Bible, in the hands of the poor priests, "became an engine of wonderful power;" that "the new doctrines insensibly acquired partizans and protectors in the higher classes;" that "a spirit of inquiry was generated, and the seeds were sown of that religious revolution, which, in a little more than a century, astonished and convulsed the nations of Europe."*

Lingard, in imitation of others of his faith, has endeavored to connect the fearful, and for a season completely successful rebellion of the common people under Watt Tyler, Jack Straw, and John Ball, in 1380, with the spread of Wickliffe's doctrines and the labors of his poor priests. But Fuller effectually silences this old slander. He says, that 'this rebellion was caused by *poll money*, heavily imposed by the king, and the arrears thereof more cruelly exacted by his courtiers that farmed it."† And Collier, no partial friend of Wickliffe, surely, attributes this rebellion mainly to the persevering efforts of Ball, or Balle, "a renegade priest, who for twenty years had made it his business to debauch

---

* *Hist. Eng.* vol. IV., ch. 3. p. 196.

† *Chh. Hist. of Britain*, bk. IV., § 21, 22, 23.

the understandings of the vulgar, making them believe that servitude and villanage was a state never intended by God and Nature." * * And adds: "Though Knighton makes this Ball in the interest of the Wickliffites, yet it does not appear by Ball's confession [before his execution] that Wickliffe held any correspondence with the rebels."* Fuller says, that neither at Ball's execution nor at Jack Straw's, "was it ever charged on them any complicity with Wickliffe or his doctrines." He also alludes to the fact that John of Gaunt—the Earl of Lancaster—the great friend and patron of Wickliffe, was the object of the special hatred of the Wat Tyler and Jack Straw rebels. They sacked and burned his palace in London, and sought his life with eager vengeance. Further, he alludes to the fact that learning and wealth were the favorite objects of abuse with these rebels; and that "of all people, only some Franciscan friars found favor in their sight;" a circumstance which directs suspicion to quite an opposite quarter from Wickliffe.†

To all this, may be added the significant fact, that neither Wickliffe nor any of his disciples ever suffered for any complicity with this rebellion. *The* Church of that day would have been but too happy to have been able to connect Wickliffism and rebellion together; and we may be sure

---

* *Ecc. Hist.*, vol. III., pp. 149, 155. Netter, however, says that Ball did confess that he was a disciple of Wickliffe.—*Fasciculi*, 273–4.

† *Chh. Hist.*, bk. IV., §§ 22, 23; *Turner's Middle Ages*, vol. II., bk. II., ch. 6.

would have left no means untried to this end had there been the slightest chance of success. That this was not done — that neither Wickliffe nor any of his known disciples were either punished, tried, or accused on this account—is a sufficient proof that they could not be — that there was no connection between the labors of the faithful preachers of God's Word and the rebellious crimes of an ignorant and infuriated mob. The charge was originally made by those who hated the truth and such as spread it; and has been reiterated by those who had more sympathy with the men who made the lie, than with those about whom it was made.*

We are now approaching the end of the good man's eventful life. His last days, if his *best* days, were not the most peaceful. Though worn down by incessant labor, and harassed by opposition and persecution, and admonished by repeated attacks of sickness, he still manifested no disposition to cease from his labors; he seemed resolved to die in the harness. During the last three years of his life, his mind, his tongue—when he could speak—and his pen, were incessantly busy in the great work to which he had consecrated his life — the reform of the church. His search into the Scriptures and into ecclesiastical antiquity opened the eyes of the Reformer to see more and more of the anti-scriptural character of the entire hierarchal

* Turner gives a very satisfactory view of this entire question of the rise, progress and cause of this rebellion. — *Hist. Eng.*, vol. II., bk. II., ch. 6; so does Vaughan, *Life of Wycliffe*, II., ch. 2.

system of those days. He boldly attacked the wealth, and pride, and pomp, and ornaments of the established order, and his thundering artillery threatened the utter overthrow of the ancient fortress of popery itself.

Hitherto Wickliffe seems to have enjoyed the protection and patronage of the court; and God had used this to keep at bay the bulls of Rome. But now, John of Gaunt openly forsook his old and faithful friend. Le Bas attributes this to the doctrine about this time (1381) advanced by Wickliffe respecting the sacramental symbols, viz: that "the consecrated host we see upon the altar is neither Christ nor any part of him, but an effectual sign of him; and that transubstantiation, identification, or impanation, rest upon no scriptural ground."

A more probable solution of this matter may be found in the fact, that Wickliffe's doctrines were beginning to threaten the *English*, as well as the *Romish* hierarchy.* The duke of Lancaster, the earl marshal of England, and other noblemen, were ready to support the Reformer so long as his labors tended to break down the despotic and destructive power of the pope over the kingdom; but when his labors began to threaten a complete reformation of the church, then courtiers were among the first to cry — "Hold! Enough!"

* See a valuable article upon "Congregational Dissenters," in the *London and Westminster Review* for October, 1837. American Ed., vol. IV., No. 1.

What Wickliffe's ecclesiastical views were, we shall presently consider. And in the course of this history we shall have occasion to remark the same courtly policy in staying the hands of later reformers. For the present, we will pass on to notice the immediate effects of the things to which allusion has just been made.

The protection of the great being withdrawn from the venerable Reformer, the whole pack, —

> "The little dogs and all,
> Tray, Blanch, and Sweet-heart * *
> Mastiff, grey-hound, mongrel grim,
> Hound, or spaniel, brach, or lym ;"

— the pope, the king, the archbishop, the bishops, the mendicants, and friars — were immediately in full chase. Their noble game was driven from the covert of Oxford by order of the king; the archbishop procured the condemnation of his doctrines in a synod of the clergy; the bishops, by "letters mandatory" to their abbots and priors, clergy and ecclesiastical functionaries, required the immediate suppression of the impious and audacious doctrines of the Reformer. In addition to all this, parliament was petitioned to provide a remedy against "the innumerable errors and impieties of the Lollards;" a royal ordinance was surreptitiously obtained by the clergy, empowering the sheriffs of counties to arrest such preachers and their abettors, and to detain them in prison, until they should justify themselves according to law and reason of holy Church; and, to cap the climax, the pope himself summoned the heretic to appear at Rome, and give account of himself to the vicar of God.*

Well might Wickliffe have adopted the words of his Master: "They gaped upon me with their mouths, as a ravening and a roaring lion." * * "Dogs have compassed me: the assembly of the wicked have enclosed me." But amidst the gathering storm the good man labored on. When driven from the university, he found shelter among his affectionate parishioners at Lutterworth. Here he preached and wrote with unflinching boldness and untiring activity. But the servant was doing his last work for his Master. God protected him and preserved his life while he had work for him to do; but, his task finished, he was soon to be called home. The incessant labor of thirty years had shattered the earthly tabernacle, and brought upon the faithful laborer a premature old age; and finally, produced a paralysis of all his powers, which terminated his invaluable life on the 31st day of December, Anno Domini 1384. When the summons came, he was where a soldier would always choose to die — at his post. He fell as a warrior would wish, on the field of battle, sword in hand. He was in his church, administering the sacrament, when a paralytic shock deprived him of speech and motion. He lingered two days; and then, as we have the best reason to believe,

---

* See *Wilkins' Concil.*, III., pp. 152—172.

slept in Jesus. "Admirable," exclaims the quaint and candid Fuller, "that a hare so often hunted, with so many packs of dogs, should die, at last, quietly sitting in his form."*

Thus died John Wickliffe; the most remarkable man of his age, and one of the most distinguished reformers of any age. His name and works have long been the subjects of the most unqualified abuse by the violent Papist; and of the *semi*-hearty praise of the devoted Churchman.† The Congregational Dissenter, while he admits that Wickliffe was subject to human infirmities, and like other men liable to error; that the truth gradually opened upon his mind; and that, even to his death, some of the shreds of popery may have clung around him;—while, I say, he admits all this, still must revere John Wickliffe as "*the modern discoverer of the principles of Congregational Dissent.*"

---

* *Chh. Hist.*, bk. IV., § 26.

† I refer to such men as Mr. Milner, whose extended notice of Wickliffe's life and labors is open to many objections, and in some points is manifestly unjust and injurious to the memory of the Reformer. In reading Milner's account, one is almost provoked to say—He damns Wickliffe with faint praise. Prof. Le Bas' work is a very different affair; he corrects "the historian of the Church" in several particulars; he might have done more.

Collier's mode of treating Wickliffe gives one the impression, that he would willingly say less in Wickliffe's favor, and more against him, if he could honestly.

Many of the original documents which illustrate the treatment of Wickliffe after Lancaster forsook him may be found in the *Fasciculi Zizaniorum* of Netter. See particularly, pp. 110–13, 115–32, 277–82, 283–85, 298, 317.

CHAPTER VIII.

ECCLESIASTICAL OPINIONS OF WICKLIFFE.

HAVING claimed Wickliffe as a remote ancestor of the denomination whose history occupies these pages, it will be expected that I give more fully than has yet been done, the grounds on which this claim rests.*

1. The prominent doctrine of Wickliffe's creed which allies him to modern Congregationalists was — THE ALLSUFFICIENCY OF THE SCRIPTURES.

His habit of "*postillating*," or expounding a portion of Scripture to his parishioners on the Sabbath, instead of "*declaring*," or preaching a sermon from a single text, or uttering an oration upon a particular subject — is a decisive evidence of his high regard for the Scriptures. His translation of the Bible into English, is a still stronger evidence of his veneration for the inspired writings. Add to

* In drawing up the following summary of Wickliffe's ecclesiastical opinions, in addition to the authorities so often quoted in preceding pages, I have availed myself of a valuable work, entitled "*Tracts and Treatises of John De Wycliffe, D. D.*, with Selections and Translations from his Manuscripts and Latin Works. Edited by The Wycliffe Society; with an Introductory Memoir, by the Rev. Robert Vaughan, President of the Lancashire Independent College, Manchester. London: 1845," 8vo., pp. xciv. and 332.

the above, the Reformer's own words upon this important point.

In a statement of his opinions, addressed to a Synod assembled at Lambeth, "on the thirtieth court day," 1378, in obedience to a bull from the pope, dated June 11th, 1377, and addressed to the Archbishop of Canterbury and the Bishop of London, directing them to commit Wickliffe to prison, and obtain secretly whatever they could of his principles and opinions, and secretly to transmit the same to Rome * — the Reformer thus speaks of his principles, and particularly of his attachment to the "Law of Christ," "the Sacred Scriptures:"

"In the first place, I protest publicly, that I resolve with my whole heart, and by the grace of God, to be a sincere Christian; and while life shall last to profess and to defend the *Law of Christ*, as far as I have power. If through ignorance, or from any other cause, I shall fail in this determination, I ask forgiveness of God, and retracting the error, submit with humility to the correction of the church.† And to prevent the Christian from being scandalized on my account, since I am prosecuted for my faith; and since the notions of children and of weak persons concerning what I have taught, are conveyed by others, who are more than children, beyond the seas, even to the court of Rome, I am willing to commit my opinions to writing. These also, I am now ready to defend,

* See *ante*, p. 254.

† The same protest may be found in *Libellus Magistri, J. W.* — *Fasciculi*, 245.

even unto death, and the same duty I regard as binding upon all Christians, but particularly on the bishop of Rome, and on the whole priesthood of the church. In my conclusions, I have followed the sacred Scriptures and the holy doctors, both in their meaning and in their modes of expression; this I am willing to shew. But should it be proved that such conclusions are opposed to the faith, I am prepared very willingly to retract them."

Such confessions to the value of the Scriptures are very frequent in the Reformer's writings. It is thus he concludes a passage in which he denies priestly absolution:

"If any man would show more plainly this sentence, by the *Law of God*, I would meekly assent thereto. And if any man prove this to be false, or against the Law of God, that I have now said herein, I would meekly revoke it."*

In another part of his statement of his principles, he says: "God forbid, that truth should be condemned by the church of Christ because it sounds unpleasantly in the ear of the guilty or the ignorant; for then the entire *faith of the Scriptures* will be exposed to condemnation."

In one of his treatises, Wickliffe gives the following as the signs of freedom from the guilt of mortal sin: "When a man will gladly and willingly hear the *Word of God;* when he knoweth

* *Vaughan*, vol. I., p. 362, note 7.

himself prepared to do good works; when he is prepared to flee sin; when a man can be sorry for his sins."*

In this same statement of his views, Wickliffe says in reference to "the power of the keys": "We ought to believe, that then only does a Christian priest bind or loose, when he simply *obeys the Law of Christ;* because it is not lawful for him to bind or loose, but in virtue of that law; and by consequence, not unless it be in conformity to it."†

In relation to this statement, Dr. Vaughan says: "It appears that the ministerial, or more properly, subordinate character asserted of all human decisions, in the fourteenth article [the one just quoted] was connected in the mind of Wycliffe with the important maxim of appeal to the Word of God, as the only absolute authority."‡

In "A Sort of Answer to the Bull"—as Wickliffe terms his review of the accusations made against him by the Lambeth Synod, and published immediately after his arraignment—he thus speaks of the "reading of the sacred Scripture," and of "a scriptural faith." Adverting to the pope, he says: "Let him not be ashamed to perform the ministry of the church, since he is, or at least ought to be, the servant of the servants of God. But a prohibition of reading the sacred Scriptures, and a vanity

* *Vaughan,* vol. I., p. 372, note. † *Vaughan,* vol. I., p. 376.
‡ Vol. I., p. 373, note 13.

of secular dominion, and a lusting after worldly appearances, would seem to partake too much of a disposition toward the blasphemous advancement of antichrist; especially while the truths of a scriptural faith are reputed tares, and said to be opposed to christian truth, by certain leaders who arrogate that we must abide by their decision respecting every article of faith; notwithstanding they themselves are plainly ignorant of the faith of the Scriptures. But by such means there follows a crowding to the court of Rome to purchase a condemnation of the sacred Scriptures as heretical; and thence come dispensations, contrary to the articles of the christian faith."

In the closing paragraph of the same work, the Reformer adds: "These conclusions have I delivered, as a grain of faith separated from the chaff, by which the ungrateful tares are set on fire. These, opposed to the Scriptures of truth, like the crimson blossoms of foul revenge, provide sustenance for antichrist."* etc., etc.

In another place, Wickliffe says: "The Law of God, and of reason, we should follow more than that of our popes and cardinals: so much so, that if we had a hundred popes, and if all the friars were cardinals,—to the Law of the Gospel we should bow, more than to all this multitude."†

In the closing chapter of the third book of his *Trialogus*, Wickliffe thus speaks of the authority

---

* *Fasciculi*, 248, 257; *Vaughan*, vol. I., p. 382. † Ib. II., 347.

of the Scripture: "We do not sincerely believe in our Lord Jesus Christ, or we should hold the authority of the Scripture, and especially that of the evangelists, as of infinitely greater weight than any other."

"Inasmuch as it is the desire of the Holy Spirit," he proceeds to say, "that our attention should not be dispersed over a large number of objects, but be concentrated on one necessary matter; it is his will that the books of the old and new law should be read and studied; and that men should not be taken up with other books, which, true as they may be, and containing Scripture truth as they may by implication, are not to be confided in explicitly. Hence Augustine (Book II. De Ordine Rerum) often enjoins it on his readers, that none should give credit to his writings or his words, except in so far as they have their foundation in Scripture, wherein, as he often saith, is contained all truth, either explicitly or implicitly. Of course, we should judge in the manner concerning the writings of other holy doctors; and much more so concerning the writings of the Romish Church, and doctors of a later date.

"Accordingly, that the Holy Scriptures may be more duly estimated, every truth which is not manifest to the Christian from the single evidence of his senses, should be deduced from Scripture, at least if the faithful are to place credence in it. And then the Scriptures would be held in reverence, and the papal bulls superseded, as they ought to be, and the veneration of men for the laws of the papacy, as well as for the doctrines of our modern doctors, promulgated since the loosing of Satan, would be kept within due bounds. How do writings of this sort concern the faithful, save as they are honestly deduced from the fountain of Scripture? By such a course, we should not only reduce the mandates of the popes, and of other prelates, to their just place, but the errors of the new orders would be corrected, and the worship of Christ would be purified and elevated. In this view, those upstart doctors are to be accounted as especially worthy of all detestation, who endeavor to maintain, that Holy Writ, of all writings or sayings, is the most false, and especially the words of Christ in the Gospel of John, which they think they can clearly demonstrate by their logic. In truth, of all heretical doctrines, I know of none more damnable than this, of none more fit for the purposes of Antichrist, none more hurtful to the faith of Christ. All the sophistries of Antichrist on the subject, lie concealed under this foul covering:—'I understand Holy Writ in this way, and according to my logic it ought so to be understood; but the sense which I attach to it amounts to an impossibility; therefore Scripture, if logically interpreted, and by consequence the author of Scripture, must be accounted false, and most unworthy of credit.'"

"It is no fault of the Scripture, if the heretic be found understanding it in a wrong sense. It is not subject to his judgment. On the contrary, it condemns him. The error of his understanding lies mainly in his pride, in his foolish confidence in his own logic; whereas the logic of Scripture itself is the most correct, the most subtle, and to be most followed."*

Extracts from Wickliffe's writings, of like import with the above extracts, illustrative of his profound regard for the Scriptures, might be furnished to almost any extent; but those already given must be deemed ample. They show, in connection with other extracts hereafter to be given, most conclusively, that the great Reformer regarded the Scriptures of the Old and New Testaments, not only as God's Word, but as literally an *all-sufficient guide* in matters of ecclesiastical order and practice, as well as of religious faith and duty; and that he considered nothing absolutely binding on his conscience, except what the Scriptures commanded, or at least authorized or justified.

In the maintenance of this great principle, Wickliffe outwent not only his own age, but the great majority of churchmen of subsequent ages, even to the present day. It was, however, for this great principle that the Paulicians of the tenth and subsequent centuries labored, and suffered, and died; as have other good men, in all ages of the church since apostolic times. It is, too, the fundamental principle which the Independents and Congregation-

---

* *Tracts and Treatises* of *John De Wycliffe*, pp. 129, 130.

alists of England and America for centuries past have professed, and in behalf of which they have argued, and labored, and suffered; and which they hope yet to see, under the smile of Him by whose inspiration all Scripture was originally given, pervade and bless the whole christian world.

2. A second principle of Congregationalism, recognized by Wickliffe and abundantly developed in his voluminous writings, is the necessity of piety to true church-membership.

He defines the church to be "a congregation of just men for whom Christ shed his blood" — "an assembly of predestinated persons" — "Christ's members, that he hath ordained to bliss;" and he calls them "true men" — "just men" — "religious men" — "devout men"; and says, "no man can possibly know himself to be a member of the church of Christ except as he is enabled to live a holy life."

It would be easy to fill a volume with proofs and illustrations, that Wickliffe considered personal piety indispensible to true church-membership. Take the following extracts from his writings as a sample of his teachings on this head:

In a work entitled *The Great Sentence of the Curse Expounded*, he thus defines a christian church: "Christian men, taught in God's law, call holy church, the congregation of just men, for whom Jesus Christ shed his blood; and they do not so call stones, and timber, and earthly rubbish, which Antichrist's clerks magnify more than God's righteousness, and the souls of Christian men." * And in another place he says, the church consists not of the clergy, "but of all men and women who shall be saved." †

In his work *De Ecclesiæ Dominio*, the Reformer says: "Christ's church is his spouse, that hath three parts. The first part is in bliss with Christ, head of the church, and containeth angels and blessed men that now be in heaven. The second part of the church be saints in purgatory, and these sin not anew, but purge their old sins. And many errors follen in praying for these saints; and since they all are dead in body, Christ's words may be taken of them: sue [follow] we Christ as our life, and let the dead bury the dead. The third part of the church are true men that here live, that shall be afterwards saved in heaven, and who live here the life of christian men. The first part is called the *overcoming* part, the middle is called the *sleeping*, the third is called the *fighting*. And all these make one church, and the head of this church is Jesus Christ, both God and man. This church is mother to every man who shall be saved, and containeth no other." ‡

He then derides the folly of regarding the church as the spouse of Christ and supposing that the offspring of Belial can be among its members. "In the present world, no man can possibly know himself to be a member of the church of Christ ex-

---

* *Tracts*, &c., p. 32. † *Ib.* 41. ‡ *Tracts and Treatises*, p. 74.

cept as he is enabled to live a holy life; few, if any, being so taught of God as to know their ordination to the bliss of heaven."

In another work entitled *De Episcoporum Erroribus*, Wickliffe says: "When men speak of holy church, they understand anon prelates and priests, monks, and canons, and friars, and all men who have crowns [tonsures—referring to the manner of wearing the hair peculiar to ecclesiastical persons] though they live never so cursedly against God's law; and they call not secular men, of holy church, though they live never so truly after God's law, and in perfect charity. Nevertheless, all who shall be saved in bliss of heaven are members of holy church, and no more." *

In the maintenance of this doctrine, the Reformer of the fourteenth century was but the forerunner of those great and good men who, in subsequent centuries, separated themselves from the impure fellowship of the church of England, banished themselves to a foreign land, and finally buried themselves in a distant wilderness, that they might, unmolested, erect a tabernacle for God's service according to the pattern furnished to them in the sacred revelations of His holy mind and will.

3. Another ecclesiastical topic on which Wickliffe symbolized somewhat with Congregationalists, relates to the christian ministry.

The hierarchy and its officials he rejected en-

* *Tracts*, &c., p. 45.

tirely — popes, cardinals, patriarchs, archbishops, bishops, archdeacons, officials, deans, etc., etc. His idea of a christian minister was, that he should be simply a preacher of the gospel. And there were few things against which he protested more vehemently than the lordly power and worldly character of the higher orders of the hierarchy. In fact, the only preëminence which he willingly recognized in the ministry of the church was, that of eminent holiness and devotion to the cause of Christ. In conformity with this general view of the nature and work of the christian ministry, Wickliffe sent forth, without license or leave from pope or prelate, his "poor priests" as they were called, to preach the gospel in the market places, in the fields, the highways, or wherever they could find hearers; thus conforming, as nearly as might be, to the primitive example of Christ and his apostles.

In his work *De Ecclesiæ Dominio*, Wickliffe, after describing the earnest and successful labors of the apostles among Jews and Gentiles, continues: "And thus the apostles of Christ filled the world with God's grace. But long after, as chronicles say, the fiend had envy thereat, and by Silvester, priest of Rome, he brought in a new guile, and moved the Emperor of Rome to endow the church. When the life of the priest was thus changed, his name was changed. He was not called the apostle, or the disciple of Christ, but he was called the pope, and head of all holy church: and afterwards came other names, by the feigning of hypocrites, so that some say he is even with the manhead of Christ, and highest vicar of Christ, to do on earth whatever he liketh; and some flourish other names, and say that he is most blessed father — because hereof cometh benefices which the priest giveth to men; for Simon Magus never more labored in simony than do these priests." *

Though in theory he admits of two orders in the ministry — presbyters and deacons, utterly repudiating the third, or episcopal order — yet in point of fact, he seems to recognize but one order. A priest, he maintains, is as competent to the ministry of every sacrament as a bishop; for "the power of priesthood is a matter which may not exist, in a degree, either more or less;" and the distinction between what were termed the superior and the inferior clergy, he insists is simply a difference of jurisdiction, and not a difference of character.† And though he admits of a distinction of order between bishops and deacons, he yet speaks of deacons, and the reason for their appointment in the apostolic churches, very much as every Congregationalist would.

In his *Trialogus*, which consists of a series of colloquies between Alithia, Pseudis, and Phronesis, — Truth, Falsehood, and Wisdom — the Reformer discusses, in a summary and comprehensive manner, the great doctrines of his creed; Alithia and Phronesis stating the several topics, and answering

---

* *Tracts,* &c., p. 75.

† See *Vaughan,* vol. I., p. 373.

the arguments of Pseudis against them. In Book IV., chap. 13, the subject of the "sacrament of orders" in the ministry of the church is thus disposed of by Phronesis:*

"In my opinion, this sacrament of order is sufficiently analogous, and its sign accordingly is very equivocal." After speaking of the use of the term "order," in two different senses, Phronesis proceeds to say: "Thirdly, with greater strictness, and more to the purpose, that power given to the priest by God, through the ministry of the bishop, in order to his due ministering in the church, is called order.

"This ordination is commonly conferred at a holy time, with a solemn fast, and accompanied by masses and other ceremonies: whence it is commonly said, that ordination is not conferred on a priest, save when the bishop imparts to him the Holy Ghost, and impresses the priestly character on his mind. And so indelible is this last, that be the priest degraded, or happen what may to him, this character is inseparably attached to him. Similar is the opinion concerning the character impressed in baptism.

"One thing I confidently assert, that in the primitive church, or the time of Paul, two orders were held sufficient — those of priests and deacons. No less certain am I, that in the time of Paul, presbyter and bishop were the same, as is shown in

---

* *Tracts*, &c., pp. 163–169.

1 Tim. iii., and Tit. i. That profound theologian, Jerome, attests the same fact. — See lxxxvii. *Dis. ea Olim.* For there were not then the distinctions of pope and cardinals, patriarchs and archbishops, bishops, archdeacons, officials, and deans, with other officers and religious bodies without number or rule. As to all the disputes which have arisen about these functionaries, I shall say nothing; it is enough for me, that, according to Scripture, the presbyters and the deacons retain that office and standing which Christ appointed them; because I am convinced that Cæsarean pride has introduced these orders and gradations. If they had been necessary to the church, Christ and his Apostles would not have held their peace about them. So that those blaspheme who extol the rights of the pope above Christ. But the office of the clergy, the catholic may best learn from Scripture, in the epistles to Timothy and Titus. Nor must he, on pain of incurring serious guilt, allow admission to Cæsarean innovations. But here I doubt not vast numbers are guilty."

In a work *On the Seven Deadly Sins*, Wickliffe divides the church into three parts — preachers; defenders, or the nobility; and laborers, or the common people. He then states that the only gradation, rank, or office, known in the church of Christ in its early history, was that of "priests and deacons, living clerks' lives" [clergymen's lives]. "By ordinance of Christ," he says, "priests and deacons were all one; but afterwards the Emperor departed [separated] them, and made bishops, lords, and priests their servants; and this was the cause of envy, and quenched much charity."

It has been the work of the fiend, he observes, to change this simple state of things into one of "many colors, as secular and religious; and both have many parts, as popes, and cardinals, and bishops, and archdeacons; monks, canons, hospitalers, and friars," etc., etc.*

These extracts show that Wickliffe did not regard Episcopacy as a Divine Institution; and that his views of the ministry of the church much more nearly accorded with modern Congregational views, than with those of Churchmen, high or low, ancient or modern.

4. Wickliffe's views respecting the order, government and worship of the church, harmonize in several other particulars with those of Congregationalists.

For example: he maintained that Christ is the only head of the church — the pope of Rome being Antichrist; that christian men should practice and teach only the laws of Christ — the laws of Antichrist being contrary in every respect to the laws and the office of Christ; that all human traditions are superfluous and sinful, and that mystical and significant ceremonies in religious worship are unlawful; episcopal confirmation he rejected; set forms of prayer he disapproved of; and even

---

* *Tracts*, &c., pp. 68, 69.

the imposition of hands in ordination it is said he disallowed. He did not believe that any other license to preach the gospel was necessary, than a conformity of life and character to Christ's example and an inward call to the work; and it was charged, that he even went so far in his notions of Christian freedom as to admit that women might lawfully preach. To all the clergy he allowed the privilege of marriage; the right to preach wherever they pleased (as his poor priests did), and the power to ordain others to the same work. He gave to the body of the church the right to call to account their clergy, and even the pope himself, for unchristian deportment. In short, taking the New Testament for his unerring and all-sufficient guide in all matters of church interest, Wickliffe regarded as erroneous, or entirely non-essential, whatever in the order, government, and worship of the church, had not scriptural warrant; and in regard to all such matters, allowed the largest liberty which either the teaching or example of Christ and his apostles would justify.

Wickliffe seems to have taken very nearly the same view of excommunication, as a church censure, which Congregationalists do. He held that no prelate ought to excommunicate any man except he knew him first to be excommunicated of God. While modern Congregationalists hold that no man should be cast out from the church, as "a heathen man and publican," who has not first forfeited his standing as a christian man.

In regard to the maintenance of the clergy, Wickliffe agreed with modern Congregationalists, that it should be by the voluntary contributions of the faithful. He insisted that the clergy should receive but a very moderate support from their parishioners, saying: "Priests owen [ought] to hold them [selves] paid with food and hiling [clothing] as St. Paul teacheth." * And even this moderate stipend, he argued should be continued only so long as the priests were faithful to their ministerial duties. And what he taught in these respects, he practised. He lived in very humble style among his parishioners; wearing, for the most part, a coarse woollen gown, and travelling about his parish staff in hand and bare footed.†

* *Why Poor Priests have no Benefices*, chap. 2.

† Wickliffe was the contemporary and personal friend of the father of English Poetry, Geoffrey Chaucer. The poet is said to have been a Wickliffite, and to have suffered for his principles. Hippisley, in his *Chapters on Early English Literature*, has collected sundry particulars respecting this friendship between the *Poet* and the *Reformer*. Chaucer's *Court of Love* was dedicated to Anne, the first queen of Richard II.; and the poet was one to whom the protection of the king was extended. In the *Vision of William*, the characteristics of a Lollard parson are described under the allegorical character of *Dobet* — do better:

"He is low as a lambe, and lovelich of speech,
And helpeth alle men after that hem nedith."

"From a subsequent expression — 'and hath rendrid (translated) the Bible' — one would be inclined to suppose Wickliffe himself here intended." — "It has been imagined that the poet, under the character of the Loller (for so he is called by the Host in the *Shipman's Prologue*), has portrayed his contemporary, and political associate, Wickliffe, as rector of Lutterworth:"

In support of the allegations now made respecting Wickliffe's ecclesiastical tenets, my appeal is generally to the Reformer's own words, as they appear in his published works; though but a few fragments of his voluminous writings have ever been printed. On some few points it has been necessary to rely on the testimony of Wickliffe's biographers, friends or foes.

In relation to the headship of the church, the Reformer holds the following language in one of his Postils:* "True men say, that so long as

---

"A good man there was of religion,
He was a poor parson of a town,
But rich he was of holy thought and werk.
He was also a learned man, a clerk,
That Criste's gospel trewely wolde preche;
His parishens devoutly he wolde tech.
Benigne he was, and wonder diligent,
And in adversitie full patient;
And swiche he was yproved often sithes,
Ful loth were him to cursen for his tithes,
But rather wolde he geven out of doute
Of his offring and eke of his substance.
He could in letle thing have suffisance;
Wide was his parish and houses far asonder,
But he ne left nought for no rain ne thunder.
In sickeness and in mischeefe to visite
The ferrest in his parish, moche and lite,
Upon his fete and in his hand a staff.
But it [if?] were any person obstinat,
What so he were of highe or low estat,
Him wolde he snibben sharply for the nones."

See Hippisley's "*Chapters on Early English Literature*," pp. 99, 151, 152–156. Lond. 12mo, 1837.

* *Tracts*, &c., p. 90, note *b*.

Christ is in heaven, the church has in him the best pope, who is head of all saints; and distance, either more or less, hindereth not Christ to do his deeds as he promiseth; and he saith he is with his own always, to the end of the world. It is granted that the church beneath hath a head, that is Christ, head of angels and of men, all that are or shall be saved; and we dare not put two heads, lest the church be monstrous. Peter was not head of the church, but captain of the church; and surely warriors would scorn the reasoning which saith that if a man is captain he is head. Peter was captain for a time, and afterwards Paul was captain. But these blind buzzards [the Papists] should first know what Christ's church truly is. There are three churches of Christ. One that hath vanquished and is above; another that sleepeth in purgatory; and neither of these requireth such a pope. But the third is fighting here; and this, with the others, require Christ as their head. And the man who is most meek, most poor, and most serviceable to the church, is its captain, by the judgment of the Head above. If men seek well, they shall find that it may not be proved that it is reasonable to have such a pope; for nothing should prove it except of these three: — a right understanding of the words of Christ; evidence of man's law; or custom, with the opinion of much people. But none of these may prove anything in this case." — *Postils*, p. 181. See also the passage from *De Ecclesiæ Dominio*, on page 282.

In the seventeenth chapter of the *Trialogus*, Book III., the Roman pontiff is thus spoken of as the great Antichrist:* "It is supposed, and with much probability, that the Roman pontiff is the great Antichrist, for he falsely asserts that he is in a direct sense the vicar of Christ, most conformed to him in his life, and by consequence the most humble of Christians, the poorest of men, and one separated more than any man beside from the thraldom of secular things. But the falsehood and blasphemy of such assertions are manifest in the fact that his life is the reverse of all this, that he is the most powerful and the most wealthy man in the whole world; and what can be more contrary to the poverty of Him who had nowhere to lay his head? How can such an Antichrist be described as a vicar bearing resemblance to Christ? From the fact of what we see in him, it is clear, that so far from being the most humble of men, he is vicar to the king of pride, set up over us all. The great mart in respect to worldly possessions lies in the hands of the pope; and yet Christ declared that he was not a ruler or divider in a case between two brethren, when the worldly matter in dispute was comparatively small.

* * * * * *

"After this great Antichrist, come the lesser Antichrists—the prelates, who desert the office which Christ has assigned to them, and take up another

---

* *Tracts*, &c., p. 124.

office according to another law. The injunction of Christ to Peter was — 'feed my sheep;' but if you wish to bring this point to a test, look well to the life of Christ and his apostles, and see how ill they are followed by our spiritual leaders. The duty of preaching is set aside, and the practice of fleecing those committed to their care is introduced in its place. Let a man bestow only slight attention on what is doing in modern times, and on the laws of Antichrist, and he will see that they are contrary in every respect to the laws and the office of Christ."

In regard to human traditions and divers religious rites and ceremonies introduced by the hierarchy, and on the right of private judgment, Wickliffe's language is quite explicit:

In commenting, in one of his sermons, on the words of the Apostle, 1 Cor. 4: 1--3, "Let a man so guess [account] of us, as of the ministers of God and dispensers of his services," etc., etc., he remarks: "If each christian man should be found true in this respect, priests, both high and low, should be more true." And on the words (vs. 3) "To me it is for the least thing that I be judged of you, or else of man's judgment, but I judge not myself," the preacher adds: "Paul chargeth not the judgment of men, whether priests or lords; but the truth of Holy Writ, which is the will of the first judge, was enough for him until doomsday. And thus stewards of the church should not judge wickedly by their own will, but merely after God's law, in things of which they are certain. But the laws and judgments which Antichrist hath brought in, putting God's law behind, mar too much the church of Christ. For to the stewards of the church, the laws of Antichrist are rules to make officers therein, and to condemn the laity." *

In other places he speaks on this wise: "In the sacrament of baptism, in that of confirmation, and in all the rest, hath Antichrist invented unauthorized ceremonies; and to the burden of the church, without warrant from Scripture, hath heaped them on subjected believers." †

And again: "We ought to know that Christ will not fail in any ordinance or law sufficient for his church; and whosoever reverses this sentence blasphemes against Christ." ‡

Of the episcopal rite of confirmation Wickliffe thus expresses himself: "This sacrament does not appear to me necessary to the believer's salvation, nor do I believe that those who pretend to confirm youths, do rightly confirm them, nor that this sacrament should be restricted exclusively to the Cæsarean bishops. Further, I think it would be more devout, and more in accordance with Scripture language, to say that our bishops do *not* confer the Holy Ghost, or confirm the previous bestowment of the Holy Ghost; for such expressions, however glossed by our doctors, are still lia-

* *Tracts,* &c., pp. 82, 83.

† *Trialogus,* bk. IV., ch. 18, in *Tracts,* &c., p. 183.

‡ *Tracts,* &c., p. 73, note.

ble, if once admitted, to misconstruction, while, at the same time, they want authority to sanction them.

"Hence some are of opinion that this slight and brief confirmation, performed by the bishop, with the rites which are attached to it, with so much solemnity, was introduced at the suggestion of the devil, with a view to delude the people concerning the faith of the church, and to give more credence to the solemnity, or as to the necessity of bishops. For according to the common opinion, while our bishops administer this sacrament of confirmation, retaining it in common with many other things exclusively in their own hands, and while there is no salvation for believers apart from the reception of these solemn sacraments, how could the church preserve her station uninjured without such bishops? But one thing appears to hold, in the greater part, that for any bishop whatever, baptizing in such a way, to bestow the Holy Spirit, according to God's covenant, implies a blasphemy. But I leave to others the more subtle discussion of this topic." *

In one of his sermons, Wickliffe thus speaks of christian freedom in contrast with the thraldom of Antichrist: † "Freedom is much coveted, as men know naturally, but much should christian men covet the better freedom of Christ. But it is known that Antichrist hath now more enthralled the church

* *Tracts and Treatises*, p. 163.

† *Tracts*, &c., p. 88.

than it was under the old law, while men might not bear that service. And Antichrist maketh new laws now, and groundeth them not on God and man; for more ceremonies are now brought in than were in the old law; and more do they tarry [hinder] men to come to heaven than did the Scribes and Pharisees by their traditions. And the root of this thraldom is the lordship which Antichrist hath, for he challengeth to be full lord, both of spiritual and temporal. He so preventeth christian men from serving Christ in freedom, that they may say, as the poet saith in his proverb, the frog said to the arrow—'Cursed be so many masters!' For now christian men are oppressed, now with popes, and now with bishops, now with cardinals under popes, and now with prelates under bishops, as one would buffet a football. But surely if the Baptist were not worthy to lose the latchet of Christ's shoe, Antichrist hath no power thus to hinder the freedom which Christ hath bought. Christ gave this freedom to man to come lightly [easily] to the bliss of heaven; but Antichrist wearieth men to give him money. Ever do these hypocrites fear lest God's law should be shown, and they be thus convicted of their falsehood. For God and his law are stronger than they, and these hypocrites may only hold man for a time in this fiend's thraldom."

On the right and duty of men to preach without episcopal license, the Reformer holds the following plain and bold language: "Worldly prelates command that no man should preach the gospel, but according to their will and limitation, and forbid men to hear the gospel on pain of the great curse. But Satan, in his own person, durst never do so much despite to Christ and to his gospel, for he alleged holy writ in tempting Christ, and thereby would have pursued his intent. And since it is the counsel and commandment of Christ to priests generally, that they preach the gospel, and as this they must not do without leave of prelates, who it may be are fiends of hell; it follows, that priests may not do the commands of Christ, without the leave of fiends. Ah! Lord Jesus, are these sinful fools, and in some cases fiends of hell, more witty and mighty than thou, that true men may not do thy will, without authority from them? Ah! Lord God Almighty, all wise, and all full of charity, how long wilt thou suffer these Antichrists to despise thee, and thy holy gospel, and to prevent the health of the souls of christian men? Lord of endless righteousness, this thou sufferest, because of sin generally reigning among the people; but of thine endless mercy and goodness, help thy poor wretched priests and servants, that they possess the love and reverence of thy gospel, and be not hindered to do thy worship and will by the false feignings of Antichrist." *

William Thorpe, one of Wickliffe's oldest, most intelligent, reasonable and laborious "poor priests,"

---

* *Vaughan*, vol. II., pp. 279, 280.

who travelled and preached more than twenty years, before he was arrested and imprisoned by Archbishop Arundel, in 1407, told the Archbishop, on his examination: "For that He [Christ] commandeth us to do the office of priesthood, He will be our sufficient letters and witness, if we, by example of His holy living and teaching, specially occupy us faithfully to do our office justly; yea, the people to whom we preach (be they faithful or unfaithful) shall be our letters; that is, our witness-bearers; for the truth where it is sown may not be unwitnessed."*

Purvey, one of the most learned of Wickliffe's disciples, taught substantially the same doctrine: "God knoweth how, and can make, when it pleaseth Him, priests (without man's working and sinful signs, that is to say, without either sacraments or characters) to be known and discerned of the people by their virtuous life and example, and by their true preaching of the law of God. For so made he the first-made priests and elders before the law of Moses; and so made he Moses a priest before Aaron, and before the ceremonies of the law, without man's operation at all; and even so hath God made all such as are predestinate to be priests." †

---

* *Fox,* vol. I., p. 606.

† *Fasciculi,* 387–88; *Fox,* vol. I., p. 620. Purvey was perhaps the leader of the Lollard party after Wickliffe's death. He revised Wickliffe's translation of the Bible, and wrote a general prologue to it. He was probably the author of the famous petition of the Lol-

Wickliffe, for some twenty years of his life, was almost incessantly engaged in controversies. Among his earliest and ablest opponents was a Carmelite monk, who became provincial of his order, and confessor to the duke of Lancaster, named John Cunningham — *Frater Johannes Kynyngham*, as Netter styles him. To this monk, probably, we are indebted for the first list of Wickliffe's "heresies," drawn up sometime before 1372. There are thirteen heresies in this list, and they are said to be the first which he promulgated — "hæreses quae primo jactavit in æra." Most of these are philosophical or metaphysical in their character. Others, however, contain the germs of opinions on ecclesiastical matters which were more fully developed in subsequent years.* For example, the ninth of the series, in which he denies

---

lard's to parliament, in 1395, and of a work entitled *Ecclesiæ Regimen*, to which reference is probably made, as the book in which the same matters are treated more at large. Judging from the "heresies and errors" extracted from this book by his opponent, Lavingham, and preserved in the *Fasciculi*, and from his prologue to the Bible, Purvey was very radical in his opposition to the order and government of the church of Rome. For example: — he denied that the Scriptures made any distinction between presbyters, priests, and bishops; he asserted that all good, predestinated christians were constituted priests by God, and might administer all the necessary sacraments,— as baptism, preaching, matrimony, etc., etc. See *Fasciculi*, pp. 383, 406, compared with the Prologue to *The Holy Bible*, made from the Latin of John Wycliffe and his Followers. Preface, pp. XXV.-XXVIII.

* See particularly "*Libellus Magistri Johannis Wycclyff*," *etc.* —*Fasciculi*, 245–57.

that any man living in mortal sin is a *dominus*, a priest, or a bishop; the tenth and eleventh, in which he protests against the civil dominion and the property-holding of the clergy; the twelfth, in which he asserts the right of temporal rulers to control the temporalities of the clergy; and the thirteenth, in which the right of the people to withhold tithes and oblations from unworthy curates is asserted.*

Fox has preserved another catalogue of Wickliffe's errors, of a somewhat later date, about 1377, as follows:—"That the Holy Eucharist, after consecration, is not the very body of Christ, but figuratively.†—That the Church of Rome is not the head of all churches, more than any other church is: Nor that Peter hath any more power given of Christ, than any other apostle hath.—*Item.* That the Pope of Rome hath no more in the keys of the Church, than hath any other within the order of priesthood.—*Item.* If God be, the lords temporal may lawfully and meretoriously take away their temporalities from the churchmen offending *habitualiter.*—*Item.* If any temporal lord do know the church so offending, he is bound, under pain of damnation, to take the temporalities from the same.—*Item.* That all the Gospel is a rule sufficient of

---

* *Fasciculi,* 2, 3.

† Wickliffe's mature sentiments on the sacramental question are given, at length, in his "Confessio Magistri Johannis Wycclyff," put forth in 1380 or 1381.—*Fasciculi,* pp. 115–32, compared with Introduction, pp. IX.–LXII.

itself to rule the life of every christian man here, without any other rule.—*Item.* That all other rules, under whose observances divers religious persons be governed, do add no more perfection to the Gospel, than doth the white color to the wall.—*Item.* That neither the pope, nor any other prelate of the church, ought to have prisons wherein to punish transgressors."*

The following "conclusions" were exhibited, among others, in the convocation of the clergy at Lambeth, 1377–8, as among Wickliffe's errors:—"A man cannot be excommunicated to his hurt or undoing, except he be first and principally excommunicate of himself.—No man ought, but in God's cause alone, to excommunicate, suspend, or forbid, or otherwise to proceed to revenge by any ecclesiastical censure.—An ecclesiastical minister, and also the bishop of Rome, may lawfully be rebuked of his subjects, and for the profit of the church be accused, either of the clergy or of the laity."

Wickliffe explained this thus: "The proof of this is manifest hereby, because the said bishop of Rome is subject to fall into the sin against the Holy Ghost, as may be supposed, saving the sanctitude, humility, and reverence due to such a father. For so long as our brother is subject unto the infirmity of falling, he lieth under the law of brotherly

* *Fox's Acts and Monuments,* vol. I., p. 491 : Lond. 1684. By a canon of the synod of Lambeth, A.D. 1216, the English bishops were required to have prisons.—*Henry's England,* vol. VIII., p. 14.

correction. And when the whole college of cardinals may be slothful in ministering due correction for the necessary prosperity of the church, it is apparent that the residue of the body of the church, which possibly may stand mostly of laymen, may wholesomely correct the same, accuse, and bring him to a better way." *

The veriest Independent could not exceed this.

Harpsfield accuses the Reformer of saying, that "the tying of people to set forms of prayer, is abridging the liberty which God has given us." † And Collier describes his views thus: — "He disallows imposition of hands in ordination, and all other signs and ceremonies of an outward call; and maintains, that, when the antichristian and insignificant prelates fail to do their duty, our Savior will give a mission himself, and determine the circumstances of person, time, and manner, as He shall think fit; for let but a man imitate the example of our Savior, and he need not question his being ordained by Him, though he never received his character from State prelate." ‡

Fox (A. D. 1393, vol. I., p. 576,) gives an account of "certain godly persons of Leicester, persecuted for the truth," who "followed Wickliffe," and held sundry "heresies and errors, of the church

---

* *Fox*, vol. I., p. 593; *Tracts and Treatises*, XXXVII.-li.; also, *Fasciculi*, 245-57.

† *Collier's Ecc. Hist. Great Britain*, vol. III., p. 183. Lond., 8vo. 1852.

‡ *Ecc. Hist.* vol. III., p. 186.

of Rome condemned," among which were the following: "That every layman, may in every place, preach and teach the gospel;" "that every good man, although he be unlearned, is a priest."

The real doctrine of Wickliffe and his followers on this point was, doubtless, that every good man was bound to do what he could to spread the gospel; and in default of any one better qualified, even to preach and administer the ordinances of the gospel: a good and wholesome doctrine.

According to Collier, (vol. III., 180--89) Wickliffe was even accused of giving women the privilege of the priesthood and the pulpit. And to every priest he granted the liberty of marriage, of preaching where he pleased, and of ordaining others to their own order.

Though I have not been able to discover in Wickliffe's own writings anything to justify the assertion, that he gave to women "the privilege of the priesthood and the pulpit;" yet, in the writings of Walter Brute, a learned layman who embraced Wickliffe's views, and wrote very ably against Romish errors, it is argued, that, "*in defect of the clergy*," women may exercise the action of prayer and administration of sacraments belonging to priests; and referring to the custom received in the Popish church for women to baptize, which, saith he, cannot be without the remission of sins, he asks: "Wherefore, seeing that women have power by the pope to remit sin, and to baptize, why may not they as well be admitted to minister the Lord's Supper, *in like case of necessity?*"*

It is apparent hence, that the Wickliffites gave to women the privileges of the priesthood and the pulpit, only "in defect of the clergy;" only "in cases of necessity;" and so it is presumed would any intelligent Congregationalist.

Waldensis, or Walden, or Netter, as he is indifferently called, enumerates *eighty* errors of doctrine into which Wickliffe had fallen, and for which he was condemned by the Pope and his hierarchy. Among these, are the following, numbered as they are given by Fuller, in his Church History of Briton, book IV, sec. 6.

"1. That it is blasphemy to call any the Head of the Church, save Christ alone.—9. That he often calleth the Pope Antichrist.—10. That Christ meant the Pope, by the Abomination of Desolation standing in the holy place.—13. That plain deacons or priests may preach without license of Pope or Bishop.—14. That in the time of the Apostles there were only two orders, namely, priests and deacons; and that a bishop doth not differ from a priest.—17. That priests of bad life cease to be any longer priests.—18. That he defineth the church to consist only of persons predestinated.—24. That tithes are pure alms; and that pastors

* See "Walter Brute's Declaration Concerning the Priesthood," etc., in *Fox*, bk. V., A.D. 1391, vol. I., p. 566. Also, the letter to Nicholas Hereford, "by a Lollard" (probably Walter Brute), in *Fox*, vol. I., p. 571.

ought not to exact them by ecclesiastical censures. — 30. That to bind men to set and prescript forms of prayer doth derogate from that liberty God hath given them. — 33. That Chrisme [anointing with oil] and other such ceremonies are not to be used in baptism. — 35. That baptism doth not confer grace, but only signifies grace which was given before. — 37. That the substance of bread and wine still remain in the sacrament."

Sentiments like these, though regarded by the popish historian, and by the hierarchy generally, as "guilty of fire" — deserving to be burned with their author — cannot be considered by modern Protestants of any denomination, as very heinous. Yet it was for the maintenance of sentiments like these that the reformers of the fourteenth century were hated, and hunted to death by the papal hierarchy.

A comprehensive summary of Wickliffe's opinions, may be found in one of the publications of the Camden Society, entitled "An Apology for the Lollards." * This Apology seems to have been ad-

---

* Its title in full reads thus: — "An Apology for Lollard Doctrines, attributed to Wicliffe. Now first printed from a Manuscript in the Library of Trinity College, Dublin: With an Introduction and Notes, by James Henthorn Todd, D.D., V. P. R. I. A., Fellow of Trinity Coll. and Treasurer of St. Patrick's Cathedral, Dublin. London: Printed for the Camden Society. 1842." Small quarto, lxiii and 207 pages. A copy may be found in the Boston City Library, and is well worth an examination, as a sample of Wickliffe's mode of reasoning, the abundance of his treasures of reading — the pages abounding in quotations in support of his positions, from the

dressed to some body of men — perhaps one of the convocations appointed to try him — who had preferred sundry charges against Wickliffe. These charges are numbered up to twenty-nine or thirty, and each one is briefly considered and defended by him. They are in substance as follows: —

1. The Pope is not the vicar of Christ, nor of Peter. — 2. The Pope has no power to give indulgences, either to men dead or alive. — 3. Ministers of the church ought never to curse men from ill will or for worldly purposes, but for breaking God's law only; and the church should never curse a righteous man. — 4. That Christ was cursed. — 5. That each priest may use the key to every man; — i. e. every priest has power to do the work of a minister of Christ, independently of Episcopal license, and even in spite of the bishop's prohibition. — 6. Every priest is bound to preach the gospel. — 7. Every person who heareth the mass of a priest who liveth in lechery, and knoweth this, is guilty of deadly sin. — 8. He that curseth any man — i. e. pronounceth an ecclesiastical sentence to this effect — when he is not cursed of God, breaketh God's commandments, by bearing false witness against his neighbor. — 9. It is a taking

Scriptures, from the Fathers, the Decretals of the Church, etc., etc.; — and above all, as a fair specimen of his English, the manuscript having been copied almost exactly, in the printed page. The work has been edited with great care and labor; and when all Wickliffe's important works are printed and edited in like manner, the world will have a better appreciation of the energy, ability, learning and piety of the great Reformer, than it now has, or can have now.

of damnation, that a man lead his life in poverty — i. e. that a man become a mendicant, is like taking damnation to his soul. — 10. Fasting is unnecessary while men abstain from sin — i. e. the most essential part of a fast is abstinence from sin. — 11. A priest is more bound to preach and do the work of a minister than to observe canonical hours. — 12. In the sacrament of the altar, after the consecration, remaineth the substance of the bread. This was one of Wickliffe's most heinous heresies. — 13. Churches are not to be worshipped, nor candles or tapers to be multiplied therein. — 14. That priests to sing may not first make covenant without simony — i. e. a priest may not lawfully require pay for his religious services. These must be paid for, or rather the priest must be supported, by the voluntary contributions of the people to whom he ministers. — 15. The pope, cardinals, bishops and other prelates of an inferior order, are disciples of Antichrist, and sellers of merit. — 16. The only true pope or vicar of Christ is a holy man. — 17. A judge giving sentence against an innocent man, sinneth mortally; referring, doubtless, to the hard and unjust decisions of the ecclesiastical courts against the innocent Lollards. — 18. A priest assoiling a feigner (pronouncing absolution over a hypocrite) sinneth mortally. — 19. Marriages within the third or fourth degrees of consanguinity, though forbidden by the church, are yet valid; but nevertheless, are not to be encouraged. — 20. The church by solemnizing matrimony in a degree forbidden, erreth.—21. Canon Law is contrary to God's Law; and it were well if the science of canon law were driven as chaff out of the church.—22. No man is Christ's disciple unless he keeps Christ's counsel.—23. Every man is holden to do the better — i. e. to choose God's law and obey it, rather than the canon law. —24. Images of saints are not to be worshipped. —25. The written Gospel is not to be worshipped —i. e. the words of the gospel are not to be regarded as the heathen do charms, and hung around the neck, to keep off evil.—26. Charms in no manner are lawful; and it is superstitious to hang words at the neck.—27. (Numbered 28 in the manuscript) The vow of religion is against Christ's Gospel. The meaning of which seems to be, that the special vows taken by monks and others, on entering into their orders, or religions, are generally inconsistent with the gospel spirit.—28. Religious men (i. e. monks and the like) are bound to bodily works—to do something by which to earn their living.—29. It is not lawful for the religious (orders) to beg—to get their living and wealth by beggary.

Thus it will be seen, that the "Apology" covers nearly the whole ground of Wickliffe's peculiar belief; and from this alone, the careful reader will get a very good notion of the peculiarities of Wickliffism or Lollardism, against which so many church thunders were uttered, and for the extirpation of which so many laws and constitutions were framed, and so much innocent blood shed by the Romish prelates of the fifteenth and sixteenth centuries.

The exposition which has now been given of the ecclesiastical tenets of the Great Reformer of the fourteenth century must satisfy every reader that, whether right or wrong in his views, John Wickliffe much less resembled a Romanist, or Prelatist, ancient or modern, than a Congregationalist of the apostolic model.

Wickliffe exerted a mighty and extensive influence in preparing the way for the Great Reformation, which took place in England some ages after he had been gathered to his fathers. His writings, many of which were small tracts, were exceedingly voluminous, and were scattered by hundreds all over the kingdom. These breathed into the nation a spirit as adverse to Popery, as it was favorable to genuine Protestantism.*

---

* Fox tells us that no less than *two hundred* volumes of Wickliffe's writings were burned at one time, in 1410, by order of the Church of Rome. And yet, notwithstanding the diligence of the Roman inquisitors, there have come down to our day in manuscript, no less than three hundred of Wickliffe's sermons ; and the whole number of volumes of manuscripts of his composition, preserved in the libraries of England and elsewhere, is very large. Dr. Vaughan, in his *Tracts and Treatises of John De Wycliffe*, furnishes a catalogue of *sixty-nine volumes* of manuscript works of Wickliffe, still preserved in different European libraries — chiefly the British Museum, and in the libraries of Oxford, Cambridge and Dublin Universities. Many of these volumes are very large, embracing several hundred pages folio, and contain numerous distinct works or tracts. We have, also, a catalogue of extinct works of

It cannot be questioned, that had Wickliffe been permitted to reform the English church as he wished, he would have laid the axe at the root of the tree. He would never have been contented with rejecting the *mother*, and adopting the *daughter*. Had his brawny arm been employed in cleaning the Augean stable of the English Church, he would have made clean riddance of all the filth of Popery. There would have been none of that timid, temporizing, trimming work which was seen in later reformers. He would, undoubtedly, have taken the beautifully simple model of an apostolic church for his pattern; and have constructed the outward order, as well as the religious faith of the church, after the same divine pattern. Milner's estimate of the Reformer's notions of "external reformation" seem clearly to intimate his belief of this. He tells us, that Wickliffe would have "erred in the extreme of excess," had he been permitted to carry out his notions of church reform. Le Bas evidently rejoices with trembling, to think what the church of England escaped by not having been reformed by Wickliffe. He says: "Had he succeeded in shaking the established system to pieces, one can scarcely think, without some awful misgivings, of the fabric which, under his hand, might have risen out of the ruins." And the ground of these *awful misgivings* of the good churchman

---

the Reformer, which number up to *one hundred and fifty-two.* — See *Tracts and Treatises,* part II., bk. I., pp. 1–107.

are very clearly exhibited, when he says: "If the reformation of our church had been conducted by Wickliffe, his work, in all probability, *would nearly have anticipated the labors of Calvin;* and the Protestantism of England might have pretty closely resembled the Protestantism of Geneva." And when he adds, that as one fruit of this reformation — "Episcopal government might have been discarded," one who has contemplated the manifold evils of that "Episcopal government" which the Reformation entailed upon England, can hardly refrain from exclaiming — O that Wickliffe had succeeded in his scriptural labors!

And when the professor speaks of another of the *evils* which might have resulted from the execution of Wickliffe's plan of reformation — "the clergy might have been consigned to a degrading [!] dependence on their flocks" — no good Congregationalist can sympathize at all with his "awful misgivings;" least of all, could any of the thousands who for centuries groaned under the oppressive burden of the English national church establishment.

Le Bas further says: "Had Wickliffe flourished in the sixteenth century, it can hardly be imagined that he would have been found under the banners of Cranmer and of Ridley. Their caution, their patience, their moderation, would scarcely have been intelligible to him; and rather than conform to it, he might, perhaps, have been ready, if needful, to perish, in the gainsaying [!] of such men as

Knox or Cartwright. At all events, it must plainly be confessed, that there is a marvellous resemblance between the Reformer, and his poor itinerant priests, and at least the better part of the Puritans, who troubled our Israel in the days of Elizabeth and her successor. The likeness is sufficiently striking, almost to mark him out as their prototype and progenitor; and therefore it is, that every faithful son of the church of England must rejoice with trembling, that the work of her final deliverance was not consigned to him." *

The men who are thus sneered at as *gainsayers*, by an English churchman of the nineteenth century, are the very men whom an infidel historian is constrained to honor, as the preservers of the precious spark of English liberty! Yes, and of English Protestantism too. But more of this anon.

Such was John Wickliffe — in character and in principle — a great man and a good man. A reformer of the purest intentions and of the soundest general principles. The Bible was the lamp by which he sought for truth. The Bible was the rod by which he measured everything pertaining to the church. This was the standard to which he would have reduced the outward form and order, and indeed the entire polity of the church. Had he succeeded in his reformatory labors, the church of England would have been saved from the taunt of one of her most eloquent statesmen — of hav-

* *Le Bas Life of Wiclif*, p. 325.

ing "an Arminian clergy and a Popish liturgy." He would have left none of the elements of popery in the constitution and ceremonies of the church; he would have purged out thoroughly all that leaven of impurity which to this very day is working death in the English church. The Oxfordism which now threatens her peace, yea, her very Protestantism, would have found no hiding places in the plain, and simple, and scriptural building which Wickliffe would have reared.*

But the time had not then come for the English nation to receive so great a deliverance. Neither indeed has it yet fully come. But the day of her redemption is gradually advancing, and the time of deliverance will yet come.

The manner in which the principles of Wickliffe were treated, and his followers persecuted, must receive attention before we enter upon other scenes to which the labors of the Reformer were a prelude.

---

* It was not long since asserted in the public prints, that it was no uncommon thing to find crucifixes and pictures of the Virgin Mary in the rooms of the students of Oxford University.

NOTE.—"The reformation attempted by Wycliffe originated in purer and more elevated motives; and with him the history of English Protestantism properly begins."—*A Retrospect of the Religious Life of England, etc.*, by J. J. Taylor, B.A. Lond. 1845.

"In essential points it [Wickliffe's system] was an anticipation of the extreme form of the later Puritanism"—*Ibid.*, p. 485.

CHAPTER IX.

THE LOLLARDS. — PERSECUTING EDICTS. — WRITERS AGAINST LOLLARDISM.

THE promulgation of sentiments like those enumerated in the preceding chapter could not fail to attract attention in the fourteenth century. It was like kindling a blazing fire at midnight, when there was neither moon nor stars to lighten the earth. England had so long been entombed in the darkness of Popery, that the voice of John Wickliffe and his "poor priests," proclaiming the all-sufficiency of the sacred Scriptures, and reading aloud their precious truths in a language which the people could understand, was like the voice of Him who commanded the dead to come forth.

The history of Lollardism is one of the most interesting and important chapters in English history. Wickliffe was far more than the "Morning Star of the Reformation," as he is usually called. He rose rather as the Sun of that glorious day. His doctrines included nearly all the essential truths of Protestantism; and he and his followers were, in several particulars, more thoroughly consistent Protestants than were the men who, in subsequent centuries, entered into Wickliffe's labors and secured for themselves the enviable title of Fathers of the Reformation.

Yet, how little is known of these good and suffering Lollards! Of the Puritans, we know everything that can be known, and almost everything that we desire to know. But how little has been written expressly to make known the men whose creed was as pure, and whose lives were as consistent, and whose sufferings were as great for the truth's sake, as were those of the good men who lived and labored and suffered for the cause of truth in the sixteenth and seventeenth centuries! It will be the object of this chapter to make the Lollards better known.

The piety energy and learning of Wickliffe, and of some of his early disciples and poor priests, aided by the purity of life, simplicity of character and popular address which distinguished them, gave them great influence over the public mind of England. The fact, too, that Wickliffe was early distinguished by his King, Edward III., one of the most popular monarchs of England, and made his ambassador on an important occasion; and that he was the advocate of the people's rights and those of the crown against the excessive pecuniary exactions of the court of Rome—all these things combined to give notoriety to Wickliffe's reformatory doctrines, and to gather around him disciples from all classes in Society. Accordingly, we find that in the course of a few years almost the entire English nation was made to feel the influence of the Reformer's teachings. A measure of his spirit, too, permeated through the nation, quickening, if not actually converting vast numbers, of all orders, from the occupants of the palace down to those of the peasant's hut. Edward III. and Richard II. felt and acknowledged its power; and Richard's first queen, Anne of Bohemia, was probably a sincere believer.* Numbers among the soldiery and the nobility of the Kingdom — Dukes, Lords, Counts and Knights; among the learned — as the chancellor, one or more professors, and many masters and bachelors of Oxford University; and great numbers of the common people; and even many monks and priests, embraced the doctrines of Wickliffe; or at least, became convinced of their general truthfulness. Thus Knighton, a contemporary of Wickliffe and his bitter enemy, complains, about the year 1394, that the Reformer's friends and disciples were everywhere and among all classes. There were even soldiers, he tells us, as masters Latymer, Trussell, L. Clyfforde, J. Pecche, R. Story, R. de Hylton; together with dukes and counts (*ducibus et*

* Anne, the first queen of Richard II., the sister of Wenceslaus, king of Bohemia, appears to have been a devout, good woman. Fox tells us, that she kept for her private instruction, the four gospels in English, together with sundry commentaries on the same; and that through her, the writings of Wickliffe were spread into Bohemia. — See *Acts* and *Monuments*, vol. I., pp. 577–78. See also *Neander's Hist. Chris. Relig. and Chh.* vol. V., 241–248., Torrey's Translation.

27

comitibus) — who were conspicuous adherents and favorers, and most strenuous promoters and most powerful defenders of this sect; and were ready to welcome the false preachers, to secure congregations for them, and to defend them, with sword and shield, while preaching, against all resistance or interruption.* And he tells us, further, that the people who became believers in this doctrine increased in number, and like germinating seeds multiplied beyond measure, until they filled the whole kingdom; and furthermore, that they made themselves quite at home in the country, and were audacious to the last degree, and were not ashamed to show themselves anywhere, and shamelessly kept up their ceaseless barking in public as well as in private. And he further tells us, that by the common people these disciples of Wickliffe were called Wickliffites, or *Lollards;* and that their doctrines prevailed to such an extent, that half of the nation or more embraced them; and the sect was held in such honor in those days, and was so greatly multiplied, that you could scarcely see two persons in the way together, but that one of them was a disciple of Wickliffe.† This,

* *Henr. de Knyghton,* (or Knighton) *de Eventibus Angliæ,* lib. v. columns 2661, 2662.

† *De Eventibus* etc. lib. v., column 2663, line 29—; 2664, l. 1—; 2666, l. 60—; 2706, l. 69—. See also, *Walsingham,* 191 l. 46.

Why the disciples of Wickliffe were called *Lollards,* I cannot tell. It was a nickname invented by the worshippers of the pope for the friends of God. Fuller says the Lollards were so called from Walter Lollardus, one of their teachers in Germany. — *Chh.*

in substance, is Knighton's representation of the state of things in England within about ten years after Wickliffe's death.

Hist. p. 163, folio ed. *Mosheim* supposes the name to be derived from the German word *lullen* or *lollen*, which signifies to *sing with a low voice*, whence our English word, *lull*. A *Lullen* or *Lullenhard, Lollard*, he thinks denoted one much engaged in singing — in religious worship. And when applied to "heretics," it was equivalent to *hypocrite*; just as *praying ones*, and *godly ones*, are used to this day. — Cent. XIV., pt. II., ch. 2, n. 68. The way the word *lolium*, or *lollium* (darnel, cockle, tares) is substituted for Lollardum, in some of the official documents of that day, suggests, at least, the probability that Lollard may have been derived from *lolium*. Thus Gregory XI., in 1378, rebukes the university of Oxford for suffering "wild cockle" (*lolium*) to grow among the pure wheat; and commands them to pluck it up by the roots, and especially to apprehend one John Wickliffe, etc. — So, also, the raving bishop of Worcester, in his profane denunciation of the Lollards, accuses them of sowing *cockle* (*lolium*) instead of corn, in the Lord's field. — See also, *Fox, Acts and Monuments*, I., 531. Chaucer evidently understood the title of Lollard to be derived from *lolium* — cockle. In the Shipmannes Prologue, in the Canterbury Tales, "our hoste" being reproved by the parsŏn for swearing, cries out:

* * * * "O, Jankin, be ye there?
Now, good men, quod our hoste, herkeneth to me:
I smell a *loller* in the wind, quod he.
This loller here wol prechen us somwhat.
Nay by my fathers soule, that shal he not,
Sayde the Shipman, here shale he not preche,
He wolde sowen som difficultee,
Or springen *cockle* in our clene corne."

But the Loller did preach to them, and his sermon finishes the Canterbury Tales. And Knighton speaking of Lollard preachers, says: "ubique in ecclesiis regni prædicans *lollium* cum tritico seminavit" — preaching everywhere in the churches of the kingdom, he sowed wild cockle (*lollium*) with the wheat. — *De Eventibus*, 2659 line 12.

Speed says: "His (Wickliffe's) followers were, in the phrase of

Walsingham, another of Wickliffe's enemies, notices this fact — that many of the nobility favored and supported the Reformer and his erroneous doctrines.* And in the convocation of the prelates and clergy of Canterbury, in 1413, complaint was made, that it would be impossible to repair the rent in the Lord's tunic — or, in other words, to suppress Lollardism — unless, first, certain *magnates* of the kingdom, who were leaders, favorers, defenders and harborers of these heretics called Lollards, were resolutely apprehended.†

In the University of Oxford, the Chancellor, Dr. Rigge; Thomas Brightwell, professor of theology; Doctors and Bachelors of Divinity, Repyngdon, Hereford and Ashton, and several Masters and graduates, were among the denounced or suspected Lollards of their day.‡ Among the

---

those dark daies, called *Lollards* (*lollium* signifieth cockle and such weeds), whereas, in truth, they endeavoured to extirpate all pernicious weeds, which thro time, slouthe and fraude, had crept into the field of God's church." — *Walsingham,* p. 588, folio ed.

* "Quod domini et magnates terræ multique de populo ipsos (Wiclefitas) in suis prædicationibus confoverunt, et faverunt prædicantibus hos errores." — *Hist. Angl.*, pp. 191, 540.

† *Wilkins' Concilia Magnæ Britanniæ et Hiberniæ,* vol. III., pp. 352–53, folio, London, 1738.

‡ See Arch. Courtney's *Mandatum contra Hereticos,* A.D. 1382, in *Wilkins' Concilia,* vol. III., pp. 158–165; and "Mandatum ad Denunciand. Magistros Hereford et Ryppyndon, excommunicatos" — *ib.* 165, 166; "Mand. cancellor. Univ.," — *ib.* 166; and the King's (Rich. II.) *Breve* to the Chancellor of Oxf., against suspected persons — *ib.* 166. Also, *Walsingham,* 285, 286.

Most of the important official documents relating to the persecution of Wickliffe and his followers may be found in Fox's *Acts and Monuments,* books V. and VI., of the folio edition of 1684. The

Magnates of the kingdom, who at different times favored Wickliffe and his followers, were the Duke of Lancaster, uncle to Richard II.; Lord Percy, lord marshal of England; Earl of Salisbury, one of Richard's favorites; Lord Cobham, a brave and trusted soldier; Sir Richard Story; Sir Lewis Clifford, the messenger who stopped the proceedings of the clergy against Wickliffe, mentioned *ante* p. 254; Sir Thomas Latimer; and Sir John Montacute, who ordered all the images removed from his church in Shenly, Buckinghampshire.* Some of these men suffered for their attachment to Lollardy, and one perished a martyr for the truth. With such examples before them in the chancellor, professors, doctors of divinity, and masters of the university, we need not wonder that many of the younger members of the university became "tainted with damnable Lollardy." Accordingly, we find Archbishop Arundel, in 1409, addressing a *Mandatum* to the University of Oxford, in which he complains of certain unworthy graduates of the university, who, according to his account, had not even mastered the simplest rudiments of learning, scarcely having yet got clear of the swaddling clothes of youth, but yet, swollen

originals of these documents, in Latin and French chiefly, are to be found in Wilkins' Concilia. A fine copy of this scarce and valuable book may be found in the library of Harvard University. The laws against the Lollards may be seen in the Rolls of Parliament, and Statutes of the Realm, and Statutes at Large.

* See Bishop Kennet's *Hist. Eng.*, vol. I., p. 287; *Walsingham*, 328, 548.

with ambition, were not afraid to hold and defend, as well as publicly to assert, certain damnable conclusions, collected from Wickliffe's writings.*

And three years later (in 1412) the same Archbishop, in a letter to Pope John XXIII., mourns over the prevalence of the pestiferous doctrines of that most miserable, pestilent fellow, of damnable memory, that son of the old serpent, yea more, that predecessor and alumnus of Antichrist himself — John Wickliffe. And most especially does he mourn, with bitterness of heart, that in that most beautiful garden of the glorious university of Oxford, which but lately was wont to produce sons conspicuous among all the faithful for their learning and doctrine, growing up like olive plants around the table of the Lord — now were suffered to grow plants poisonous and infectious, whose seeds being allowed to mature, were scattered by the winds of presumption and pride over the pleasant fields of the English realm. And he adds, that on account of the growth of these hurtful plants, there remained in this garden of Oxford university scarcely any plants of truth worth gathering.†

---

* *Wilkins' Concilia,* vol. III., p. 322. *Walsingham,* 285.

† *Wilkins' Concilia,* vol. III., pp. 350, 351. I have aimed to give the spirit, rather than the exact phraseology of the Archbishop's bitter letter. That I have not intensified this bitterness, will be evident to the classical reader, from the following sentence in the original Latin, which follows the complaints of the prelate about the deplorable condition of the university: —

The interest of the common people in Wickliffe's doctrines is sufficiently apparent from what Knighton and other ancient chroniclers say of the number of Lollards in the kingdom; * and from the fact that a petition was prepared by them, to be presented to Parliament in 1394–5, praying for a reformation in the church, based on Wickliffism; which, though it came to nothing, yet proved that the number of Lollards must have been very large at that date, and their strength in the nation very considerable; for otherwise, they would not have ventured thus before the government.† The prevalence and power of Lollardism yet further appears, from the complaint of Walsingham, about this time, (1394) that, though the followers of Wickliffe had reached such a pitch of temerity, that their preachers, after the manner of the pon-

---

"Hic enim ille pestilens et damnandæ memoriæ misserimus Johannes Wycliff, serpentis antiqui filius, imo et ipsius antichristi prævius et alumnus, qui dum vixerat in vanitate, sensuo ambulans, nesciens in semitis justitiæ dirigere gressus suos, non solum canones sacros, et monita paterna despicere, sed piæ matris uterum, quantum in ipso fuerat, viperinis elegit conatibus laniare."

* See *Ante* pp. 314, 315.

† *Wilkins' Concilia*, vol. III., p. 221. *Fox*, (I., 578), gives this petition in English; and says it was presented to parliament in 1395. It was entitled: — "The Book of Conclusions of Reformation." At the same time satirical papers, we are told, were posted up in London, by the Lollards. *Bale* says that "Sir John Oldcastle put into the parliament house certain books concerning their [the clergy's] just reformation, both in the year of our Lord 1395, and in the year 1410." One of these was doubtless "The book of Conclusions," etc., above mentioned. — *Brefe Chronycle*, etc., p. 11. Pref. Parker Soc. Pubs.

tiffs, created new presbyters, asserting that any priest had as much power to confer ecclesiastical sacraments as the pope himself; and that notwithstanding the prelates of the kingdom heard and knew all this, one went to his farm and another to his merchandise, and only the bishop of Norwich dared to be a good man in evil times; — that is, dared to persecute the followers of the Gospel Doctor, when all his brother prelates feared to do this.*

In one of the older histories of England, we read: — "The followers of Wickliffe were not insensible how happy a juncture it was [about A.D. 1389] for them to promote their doctrines, while their enemies were employed; and accordingly had so bestirred themselves, that they were become a formed church, and in many parts of the nation had regular congregations, with pastors, well qualified, and chosen to administer sacraments and preach to the people. The bishop of Salisbury, John Waltham, had gotten a very particular account of all their party, and their present condition, by one that had been of their society; and though he acquainted his brethren with the great increase of them, yet, neither himself nor any of the bishops raised any persecution against them. The bishop of Norwich, Henry Spencer, threatened them loudly, that if they were found in his diocese he would make them, as he termed

* *Ypodigma Neustriæ*, 544, and *Hist. Angl.*, 339–340. Franc. ed. 1603.

it, "*hop headless, or fry a faggot.*" And 'tis very probable that he, being a rough and warlike prelate, would have made good his words; but they had wit enough to keep out of his way."*

These things, and indeed the whole current of history from the time of Wickliffe's first public appearance as a church reformer, go to show that the common people heard him and his poor priests most gladly.† The subsequent pages of this history will illustrate very fully this fact — that multitudes, in all parts of the kingdom, received with joy the doctrines of the Great Reformer;

* *Kennet's Hist. Eng.*, vol. I., p. 265, folio ed. *Wals.*, 340, l. 17.

† *Knighton* acknowledges the learning, eloquence, and power in disputation of Wickliffe and some of his poor priests; though he is disposed to regard them as bearing a stronger resemblance to fighting Mahommedans than to good Christians. — *De Eventibus*, col. 2554–65. He calls Wickliffe, *Doctor in Theologia eminentissimus in diebus illis* — the most eminent doctor in theology of those days; and says that in philosophy he was reputed second to no one; in scholastic learning incomparable. — *Ib.* 2644. And he describes one of Wickliffe's preachers, John Ashton, as accustomed to travel about everywhere in the kingdom, on foot, staff in hand, having no hindrance to his journies arising from the preparation of his horse etc., but like a dog leaping up from his bed ready on the slightest noise to bark, so this poor priest was ever ready for his work. — 2658, l. 62. In another place he says, at the introduction of this nefarious sect, the principal *pseudo Lollardi* were accustomed to go about in russet garments, for the most part; in order, as he says, to deceive the people with the idea that their hearts were as simple as their dresses. But he does not hesitate to call them wolves in sheep's clothing. — 2663, l. 40. And in another place, alluding to their seductive power in making disciples among the people, he says, these preachers carried the sweetness of honey in their head of eloquence, in their tail, poison. — 2664, l. 32. *Wals.*, 192, l. 2.

and that even many priests embraced the new doctrine, and for it suffered, and some even dared to die; though many, alas, in time of trial, fell away and denied the faith.

This state of things, neither the pope, nor his prelates in England could be expected to submit to willingly. We have seen, that during the lifetime of Wickliffe they showed their will to quench the dangerous flame of truth which he was spreading through the kingdom. But the bulls of popes and the mandates of bishops alone, are of little avail against the truth among a people who have the Bible in their hands. These edicts must be backed by the strong arm of the State, to make them effectual. During the long reign of the gallant Edward III., the hierarchy could not get hold of the secular arm; and the Lollards laughed at the harmless thunders of the pope and his prelates. And during Richard's reign there was little hearty coöperation of the crown with the crosier in persecuting the Lollards. Besides the surreptitious law of 1382, entitled, "An Act against preachers of Heresy," which will be noticed more fully in another place, we find occasionally a *breve*, or letter, from the king against the Lollards; and we read of his reprimanding some of his nobility, on his return from Ireland in 1394, for their attachment to the new learning.* Something he could not

* The *King's Breve* (Rich. II., 6, A.D. 1382), to Chancellor of Oxford, against suspected persons, especially those embracing the

well avoid doing for the clergy, after having been sent for by them, in hot haste, to return home to save the Church of England from utter destruction by the Lollards.* But Fox tells us that, "following his father's steps," Richard "was no great disfavorer of the way and doctrine of Wickliffe;" and that during his reign none were put to death for religion's sake; "whereby it appears of this king, that, although he cannot utterly be excused for molesting the godly and innocent preachers of that time, (as by his briefs and letters aforementioned may appear,) yet, neither was he so cruel against them as other that came after him; and that which he did, seemed to proceed by the instigation of the pope and other bishops, rather than either by the consent of his parliament, or advice of his council about him, or else by his own nature."†

---

errors of Wickliffe, Hereford, Repyngdon, and Jno. Ashton.—*Wilk. Conc.*, vol. III., p. 166; *Fox*, I., 504–5. *Mandatum Regium*, (Rich. II. 11, A.D. 1387)—*Wilk.* III., 204. Also the letter of Rich. II. in answer to Archbishop Courtney's, July 12, 1382, granting power to the clergy to arrest and imprison heretics.—*Wilk.* III., 156.

* *Fox*, vol. I., p. 578, says, that shortly after the good queen Anne's death, Richard being in Ireland, two bishops, either on their own account, or as messengers of the archbishop of Canterbury, went over, "to desire the king, in all speed-wise, to return and help the faith and church of Christ against such, as holding of Wickliffe's teaching, went about (as they said) to subvert all their proceedings, and to destroy the canonical sanctions of their holy mother church." See also *Collier, Ecc. Hist.*, III., 213; *Wals.*, 351, 547.

† *Acts and Monuments*, vol. I., pp. 490, 577, bk. V., A.D. 1376–82 and 1394–95.

So great, in fact, was Richard's unwillingness to persecute the Lollards, so much sympathy had he with their reformatory labors, or so little with the persecuting spirit of the English church, that, in the opinion of a master of English history, the Papal Church in England would have been shaken, and the Reformation hastened a hundred years, had not Richard II. been deposed.*

The clergy of Richard's day seem to have appreciated their danger, to some extent at least. They perceived that they had no hearty support from government in their attempts to suppress Lollardism. And to save their hierarchy, they finally sacrificed their king. They sympathized with the rebellion which dethroned and murdered Richard II., and enthroned Henry IV. as king of England. Indeed, "they were the *first* that led this dance of disloyalty."†

Archbishop Arundel, then in banishment on the charge of high treason, took an active and leading part in stirring up the Duke of Lancaster to head the rebellion against Richard, assuring the Duke of the readiness of the English nation to second his efforts. The archbishop attended Lancaster on his return to England, and contributed all his influence and aid to promote the success of the rebellion. And after Richard's forced abdication, Arundel and his clergy were prompt to welcome

---

* *Turner's Hist. Middle Ages*, vol. III., p. 117, note.

† *Fuller's Chh. Hist.*, p. 153, folio ed. Also, *Walsing.*, 554, 555.

Henry IV. to the throne of England.* And that Henry was not unmindful of his obligations to the clergy, his subsequent subserviency to their wishes quite clearly proves.

Henry V. and VI. were in sympathy with the founder of the Lancasterian dynasty, and emulated the persecuting spirit of the fourth Henry.† During the reign of the house of York, including the reign of Edward IV., and the brief reigns of Edward V.

* See Arundel's letter to the Duke, in *Collier*, III., 232, 233, which Collier denominates a "treasonable harangue."

Cobbett's Parliamentary History informs us that to the Duke of Lancaster, then in banishment in France, "the discontented nobility and gentry of England applied themselves, as the only man that by his birth, power, and popularity, could redress their grievances. The duke received their addresses at first very slightly; but *being settled at last in his resolutions by Thomas Arundel, archbishop of Canterbury*, who came to him in disguise for that purpose, he determined to try his fortune in England on the first opportunity."—Vol. I., 241. See also the archbishop's coronation discourse, in *Collier* III., 238–240.

† *Turner's Middle Ages*, vol. III., pp. 4 and 5, compd. with p. 96. Turner says: "The house of Lancaster, having been greatly indebted to the clergy for its revolutionary elevation to the throne, had, under Henry IV., the founder of its royal dynasty, and still more under Henry V., distinguished itself for its severe hostility to that reforming spirit, which, from the reign of Edward I., had been annoying and menacing the ecclesiastical establishments." See also *Fuller*, p. 155; and *Fox*, I., 593, 595. *Collier*, III., 447–48, says: "It is observed that there were few prosecutions [against the Lollards] in Henry VII.'s reign, and those that were went seldom any further than penance and carrying faggots." Henry VI. the same historian represents as "a prince of very gentle, religious disposition, and rather formed for a cloister than the government."—*Ecc. Hist.* III., 396. We shall see how nearly these representations agree with truth. Bale says: Henry VI. was "a childish thing all the days of his life."—*Brief Chronicle*, preface.

and Richard III., or from about 1461 to 1485, the civil wars, if not the dispositions of the reigning sovereigns, prevented the severe persecution of the Lollards. But when the Tudors ascended the English throne, in 1485, the Papists had again a willing civil arm at their disposal. "To the Lollards," says Fuller, "(so were God's people nicknamed,) Henry VII. was more cruel than his predecessors." Thus the founder of the Tudor line imitated the founder of the Lancasterian dynasty; and for about a hundred and fifty years, or till the Reformation in the days of Henry VIII., the people of God in England, were liable to the curse of the church, to fines, imprisonment, hanging, and burning, for believing the Bible and endeavoring to conform their faith and practice to its infallible teachings.*

---

* The curse of the church in those days was as comprehensive and complete an expression of ill-will towards the subject of it, as can well be conceived of. It was distilled hate — yea, the very oil of hate — poured out on the devoted head of a "heretic," with all the formalities adapted to impress the superstitious — with bell, book, and candles; the latter being thrown upon the ground at the close of the ceremony, and trampled out, to signify the utter destruction of the person cursed by the church. This curse extended to all the heretic did, and all that he was. He was cursed in body and soul, for time and eternity.

The following was the curse in full: "Let them be accursed eating and drinking, walking and sitting, speaking and holding their peace, waking and sleeping, rowing and riding, laughing and weeping, in house and in field, on water and on land, in all places. Cursed be their head and their thoughts, their eyes and their ears, their tongues and their lips, their teeth and their throat, their shoulders and their breasts, their feet and their legs, their thighs and their inwards. Let them remain accursed from the bottom of the foot to

Having taken this general survey of Lollardism, —its progress and its persecution—it may be satisfactory now to examine the matter a little more in detail, and see what were some of the chief instruments of persecution devised, how these were used, and who, and how many were sufferers among the Lollards.

All this, it is obvious, can be done but very superficially; for the laws, and bulls, and mandates, sent forth by kings, and popes, and bishops, against the Lollards, would alone fill a good-sized volume. Little else, therefore, must be expected than an enumeration of most of these and a description of the principal of these cruel edicts of persecution, prepared by ecclesiastical hands, and made effectual by the strong arm of the State. And so, likewise, must we deal with the stories told in ancient records of the sufferers under these cruel and unrighteous laws and mandates. We can only notice most of them very briefly, while we enlarge on a few prominent cases.

But even this kind of notice of what our ancestors suffered in defence of the truth, cannot but be instructive to all who recognize in these sufferers their own ecclesiastical precursors — the men who took the first step towards the introduction of Protestantism and Independency into England, even at

---

the crown of the head, unless they bethink themselves and come to satisfaction. And just as this candle is deprived of its present light, so let them be deprived of their souls in hell." — *Wanly's Catalogue*, in Henry, vol. VIII., p. 37.

the cost of their property, their liberty, and their lives.

The first instruments used by the church against Wickliffism were the censures of the ordinary ecclesiastical courts of the kingdom, the special mandates of the prelates, the briefs of the kings, and finally the bulls of the popes. Several of these were tried during the lifetime of the Great Reformer, and have been alluded to on preceding pages of this volume.

The earliest of these documents are "Letters Apostolical," from Pope Gregory XI., bearing date the sixth of Gregory's reign, and the fifty-first of the reign of Edward III., A.D., 1377. They are three in number. One is addressed to the Archbishop of Canterbury and the Bishop of London, directing them to proceed against John Wickliffe for his pernicious heresies, etc. Another is addressed to the king and his nobles, to incite them against Wickliffe; and the third cites the bold reformer to appear before his holiness, at Rome, to answer for his errors and heresies.* These edicts were all sent forth in the last year of Edward's reign, when the king was old and broken, and just ready to pass away. He died June 12, 1377.

The next year, June, 1378, the first of the reign of the youthful Richard II., Gregory addressed a letter to the University of Oxford, "rebuking them sharply, imperiously, and like a pope," as Fox

---

* See *ante*, p. 251 *et seq*; *Wilkins' Concilia*, III., 116–18.

says, "for suffering so long the doctrine of John Wickliffe to take root, and not plucking it up with the crooked sickle of their Catholic doctrine." In this bull the pope tells the governors of the university: "We are compelled not only to marvel, but also to lament, that you, by your great negligence and sloth, will suffer wild cockle, not only to grow up among the pure wheat of the flourishing field of your university, but to wax strong and choke the corn." And he commands the chancellor, and the faithful in the university, to extirpate and pluck the filthy weed up by the roots. And especially to apprehend and detain in safe custody, one John Wickliffe, who had sown this wild cockle, "vomiting out of the filthy dungeons of his breast diverse professions, false and erroneous conclusions, and most wicked and damnable heresies."* Letters of like import were addressed by the pope to the king and to the bishops of England.

The year 1382 was one of uncommon activity among the rulers of the hierarchy. It was the first year of Archbishop Courtney's reign, and the sixth of Richard II. The briefs, mandates, and judgments against Wickliffe and his disciples followed each other in quick succession. It was about this time that Wickliffe came out impugning the popish doctrine of transubstantiation, and denying that the sacramental emblems, after consecration, became the actual body and blood of

* *Fox*, vol. I., p. 491.

Christ. It was about this time, too, that the Duke of Lancaster, John of Gaunt, the king's uncle, and one of the most influential noblemen in England, for some unexplained reason, forsook the Reformer and left him unshielded from the attacks of his enemies. To these things must be added, perhaps, a measure of odium, unjustly attached to Wickliffe and his followers, by reason of the peasants' insurrection in 1380. All these things emboldened the hierarchy to commence in earnest the work of persecution.*

Among the instruments employed by the prelates at this time was, first, the king's *Breve*, addressed to the chancellor of Oxford, against suspected persons in the university; especially such as embraced the errors of Wickliffe, Hereford, Repyngdon, and Ashton.† The same year mandates were issued by Archbishop Courtney against heretics, or the Lollards — for no other heretics make any figure during this period — and against Hereford and Repyngdon, *excommunicatos*. By these commands the chancellor of the university was compelled to issue his mandate also against the excommunicates; and following these denunciatory documents came the judgment of the uni-

* Knighton gives substantially the same account of the Jack Straw insurrection, as Fuller does, (see *ante*, p. 262,) attributing it to the irritation of the common people in consequence of the heavy taxes laid on them; and especially the cruel and indecent methods adopted by the tax-gatherers to collect some of their dues. — *De Eventibus*, columns 2633–2644, inclusive.

† *Wilkins' Concilia*, III., 166; *Knighton*, colls. 2708–2710

versity, in answer to the order of the convocation of Canterbury, against the books of John Wickliffe. According to this judgment, numerous errors and heresies had been discovered by the learned doctors to whose examination the Reformer's writings had been submitted. These heresies and errors were proclaimed and condemned with all due solemnity, and their author and their favorers were suitably denounced.

Knighton furnishes a list of *nine* of Wickliffe's heresies, and *fifteen* of his errors, discovered and condemned, as he tells us, by the archbishop, the bishops, and the chancellor of the university, and many doctors and other clergy, assembled at Oxford for this purpose. After the publishing, and denouncing, and damning of these heresies and errors, and declaring that all who defended them were excommunicate, he tells us that, "in evidence of this," (i. e. in order to make a deeper impression on the public mind,) a procession was made through the city of London, and all the clergy, and many of the laity of different ranks, walked with naked feet *pro statu.* And after the procession, one of the Carmelite brothers preached, and in his discourse pointed out the heresies and errors condemned; and pronounced by the archbishop's authority, all those excommunicate who taught, or held, or preached these doctrines, and all who favored, or adhered to those who preached, or held them, and all who heard these teachings.*

* *De Eventibus,* 2648–2651.

We next have the sentence of the chancellor of Oxford against Wickliffe himself, residing then in the cathedral church of Oxford.

But all these ecclesiastical fulminations would have had little effect, had not the civil arm been secured about this time to aid the church. It was in July of this same year, 1382, that the clergy found means to smuggle through parliament the first law which made the secular arm of the English government subservient to the will of the priesthood in persecuting "heretics," so called.

This act sets forth, that forasmuch as it was well known that "there were divers evil persons within the realm, going from county to county, and from town to town, in certain habits, under dissimulation of great holiness, and without the license of the ordinaries of the places, or other sufficient authority, preaching daily, not only in the churches and churchyards, but also in markets, fairs, and other open places, where a great congregation might be found, divers sermons containing heresies and notorious errors," etc. etc., — therefore, "it is ordained and asserted in this present parliament, that the king's commission be made and directed to the sheriffs and other ministers of our sovereign lord the king, or other persons sufficiently learned, and according to the certificates of the prelates, to be made in chancery from time to time, to arrest all such preachers, and also their favorers, maintainers, and abettors, and to hold them in arrest and strong prison till they justify themselves according to the law and the reason of holy church,"* etc., etc.

This was a most important Act for the persecuting prelates. It gave them the use of the State machinery for arresting and punishing criminals, to stop the labors of the "poor priests," who were indefatigable in their self-denying labors, traversing the entire kingdom, staff in hand, preaching the Word, in season, out of season, in churches, when they could, in churchyards when shut out from the churches, in the market places, in short, wherever they could find people to hear the truth; and thus, "with their depraved doctrine," according to Walsingham, "infecting almost the whole kingdom."†

It was, therefore, a great point gained, to be allowed to use the sheriffs and other ministers of criminal justice, and the common prisons of the land, in stopping these dangerous innovators. Being allowed to arrest these preachers of the gospel, as criminals would be arrested, was, for popular effect, the next thing to having them proved criminals.

The Commons, at a subsequent parliament, declared this act *invalid*, because issued without their consent; but the clergy had sufficient influence to prevent its repeal, or, at least, to prevent the repeal from being published; and it long re-

* *Fox*, vol. I., p. 502; *Wilkins' Concilia*, III., 156; *The Statutes at Large*, and *The Statutes of the Realm*, 5 Richard II.

† See what Knighton says, *ante*, pp. 313–314, and 321, note.

mained a blot on the statute book of England.* That the clergy were fully alive to the value of this persecuting act, is apparent from their doings in November of the same year. For Walsingham tells us, that in the parliament held in London, about the time of the feast of St. Michael, 1382, a *tenth* was conceded by the clergy for the king's use, and a *fifteenth* by the laity; "with the understanding on the part of the clergy, that the king shall faithfully exert himself in defence of the

* Fox shows quite satisfactorily the surreptitious character of this pretended act of Parliament. The Commons never gave their consent to this act, and protested against the same. — *Acts and Monuments*, I., 502. *The Parliamentary, or Constitutional History of England*, in describing the doings of the Parliament of 6 Richard II., says of this statute, that it "had been *surreptitiously obtained by the clergy*, and had the formality of an enrolment without the consent of the Commons. In this Parliament, therefore, [6 Rich. II., A.D. 1383,] that body justly complained, and humbly petitioned the king, that, 'forasmuch as that statute was made without their consent, and never authorized by them; as it never was their meaning to bind themselves, or their successors, to the prelates, no more than their ancestors had done before them,' they prayed the aforesaid statute might be repealed, and it was done accordingly. But by the artifice of the bishops even this Act of Repeal was suppressed, and prosecutions carried on by virtue of the former; which is the reason that the other [the Repeal] is not to be found in the statute books. This is a piece of ecclesiastical collusion too glaring to be overlooked by any except the prelatical writers of this and the last age." — Vol. I., pp. 397, 398. Lond. 8vo., 1762. *Viner*, in his abridgement, calls this statute "the *supposed* statute of 6 R. II." — Vol. XIV., p 293. *Prynne*, in his commentary on Coke's Institutes, calls this "the *pretended* statute," p. 395, — the "*forged* statute," 396. Bishop *Gibson*, however, argues against the current opinion, that this statute was surreptitiously obtained. — *Codex*, vol. I., p. 327.

church, and stand forth with aid to suppress the heretical Wickliffites, who already, with their depraved doctrine, had infected almost the entire kingdom." *

Altogether, the year 1382 was a memorable year in the history of the Lollards. After 1382 there appears to have been a lull in the storm against the reformers, for a few years. The bishops, no doubt, used the authority of the king when and where they could; but, for some reason, there is but little on record illustrative of the spirit of the church towards the Lollards, during some five or six years. Perhaps the abandonment of their cause by some of the nobility, the vigorous movements of Archbishop Courtney, the threatening and harrassing act already commented on, the banishment from Oxford of their leader, and his sudden death in 1384, may have combined to make the Lollards more cautious in their movements, if not to discourage them somewhat; and therefore it may be that we hear so little of them from about 1383 to 1387. And, on the other side, the clergy may have become satisfied that they could not — despite their contributions, *condition-*

---

* *Walsingham, Ypodigma Neustriæ,* p. 535, lines 45–49. His words are: "In parliamento, facta Londoniis circa festum sancti Michaelis (1382), concessa fuit Regi per Clerum una decima, et a laicis quinta decima; conditionaliter tamen ex parte Cleri, ut videlicet Rex manus apponat defensioni Ecclesiæ, et præstet auxilium ad compressionem hæreticorum Wicklivensium, qui jam sua prava doctrina peene infecerant totum regnum."

aliter — rely on the hearty support or concurrence of the king, in any persecution of the church reformers; and even had the king concurred with the clergy, the unpopularity of the persecuting act of 1382 was so great, that it could not have been easy to enforce it, particularly after the remonstrance of the Commons; and it might have been deemed inexpedient to attempt a general enforcement of the law, even had it been possible. For some reason, certainly, the Lollards are but little noticed in history for about five years.

But in 1387 a new impulse was given to the clerical work of denouncing and persecuting the friends of the gospel. The first document which meets our eyes, among the official papers of the times, is the mandate of the Bishop of Worcester. On the 10th of August, 1387, the eleventh year of Richard II., this prelate issued a mandate against the preaching of the Lollards in his diocese. In this document — so characteristic of the spirit in which the believers were persecuted at that time — the bishop complains of the frequent clamor of "the eternally damned sons of antichrist," whom he designates as the disciples and followers of Mahomet, and accuses of "conspiring together, under the instigation of the Devil, in illicit fellowship, with reprobate oaths, under the name or religious usage of Lollards." He mentions particularly masters Nic. Hereford, John Ashton, *duo*, John Perney, John Parker, and Rob. Swinderley, as persons who, "led by insanity, and utterly unmindful of their own safety, under the veil of great sanctity, were pouring poison from their lips with a honeyed mouth, and were sowing cockle instead of corn in the Lord's field," etc., etc. "These diabolical sons of antichrist" are forbidden to preach in any church, churchyard, or consecrated place in the bishop's diocése; and all people are prohibited from going to hear them.*

From the bishop's violent and profane language we are compelled to infer, "that these reformers were men of virtuous lives, and mild manners, as well as of intelligent minds;" † all which it was very far from his lordship's intention to have inferred.

Another weapon formed against the church in 1387 was the king's mandate — *Mandatum Regium* — against "heretical books," especially those of Wickliffe and Hereford. ‡ In 1389 we find Archbishop Courtney's *Processus contra Lollardos*, by which sundry good men in Leicester were arraigned, and condemned, and excommunicated, for their attachment to the gospel. And on the

---

* *Wilkins' Concilia*, III., pp. 202, 203: — "Frequente clamore, ad æternum damnati filii antichristi discipulis et Machumetæ sequaces instigatione diabolica conspirati in collegio illicito, et a jure reprobato, nome sue ritu Lollardorum confæderati, magistri Nic Hereford, Joh. Ashton, duo, Joh. Perney, Joh. Parker, Rob. Swinderley, insania mentis perducti, ae suæ salutes immemores, sub magnæ sanctitatis velamine venenum sub labiis in ore mellifluo habentes, zizanian pro frumento in agro dominico seminantes," *et cet.*

† *Turner's Hist. Eng.*, V., 198.

‡ *Wilkins*, III., 204.

7th of November of the same year, we have from the same source, "Mandatum ad denunciandos Lollardos excommunicatos;" and immediately afterwards, a mandate for arresting these denounced and excommunicated Lollards.*

But, in spite of all these mandates and processes, the hated saints continued to live and grow; and about 1394 Pope Boniface IX. thought it necessary to address his "sweet son," Richard, and his "reverend brethren, Canterbury and York, archbishops," and exhort them to "stand up against this pestilent sect; and that they lively persecute the same in form of law; root out and destroy those that advisedly and obstinately refuse to withdraw their foot from the same stumbling-block, any restraint to the contrary, notwithstanding." And the persons to be dealt with, are described by the pope, as "a certain crafty and hair-brain sect of false Christians, whom the common people call *Lollards*, (as a man would say, *withered darnel*,) according as their sins require, and whom we cannot call men, but the damnable shadows or ghosts of men." †

Between the years 1394 and 1396 we notice occasional documents which indicate the tone of feeling in the churchmen towards the Lollards, such as, "Conclusiones Lollardum in quodam Libello"; "Juramentum Lollardes impositum"; and especially "De Conclusionibus (18 in numero)

---

* *Wilkins*, III., 208 and 210.

† *Fox*, vol. I., p. 574.

damnatæ memoriæ Johannis Wycliff." These conclusions of John Wickliffe, of damnable memory, were condemned in the convocation of the prelates and clergy of Canterbury, in St. Paul's cathedral, in 1396, in the twentieth year of Richard II., and the first year of the administration of that noted persecutor of the Christians, Thomas Arundel.*

The history of the years now reviewed, shows that all the mandates of popes, kings, and prelates accomplished very little, if anything, towards the suppression of Lollardism. In fact, "the Gospellers" rather gained ground than lost it between 1384, when Wickliffe died, and 1399, when Richard was dethroned. It was, doubtless, a knowledge of this fact, coupled with a full conviction that merely ecclesiastical punishments would never check the growing freedom of the people in regard to religious matters, which induced the papal clergy of England, about this time, to sacrifice their hereditary faith in the divine right of kings, and become traitors to their sovereign, Richard II. Mainly to preserve their hierarchy from that dreaded reformation which was impending over them, the clergy of England contributed to the dethronement of their lawful sovereign, and the enthronement of an usurper, who, in addition to his crimes in persecuting the church of God, inaugurated those civil wars between the houses of Lancaster and York — the red and the white

* *Wilkins*, III., 221, *et seq.*

roses — which kept England in commotion during the greater part of the fifteenth century, or until the accession of Henry VII., in 1485; who, by intermarriage with a daughter and the heiress of the house of York, blended the roses, united the rival houses, and stopped the fratricidal wars of England.

Richard II. gets but a small meed of praise from historians; and perhaps he does not deserve much. Yet there is something to be said in palliation of his short-comings and many of his overt acts. Richard, when a child, had the misfortune to lose his father, the accomplished and celebrated Black Prince. He was brought to the throne when a mere boy, eleven years old. Of uncommon personal beauty, for which he was admired and flattered; crowned as a king, yet treated as a child; his education neglected, and he left by his natural guardians to choose his own associates: — it is not strange that he was betrayed into sundry acts of indiscretion, if not of actual tyranny and oppression, which finally provoked a rebellion among his powerful nobles, which, by the aid of the clergy, was made successful. To save the kingdom from a civil war, Richard consented to resign his crown, on condition that an honorable provision should be made for him, and protection afforded to certain friends.

This resignation was readily accepted on the conditions proposed; though, as events showed, without any intention, on the part of Henry, of complying with the conditions. The unhappy monarch was confined, first in the Tower; then removed to Pomfret castle. There he remained but a short time before his miserable life was ended, probably by starvation, and the usurper was relieved of the presence of the legitimate sovereign.*

Henry the IV., though the son of John of Gaunt, who was the early friend and efficient protector of Wickliffe, proved himself not ungrateful to his clerical supporters, by becoming a ready instrument in their hands to persecute unto death the disciples of the Great Reformer.† The king had

* For the particulars briefly alluded to in the text, see *Howell's State Trials*, vol. I., pp. 135–162; *Parl. or Const. Hist. Eng.*, vol. I., p. 522; vol. II., 1–50. *Tyrell* says: "This prince never showed himself more worthy to govern, than when he was deposed as unworthy of it." — In *Parl. or Const. Hist. Eng.*, I., 528. — *Stow* says, Richard was kept *fifteen days* together, in hunger, thirst, and cold till he died. And *Polydore Virgil* says, he was not suffered to touch or taste the victuals which lay before him. — See *Howell*, vol. I., p. 162.

† Fox thus speaks of Henry IV.: — "The king, after the shedding of so much blood [in getting possession of the kingdom], seeing himself so hardly beloved of his subjects, thought to keep in yet with the clergy, and with the bishop of Rome, seeking always his chiefest stay at their hands. And therefore he was compelled in all things to serve their humor." — *Acts and Monuments*, vol. I., bk. V., p. 593, compd. with p. 595. See also *Parl.* or *Const. Hist. Eng.*, vol. II., 59, 60.

At the coronation of Henry IV. Archbishop Arundel made an oration, or sermon, laudatory of the new king, on this text of Scripture: "A man shall reign over the people;" from whence he took occasion to describe the happiness of that kingdom which was governed by *a man*, and the infelicity of that which was governed by *a*

hardly got seated on his usurped throne, before the clergy approached him with a petition of the most inflammable character against the Lollards. With words of flattery from honeyed lips — "Excellentissimo ac gratiosissimo principi domino nostro regi!" — they first praise him and his most noble progenitors for their princely care of the Church of England, and then proceed to say, that notwithstanding all this care, divers perfidious and perverse persons, belonging to a certain new sect, entertaining damnable sentiments respecting the sacraments of the church and her authority, and rashly usurping the office of preachers, contrary to the divine and the ecclesiastical law, had perversely and maliciously preached and taught in divers places, publicly and secretly, under cover of feigned sanctity, divers new doctrines and iniquitous opinions, heretical and erroneous, contrary to the sound determinations of holy church; and held unlawful conventicles and confederacies (*confœderationes*) for the propagation of their nefarious doctrines and opinions; and supported schools, and made and wrote books, and craftily instructed and informed the people, and excited them to sedition and insurrection as much as they could, and made great dissensions and divisions among the

---

child, whether in age or discretion; and, whereas they had dangerously felt the evils of the latter, under king Richard, so they hoped abundantly to enjoy the blessings of the former, from king Henry." —*Echart's Hist. Eng.*, vol. I., p. 413. See also *Collier*, vol. III., pp. 238, 239.

people, and daily perpetrated and committed divers other enormities, horrid to be heard, tending to subvert the doctrines of faithful Catholics and of most holy church, to diminish religious culture, and even to destroy the constitution, courts, and liberty of the English Church, etc., etc.

The clergy finally declare their inability to correct or restrain these terrible evils, without the aid of his royal majesty's arm — that is, without authority from the State to fine, imprison, and even burn to death the obstinate believers in the supremacy of the Scriptures; and they therefore beseech him, for the preservation of the Catholic faith, and the sustenance of divine worship, etc., etc., that he would provide a remedy for these horrible evils; and then humbly point out to the king what that remedy should be.*

In answer to this petition of the Archbishop of Canterbury, his brother prelates and their clergy, was given to the English hierarchy the famous *Statute Ex Officio*, the first penal enactment against dissenters from the English Church; the first statute which gave the English prelates the power to burn to death men and women of spotless morals, devout lives, and a faith based entirely on the teachings of God's Word.

This statute denounces fines, imprisonment, or death by burning, against every one within the

---

* *Statutes at Large*, 1 Henry IV.; *Wilkins' Concilia*, vol. III., pp. 252–254; compare pp. 328, 329; *Fox*, I., 596.

realm who shall "presume to preach, privily or openly, without license of his diocesan;" * * or "maintain, teach, hold, or inform, openly or secretly, or make or write any book contrary to the Catholic faith and determination of holy church;" * * * or "hold conventicles or assemblies; or keep or carry on any schools for the promotion of this sect, their wicked doctrine and opinions."

It further provides that no man shall, by any means, favor any such preacher; any promoter of such or similar conventicles, or holder or worker of such schools, or maker or writer of any such books; or any such teacher, informer, or stirrer-up of the people. * * * And enjoins, that all persons having any of the said books, writings, or schedules, containing the said wicked doctrines and opinions, shall, within forty days, deliver up said books and writings to the ordinary of the place in which he resides.

Every person who should violate this statute, or attempt to violate it, in any way, or should even be *suspected* of such violation or attempt, was to be arrested, and imprisoned until he had purged himself from the charge or suspicion, or had denied or recanted; or, if convicted on trial before the bishop or ordinary, or his commissary, then the ordinary, or his commissary, might cause the person so convicted, to be confined in any of the bishop's prisons, and there kept so long as, in his judgment, should be expedient. And further, the said ordinary, or commissary is required to charge the said convicted person with such a fine of money, to be paid unto the king's majesty, as the ordinary should think competent.

This infamous statute yet further provides, that any person convicted of any of the crimes set forth therein, or who should refuse to abjure these crimes, or should relapse after having abjured them, should be taken by the sheriff of the county, or the mayor or bailiff of the city, village, or borough where said crime was committed, and *burnt in sight of all the people;* that thus the victim might strike fear into the hearts of all others.*

Such was the Statute Ex Officio, framed by the prelates of England for the extirpation of what they were pleased to call *heresy;* but what was really a humble attempt of conscientious men to conform their faith and lives to the teachings of God's Word. For this dangerous and revolutionary crime, the property, the liberty, and even the lives of innocent, good men and women, were placed at the absolute disposal of the bishops of England and their commissaries. And this law, which was passed in 1401, remained on the statute book until the 25 Henry VIII., A. D. 1533. And the writ, *De Hæretico Comburendo*, was not taken away until 29 Charles II., A.D. 1677.†

---

* *Rotuli Parliamentorum*, vol. III., pp. 466, 467; *Statutes of the Realm*, or *Statutes at Large;* and *Gibson's Codex*, I., 328, 329.

† *Gibson's Codex*, vol. I., pp. 336, 352 *statutes*. Ch. 14.

Previous to the passage of this statute, "no bishop could convict of heresy as to loss of life, but only as to penance and *pro salute*

With this "new, sharp threshing instrument, having teeth," the prelates thought to thresh the poor Lollards (who were like mountains before them)," and beat them small, and make them as chaff." And much of this they were able to do; for, though the law failed to root up utterly and destroy the Lollards, as the prelates hoped and expected it would do, yet it filled the prisons of England, and brought many good men to untimely ends.*

But even this statute, made to order, and apparently the exact thing to effect the purposes of the clergy, did not long satisfy them. For, in 1406,

---

animæ; but in case of life, the conviction by the common law ought to have been before the archbishop in convocation. — See Pelet's Collection, 72, 73; the writs and process for burning Barth. Legate, and Anne Wightman, *temp.* Jac. I." — *Fitzherbert's New Natura Brevium*, 269 D., 9th ed. 8vo., 1794.

Hargrave says: That by ancient law, burning was the punishment of heresy; but the party accused was first to be tried and convicted by the archbishop and clergy of the province in convocation; then delivered to lay hands. It being inconvenient to summons convocations, the law of 2 Henry IV. gave every diocesan, or bishop, power to try and convict. If a person was convicted in the presence of the sheriff, the sheriff could burn him without the writ *de comburendo*. Otherwise, he must wait for the writ to be issued. — See *State Trials*, vol. VI., pp. 1, 2. appendix. The writ *de heretico comburendo* is thought by some to be as ancient as the common law. By the common law a convicted heretic might be burned, by virtue of the writ issued out of chancery. But he did not forfeit lands, etc., because the proceeding was only *de salute animæ* — for the good of his soul. — *Law Dictionary*, art. heresy; also *Bacon's Digest*, art. heresy; and *Gibson's Codex*, vol. I., pp. 328, 329, ed. 1761.

* *Fuller, Chh. Hist.*, p. 164.

we are told, that "the clergy suborned Henry, Prince of Wales, and Sir John Tibetot, the speaker, to exhibit a long and bloody bill against certain men called Lollards, namely, against those that preached or taught anything against the temporal livings of the clergy." The king is told in this bill, that in case this evil purpose be not resisted," it is very likely that, in process of time, they will also excite the people to take away from the said Lords Temporal, their possessions and heritages." The clergy also artfully confound the Lollards, who opposed the lordly power and dignity of the prelates, with those who published, evilly and falsely, that Richard, late king of England, was alive. Wherefore, they petition his royal majesty, in maintenance of the honor of God, conservation of the laws of holy church, as also in preservation of himself and his children, and the lords aforesaid, and for the quiet of all his kingdom, to ordain by statute, that, in case any man or woman preached, published, or maintained; held, used, or exercised, any schools against the Catholic faith; or wrote any schedule against the temporalities of the prelates, or that Richard, late king, was alive; or wrote any prophecies, to the commotion of the people; that they be taken and put in prison, without bail, except by good and sufficient mainprize before the Chancellor.*

* *Prynne* and *Fuller*, in Parl. or Const. Hist. Eng., vol. II., pp. 101–103. — *Tyler* defends Henry from everything dishonorable in this affair. — *Memoirs of Henry V.*, vol. II., pp. 333–338.

Though this petition does not seem to have met with a favorable response from the king and parliament — both being quite inclined to lay their hands on the superfluous temporalities of the clergy — yet it marks the spirit of the hierarchy towards the dissenting Lollards. This spirit of bitter enmity was, however, more perfectly displayed by the doings of the clergy in convocation, a year or two after the presentation of the above-mentioned bill.*

In the convocation of the prelates and clergy of Canterbury, whose sessions began on January 14th, 1408, it was thought necessary to pass certain "Constitutions against Heretics," in order to give a sharper edge to the law of 1401. In these, all preaching without license after special examination by the Episcopal authority of the diocese, was forbidden; no book of Wickliffe's could be lawfully read by the people, until it had first been examined, by authority of the archbishop, and pronounced safe; it was made a crime even to translate a text of Scripture into English; and furthermore, all disputations about the sacrament of the altar, or other sacraments ordained by the church, were strictly forbidden; as well as all questioning of any decrees, or canons, or usages of the church. In fact, absolute and abject submission to ecclesiastical authority, in all things, and in all places, and under all circumstances, was

* Hallam suspects this petition was intended to favor the Lollards. — *Middle Ages*, part III., chap. 8.

demanded, under severe pains and penalties. The following abstract contains the substance of these abominable constitutions.

They are addressed "to all and singular our reverend brethren fellow-bishops, and our suffragans, to abbots and priors, deans of cathedral churches, archdeacons, provosts and canons, rectors of parish churches, vicars and chaplains, and to all clergymen and laymen within our province of Canterbury." Then, after a long, rambling preface, in which the archbishop indulges in the bitterest denunciation of all who, "trusting to their own wits, are so bold to violate, and with contrary doctrine to resist, and in word and deed to contemn, the precepts of laws and canons, rightly made and proceeding from the Key-Bearer and Porter of Eternal Life and Death, occupying the place (*vicem*), not of simple (*puri*) man, but of True God dwelling here on earth"—the archbishop proceeds to say, that, "willing to shake off the dust from our feet, and to see to the honor of our holy mother church, * * by the advice and assent of all our suffragans and other prelates, for the better fortification of the common law in this part, adding thereunto punishments and penalties condign, as be hereunder written, we will, and command, ordain, and decree," etc., etc. Then follow thirteen articles, or constitutions, to this effect:—

1. No person, secular or regular, shall preach, either within or without the church, in Latin or in English, except licensed, after examination by the

ordinary of the place, and by him assigned to some particular church or churches; not even though said person may have been previously authorized to preach by the laws prescribed, or licensed by special privilege. And any persons convicted of a violation of this constitution, are first to be excommunicated; and if they still persist in such preaching, to be pronounced, reputed, and taken, as heretics and schismatics; and to incur, *ipso facto*, the penalties for these crimes expressed in the law. And all favorers, receivers, and defenders of these preachers, are made liable to like punishments. — 2. A clergyman or inhabitant of any parish, admitting an unauthorized person to preach in the parish church or churchyard, subjects the place so used to an "ecclesiastical interdict." — 3. Preachers are required to touch chiefly the vices of the clergy and the sins of the laity, as they may have occasion to address one or the other of these classes. — 4. Preachers and others are forbidden to teach, preach, or observe anything concerning the sacraments, or any article of faith, otherwise than holy mother church has already found out (*reperitur*), decided, and determined; or preach, teach, or observe, anything contrary to the wholesome doctrine of the church, under the pains and penalties,on a second offence, of excommunication, *ipso facto*.—5. All school-teachers are forbidden, either to mingle anything concerning the Catholic faith, with their secular instructions, or to allow their scholars to expound any text of holy Scriptures (except according to ancient method), or dispute concerning the Catholic faith or sacraments, even privately. — 6. No book written by John Wickliffe, or other person about his time, or since, to be read in schools, halls, hospitals, or other places within the province of Canterbury, unless it has first been examined and authorized by at least twelve persons, appointed by one of the universities and approved by the archbishop. — 7. No man shall, by his own authority, translate any text of Scripture into English, or other language, by way of book, tract, or treatise. Neither shall any one read any such book, tract, or treatise, privately or publicly, under pain of the greater excommunication.—8. All asserting or propounding of doctrines, or propositions, or conclusions, contrary to the Catholic faith, though these doctrines can be defended with never so curious terms and words, are strictly forbidden, under penalty of the greater excommunication. — 9 Forbids all disputes, public or private, on all articles determined by the church: such as decrees, decretals, constitutions, provincial or synodical; and also forbids any one to call in doubt the authority of said decretals or constitutions, or the authority of him who made them; or to teach anything contrary to the determination thereof; "and more especially, concerning the adoration of the glorious cross, images, veneration of saints, pilgrimages to certain places, or to the relics of saints," etc., etc. * * All persons who shall disregard this constitution, shall incur the penalty of heresy. —

10. No chaplain is allowed to celebrate religious rites in any diocese in which he has not either a special appointment or is about to be ordained — *ordinandus sive ordinatus non fuit* — unless he bring letters of orders, and letters commendatory from his own diocesan, or other bishops in whose dioceses he was well known, whereby his manners and conversation may appear; otherwise, as well he that officiates as he who permits him to officiate, shall be sharply reproved at the discretion of the ordinary.

The remainder of this long and bitter paper is chiefly devoted to the University of Oxford. After complaining of the heresies and errors in that ancient seat of learning, the archbishop proceeds to tell the wardens, provosts and masters of the several colleges, how to proceed, by monthly examinations, etc., in finding out and extirpating heresy from the university; and how to deal with "the defamed, detected, denounced, or vehemently suspected" heretics or errorists among the members of their respective colleges. They were to be excommunicated and expelled from college. And all neglect on the part of the heads of colleges to enforce these constitutions, exposed them to excommunication, deposition from office, deprivation of benefices, and summary proceedings, at the discretion of the ordinary.*

* *Wilkins' Concilia*, vol. III., pp. 314–319; *Fox, Acts and Monuments*, vol. I., pp. 597–600. A very good abstract of these constitutions may be found in *Collier*, vol. III., pp. 378–383. See also *Gibson's Codex*, vol. I., pp. 329–336.

Such were Arundel's constitutions; minute and severe enough to have accomplished the end whereunto they were sent — the utter suppression of Lollardism — if laws and constitutions could have done this. But the archbishop soon had experience of the difficulty of executing his constitutions. The very next year (1409) he complains to the governors of the University of Oxford, of certain masters of art, "or rather disciples of error," who disregarded his conventional constitutions. And the clergy, moved doubtless by the archbishop, petitioned the king (Henry IV.) and the parliament for further help against the heretics; since, as they say, the power of the church had proved insufficient to extirpate them.*

In this petition to the king and parliament, the clergy denounce the Lollards, as a *new* religious sect,† which entertained diverse, perfidious, and perverse sentiments concerning the faith, and damnable opinions about the authority of the church and its sacraments; and which had rashly usurped the office of preaching, and, in opposition to the divine and ecclesiastical law, preached and taught, publicly and privately, diverse new doctrines and iniquitous opinions, errors, and here-

* *Wilkins' Concilia*, III., 323 and 328.

† The Lollards had been well known throughout England for about thirty years, when this petition to the king was penned; but it suited the ends of the persecuting prelates and clergy to persevere in calling them "a *new* sect." Many other illustrations of this policy may be seen in the official documents quoted in these pages.

sies, contrary to the faith and the holy determinations of the most holy church, perversely and maliciously, under the cover of pretended sanctity; and who made unlawful conventicles and confederations with their nefarious doctrines and opinions, held and supported schools, made and wrote books, wretchedly (*nequiter*) instructed the people, and, as much as they could, excited to sedition and insurrections, and made great divisions and dissensions among the people, and committed various other horrid enormities (*auditui horrenda*), to the subversion of the Catholic faith, and the doctrines of most holy church, the diminution of religious culture, and even to the destruction of the civil laws, and of the liberty of the Church of England. And in view of these "horrid enormities" and threatening dangers, the clergy pray for a law to authorize the bishops to arrest and imprison all persons suspected of these errors and heresies.* This petition, for a wonder, does not appear to have been regarded by the king. He probably thought that there were laws enough already against the Lollards.

The next year (1410) the university demonstrated to the archbishop its fealty to mother church, by publicly burning several of Wickliffe's works. "And not only in England, but in Bohemia likewise, the books of Wickliffe were consumed by the Archbishop of Prague, who made

* *Wilkins' Concilia*, vol. III., pp. 328, 329.

diligent inquisition for them, and burned them. The number of volumes which he is said to have burned, most excellently written, and richly adorned with bosses of gold (as Eneas Silvius writes), was about two hundred."* The books burned at Prague were, probably, those which were sent out by Lord Cobham, at the request of John Huss; Cobham having had all Wickliffe's writings copied for Huss, and sent to Bohemia.†

The same year, 1410, the 11th of Henry IV., the Commons showed their good will towards the Lollards by presenting two petitions to the king: one against the clergy, and the other for some relaxation of the *Ex Officio* statute. In the first, they tell the king that the "temporalities disordinately wasted by men of the church, might well suffice to furnish the king with fifteen earls, fifteen hundred knights, sixty-two thousand esquires, and one hundred almshouses for the relief of poor people—more than there were then in England. * * * And, over and above all these, the king might put

---

* *Acts and Monuments*, vol. I., bk. v., p. 509.

† This is asserted explicitly by Bishop Bale, "*Brefe Chronycle Concerning Sir John Oldcastell,*" etc. etc., preface.

Bale says, in another work, in allusion to the destruction of Wickliffe's books: "Great slaughter and burning hath been here in England for John Wickliffe's books, ever since the year of our Lord 1382; yet have not one of them thoroughly perished. I have at this hour, [November, 1546,] the titles of *one hundred and forty-four* of them, which are many more in number, for some of them, under one title, comprehendeth two books, some three, some four; yea, one of them containeth *twelve*."—*Examination of Anne Askewe*, preface.

yearly into his own coffers £20,000." They further assert "that the temporalities, then in the possession of spiritual men, amounted to 322,000 marks, yearly rent," and "that over and above the said sum of 322,000 marks, several houses of religion in England possessed as many temporalities as might suffice to find fifteen thousand priests, every priest to be allowed, for his stipend, seven marks a year." *

In relation to the Lollards, the Commons put up the following petition: — "Also the commons pray, that it may please our sovereign lord the King to grant, that if any one may have been or shall be arrested by virtue of the statute enacted the second year of your reign, on motion of the prelates and clergy of your realm of England, he may be set free upon surety, and clear himself of the charge without annoyance from any, in the same county where he was arrested; and that such arrests may be henceforward made in due form of law, by the lieutenant, mayors, bailiffs, or constables [of] our lord the King, without violent affray of force and arms, or spoiling of their goods, or other exaction or injury whatsoever [wont] in such case to be made."

To this last petition the king replied, according to the record, that *he would be advised;* which was equivalent to a denial of the petition. The other petition which is said to have been presented by Lord Cobham, and for which the prelates never forgave him, is not on the roll of that parliament,

* A *mark* was about $3.20, Federal money.

and may, like other obnoxious papers, have been suppressed by the influence of the clergy. But Rapin tells us, that the king rebuked the Commons very sharply, and told them "he neither could nor would consent to their petitions; and expressly forbade them to meddle any more with the church's concerns. As for the Lollards, he added, that far from permitting the statute against them to be repealed, he wished it more rigorous, for the utter extirpation of heresy out of the land." *

In 1412 Arundel addressed a letter to that odious sinner, Pope John XXIII.,† respecting the "pestiferous doctrines" of Wickliffe; and besought his holiness to use his apostolic authority against the doctrines, and books, and writings, and disciples, and followers of Wickliffe; and to inhibit every one, however eminent, of whatever condition, or dignity, or order, or honor, he may be, to hold, approve, defend, preach, teach, or learn, publicly or privately, in schools or out, these doctrines of Wickliffe, under pain of heavy censure and punishment, and under the penalty of heretical pravity. In this same letter this busy persecutor and hearty hater of the Lollards, beseeches the pope to

---

* *Rot. Parl.*, vol. III., p. 626; *Parl. or Const. Hist. Eng.*, vol. II., pp. 113–116; *Acta Regia*, vol. II., pp. 105, 106; *Walsing.*, 379, l. 11.

† "Infamous for crimes of all sorts." — *Gieseler*, IV., 283. He was charged before the council of Constance with "every species of vice and crime, and which, for the most part at least, were too true." — *Neander*, V., 104, 105.

have the bones of Wickliffe dug up and thrown upon a dung-hill, or burned.*

On the 20th of March, 1413, Henry IV. died, after a turbulent reign of fourteen years. "Such was the reign of this prince, that he was ever terrible to the godly, immeasurable in his actions, and really beloved by very few men. But princes never lack flatterers.

"Neither was the time of his reign quiet; but full of trouble, of blood, and misery. * * * For the space of six or seven years together, scarcely a year passed without some conspiracy against the king. Many of the nobles joined in these rebellions, and many of them were beheaded, or otherwise slain; but still the rebellions continued."†

In addition to all his cares and troubles of State, the king had domestic anxieties, arising from the conduct of his children, particularly the Prince of Wales, ‡ and from the state of his own health,

---

* *Wilkins*, III., 350, 351.

† *Fox*, vol. I., bk. V., p. 590.

‡ Shakespeare's Henry IV., illustrates very aptly, and probably truly, the uneasy and even wretched state of mind in which the king spent his last days, in consequence of outward tumults and inward distresses. Take, for example, Henry's soliloquy on sleep, Act III., Scene 1; and his address to Prince Henry, on his removing the crown from the king's pillow while asleep; and his dying address to the Prince, Act IV., Scene 4. The traditional character of the Prince is portrayed in those scenes in which he figures in the company of Falstaff, Poins, Bardolph, and their riotous associates.

The authors of the Parliamentary, or Constitutional History of England, think the fact that the Prince of Wales was honored with

and the reproaches of his conscience. Afflicted with epileptic fits, his face covered with a loathsome eruption, and his conscience scourging him for his usurpations and his bloody reign, this monarch, at the age of forty-six years, bore about him all the symptoms of declining age, and at length sank into an untimely and unhonored grave.*

With the commencement of the reign of Henry V., we shall find new life infused into the persecutors of the Lollards. Much of this activity may be safely attributed to Walden, or Waldensis, or Nutter — as he is indifferently called. He was prior of the Carmelites, a learned man, a bitter hater of Wickliffe and his doctrines, against which he wrote more fully and ably than any contemporary; and withal, he was confessor to Henry

---

sundry marks of respect by the Commons in Parliament, and made President of the Council, "does not, by any means, suit with the light character which most historians have given of this prince in his younger days." And "that it was the king's jealousy of his his son's growing greatness and popularity, and his neglect of him for that reason, which threw the prince on the dissolute courses which are laid to his charge." — Vol. II., p. 113.

The heroic character and daring deeds of Henry are duly celebrated by a contemporary of that prince, a chaplain in his army during his celebrated French campaign, on which the Archbishop of Canterbury sent him, to divert his attention from church reforms. In the preface to this old work the editor gives an account of numerous and important honors conferred on Henry when Prince of Wales, and some of them even when he was quite young; and hence infers his capacity and popularity. — See *Henrici Quinti Regis Angliæ Gesta*, a beautiful edition of which may be found in in our City Library. — See also *Tyler's Memoir of Henry V.*

* *Lingard's Eng.*, vol. IV., pp. 317–321.

V., and keeper and director of his conscience.* Immediately after this king's coronation, parliament was held at Westminster, "at which time (A.D. 1413) Thomas Arundel, the archbishop of Canterbury, collected in St. Paul's church, in London, an Universal Synod, of all the bishops and clergy of England. The chief and principal cause of the assembling of this Synod, as the Chronicle of St. Albans reports, was to repress the growing and spreading of the gospel, and especially to withstand the noble and worthy Lord Cobham, who was then noted to be a principal favorer, receiver, and maintainer of them whom the bishop misnamed to be Lollards; especially in the dioceses of London, Rochester, and Hereford."†

In the minutes of this convention, mention is made of the burning of certain heretical tracts, doubtless in English, at St. Paul's church-yard, London; the *auto-de-fe* being prefaced with a speech from the archbishop, explaining the reason why the tracts were burned.‡ These tracts contained, probably, portions of the sacred Scriptures, discourses by Wickliffe or some of his poor priests, or treatises on topics of current interest in the church at that time. Such writings, in English, scattered through the nation, were the terror of the hierarchy. They were sought out everywhere, and wherever found, instantly seized, made witnesses against those in whose possession they were found,

* See *Gieseler*, IV., 256, 257. † *Fox*, vol. I., bk. V., p. 635.
‡ *Wilkins*, III., p. 351.

or to whom they belonged, even though the tracts had never been read by those who owned them, and never could be, by reason of the possessor's ignorance of the art of reading—and then destroyed as things most dangerous to "holy mother church!"

A canon was also passed in this Synod, by which not only every person who preached without license from the bishop or his commissary, but all the adherents, counsellors, promoters, favorers, defenders, and managers of such preachers, incurred the sentence of the greater excommunication, *ipso facto* — for the very act.*

The Oxford inquisitors made a report to this synod, in a communication addressed to the archbishop, of their success in hunting out heresies and errors in Wickliffe's writings, of whom they facetiously speak, as, "Doctor quidam novellus dictus Johannes Wycliff, *non electus, sed infectus;*" while the twelve inquisitors themselves are termed, "*electissimos viros* magistros et doctores." These most select masters and doctors were able to report the discovery of no less than *two hundred and sixty-six* heresies or errors in the works of this certain new, *infected,* rather than *elected* doctor, John Wickliffe.†

At the opening of parliament in this the second year of Henry V., April 30th, 1414, the chancellor,

---

* *Wilkins,* III., 351–353.

† *Wilkins,* III., 339–349; *Bale's Brefe Chronycle,* pp. 15, 16.

the Bishop of Winchester, the king's uncle, inveighed bitterly against the Lollards, charging them with traitorous intentions, and the general purpose of overturning Church and State. And he assigned this as one of the reasons for which parliament had been called together, that some check might be put to the progress of Lollardism.* Accordingly, a statute was obtained from this parliament, by which it was hoped and expected this object would be effectually secured.

The special end contemplated in this new law, as will be seen, was to secure the hearty coöperation of the king and all his officers of justice, in the arrest and conviction of the heretics, by giving the king and these officers a pecuniary interest in the work of persecution. It was a great point gained by the hierarchy, to be allowed to employ the officers of State to do the persecuting work of the church. But this vile work, these administrators of secular justice could not be expected to do heartily, without pay, or, at least, the king's special approbation. Both of these points, as will be seen by the outline of the law which follows, are provided for in the new statute: the officers are to be paid by the bishops, and the king is to be made willing to have his subjects prosecuted and convicted as heretics, by the bribe of their possessions, which are to be forfeited to the king, as in cases of treason. In fact, the law is drawn up as though

---

* *Rotuli Parliamentorum*, vol. IV., p. 15.

Lollardy and treason were synonymous terms; and we shall see, in the progress of this history, that those convicted under its administration were treated as traitors and heretics both, being hanged and burned, and their goods confiscated. But let us look more particularly into this crafty and bloody statute.

The statute sets forth, first of all, that, "forasmuch as great rumors, congregations, and insurrections, had been made of late, by those who were of the sect of heresy called Lollardy, to the intent to annul and subvert the Christian faith and the law of God within the realm, as also to destroy our sovereign lord, the king himself, and all manner of estates of the realm, as well spiritual as temporal, and also all manner of policy and the laws of the land; therefore, our lord the king, willing to provide a more open and due punishment against the malice of such heretics and Lollards than hath been had or used heretofore, so that, for fear of the same laws and punishments, such heresies, etc., may cease in time to come; by the advice and assent, and at the prayer of the Commons, hath ordained and established, that the chancellor, the treasurer, the justices of the king's bench, justices of assize, justices of the peace, sheriffs, mayors and baliffs of cities and towns, and all other officers having the government of people — make oath, in taking their charge and offices, to exert their utmost pains and diligence to put out, to cause to be put out, to make to cease, and to destroy, all manner of heresies and errors, commonly called Lollardies; and that they assist, favor, and maintain the ordinaries, or their commissaries, as often as required by said ordinaries or their commissaries." * For this assistance the officers were to be paid reasonably by the ordinaries and commissaries.

And it was further provided, that all persons convicted of heresy by said ordinaries and commissaries, and left to the secular power, *should lose and forfeit all their lands and tenements;* the king to have all the lands and tenements which the convicts held in fee simple, and which were immediately holden of him, as forfeited; and the other lords, of whom the lands and tenements of such convicts were held immediately, to be satisfied as in cases of attainder of felonies, except such lands and tenements as were held of the ordinaries or commissaries before whom the impeached of heresy were convicted, which were wholly to remain to the king as forfeit; to whom, also, *all the goods and chattels of such convicts were likewise to be forfeited.*

And moreover, it was provided, that the justices of the king's bench, the justices of the peace, and justices of assize, have full power to inquire

* This oath was required of all State officers until the time of Charles I., when Sir Edward Coke, being about to be made sheriff, objected to the oath; and on consultation, the judges decided, that, as the statute itself had been repealed, the oath, which was required in it, ought to be discontinued; and so it was from that day.—*Gibson's Codex,* vol. I., pp. 330, 331.

of all such Lollards, who were the maintainers, receivers, favorers (*fautores*), and sustainers, common writers of their books and sermons; and respecting their schools, conventicles, congregations and confederacies; and that this clause be put into the commissions of the justices of the peace. And that said justices have power to issue against such indicted persons, a *capias*; and that the sheriffs be bound to arrest such persons as soon as they can be found, and deliver them to the ordinaries or commissaries, to be imprisoned and tried by them according to the laws of holy church.

And yet further, it was provided, that if such arrested person should escape from prison, either before or after his conviction, then all his goods and chattels should be forfeited to the king, and all his lands and tenements be seized into the king's hands, and the king have all the profits of the same until the escaped rendered himself unto the same prison whence he had escaped.*

Bishop Bale, in describing the doings of this parliament, which, he says, was held at Leicester, because of "the great favor which Lord Cobham" — who had just been condemned to death by the convocation of clergy in London — "had both in London and about the city," adds: "In the said parliament, the king made this most blasphemous and cruel act, to be as a law forever: That what-

* *Fox*, vol. I., pp. 649, 650; *Rotuli Parliamentorum*, IV., pp. 24, 25; *Statutes at Large*, 2 Henry V.

soever they were that should read the Scriptures in the mother tongue, (which was then called Wickliffe's learning,) they should forfeit land, cattle, body, life, and goods, from their heirs forever, and so be condemned for heretics to God, enemies to the crown, and most errant traitors to the land. Besides this, it was enacted, that never a sanctuary, nor privileged ground within the realm, should hold them; though they were still permitted both to thieves and murderers. And if, in case they would not give over, or were, after their pardon, relapsed, they should suffer death in two manner of kinds; that is, they should first be hanged for treason against the king, and then be burned for heresy against God; and yet neither of both committed."

He adds: "Anon after was it proclaimed throughout the realm; and then had the bishops, priests, monks, and friars, a world somewhat to their minds. For then were many taken in divers quarters and suffered most cruel death. And many fled out of the land, into Germany, Bohemia, France, Spain, Portugal, and into the wilds of Scotland, Wales, and Ireland, working there many marvels against their [the Papists'] false kingdom, too long to write."*

Walden — sometimes called Waldensis, and sometimes Nutter — the confessor of Henry V.,

---

* *Brefe Chronycle.* Bale quotes Walden and Polydor Virgil among his authorities for this statement.

confirms this statement of Bale's, so far as the statute is concerned. After praising Henry, as the most commendable of kings, in that, at the commencement of his reign, he rejoiced to erect a standard against the heretical Wickliffites, especially after their conspiracy [?] against their excellent king, under the leadership of John Oldcastle, he adds: "That no great time elapsed before the council spread abroad, by public proclamation, through the whole kingdom, a general statute, that all Wickliffites, inasmuch as they were betrayers of God, so as betrayers of the king and the kingdom, they were judged to have incurred forfeiture of goods, and to be deserving of a double punishment — burning for God's sake, hanging for the king's sake — and so it is ordained. The thing stands as a perpetual law." *

---

* Walden's words, of which I have tried to give a pretty literal translation, are as follows: — "Nec mora longa processit, quin statutum publicum per omne regni concilium in publico emanavit edicto, quod omnes Wiclevistæ, sicut Dei proditores essent, sic proditores Regis et regni proscriptis bonis censerentur, duplici pœnæ dandi, incendio propter Deum, suspendio propter Regem: factumque est ita. Stat res jure perenni." — *Walden*, in Gieseler, IV., 256, note 29.

I suppose Walden to be unexceptionable authority for the statement in the text from Bale. The same account is given of this law in the Parliamentary, or Constitutional History of England; and in Cobbett's Parliamentary History, and by other writers of standard authority. But I am bound to say, that after most diligent inquiry, I have been unable to find any such statute as Walden and Bale and others describe. It is not in the Rolls of Parliament, nor among the Statutes of the Realm, nor in the collection of the Statutes at Large; neither is it to be found in Rymer's Fœdera,

With a statute like this, in addition to that given them by Henry IV., what more could the

---

in Wilkins' Concilia, nor Gibson's Codex. There is nothing of the kind in Bacon's Abridgment, nor in Viner's Abridgment of the Laws of England; nor in any of the old chronicles to which I have had access. If, therefore, such a law passed at the time mentioned, it must have been lost. The authors of the Parliamentary or Constitutional History, indeed, suggest that the roll of this parliament may have been lost; as they say, "there is no account of the proceedings of this parliament (the 2 Henry V.) to be met with on the rolls." — Vol. II., p. 135. The printed rolls of parliament, nevertheless, contain several other laws, said to have been passed by this parliament; and why not this? It is possible that what Bale speaks of as an *act of parliament,* may have been a proclamation of the king. In Rymer, vol. IX., p. 46, there is a proclamation by the king, dated Aug. 21, 1413, which forbids and condemns the assemblies of the Lollards, and threatens those clerks, of every grade, who shall have anything to do with these assemblies, with imprisonment and forfeiture of all their goods, cattle, etc. This proclamation was made more than eight months previous to the passage of the first statute, above described, or even the meeting of the parliament which passed either that, or the statute mentioned by Bale. And it is barely possible, that what is described by Bale, and Walden, and others, as *a statute,* may have been *a royal proclamation* merely, in explanation and interpretation of the several laws against the Lollards, and having the force of a statute. But why Rymer should not have it among his collections, in that case, is more than I can tell.

Hargrave, in his complete Collection of State Trials, takes it as a settled point, that reading the Bible was made treason in the reign of Henry V. But he speaks of the taking away of the right of sanctuary as the work of another act. — See *Hargrave's Trial of Lord Cobham,* vol. I., p. 50, and onward; also appendix to vol. VI., pp. 1, 2; and Index to the whole work, article, Treason.

There is still another difficulty about this account by Bale. He describes the statute in which reading the Scriptures is made treason and heresy, and punishable by hanging and burning, etc., as commencing just as the statute does which is given on page 363, and

Papists ask! The fourth Henry gave them power to fine, imprison, and burn the Lollards; the fifth Henry puts into the hands of the bishops all the criminal machinery of State, to aid them in detecting, fining, imprisoning, and burning to death, the poor Christians in their respective dioceses!

These persecuting churchmen could make no headway against the "Gospellers" while there were only ecclesiastical courts and punishments with which to awe the simple believers in God's Word. And even when, by protesting that the church was in danger of utter subversion, and declaring that the Lollards laughed to scorn all the excommunications and anathemas of the church, saying that no man could be really excommunicate unless he had first excommunicated himself by false doctrine and wicked works — even when, I say, by such representations, the bishops had persuaded the king to let them use the arm of the State — they could not suppress the Gospel; they must bribe the king and the officers of the State to do the Church's bloody work. The king must be made to believe, or to pretend to believe, that the Lollards are a race of traitors, who are plotting in their conventicles and schools, the destruction of their sovereign and the utter overthrow of the whole fabric of State; and therefore should be

---

onward, in this volume. If Bale spoke from actual inspection of the law, as he appears to have done, then it has been mutilated since he wrote — near the middle of the sixteenth century; for no copy of it now contains those clauses which he mentions.

persecuted *rigidly*. And to make this more apparent to the king, a substantial bribe is offered to him, in the proposed forfeiture to him of all the lands and tenements of the convicted Lollards!

And now, surely, we may regard the machinery of persecution as complete. Can pope, cardinal, or bishop, ask for anything more? Between these two laws of the two Henries — the upper and nether millstones of the English church — the poor dissenting saints must certainly be ground to powder!

These laws were, doubtless, most admirable devices; as good for their purpose as the most cunning priest could invent; yet it was not two years after the passage of the second of these laws, before Archbishop Chicheley — "the fire-brand of the age," as he has been appropriately called — the prime mover, and the indefatigable superintendent of this persecuting machinery, thought that it required some improvement. The stones of his mill he thought needed picking; the teeth of his threshing instrument, sharpening. Accordingly, in the convocation of the prelates and clergy of Canterbury, in 1416, the archbishop caused to be enacted a series of ecclesiastical laws, which Dominic himself could not have improved, and which the Spanish Inquisition could have adopted without discredit to its taste for heretical blood.

In these "Constitutions," as they are called, the archbishop denounces the Lollards as "little foxes, which hide themselves in the Lord's vineyard."

To the end, therefore, he proceeds to say, "that the dust of negligence may be thoroughly shaken from our own feet and our brethren's, * * * we have ordained in this convocation of bishops and clergy, that our brethren, our suffragans, and archdeacons of our province of Canterbury, by themselves, their officials, or commissaries, twice every year, at least, do diligently inquire for such persons as are suspected of heresy; and that in every archdeaconry, and in every parish in which it is reported that any heretics live, they cause three or more men of the best reputation, to take their oath upon the holy evangelists, that, if they shall know of any who are heretics, persons frequenting secret conventicles, or differing in life and manners from the common conversation of the faithful; or holding either heresies or errors; or having any suspected books, written in the English language; or in the habit of receiving persons suspected of heresies or errors; or favoring them or their associates; or conversant in any way with them, * * * they shall denounce such persons, in writing, with all the circumstances which cause them to be suspected, to our suffragans, archdeacons, or their commissaries, with the least possible delay."

The information thus gathered, the archbishop directs his suffragans or their archdeacons, to send to him secretly, under their seals, while they proceed forthwith against the accused or suspected persons. And should the bishops or their commissaries fail to convict the accused Lollards, "yet, notwithstanding," continues the archbishop, "let them commit them to perpetual or temporary prisons, as the nature of the case may require, until the next convocation of the prelates and clergy of our province of Canterbury." Then and there a full relation of each such case of heresy or error, with all the particulars connected with the suspicion, arrest, trial, etc., etc., of the party, was required to be certified to the archbishop and the official of his court.*

Such were Archbishop Chicheley's "Constitutions." The hand of the cunning fisherman has here made the net so fine, and yet so strong, that nothing, great nor small, can escape through its meshes. The cup of bitterness which the poor Lollards had long been drinking from the hands of the priests, was now made to brim over with wormwood and gall. "By this accursed ordinance the horrors of the writ for burning heretics were completed. It set up an inquisition in every parish. It sent terror and distrust into every family. Every dwelling was haunted by discord and suspicion; so that a man's bitterest foes were often those of his own household and blood. And the fruits of this flagitious system were, that multitudes were consigned to the dungeon or the stake, by the treachery or the weakness of their nearest kindred, or their dearest connections."†

* *Wilkins' Concilia*, vol. III., pp. 378, 379; also *Fox*, I., 728, 729

† *La Bas' Life of Wiclif*, p. 369, Harper's edition.

Turner, in speaking of the persecuting edicts of this period of English history, says: "Few Roman Emperors, most decried for their persecutions, outdid these severities. If the Papal church was not able to stand against the reason and moral principle of the fifteenth and sixteenth centuries, it was not for want of the most tyrannous exertions of the most arbitrary power, and the most vindictive hostility." *

One feature of these persecuting enactments deserves special notice, as it was the harshest and most oppressive, in some respects, of them all: I mean the authority given the civil judges, by the law of Henry V., and taken in all the bishops' courts, to question the accused or suspected heretic. If he answered, he became his own accuser, and was sentenced to prison or the stake; if he refused to answer — to be a witness against himself — then he was condemned for contumacy. Thus there was no escape for a conscientious, truthful man. By one or the other of these horns he was sure to perish.

We have now briefly noticed the chief laws, and some of the more important ecclesiastical constitutions, canons, and mandates, together with the briefs, and letters — royal and episcopal — which were contrived and promulgated in England between the years 1377 and 1416, for the

---

* *Hist. Middle Ages*, vol. III., p. 142.

suppression of the free, Protestant, and Scriptural doctrines and sentiments of John Wickliffe and his numerous followers, commonly called Lollards; and for the punishment of such as would insist on taking God's Word for their rule of faith and practice, contrary to the bulls of popes, mandates of prelates, canons of convocations, and even the laws of the State.

I am not aware that there were any laws, other than those already described, made against heresy, during the fifteenth century. Popes and bishops continued, from time to time, to fulminate their thunders and let loose their bulls and mandates against the heretics, some of which may be noticed in the progress of this history; but the reader has now before him the chief instruments employed by the Romish hierarchy, to reduce to obedience the refractory believers in the Gospel. And under some or all of these merciless laws, and constitutions, and provisions, the Wickliffites groaned, languished in prison, or died at the stake, during more than one hundred years; or to the time of the English Reformation in the days of Henry VIII.

There are two other topics which must be briefly touched upon, in this connection, before we are prepared to appreciate fully the bitter hatred of the papal hierarchy against the Lollards, and the varied and unremitting devices of that hierarchy to destroy these dissenters. One of these topics is suggested by the doings of the Council of Constance.

On November 5th, 1414, a famous — or rather infamous — General Council of the Papal Church commenced its sessions in the city of Constance, Germany, to be continued, as the result proved, until April 22, 1418. For nearly forty years there had been two, and part of the time three popes reigning over Christendom, each claiming to be the especial vicar of Christ and the infallible head of His church; and each ready to denounce his fellow-popes as usurpers and antichrists.* This state of things occasioned so much scandal, made so ridiculous the claims of the papal hierarchy, and, in the meantime, gave the Protestants such vantage-ground in their contests with the Papists, and withal raised so loud a cry among the Papists themselves for reformation, that the rival popes were compelled at last, though very reluctantly, to submit to the authority of a General Council. Two of them were deposed, and one resigned his papal authority; and thus the way was prepared for a single head to be placed on the bleeding body; and, in the language of the times, the body itself, in its limbs as well as its head, to be healed and restored to health.†

* See an account of this schism, in *Neander,* vol. v., pp. 47–112.

† In *Wilkins,* III., 366, 367, may be found: "Bulla papæ Johannes XXIII., cum Archiepiscopi Cant. certificatorio, pro concilio generali Constantiensi."

Neander gives a somewhat particular account of the manœuvering of the infamous Pope John XXIII., in connection with the Council of Constance. This monster was finally induced to sign his resignation of the popedom, perhaps as much through fear of exposure

The complete settlement of the papal schism, and the thorough reform of the church were the avowed, and with many, doubtless, the real objects and ends of this General Council. The schism was indeed healed, and pope Martin V. was elected to fill the papal throne. But beyond this, little was done by the council towards reforming the errors and abuses of the church. While the world was deluded with mere promises of reformation, the council actually employed itself mainly in attempts to suppress all real, radical reformatory measures; more particularly those promulgated by Wickliffe, Huss the Bohemian reformer, and Jerome of Prague. The council not only condemned the doctrines of these reformers, and doomed their writings to the flames, but sentenced Huss and Jerome themselves to the stake; and the members had the satisfaction of seeing these good men burnt to ashes, before their reformatory sessions were ended.*

On Wickliffe, who was considered the master

---

as anything else, sundry charges against him having been presented to the council. Neander, however, thinks the council would not have gone to extremes with the hardened sinner; because the crimes charged on John were so infamous, that the public discussion of them could not fail to disgrace the papacy and the church. — *Hist. Christ. Relig. and Chh.*, vol. v., pp. 100–128; see also, *Gieseler*, IV., 293 Gillet's Life of Huss, I ch. 12.

* *Fox* gives an extended account of this council, and more particularly of the trial and condemnation of Huss and Jerome. — Bk. v. *Milner* gives quite a full account of the council, — Cent. XV., ch. 2; comp. *Mosheim*, cent. XV., pt. II., ch. 2; *Gieseler*, vol. IV., pp. 285–311; and *Walsingham*, 387, l. 52, and 579–80.

and teacher of these Bohemian reformers, from whose writings they doubtless derived many valuable suggestions,* and whose sentiments they adopted and defended in part,† the council could not lay their bloody hands, since for thirty years his precious dust had slept by the side of his affectionate parishioners in the church of Lutterworth. The council, therefore, could only condemn his writings to the flames; and, in their impotent wrath, order that "his body and bones, if they could be distinguished from other bodies of the faithful, should be exhumed and thrown far away from consecrated ground, according to canonical and lawful decrees."‡ This spiteful decree could

* *Neander* gives a very interesting and full account of "The Movements of Reform in Bohemia," including the forerunners of Huss: Militz, who gave the first impulse to the reformatory movement in that country; Conrad of Waldhausen; and Matthias of Janow, in whose works are said to be, not only the reformatory ideas which were developed by Huss, but also the germs of those Christian principles which were subsequently unfolded by Luther. Neander also notices the connection of Huss with Wickliffe; and the history, writings, trial, and execution of Huss, and also of Jerome of Prague.—*Hist. Christian Chh.*, vol. v., sec. II., pp. 173–235, 235–255, and 255–380.

† See the defence of Wickliffe's sentiments, by Huss, in *Fox*, vol. I., bk. v., pp. 517–520.

‡ *Fox*, vol. I., p. 512. *Fuller* says, that this sentence against Wickliffe's bones and dust, was passed by the council of *Sienna*, in 1428, and not by the council of Constance, as Fox reports.—*Chh. Hist.*, p. 171, folio ed. But *Gieseler* says: "The council of Constance in its eighth sitting, 4 May, 1415, condemned forty-five articles of Wycliff's, adjudged his works to the flames, and decreed at last, 'corpus ejus et ossa, si ab aliis fidelium corporibus discerni possint, exhumari, et procul ab ecclesiastica sepultura jactari secun-

not be executed immediately; though its moral force was nearly the same as though it could have been. It was designed to be, and it was, a most emphatic condemnation, by a general council of the papal church — a body which claimed to be above even the pope himself — by the highest ecclesiastical authority then recognized in the world — of the doctrines of John Wickliffe, the Gospel Doctor. It was, too, a virtual sanction, yea, *sanctification*, of all the bloody laws and persecuting constitutions, canons, mandates, and briefs, which the English prelates and kings had for thirty years and more been accumulating for the punishment and utter extirpation of the simple believers in the supremacy of God's Word as the rule of faith and practice in the church of Christ. And from this date we may consider the whole machinery of persecution in England, as not only complete, but as recognized and approved, in the most emphatic manner, by the whole papal church.

Thirteen years after the passage of this decree for the violation of Wickliffe's grave, the will of "*the* church" was done; the chancel of the church of Lutterworth was searched by the servants of the hierarchy; the remains of Wickliffe — if perchance the resurrectionists did not get hold of some other person's — were thrown out, consumed by

---

dum canonicas et legitimas sanctiones.'" — Vol. IV., p. 257, note 30. This command, however, had to be enjoined over and over again by Martin V., upon the Bishop of Lincoln, so late as 1427, before its accomplishment could be secured.

fire, and the ashes cast into a neighboring brook. "The brook," says Fuller, "did convey his ashes into Avon, Avon into Severn, Severn into the narrow seas, they unto the main ocean; and thus the ashes of Wickliffe are the emblem of his doctrine, which now is dispersed all the world over."

There is yet one more topic which must be adverted to, in illustration of the spirit of the popish persecutors of the Lollards: I mean the literary element of this persecution.

It cannot have escaped observation, that the bulls and mandates, and even the laws which were issued against the Wickliffites, were prepared with a special regard to rhetorical effect. These documents abound not only in bitter words, but also in rhetorical flourishes, in which the poor Lollards are held up to the execration of Christendom, as the perpetrators of crimes innumerable, against Church and State—crimes even too horrible to be mentioned! And all through this bloody controversy, the power of the pen was constantly invoked, to aid the crosier and the sword. Bitter words and rhetorical denunciations were counted next best to dry faggots. They were relied on as the kindling materials of the pyre.

But it was not in the official documents alone that the pen of the persecutor was used. Between the years 1382 and 1412, the number of literary opponents of Wickliffe and his doctrines was very large. Among the chief of these were Th. Ashburn;

Bankinus, a Dominican; Gaulter Dysse, a Carmelite; R. Lanynfans, and R. Maydesley; and above all these, W. Woodford, who composed many works against Wickliffe, some of which are still extant. In 1400, Alyngton vigorously defended image worship against Wickliffe's attacks. But the most able, active, and persevering literary opponent of Wickliffe and his disciples was Thomas Nutter, of Walden, a Carmelite, usually quoted as *Walden*, or *Waldensis*. His works, particularly his *Doctrinale Antiquum*, are the great thesaurus from which the enemies of Wickliffe, ancient and modern, have drawn their materials.*

To these names must be added that of Knighton, or Knyghton, a contemporary chronicler, whose sayings are often quoted in these pages; and Walsingham, who, though not a contemporary of Wickliffe himself, lived and wrote his History of England during the prevalence of the Lollard persecution, or about the middle of the fifteenth century. It is this historian who exults with such malicious satisfaction over the death of Wickliffe, thus: "In the year 1385 * * that devil's organ, enemy of the church, confusion of the people, idol of heretics, image of hypocrites, renewer of schisms, distributor of lies, sink of flattery, John Wycliff, smitten by the awful judgment of God with paralysis in his whole body, breathed out his wicked spirit to the abodes of darkness," *et cet.* †

* *Turner's Middle Ages*, III., 139, 140, and notes.

† *Ypod Neust.*, 537, l. 11; *Hist. Angl.*, 312, l. 11.

"But the support of the establishment was not intrusted merely to sermons, severities, or controversial logic. The poetry of the day was called in to its aid. Metrical verses against the Lollards were part of the devices of their pageantry and State banquets; and even ballads were written to stigmatize and burlesque them."*

Among the ancient ballads, Ritson has preserved one of considerable length, which bears internal evidence of having been written between the years 1413 and 1417. It is alliterative to a considerable extent, and in rhyme; and in these particulars exhibits the hand of a somewhat skilful workman for those rude days. And though destitute of any particular merit, and anonymous, it deserves to be quoted as illustrative of the spirit of the age — or rather of the *church* — in its persecution of the Lollards. It is throughout a bitter satire on that hated sect, and particularly on Sir John Oldcastle, Lord Cobham, who was a leading Lollard, and for his faith was tried by the archbishop of Canterbury, excommunicated and condemned to the flames; but who had escaped from prison and was then at large, and on whose head a price was set. A few of the best stanzas of the ballad will be sufficient to give the reader an idea of the whole. I have added a sort of glossary, to assist in understanding the satire. The entire ballad may be found in *Ritson's Ancient Songs and Ballads, from the reign of Henry II., to the Revolution.* vol. I., p. 121–127.

---

* *Turner*, vol. III., p. 144.

SATIRE AGAINST THE LOLLARDS.

Lo he that can be Cristes clerc,
And knowe the knottes of his crede,
Now may se a wonder werke,[1]
Of harde happes to take goud heede,
The dome of deth is hevy dred,
For hym[2] that wol[3] not mercy crie,
Than is my rede,[4] for mucke ne mede,[5]
That no man melle[6] of 'lollardye.'

I sey[7] for myself, yut[8] wist[9] I never,
But now late what hit[10] shuld be,
And by my trouth I have wel lever,[11]
No more kyn[12] than my a. b. c.
To lolle so hie in suych degre,
Hit is no perfit 'polecie,'[13]
Sauf seker[14] sample to the and me,
To bewar of lollardie.

The game is noght to lolle so hie,
That fete failen fondement,[15]
And yut is a moche folie,
For fals beleve to ben brent;[16]
That the bibell is al mys went,[17]
To jangle of Job or Jeremye,

---

1 See a wonderful work.

2 *y* is generally used for *i*, sometimes *i* for *y*.

3 Would. 4 Then is my advice. 5 Without reward — free gratis.

6 Meddle with Lollard doctrines. 7 Say. 8 Yet. 9 Know.

10 It. 11 Full rather. 12 Know.

13 That is, to carry Lollard doctrines to such a height is not good policy.

14 Save, sure; or, except as, it may be a warning to thee and me.

15 The meaning of these lines I suppose to be, that it is no part of the Lollards' purpose to carry their notions so far as to have their feet fail to support them — i. e., to get hanged.

16 And yet it is equally foolish to get burned for false belief.

17 Always wont.

That construen hit after her[1] entent,[2]
For lewde lust of Lollardie.

Hit is unkyndly for a knight,
That shuld a kynges castel kepe,
To bable the bibel day and night,
In restyng tyme when he shuld slepe,
And carefoly awey to crepe,
For alle the chief of chivalrie,
Wel aught hym to waile and wepe,
That suyche lust hath in lollardie.

An old castel[3] and not repaired,
With wast walles and wowes[4] wide,
The wages ben ful yvel wared,
With suiche a capitayn to abide,
That rereth[5] riot for to ride
Agayns the kyng and his clergie,[6]
With prive peyne and pore pride,
Ther is a poynt of lollardie.

For many a man withyn a while
Shal aby[7] his gult ful sore,
So fele[8] gostes[9] to begile,
Hym aught to rue evermore;
For his sorrowe shall he never restore,[10]
That he venemed with envye,
But ban the burthe that he was of bore,[11]
Or ever had lust in lollardie.

*　　*　　*　　*　　*

---

[1] Their.

[2] Understanding. It was a great crime in the eyes of the hierarchy, for a man to exercise his own judgment in reading the Bible.

[3] A play on Sir John Oldcastle's name. [4] Windows. [5] Raiseth.

[6] Sir John was accused, though falsely, of endeavoring to raise insurrection against the king, etc.

[7] Expiate. [8] Many. [9] Guests. [10] Repair.

[11] Curse the birth that bare him.

And perde[1] lolle thei never so long,
Yut wol lawe make him lowte,[2]
God wol not suffre hem be so strong
To bryng her perpos so abowte;
With saunz[3] faile and saunz doute,
To rere riot and robberie,
By reson thei shul not long route,[4]
While the taile is docked of lollardie.

* * * * *

When falsnes faileth frele folie,[5]
Pride wol perseyn sone among,[6]
Than willerdome[7] with old envy
Can none other way but wrong.
For synne and shame with sorowe strong,
So overset with avutrie,[8]
That fals-beleve is fayn to fong[9]
The lewde lust of lollardie.

And under colour of suiche lollyng,
To shape sodeyn surreccion
Agaynst oure liege lord [the] kyng,
With fals ymaginacion.
And for that corsed conclusion,[10]
By dome of knighthod and clergie,
Now turneth to confusion
The sory sekte of lollardie.

For holy writ berith witnes
He that fals is to his kyng
That shameful deth and hard distres
Shal be his dome at his endyng;
Than double deth[11] for suych lollyng
Is hevy when we shul hennes hye,[12]
Now lord that madst of nought alle thing
Defende us all fro lollardie.

---

[1] A profane oath. [2] Bend, bow. [3] Without. [4] Hunt, riot.
[5] When falsehood deceiveth frail folly.
[6] Pride would pierce in soon among. [7] Wilfulness. [8] Avarice.
[9] Glad to take hold on. [10] Cursed experiment.
[11] That is, hanging and burning. [12] Hence go.

At the coronation dinner of Henry VI., in 1431, among other entertainments, was recited a ballad, praising the Emperor Sigismund, who, in violation of his own safe-conduct, sanctioned the burning of Huss; and Henry V. of England, who allowed his friend, Lord Cobham, to be burnt for Lollardism:

"And Henry the fifte a noble knight was founde,
For Christie his cause in actes martiall;
Cherished the church, to Lollers gave a fall;
Giving examples to kynges that succede;
And to their braunche here, in especiall,
While he doeth reigne, to love God and drede."*

And this use of poetical lampoons against the Lollards we find was continued during the reign of Henry VII. Among the poetical productions of John Skelton, poet laureate, who flourished during the latter half of the fifteenth century, there are several notices of the Lollards. In a piece entitled "A Replycacion, &c.," which is devoted to the abuse of heretics, we find the following stanzas, which may be taken as a sample:

"Ye soored ouer hye
In the ierarchy
Of Iouanyans heresy,
Your names to magnifye
Among the scabbed skyes,[1]
Of Wycliffes flesshe flyes;[2]

* *Turner*, III., p. 12.
[1] Rough clouds. [2] Evil spirits.

Ye strynged so Luther's lute,
That ye dawns[1] all in a sute
The heritykes ragged ray,[2]
That bringes you out of the way
Of holy churches lay,[3]
Ye shayle *inter enigmata*
And *inter paradigmata;*
Marked in your crudels[4]
To beare faggotes for babyls."[5]

And further on he says:

" Ye shulde take further payne
To resorte agayne
To places where ye haue preched,
And your lollardy lernyng teched." *

In another poem, entitled "The Maner of the World Now a Dayes," among the signs of degeneracy, Skelton mentions the following:

So many *lollers*,
So few true tollers,[1]
So many bauds and pollers,[2]
Sawe I never. †

These quotations will serve to show how the poetry of those times — if poetry it may be called — as well as everything else within the grasp of the hierarchy, was used against the hated and persecuted readers of God's Word.

---

[1] Dance. [2] Name of a dance. [3] Law. [4] Cradles. [5] Baubles.

* *Poetical Works of John Skelton*, vol. I., pp. 207–224. London, 1843, 8vo. 2 vols.

[1] Truth tellers. [2] Plunderers.

† *Skelton*, I., 152.

The Lollards, it must be confessed, were not always passive recipients of the hard thrusts of their enemies. Chaucer, in his Canterbury Tales, though at a somewhat earlier date, chastised the lazy, ignorant, sensual, and covetous priests. Among his pilgrims, he describes "a monk that loved venerie," — hunting; "a frere, a wanton, and a mery;" "a limitour," — a licensed ecclesiastical beggar, — "an easy man to give penance;" "a sompnour," or summoner, — an officer attached to ecclesiastical courts, — who "wel loved to drinke strong win as rede as blood;" "a gentil pardonere," or seller of indulgences, who, "with fained flattering and japes, made the persone and peple his apes.* And this treatment of the clergy was not original with him; for in "The Latin Poems of Walter Mapes," and in "The Political Songs of England from the Reign of John to Edward II.," may be found several satires on the bishops of the 12th and 13th centuries. And though I have not been so fortunate as to meet with any poetry (except a single stanza or two) attributed to Lollards, but Chaucer's, yet, from the complaints of the clergy in 1413, that the Lollards were not only suffered to preach, but "to keep schools in men's houses, compile treatises, *and write ballads;*" and from the fact that a single stanza of Latin poetry, attributed to Lord Cobham, has come down to us, we are prepared to believe that the Lollards did

* See *ante*, p. 286.

sometimes try their hands at verse, as well as prose, in exposing the errors and vices of the clergy. The Latin stanza referred to was attached to a Lollard petition to parliament, in 1394–5, praying for church reform; and was posted up, with the petition, in Westminster and London. It reads thus: —

"Plangunt Anglorum gentes crimen Sodomorum,
Paulus fert, horum sunt idola causa malorum.
Surgunt ingrati Gierzitæ Simone nati,
Nomine prelati, hoc defensare parati.
Qui reges estis, populis quicunque præestis,
Qualiter his gestis, gladios prohibere potestis?" *

Collier (*Ecc. Hist.* III., 213–18) says of the Lollards' petition and verses: — "I shall determine nothing against the honesty of their intentions; though, if the rhyming invective was part of their address, it would almost make one suspect their integrity."

---

* Bishop Bale gives the following English versification of the lines: —

"Bewail may England the sin of Sodomites,
For Idols and they are ground of all their woe.
Of Simon Magus, a sect of hypocrites,
Surnamed prelates, are up with them to go.
And to uphold them in all that they may do.
You that be rulers peculiarly selected,
How can you suffer such mischiefs uncorrected?"

Bale informs us that "these verses, copyed out by dyverse menne, and set upon their wyndows, gates, and dores, which were knowen for obstinate ypocrets and fleshly lyvers, made the prelates madde." — See *Chronycle of Sir John Oldcastell.*

For the same reason he might suspect the integrity of the whole hierarchal party; for these verses were only answering a fool according to his folly. It was, we admit, returning evil for evil; yet it was simply picking up the spent shot of the enemy and firing them back again. But before we condemn the Lollards, it will be well to remember that "oppression maketh a wise man mad," sometimes.

Fox gives some account of this "libel" on the prelates; and of a very bitter satire in prose, which appeared about the same time, in the form of a letter from "Lucifer, Prince of Darkness, * * Captain of the Dungeon of Erebus, King of Hell, and Controller of the Infernal Fire, To all our Children of Pride, and Companions of our Kingdom, especially to our princes of the church of this later Age and Time," etc., etc. In this the prelates are thanked for their coöperation with the Prince of Darkness in destroying men, and sending them to his dungeons and eternal fire, etc., etc.*

**Acts and Mons.*, I., 580–81. See also *Henry's Hist. Eng.*, VIII., 76.

CHAPTER X.

THE PERSECUTION OF THE LOLLARDS.

HAVING, in the preceding chapter, examined with some care the various instruments prepared for the suppression of Lollardy in England, let us now look at the practical application of these instruments of persecution to individuals, and see how the papal church vindicated its apostolical character in its treatment of the Lollards; how it labored, with all the appliances which could be summoned to its aid, to suppress the Gospel; to shut out the light of God's Word from the people; to bind our ancestors in chains of religious ignorance and papal superstition.

To get a vivid conception of the nature and extent of this persecution, we must consider individual cases; we must examine in detail a few, at least, of the many instances of suffering which have come down to us in authentic history. The names, and places of residence, and the circumstances attending individual sufferers for the truth, must be given; and then we shall appreciate more fully what is meant by "The Persecution of the Lollards."

But here a difficulty arises, from the very great

number of these sufferers—which to choose—of whom to write. I have collected, from different sources, the names of some hundreds of Lollards, who suffered in England during the period reviewed in the preceding chapter. The list embraces men and women; the aged and the young; the learned and the ignorant; in all ranks of society—nobles, knights, merchants, mechanics, farmers, laborers, priests, deacons, monks, and friars; together with doctors in divinity, masters of art, and professors and students of the university. There were sufferers for the truth everywhere; and there was almost every kind of suffering endured that papal superstition or malice was allowed to inflict. The timid were threatened and frightened, and made to recant; some did shameful penance, as, half-naked, they were beaten around the cathedrals and through the market-places; others were branded on the cheek; were compelled to wear a faggot marked on their sleeves for life, after suffering previous indignities; were cast into prison, and starved, and tormented, loaded with manacles, doubled up in dungeon-holes made on purpose to torment men, and thus their manhood disgraced, their hearts broken and their spirits crushed; while others, more stout-hearted, after enduring these or like torments, were smothered and crushed to death, or hanged secretly, or pined away and died in the bishops' prisons. Others still, and not a few, saintly men and women, were led forth to the stake and openly burned to death, amidst the taunts of the papists, and the lamentations of good men and women, who looked forward to a like punishment for believing and professing the Gospel of Jesus Christ. And in some of these burnings there was a refinement of cruelty practised, befitting the character of savages rather than christians: — children, after being compelled to betray their parents, were forced to set fire to the faggots which consumed them!

The official registers of the bishops' courts, the authentic documents and the reliable history of the period under consideration, have transmitted to us a great multitude of cases of individual suffering, like those just alluded to, which occurred in England between the time of John Wickliffe and that of the English Reformation, or between 1377 and 1534. And besides the persons whose names are given us, and about whom we have more or less particulars, great numbers of other sufferers for conscience sake are referred to in general terms only. Whole congregations of Lollards were discovered from time to time — betrayed by false brethren or ecclesiastical spies; and large numbers — half a hundred at a time — were sometimes arrested, imprisoned, and punished in various ways. Many of these maintained their integrity to the last extremity; but others, alas, were overcome, and recanted. And besides all these, there were doubtless very many of whose sufferings no account whatever has come to us. Then we are to take into consideration how many were compelled to flee from home and country, in order to save their lives; and how many went about in constant fear and trembling, and suffered martyrdom daily in their minds; and how many wives, and children, and brothers, and sisters, and relatives, and friends, endured grievous sorrows through those whom they loved; the husband being compelled to betray his wife, the wife her husband, parents their children, and children their parents; — all this we are to keep in mind, when trying to estimate what the profession of Protestant and Congregational sentiments cost our English ancestors; and when endeavoring to form a judgment of the true character of that unchangeable church, of which the pope of Rome was then and is now the Supreme Head. But it is time for us to pass to particular cases, illustrative of these general statements.

Wickliffe, though exposed to severe persecution, and finally driven from his professorship and living at Oxford, and compelled to anticipate and prepare himself for martyrdom, was yet suffered to die in his bed, in his own parish. But some of his chief supporters in Oxford were not so fortunate. Among these may be mentioned Nicholas Hereford, Philip Reppington, or Repyngdon, canons of Leicester and "professors of the sacred page," and John Ashton; all of whom, after having been repeatedly examined and long harassed by the archbishop of Canterbury, Courtney, were finally denounced as heretics, and excommunicated; and Ashton condemned to perpetual prison. They were all learned men, and two of them at least, doctors or bachelors of divinity. After hiding themselves from the wrath of the archbishop for some time, Repyngdon and Ashton recanted, and were restored to the university. All this took place between 1380 and 1382. Ashton subsequently, however, repented of his recantation, and either died in prison or was burned by archbishop Arundel. But Repyngdon was richly rewarded for his apostacy, and ultimately became a most bitter and notorious persecutor of the Lollards.*

Hereford and Ashton's recantations, as given by Knighton, their contemporary, relate entirely to the doctrine of "the sacrament of the altar," as it was called; both declaring their belief in the doctrine of the church — that the sacramental bread

---

* *Wilkins' Concilia*, vol. III., pp. 157–172; *Fox*, I., 498–502, 504–507; *Clarke's Martyrology*, p. 44, quarto edition. See also the preceding chapter.

Clarke says, *Ashton* was condemned to perpetual imprisonment.

In the *History and Antiquities of Leicestershire*, I find the following notice of *Repyngdon*, or Repingdon, as he is there called: — "In 1393, Philip de Repingdon was elected abbot of this house [Leicester Abbey]. * * He had the honor of being chancellor of the university of Oxford in the years 1397, 1400, 1401, and 1402. * * He was confessor to the king [Henry IV.]. * * On bishop Beaufort's translation to Winchester, in 1405, Dr. Repingdon obtained the see of Lincoln, and after this became such a persecutor of the Wicklevians that he was commonly called Philip *Ramping*don. * * He was made a cardinal by Pope Gregory XII., in 1409, resigned his bishoprick in 1419, and lived private from that time to his death, which happened in 1424." — Vol. I., pp. 264–265.

and wine, after consecration, became the *very same body and blood of Christ* which was born of the virgin Mary; and the *entire* body of Christ too. No other point of doctrine is touched in either of their recantations and confessions as given by Knighton. But from Fox we learn, that Ashton made another confession. Hereford, who appears to have been a writer of much ability—his books being repeatedly honored with a condemnation in company with Wickliffe's, and himself placed second on the list of heresiarchs by Knighton—failed to obtain pardon, and was condemned by the archbishop to imprisonment.* From this decision, Hereford appealed to the king and council; but the archbishop would not allow his appeal, and condemned him to prison. But, making his escape, he returned at once to his old work of preaching the gospel. The archbishop was, of course, much enraged by his contumacy, and appealed loudly to the king for assistance in arresting the bold heretic and effectually stopping his mouth. The king granted the required aid, and Hereford was finally arrested and condemned to imprison-

* See *Knighton*, 2655–2657. These confessions are entire in Knighton, in old English; and are dated June 19th, 1382.

John Ashton is spoken of by Knighton as one of the most active and indefatigable of Wickliffe's preachers, being placed next to Hereford. Staff in hand, he traversed the kingdom, and preached the gospel wherever he found opportunity. Knighton compares him to a dog, ever ready to leap up from his bed at the slightest noise and commence barking.—*De Eventibus*, 2658–2659.

ment. From this sentence he appealed to the pope. The archbishop admitted this appeal; and he went boldly to Rome to defend himself before the pope. His success there was just what might have been anticipated:—the pope condemned him, as an incorrigible heretic, to perpetual imprisonment. The most natural thing for his holiness to have done, would, no doubt, have been, to have burned the heretic; and the reason given by Knighton for this unwonted leniency toward Hereford is, that Pope Urban wished to show a favor to the English nation, for attaching themselves to him rather than to the "schismatic pope, Clement, who flourished in those days."

But Hereford had not long been imprisoned in Rome, before a popular tumult in the city set free the prisoners from the apostolic dungeons, and he returned to England. Here he fell again into the archbishop's hands, and was again doomed to imprisonment. This was the worst that the law then allowed the bishops to do, without an appeal to the king for a writ *de heretico comburendo*, which Richard had never granted, and for which the archbishop probably thought it useless to ask. What became of Hereford after this imprisonment, we can only conjecture.*

---

* *Knighton De Eventibus*, col. 2657; *Fox*, I., 507; *Collier's Ecc. Hist.*, vol. III., pp. 163–170.

I am not quite sure that I have not sent Hereford to prison once more than I ought. But I have done the best I can to reconcile the

Utred Bolton and John Ashwerby, fellows of Oriel College, were also among the persecuted in the university about the same time; as was also Robert Rigge, the chancellor of the university; Laurence Redman; and Thomas Brightwell, a professor in the university. But we have no particulars of special interest respecting their cases.*

In 1389, archbishop Courtney seems to have discovered a congregation of Lollards in Leicester; and we find processes for the arrest, and mandates denouncing and excommunicating Roger Dexter, Nicholas Taylor, Master Richard Waytstack, a chaplain, Michael Scryvner, William Smith, John Harry, William Parchmener, Roger Goldsmith, and many others, whose names are not given.† These men, though most of them contrived to keep out of the archbishop's hands, were doomed to suffer the curse of the church. Their

---

confused account given by Fox, with the direct statement of Knighton—that Hereford went to Rome to prosecute his appeal, was imprisoned, escaped from prison, returned to England and went to work again. Fox says, Hereford was excommunicated and imprisoned by the archbishop, escaped from prison, and returned to his "former exercises and preaching;" on which the archbishop thundered out his excommunication against him, and required the aid of the temporal sword.

* *Clarke,* 44, 45; *Wilkins,* III., 158–165.

† *Knighton* places these matters apparently under the year 1392.—*De Eventibus,* 2736; but the date of Courtney's denunciation of these Lollards, according to Wilkins, was Nov. 7, 1389.—*Concilia,* III., 210.

heresies are enumerated in the archepiscopal process against them, as follows:—They believed that after consecration, there remained at the same time, the body of Christ with material bread.—Tithes should not be given to rectors or vicars so long as they continued in mortal sin.—Images ought by no means to be worshipped, or lights placed before them.—No cross should be worshipped.—Masses and matins ought not to be sung with notes (*nota*) or with a loud voice in the church.—A curate or presbyter entangled in any crime ought not to perform any clerical office-work.—Neither the pope nor any prelate can bind any one by the sentence of excommunication, unless he know, first, that he is excommunicated of God.—No prelate of the church has power to grant indulgences.—Any layman, who will, has power to preach and teach the holy gospel anywhere.—It is sin to give to the begging friars.—Offerings should not be made for the dead.—It is unnecessary to make confession of sins to a priest; and every good man who pleases, though not educated, is a priest.

These sentiments were pronounced by the archbishop subversive of the Catholic faith, and destructive of the order of the church; and for holding them, the chief minister of the church of England denounced, and excommunicated, and cursed, eight persons, together with all their adherents. The archbishop also interdicted the whole town of Leicester, and all the churches in it, so long as any of the denounced, excommunicated, and accursed Lollards should remain in the place.*

---

* *Wilkins*, III., 208–212; *Fox*, vol. I., 576–77. *Nichols' Hist. and Antiq. of Leicester*, vol. I., pp. 263–264.

One of these men is supposed to have died in the town, an excommunicate, and to have been buried in common ground, in the back lanes, at a place which has since been called after him "Goldsmith's Grave."

Knighton describes this William Smith, who was compelled to do penance, as a despicable and deformed person, who being crossed in love, forswore the world and all the women therein; renounced the use of linen, of flesh and fish of all kinds, and refused wine as if it had been a poison, and for many years went about barefoot. Smith and a chaplain named Waytestathe, we are told, were drawn together to a certain unfrequented chapel outside of Leicester, near the house of the lepers. Thither other Lollards resorted, and there held conventicles, and consulted together, until the chapel became a sort of inn and place of entertainment for all such comers, where they brought forth and communicated their malignant doctrines and opinions and heretical errors.

These poor Christians, hiding themselves thus in the house of the lepers from prelatical persecution, were sometimes, according to Knighton, reduced to straits for food; and even when they had cabbages to eat, they had not always fire to cook them with. On a certain occasion, Knighton says, when in want of fuel, one of them, in looking into a corner of the chapel, discovered an ancient image of St. Catherine, and immediately cried out—"Behold, my dear companion, God has provided fuel with which to cook our cabbages!" So they immediately siezed on the image, and doomed it to a "new kind of martyrdom"—to be chopped up for fire-wood. But they first facetiously agreed together, that if the stroke of the axe on the head of St. Catherine brought out blood, they would regard the image as holy; but, if no blood followed the stroke, then they would make the wooden saint food for the fire, with which they would cook their cabbages. All this Knighton refers to the year 1382.

In the year 1392 Knighton tells us that the same William Smith, with other Lollards, was cited before the archbishop, and all his re-

Three of these denounced and excommunicated Lollards, William Smith, Roger Dexter, and Alice Dexter, his wife, at length recanted, and submitted to do penance, in order to make their peace with the church. As an illustration of the spirit of the persecuting church, and the ignominious treatment of the poor, faint-hearted Lollards who fell away from their profession, archbishop Courtney's sentence of penance against these three persons deserves to be copied. It is as follows:—

SENTENCE OF PENANCE.

"Seeing our holy mother the church denies not her lap to any penitent child returning to her unity, but rather proffers to them the same; we therefore receive again William, Roger, and Alice, to favor. And further, have caused them to abjure all and singular the aforesaid articles and opinions, before they received of us the benefit of absolution, and were loosed from the sentence of excommunication wherein they were involved, enjoining on them penance, according to their faults, as follows: That on the Sunday next after returning to their homes [*ad propria*], they, William and Roger, in their shirts and trousers, and Alice, cov-

---

ligious books in English, from the Gospel and Epistles, and from other sources, which he had studiously labored during eight years to write, were seized by the archbishop; who also obliged him to do penance, clothed only in his linen, and bearing a crucifix in one hand, and an image of St. Catherine in the other, because he had split up and burned an image of that saint for fire-wood.—*De Eventibus*, 2661–62, 2736–37.

ered only with her linen, with naked feet and heads, each holding an image of the crucifix in their right hands, and in their left hands a taper of wax weighing half a pound, shall go before the cross three times during the procession of the cathedral church of our Lady of Leicester: that is to say, in the beginning of the procession, in the middle of the procession, and in the latter end of the procession; to the honor of him that was crucified, in the memorial of his passion, and to the honor of the Virgin his mother; and kneeling, shall devoutly kiss the crucifix held in their hands. And entering again into the church, shall stand during all the time of the holy mass, before the image of the cross, with their tapers and crosses in their hands. And when the mass is ended, the said William, Roger, and Alice, shall make an offering to him that celebrated that day the mass.

"Then upon the Saturday next ensuing, the said William, Roger, and Alice, shall in the full and public market, within the town of Leicester, stand in like manner in their shirts, holding the aforesaid crosses in their right hands; which, three times kneeling, they shall devoutly kiss (during the market); that is in the beginning of the market, in the middle of the market, and in the end of the market. And the said William (because he is somewhat educated,) shall say one antephon, with the collect, "*Holy Catherine*" etc.; and Roger and Alice, being unlearned, shall say devoutly a Pater Noster, and an Ave Maria."

[On the Sunday following, the same indecent farce was to be repeated in the cathedral church of Leicester, as was first prescribed.]

"And because of the cold weather," says the archbishop, "that now is [it was the last of November], lest the aforesaid penitents might suffer some bodily hurt, standing so long naked (being mindful to moderate partly our rigor) we give leave, that after their entrance into the churches above said, whilst they shall be hearing the aforesaid masses, they may put on the necessary garments to keep them from the cold, so that their heads and feet notwithstanding be bare." *

This humiliating, disgraceful sentence was carried out to the very letter, on these poor recanting Lollards; and thus their peace was made with Courtney and his church: how it was with their own consciences, we have no means of knowing.

Some time about the year 1389, there lived at Leicester, diocese of Lincoln, a learned and good man, a priest, whom the common people called "William the Hermit," because he had there long lived the life of a recluse. Whence he came, or what was his origin, was not known. He was a man of rather austere notions, and preached

---

* *Fox*, I., p. 577; *Wilkins*, III., 211–12. I have copied the version of Fox, chiefly, for convenience sake; but have made some abridgment of the article, and some slight alterations, suggested by a comparison of Fox with the original in Wilkins. The sentence bears date Dorchester, Nov. 17, 1389.

against the fashionable follies and vices of society. His persistent denunciations of the pride, extravagance, ornaments, and general deportment of the women, at length so provoked them, that, we are told, they proposed to stone him out of the place. He next addressed himself to the merchants and rich men, warning them of the danger of losing heaven through the possession of the riches of this world; and this he did, it would seem, not altogether without effect; for Knighton, his contemporary and neighbor, expresses the conviction that but for the Divine interposition, certain good men of Leicester would have been drawn into his desperate errors, by his earnest preaching. He also preached, with much power and success, against the pride, and vices, and crimes of the clergy, and the corruptions of the church. He is charged with teaching, among other things: — that parishioners were not bound to pay their tithes to unchaste, immoral and inconsistent curates; or even to non-residents; or to such as were unfit or incompetent to discharge the duties of their office: under such circumstances, he held that parishioners might give their tithes and offerings to whomsoever they pleased. He is charged, also, with teaching that men were able to collect their debts by gentle means; but ought, on no account, to harrass or imprison their debtors. He condemned, as injustice and extortion, the collection of tithes by threatening excommunication against those who withheld them. And he taught that no man was a true priest who lived contrary to God's law, whoever might have ordained him.

If the preaching of this good man was austere, his mode of living was, in a good measure, conformed to his creed. He sought for himself neither honors, nor riches, nor luxuries. When not engaged in his preaching tours, he made his home generally in some solitary place; and depended on the freewill offerings of the charitable for his sustenance; refusing even these, when they exceeded his simple wants. Having food and raiment, he seems therewith to have been content; and when pinched with hunger, and destitute of other necessities of life—which was occasionally his experience—he appears to have borne his lot with patience and even cheerfulness. That he was a worthy priest, though somewhat austere and enthusiastic in character and conduct, seems evident from the interest which the Duke of Lancaster took in him; at one time supporting him, and ever, it would seem, being ready to interpose his good offices on his behalf.

This man was a Wickliffite, or Lollard, and his name was William Swinderby. The common people were greatly taken with his preaching, and declared that they had never seen nor heard such truths as he expounded to them; and around him and his companion and fellow-recluse, William Smith, others of like faith were gathered from time to time, at the chapel of St. John the Baptist, near the mansion of the lepers, outside of the town.

When the rumor of these things reached the ears of John Buckingham, Bishop of Lincoln, without delay he suspended Swinderby from preaching in the leper's chapel, or in any other church, or churchyard, or consecrated place in the diocese; and forbade the people to hear or to favor the preacher, under pain of the greater excommunication.

Being thus driven out from his chapel, and from all consecrated places, Swinderby resorted to the highway. At a little distance beyond the leper's chapel, there chanced to be a pair of mill-stones, which Swinderby turned into a pulpit: and around these stones he gathered the people, and there preached the gospel, in contempt of episcopal authority; saying, as Knighton informs us, that "he could and would preach in the king's highway, in spite of the teeth of the bishop, as long as he could have the favor of the people." And so great was his popularity as a preacher, that Knighton tells us, "you might see crowds of people from every quarter, rushing to his preaching, in spite of the inhibition" and the threatened excommunication.

In the meantime the lord-bishop of Lincoln cited Swinderby to appear at the cathedral church of Lincoln; and the preacher obeyed: and many days were spent in discussing the objectionable doctrines which he taught, and in hearing his answers to the objections urged against them. At length, being publicly convicted by his judges of diverse heresies and errors — certain friars of the

Minorite, Augustin, and Preaching orders being his accusers — Swinderby was deemed to be fit food for the flames. This decision occasioned great distress among the people who had accompanied the poor preacher from Leicester, with the hope of rendering him some aid. They wept and smote their hands and heads against the walls, we are told, in the abandonment of their sorrow; but it was all in vain.

It so happened, however, that the Duke of Lancaster, who had always befriended the Lollards, and had before shown his personal interest in Swinderby, was in Lincoln on the day of the ecclesiastical decision, and interposed his good offices on behalf of the condemned, and obtained from the bishop a commutation of the punishment decreed; the bishop consenting, that, instead of burning him, he would require only that Swinderby should publicly renounce the heresies and errors charged upon him, in the cathedral at Lincoln, in three churches at Leicester and some others in the diocese, which were named; and should no more preach in the diocese of Lincoln, unless he had license from the diocesan.

Swinderby consented to make his recantation in form and manner prescribed by the bishop; and then retired, sad and mournful, to his lonely retreat in the leper's chapel. The populace, intimidated by the threatening position of the church authorities and the narrow escape of their leader from the flames, seem to have forsaken him; and he, following apostolic examples, soon left the place and the diocese, and took up his abode in Coventry, in the diocese of Hereford. Here, in a short time he became a greater favorite with the laity than he had ever been before; and he continued about a year, preaching and teaching as he had before done, and making many proselytes, and spreading his fame and his doctrines over the whole diocese.*

Though at the time of his condemnation the good man's fears gained the mastery over him, and he was induced to make public recantation of the heresies and errors objected to him, yet he justifies his course, in part, by saying, that the errors he was called to renounce, he never held in the forms charged against him; and therefore had no scruple in renouncing them as required. His promise not to preach in the diocese of Lincoln, he seems to have regarded as binding on him; but nothing else seemed to keep him from immediately return-

---

* *Knighton, De Eventibus,* columns 2665–2671. *Collier* reproduces the old canon's gossip about Swinderby and his companion Smith, so far as this tends to the discredit of the Lollards. — *Ecc. Hist.,* vol. III., 174, 206, 171.

Thus far we have the narrative of the canon of Leicester, Knighton, for our guide. He was a contemporary, had opportunity to know the facts in the case, and it is highly probable was present at Swinderby's trial, and witnessed what he relates.

Fox tells us that the friars who were accusers and denouncers of Swinderby, actually brought faggots into town with them, for the purpose of burning the heretic: perhaps rather to frighten him and his friends and followers; which they did most effectually. Swinderby confirms this statement about the faggots in a subsequent statement of his own case.

ing to his old ways. And accordingly, we find him immediately on his removal to Coventry engaged in preaching his Lollard doctrines and making converts to the faith.

These labors he had carried on for about a year, when another Lord John, bishop of Hereford, interposed his authority, and summoned the preacher to his presence, to answer to charges of heresy and error, which were drawn out into seventeen articles. At the instance of "certain noble personages," as the bishop tells us, free access and departure were guaranteed to Swinderby; and he made his appearance in court and presented a written protestation against the charges, and a brief explanation and defence of his real views; protesting, that "it was his purpose, with his whole heart, to be a christian man, with open confession of his defaults;" and declaring, that "it was not his intent anything to say or affirm, to maintain or defend, contrary to holy writ;" and that he was ready to renounce any doctrine or opinion that could be shown to be contrary to that standard of authority. He then examined, first, the charges made against him on his previous trial at Lincoln; and declared them to be false and slanderous. He next took up the new charges against him, and defended himself with spirit but modesty.

Having read his defence, he left the court, and took himself out of the bishops' way, so that he could not be personally cited again. The bishop and his advisers being dissatisfied with Swinderby's protestation and answers, on the 5th of July 1391 issued another citation, for his appearance on the 20th of the same month, to answer more fully.

The 20th came and the court assembled and called for the heretic; but "only by a servant he sent a certain schedule of paper, made like an indenture unto us [the bishop] to excuse him." For his non-appearance he was judged obstinate, and the court assigned another day, the 29th, for his appearance. His non-appearance on that day was pronounced an evidence of his great obstinacy; nevertheless of "our exceeding favor," the bishop appoints the 8th of August for his appearance; and on that day, still another was assigned, the 16th of August, to the absent heretic; and on that day, he not appearing, the 2d day of September was assigned. Swinderby not appearing then, witnesses were examined against him, and he was pronounced and denounced as "a heretic, schismatic and false informer of the people," and all men were warned neither to believe, receive, defend nor favor him.

From this decision Swinderby appealed to the king and his council, and addressed a protest to the king and council, and an appeal to the nobles and burgesses of parliament. Nothing, however, came of this appeal, and Swinderby was compelled to flee the country, and hide himself from the vengeance of the bishop of Hereford. This he succeeded in doing probably as long as Richard II.

was on the throne. In March 1392, a commission was issued out for his arrest, and the arrest of one Stephen Bell, "a learned man," who had been excommunicated as a heretic at the same time that Swinderby was. From this document we learn, that Swinderby and his associate were supposed to be hid in the borders of Wales. But whether these poor hunted saints were arrested, or whether they succeeded in escaping the spiritual hounds, we are not informed; though Fox thinks that Swinderby, at least, was arrested, and suffered martyrdom at Smithfield, about 1401.*

The history of Swinderby has been given thus particularly, not simply on account of its intrinsic interest, but chiefly because, by means of a contemporary, we are here introduced to the domestic life and the abundant labors and hardships of one of the "poor priests," who spread the doctrines of Wickliffe through England. We may look on Swinderby as the representative of a class; as a living illustration of the self-denial, labor, suffering, and general experience of the poor preachers of the gospel, in those days of popish darkness and cruelty. All over England there were men of like spirit, who labored and suffered for the

---

* *Fox*, vol. I., pp. 530–543, gives the details of Swinderby's case, so far as the Episcopal Registers furnish information; but these are in a broken, fragmentary condition, not very intelligible nor readable. Knighton, though an enemy, seems to have taken special pains to transmit to posterity the facts of Swinderby's life and labors up to the time he left Leicester.

truth, of whom we know little or nothing, because no contemporary, as in Swinderby's case, has transmitted to us their history.

Another distinguished champion of the gospel, who was persecuted about this time, was Walter Brute, "a learned layman," of Merton College. He was examined before the bishop of Hereford and other inquisitorial dignitaries, in the cathedral church of the diocese, and defended his sentiments with much ability, for several days. One of the sins charged upon Walter at this time was, that he had declared that William Swinderby's answers to the bishop were "good, righteous, and not able to be convinced [refuted], in that they contained no error;" and that the bishop's sentence of excommunication etc., against said William, was "evil, false, and unjust." His other heresies were:— that he believed and openly taught that every Christian man (yea, and woman) being without sin, may make the body of Christ as well as a priest; that in the sacrament of the altar is not the very body of Christ, but a sign and a memorial; that no man is bound to give tithes or oblations; but if any wills so to do, he may give to whom he pleases. That he denounced as heretics and schismatics such persons as accepted the indulgences granted by the pope to all who aided the bishop of Norwich in his crusade against the French pope. That he commonly spoke of the pope as antichrist, and a seducer of the people, and utterly against the law and life of Christ.

Brute defended himself, with great ability, in a long treatise on the several points charged against him. But was at length induced to offer a sort of submission, which, perhaps, he could do with a clear conscience; and which the bishop probably thought it best to accept. It was to this effect:—

"I, Walter Brute, submit myself principally to the Gospel of Jesus Christ, and to the determination of holy kirk, and to the general councils of holy kirk; and to the sentence and determination of the four doctors of holy writ; that is Augustine, Ambrose, Jerome and Gregory. And I meekly submit me to your corrections as a subject ought to his bishop." *

It was judicious in the bishop to accept this submission; for the learning and ability displayed by Walter were such, that neither the bishop nor any of his fellow inquisitors undertook to reply; but after devoting three days to the heretic, they gathered up no less than thirty-seven propositions out of his defence, and sent them to the learned men of the university to be examined, and refuted if possible.

* *Fox* gives a very long account of Walter Brute's defence, giving his arguments, which were written out in Latin, nearly or quite entire. See vol. I., pp. 542–71.

The difference between such a submission as Brute's, and such an one as Smith and Dexter were compelled to make, and such as was required of many others, is very great. See *ante*, p. 400.

Two other distinguished advocates of Wickliffe's doctrines were brought into trouble about this time, by preaching the gospel faithfully. One was Peter Pateshal, a London preacher, once an Augustine friar, who was compelled to flee to Bohemia. The other was Henry Crump, a doctor of divinity at Oxford, who, from being an adversary, became a devoted advocate of Wickliffe's doctrines. He was persecuted by the bishops and compelled to flee into Ireland. And even there, did not long escape their malice, for he was arrested and suffered a long imprisonment.*

* *Clarke*, p. 44; Fox, vol. I., p. 577; *Wilkins*, III., 167. *Walsingham* speaks of this Lollard preacher, whom he calls Peter Pateshull. He appears to have been quite successful in making converts in London. On one occasion, when preaching in the church of St. Christopher, and exposing the secret iniquities and crimes of the monks, some of the Augustinian monks being present and interrupting and contradicting him, quite a row was produced, and the monks were attacked and driven out of the church and beaten, etc., and their house threatened with destruction. — See *Hist. Angl.*, p. 327–28.

CHAPTER XI.

THE FLAMES OF MARTYRDOM KINDLED. — WILLIAM SAUTRE, THE PROTO-MARTYR OF THE LOLLARDS. — WILLIAM THORPE'S TRIAL, IMPRISONMENT AND PROBABLE DEATH. — THE BURNING OF JOHN BADBY.

We now enter on the reign of Henry IV. in the State, and Thomas Arundel in the Church of England; and are to be introduced to a more bitter and deadly persecution of the Lollards than anything heretofore experienced. The prelates, as we have seen, had been harrassing the preachers of the gospel and others, by means of trials before the ecclesiastical courts, denunciations, excommunications, imprisonments, and forfeiture of property; but hitherto they had been restrained from taking the lives of the believers, as Satan of old was from taking the life of Job. Neither Edward III. nor Richard II. would allow this. Nor was it in harmony with the general spirit of the English government, to suffer persecution unto death for religion's sake. A few instances, only, are on record where this was done before the year 1400. Hitherto the English monarchs had kept in their own hands the lives of their subjects. The prelates might persecute, and imprison, and excommunicate, and curse the heretics, to their heart's content; and they could even denounce them to the king as worthy of fire; but the king was the ultimate judge whether to put the denounced heretic into the fire: and as most of the English sovereigns were averse to this method of benefitting men's souls — as, in the language of the church, this was done, *de salute animæ* — few got burned to death.* But when Henry IV. had given the clergy the desire of their hearts — a law by which the bishops could burn heretics without any appeal to the king for a writ — then began the reign of terror in England.

The first victim — if not of the law itself, which was passed in the second year of Henry IV. — of

---

* I have met with but *two* examples of the burning of heretics in England previous to the time of Henry IV., 1399–1400. One was an Albigensian, burned in 1210; the other was a deacon of the church, who apostatized to Judaism, in 1222. — See Preface to *Bale's Chronicle.*

Clarke tells us that as early as 1160, in the reign of Henry II., "there came above thirty of the Waldenses into England, one Gerard being their minister, acknowledged to be a learned man by the Monk of Newbury who writes the story." These good people were arrested, examined and excommunicated by a council of bishops assembled at Oxford, and given over to the civil power for punishment. By the king's order they were branded in the face, their clothes were cut off to their "girdlesteads," they were publicly whipped through Oxford, and then driven out to perish in the fields; the king commanding "that no one should presume to receive them to house, nor to cherish them with any comfort; whereby they miserably perished with hunger and cold." — *Persecution of the Eng. Chh. under the Papacy.* quarto, p. 41.

that spirit which dictated that law—was William Sautre, or Sawtree, or Chatres, sometimes called *Sir* Wm. Sautre.*

Our first introduction to this proto-martyr of the Lollards, is in 1399, when he was parish priest of the church of St. Margaret, Lynn, diocese of Norwich. In that year he was arraigned before the fiery, fighting bishop Spencer, as a heretical preacher. In answer to the charges against him, he made a bold confession of the truth. The bishop finding that he could not prevail against him in open court, doomed him to close confinement in his palace prison, at South Helingham; probably in what was called, "Little Ease"; a sort of dungeon, or hole, so contrived that a prisoner could neither stand upright in it, lie straight, nor sit comfortably. After eighteen days of suffering in the bishop's dungeon, poor Sautre was brought out, broken

* The Latin word *Dominus* is usually translated *Sir;* and as the clergy generally had received the college honor of B. A. (*Dominus*), it became common to style them *Sir.* Thus *Don* is used in some parts of Italy. At this date, Sir was rarely thus used in England. *Shakspeare* uses the term in "As You Like It," where Sir Oliver Martext, a vicar, is thus addressed: "Here comes *Sir* Oliver.—Sir Oliver Martext, you are well met: will you despatch us here under this tree, or shall we go with you to your chapel?"—*Act* III., *Scene* 3. But "*Sir* Oliver" does not appear as a very respectable character, for Jaques says to Touchstone: "Get you to church and have a *good priest,* that can tell you what marriage is: *this fellow* will but join you together as they join waistcoat; then one of you will prove a shrunk panel, and like green timber, warp, warp." *Chaucer* sometimes uses the term *Don* when speaking of ecclesiastics.—See *Canterbury Tales.*

down in spirit, and — if we may believe the bishop's account — ready to deny himself, if not the Lord who bought him. He recanted, it is said, ten articles which were charged against him; and then was suffered to go free.

The next year, however, we hear of him as parish priest of the church of St. Scithe (Osith) the Virgin, in London. Though a parish priest, he seems not to have become reconciled to the corruptions of the papal hierarchy, nor to have changed his faith, notwithstanding his reported recantation before the bishop of Norwich.

He had devised, we are told, some plan of church reform, which he sought opportunity to lay before parliament. The clergy suspecting his purpose, succeeded in getting the whole matter referred to them. The Convocation of Canterbury was then in session in St. Paul's Cathedral, with Arundel at its head; and when the reformer made his appearance before that august body, instead of getting a hearing in favor of church reform, he found himself at once confronted with charges of heresy, and of being a relapsed heretic. The charges against him were, in form, as follows:

"Sir William Sautre, otherwise called Chatres, parish priest of the church St. Scithe the Virgin, in London, publicly and privately doth hold these conclusions under-written: —

"1. That he will not worship the cross on which Christ suffered, but only Christ that suffered on the cross. — 2. That he would sooner worship a temporal king than the wooden cross. — 3. That he would rather worship the bodies of the saints, than the very cross of Christ on which he hung, if it were before him. — 4. That he would rather worship a man truly contrite than the cross of Christ. — 5. That he is bound rather to worship a man that is predestinate than an angel of God. — 6. That if any man would visit the monuments of Peter and Paul, or go on pilgrimage to the tomb of St. Thomas á Becket, or anywhere else, for obtaining of any temporal benefit, he is not bound to keep his vow, but he may distribute the expenses of his vow upon the alms of the poor. — 7. That every priest and deacon is more bound to preach the word of God than to say the canonical hours. — 8. That after the pronouncing of the sacramental words of the body of Christ, the bread remains of the same nature that it was before, neither does it cease to be bread."

Sautre finding himself entrapped by the cunning of the archbishop and his councillors, asked for a copy of the charges against him, and time to answer. This was on Saturday, Feb. 12, 1400. This request was granted, and the archbishop gave him until the next Thursday to prepare his answer.

At the appointed time Sautre presented a brief reply to the charges against him, explaining his views somewhat on the several points designated, but admitting that he held in substance the opinions charged against him.

The archbishop then commenced an examination of the prisoner, particularly respecting this point: — "Whether, in the sacrament of the altar, after the pronouncing of the sacramental words, remains very material bread or not?"

Sautre said, after some hesitation, that "there was bread, holy, true, and the bread of life."

The archbishop then asked him, "whether the same material bread before consecration, by the sacramental words of the priest, rightly pronounced, be transubstantiated from the nature of bread into the very body of Christ?"

Sautre answered, that he knew not what that meant.

The archbishop then gave him until the next day to consider the question.

The next day he was examined on the same topic — the transubstantiation of the bread into the real body of Christ; but no further replies could be obtained from Sautre than were given on the previous examination. The archbishop then demanded of him "whether he would stand to the determination of holy church, or not; which affirms, that in the sacrament of the altar, after the words of consecration, being rightly pronounced by the priest, the same bread, which before in nature was bread, ceases any more to be bread?"

Sautre replied, that he would stand to the determination of the church, where such determination was not contrary to the will of God.

Being still further pressed for his own belief in

regard to the bread after consecration; he finally replied — that it remained the same bread that it was before consecration.

This was enough. The parish priest of St. Osith was at once pronounced a heretic.

Here ended the first step. The next movement was made by the bishop of Norwich. At the command of the archbishop, he presented a sealed document to Sautre, which was afterwards read aloud, charging, "that upon the last day of April, 1399, Sir William Sautre, parish priest of the church of St. Margaret, in the town of Lynn, appeared before the bishop of Norwich, and there publicly affirmed and held the conclusions before specified" — referring to the charges already enumerated. "And afterwards, to wit, the 19th day of May, Sir William revoked and renounced all his conclusions, abjuring and correcting all such heresies and errors, taking his oath upon a book, before the bishop of Norwich, that from that time forward, he would never preach, affirm nor hold, privily nor openly, the conclusions; and that he would pronounce, according to the appointment of the bishop, the aforesaid conclusions to be erroneous and heresies, in the parish churches of Lynn and Tilney, and in other places, at the assignment of the said bishop."

This being read, the archbishop charged Sir William with having affirmed, after having once abjured, the error, that after the consecration there remained material bread in the sacrament; and he not denying that he did thus believe — though he seems to have denied that he ever recanted this — the convocation, after badgering the poor victim for about three hours, determined that he ought to be deposed and degraded from all official relation to the church, as a relapsed and incorrigible heretic; and the archbishop proceeded forthwith to pronounce in form, the sentence of deposition and degradation.

This finished that day's work with the clergy. On the 26th of February, the archbishop arrayed in pontifical attire, accompanied by six other bishops, took his place again in St. Paul's cathedral, and ordered Sautre to be brought before him, clothed in full priestly array. Arundel then made an address to the assembled multitude, and informed them of the proceedings of convocation against the prisoner; and finished by reading to them the sentence which had been pronounced against him. After this, he proceeded in form and manner as follows, to degrade Sautre, step by step, down the entire church-ladder — from every office in the church; first from the priesthood, then from the office of a deacon, a sub-deacon, an acolyte, an exorcist, a reader, and finally from even the office of sexton.

SENTENCE OF DEGRADATION.

" In the name of the Father, and the Son, and of the Holy Ghost. We, Thomas, by God's permission archbishop of Canterbury, primate of all

England, and legate of the apostolic see, do denounce thee, William Sautre, otherwise called Chatres, chaplain feigned, in the habit and apparel of a priest, as an heretic, and re-fallen into heresy, by this our sentence definitive, by counsel, assent, and authority, to be condemned: and by conclusion of all our fellow brethren, fellow bishops, prelates, council provincial, and of the whole clergy, do degrade and deprive thee of thy priestly order. And in sign of degradation and actual deposition from thy priestly dignity, for thine incorrigibility and want of amendment, we take from thee the paten and chalice, [i. e. the communion plate and cup] and do deprive thee of all power and authority of celebrating the mass; and also we pull from thy back the *casule*, and take from thee the vestment, and deprive thee of all manner of priestly honour.

[Here the poor man was stripped of all the insignia of the priestly office, and thus was made a deacon.]

"Also, we Thomas, the aforesaid archbishop, by authority, counsel, and assent, which upon the aforesaid William we have, being deacon pretensed, in the habit and apparel of a deacon, having the New Testament in thy hands, being an heretic and twice fallen, condemned by sentence as is aforesaid, do degrade and put thee from the order of a deacon. And in token of this thy degradation and actual deposition, we take from thee the book of the New Testament, and the stole [the appropriate garment of a papal deacon] and do deprive thee of all authority in reading of the gospel, and of all and all manner of dignity of a deacon.

[The official vestment and the insignia of a deacon being taken away, Sautre becomes, in the eye of the papal church, a sub-deacon — a deacon's assistant.]

"Also, we Thomas, archbishop, by authority, counsel, and assent, which over thee the aforesaid William we have, being a sub-deacon pretensed, in the habit and vestment of a sub-deacon, an heretic and twice fallen, and condemned by sentence, as is aforesaid, do degrade and put thee from the order of a sub-deacon; and in token of this thy degradation and actual deposition, we take from thee the albe [or surplice] and *maniple*, and do deprive thee of all manner of sub-deaconical dignity.

[Sautre is now reduced to an acolyte — a sort of servant or personal attendant of the bishop.]

"Also, we Thomas, archbishop aforesaid, by counsel, assent, and authority which we have over thee, the aforesaid William, an acolyte pretensed, wearing the habit of an acolyte, an heretic twice fallen, by our sentence condemned, do degrade and put from thee all order of an acolyte; and in sign and token of this thy degradation, and actual deposition, we take from thee the candlestick and taper, and also the *urceolum* [a vessel to contain water] and do deprive thee of all and all manner of dignity of an acolyte.

"Also, we Thomas, archbishop, by assent, counsel, and authority, which upon thee the aforesaid William we have, an exorcist pretensed, in the habit of an exorcist or holy water clerk, being an heretic, twice fallen, and by our sentence, as is aforesaid, condemned, do degrade and depose thee from the order of an exorcist; and in token of this thy degradation and actual deposition, we take from thee the book of conjurations, and do deprive thee of all and singular dignity of an exorcist.

[An exorcist had charge of the holy water of the church, and was instructed by the book of conjurations how to cast out devils in the most approved manner.]

"Also, we Thomas, archbishop, by assent, counsel, and authority, as is abovesaid, do degrade and depose thee, the aforesaid William, a reader pretensed, clothed in the habit of a reader, an heretic twice fallen, and by our sentence as is aforesaid, condemned, from the order of a reader; and in token of this thy degradation and actual deposition, we take from thee the book of the divine lections [that is, the book of the church legend], and do deprive thee of all and singular manner of dignity of such a reader.

"Also, we Thomas, archbishop of Canterbury aforesaid, by authority, counsel, and assent, the which we have, as is aforesaid, do degrade and put thee, the aforesaid William Sautre, a sexton pretensed, in the habit of a sexton, and wearing a surplice, being an heretic twice fallen, by our sentence definitive condemned, as aforesaid, from the order of a sexton; and in token of this thy degradation and actual deposition, for the causes aforesaid, we take from thee the keys of the church-door, and thy surplice, and do deprive thee of all and singular manner of commodities of a door-keeper.

"And also, by the authority of omnipotent God the Father, the Son, and Holy Ghost, and by the authority, counsel, and assent of our whole council provincial above written, we do degrade thee, and depose thee, being here personally present before us, from orders, benefices, privileges and habit in the church; and for thy pertinency incorrigible, we do degrade thee before the secular court of the high constable and marshal of England, being personally present; and do depose thee from all and singular clerkly honours and dignities whatsoever, by these writings. Also, in token of thy degradation and deposition, here actually we have caused thy crown and ecclesiastical tonsure in our presence to be razed away, and utterly to be abolished, like to the form of a secular layman; and here we do put upon the head of thee, the aforesaid William, the cap of a lay secular person; beseeching the court aforesaid, that they will receive favorably the said William, unto them thus re-committed." *

---

* *Fox*, vol. I., p. 589.

The circumstances attending the degradation of Sautre, will remind the reader of ecclesiastical history of another victim, and a more illustrious, if not a more sincere and valiant soldier of the Cross,

This piece of solemn mummery being finished, and the poor man being stripped of all the vest-

---

who perished at the stake, in another land, but for substantially the same truths, about fifteen years after the death of the poor parish priest of St. Osith, London. I refer to John Huss. The following account of the degradation of this eminent disciple of Wickliffe and martyr of Jesus Christ, is from *Neander*, vol. v., pp. 368–369; and from *Fox* (Seymour's ed.), p. 307 : —

"On the 6th of July [1415], Huss appeared before the assembled council, at which the emperor also was present, seated upon his throne, surrounded by the princes, and with the insignia of the empire. In the middle of the hall where the council met, stood a sort of table, and near it a wooden frame or stand, upon which were hung the priestly vestments which Huss was to put on previous to his degradation. After an introductory discourse the process was read, together with all the articles of complaint, and from the whole the conclusion was drawn that Huss was a follower of Wicklif, and had disseminated Wicklifite doctrines.

"Various errors and heresies were ascribed also to Huss himself, with various qualifications, and he was pronounced an obstinate, incorrigible heretic. One of the points here specified was the appeal of Huss to Jesus Christ, which was characterized as an overleaping of the constituted instances of ecclesiastical courts, as an act of infatuation, and a contempt of church jurisdiction. Huss attempted, more than once, to interpose a word in defence of himself against the allegations; but he was not permitted to proceed."

"At last, the seven bishops who were chosen out to degrade him of his priesthood commanded him to put on the garments pertaining unto priesthood, which, when he had done, and come to the putting on of the albe, he called to his remembrance the purple vesture which Herod put on Jesus Christ to mock him withal. So likewise in all other things he comforted himself by the example of Christ. When he had now put on all his priestly vestures, the bishops exhorted him that he should yet alter and change his mind, and provide for his honour and safety; then he (according as the manner of the ceremony is) going up to the top of the scaffold, being full of tears, spake to the people. * * * Then he was commanded to come down to the execution of his judgment, and in his coming down,

ments and insignia of office in the pope's church, and his head being shaved, and scraped where the holy oil and the bishop's fingers in ordination had been placed, and being made, after the most approved method of Roman law, a mere layman, is now prepared for the faggots; and the archbishop immediately petitions the king for a writ for burning the heretic, for the good of his soul and the terror of all such evil doers.* This the king granted

one of the seven bishops before rehearsed, first took away from him the chalice which he held in his hand, saying: 'O, cursed Judas, why hast thou forsaken the council and ways of peace, and hast counselled with the Jews? We take away from thee this chalice of thy salvation." * * * Then followed the other bishops in order, who every one of them took away the vestments from him which they had put on, each one of them giving him their curse. * * * At the last they came to the erasing of his shaven crown. But before the bishops would go in hand with it, there was a great contention between them, with what instrument it should be done, with a razor or with a pair of shears. In the mean time, John Huss, turning himself toward the emperor, said: 'I marvel that forsomuch as they be all of like cruel mind and spirit, yet they cannot agree upon their kind of cruelty.' Notwithstanding, at last they agreed to cut off the skin of the crown of his head with a pair of shears. And when they had done that, they added these words: 'Now hath the church taken away all her ornaments and privileges from him. Now there resteth nothing else, but that he be delivered over unto the secular power.'

"But before they did that, there yet remained another reproach. For they caused to be made a certain crown of paper, almost a cubit deep, in the which were painted three devils of wonderful ugly shape, and this title set over their heads, 'ARCH-HERETIC,' which, when he saw, he said: 'My Lord Jesus Christ for my sake did wear a crown of thorns, why should not I then for his sake again wear this light crown, be it never so ignominious? Truly I will do it, and that willingly.'"

* The parliament which made the statute by which the bishops

forthwith; and on the same day, February 26th, 1400–1401, William Sautre was led forth to execution, and became the first of a long line of martyrs to the faith of the gospel as preached by Wickliffe and embraced by the Lollards. So far as appears from the record of his trial and martyrdom, after he had once taken his stand, Sautre quitted himself like a valiant soldier of the cross. There were no signs of fear, no wavering in him. His repentance, like Peter's, for his first denial of his faith — if indeed he ever did deny his faith — appears to have been hearty, and his strength for the final trial sufficient to meet the fiery ordeal, not only unwaveringly, but even with a cheerful countenance.*

---

could burn heretics without the king's writ (see *ante* p. 343) was at this time in session, and the statute itself had probably been enacted; why, then, was application made for this writ out of chancery, agreeably to the old, common law of the land? The answer may be, first: that the archbishop wished to give to this initiatory step in the bloody drama of persecution all the formality and impressiveness possible; secondly, that he thought it more prudent to test the king's willingness to execute the law against heretics, and to commit him to the work, than to assume the responsibility himself, and the necessary odium of being the first to burn to death virtuous men, who merely dissented from the dogmas of the church; or, thirdly, it may have been, that, though the statute for burning heretics without the king's writ had passed, it had not been proclaimed, and therefore could not be used. This last suggestion is *Collier's*, Ecc. Hist. III., 262.

* The authorities for this account of William Sautre's trial and condemnation are *Fox*, vol. I., pp. 587–590; *Wilkins' Concilia*, vol. III., pp. 254–260; *Collier's Ecc. Hist.*, vol. III., pp. 259–262; *Richards' Hist. Lynn*, Eng., vol. I., pp. 589–615, folio.

There seems to be some mystery respecting the alleged recantation of Sautre before the bishop of Norwich. Being charged by the

minuteness — and it deserves, therefore, to be transcribed and made familiar to all who would understand the true story of the Lollards of England.

I have greatly abridged the narrative preserved by Fox, but so as to give the spirit of it, and always in Thorpe's own quaint and expressive style, though the words themselves are somewhat modernized.

THE EXAMINATION OF WILLIAM THORPE, PENNED WITH HIS OWN HAND.

"Be it known to all men that read or hear this writing, that on the Sunday next after the feast of St. Peter, that we call Lammas (A. D. 1407), I, William Thorpe, being in prison in the castle of Saltwood, was brought before Thomas Arundel, archbishop of Canterbury, and chancellor then of England. And when I came to him, he stood in a great chamber, and many people about him; and when he saw me he went into a closet, bidding all secular men that followed him to leave him soon, so that no man was left in that closet but the archbishop himself, and a physician that was called Masveren, parson of St. Dunstan's in London, and two other persons unknown to me, who were ministers of the law.

"By and by the archbishop said to me, 'William, I know well that thou hast these twenty winters or more travelled in the north country, and in divers other countries of England, sowing false doctrine, labouring with untrue teaching to infect and poison all this land. But through the grace of God thou art now withstood and brought into my ward, so that I shall now sequester thee from thine evil purpose, and prevent thee from poisoning the sheep of my province. Nevertheless, St. Paul saith, If it may be, as much as in us lies, we ought to live peaceably with all men. Therefore, William, if thou wilt now meekly and of good heart, without any feigning, kneel down and lay thy hand upon a book and kiss it, promising faithfully, as I shall here charge thee, that thou wilt submit thee to my correction, and stand to mine ordinance, and fulfil it duly by all thy skill and power, thou shalt yet find me gracious to thee.'

"Then said I to the archbishop, 'Sir, since ye deem me an heretic, and out of the faith, will you give me here audience to tell you my belief?'

"And he said, 'Yea, tell on.'

"And I said, 'I believe that there is but one God Almighty, and in this Godhead and of this Godhead are three Persons, that is, the Father, the Son, and the Holy Ghost. And I believe that all these three Persons are equal in power and in knowledge, and in might, full of grace of all goodness. For whatsoever that the Father doth, or can, or will do, that thing also the Son doth, and can, and will do; and in all their power, knowledge, and will, the Holy Ghost is equal to the Father, and to the Son. Besides this, I believe,

CHAPTER XIII.

THE PRETENDED INSURRECTION OF THE LOLLARDS, IN JANUARY, 1413–14.

HAVING finished in the preceding chapter the story of "the good Lord Cobham," so far as the facts relating to his life, trial for heresy, condemnation, escape from prison, recapture and martyrdom are concerned; we must now retrace our steps, and examine certain matters which transpired between the time of his escape, near the end of October 1413, and his recapture, in December 1417. These things were omitted in their chronological order, that the interesting story of Cobham might not be broken.

What I particularly refer to, is called "the insurrection of the Lollards;" and occurred in January, 1413–14. This is an affair of considerable historical importance, not only because it involved a large number of innocent persons in suffering and death; but because it illustrates the spirit of the rulers of Church and State, early in the fifteenth century, towards those who ventured to think for themselves, and to worship and serve God according to what they believed to be his most holy will.

But while this "Lollard Insurrection" — so

called — is intrinsically and historically quite an interesting and important matter, it is one on which historical writers are by no means agreed; and which there is reason to suspect that very few have carefully investigated; their opinions being, for the most part, the result of accidental impressions or religious prejudices, rather than of impartial examination of the facts involved. The Catholic writers are, without exception, so far as I know, on one side; while Protestants, as usual, are divided in opinion.

This difference of opinion is not, however, altogether a matter of religious prejudice, or the result of Protestant indifference. There are real difficulties in the way of coming to a perfectly satisfactory conclusion — in ascertaining exactly the truth in relation to the matter. The prominent difficulty arises from the fact, that the original authorities on this question are all Romish ecclesiastics, bitterly prejudiced against the Lollards, and ready to believe and report any evil thing about them; and, in addition to this, that their accounts are manifestly, and in some particulars confessedly popular and hearsay accounts, and not the results of careful investigation even of prejudiced persons. I refer particularly to the stories told by Walsingham, the Benedictine monk of St. Albans, who wrote his History of England about the middle of the fifteenth century; by Thomas Elmham, a contemporary and biographer (or rather eulogist) of Henry V.; by Titus Livius — not the great Roman, but another contemporary of Henry, and a chaplain in his celebrated French campaign, of which Livius has written a detailed account. Of these three writers, who are the chief original authorities on the question at issue, Walsingham is the fullest, and the one chiefly relied on by Lingard in his History of England, and by all the Romish and High-Church party. The other two contemporaries — though they agree in their general representation of the meeting in St. Giles' Field, as an insurrectionary affair — give few details, and only mention the matter incidentally, as connected with the glorious deeds of their hero, Henry V. And Walsingham, whose History of England was not written until some thirty or more years after this "insurrection of the Lollards," admits, in repeated instances, that he is giving only current rumors. He tells the story of Lord Cobham, and the pretended insurrection of the Lollards under his leadership, as it was currently reported among the ecclesiastics of his day. He may have believed every word he wrote; and yet his story, coming through such channels, and told by one bitterly and notoriously prejudiced, and this story too, more or less of it, confessedly mere hearsay — must be received with many grains of allowance. As to Elmham and Livy, they are of very little account. They evidently knew but little, and cared still less about this whole affair, except as it afforded an opportunity to glorify Henry. And Elmham, in one important particular at least, contradicts Arundel's own account, respecting Cobham's intimacy with Henry.*

In addition to the united testimony of these ancient, contemporaneous writers, to the insurrectionary character of the St. Giles affair, there are public documents — royal proclamations of undoubted authenticity, and legal papers of probable authenticity — which hold the same language on the mooted question. And besides these original authorities, the old chroniclers of the succeeding century — Fabyan, Hall, and Holinshed; and the historians of England generally, notice this matter more or less fully, though with considerable variation in respect to particulars.

Having read and compared all the various stories — or rather different versions of this one story of the insurrection of the Lollards — the following seems to me the truth, as nearly as can be ascertained: —

On or about the sixth day of January, 1413–14, Henry V., who was keeping the Christmas holidays at his palace at Eltham, about seven miles east-south-east from London, was secretly in-

---

* Thus Elmham (*Vita Hen. Quint.* p. 31) would have his readers believe, that before Henry ascended the throne, he drove Oldcastle from the royal househould on account of his insane opinions: — "Quem iste rex Henricus, anteqaum regni culmen ascenderet, causa opinionis insanæ a suo famulatu domestico repellebat." Whereas the truth was, that the great difficulty which the archbishop experienced in persecuting Oldcastle, was to get at one on such friendly and familiar terms with the king, and a noble domestic of his household. — See *ante* p. 459.

formed that an extensive and desperate insurrection was in progress among the Lollards, under the leadership of Sir John Oldcastle, the Lord Cobham. The details of their plan, he was told, were — to attack the king by surprise at Eltham, capture or kill him, and his brothers and friends; to sack and destroy the monasteries of Westminster, St. Albans, and St. Pauls, and all the religious houses of London — "et cunctorum fratrum Londoniis;" to murder the prelates, overturn Church and State, and introduce an entirely new order of things in both, under the regency of Lord Cobham.

This was certainly a frightful story to tell a young and inexperienced king, who owed his own elevation to one of those popular outbreaks for which England was proverbial in the middle ages. But, as the king had been somewhat accustomed to this wolf-cry of the clergy against the Lollards, he might not, after all, have been greatly affected by this story, had not his informant gone into minuter details, and informed his majesty, that by means of traitors among the conspirators, the very night when this work of destruction was to begin, had been discovered. On the night of January 10th, the king was told, there was to be a gathering of twenty or fifty thousand Lollards, in or near St. Giles' Field, just out of London, and Cobham was to head them and open the bloody campaign.

The definite and circumstantial character of this

information induced Henry to take immediate measures to meet the dangerous exigency. First of all, he quietly removed his court from Eltham to the palace of Westminster, where he would be nearer to London and within call of military forces.

Having promptly and noiselessly made all his arrangements, on the appointed night he first revealed the information he had received to his friends, and called on them to arm. Though attempts were made to dissuade him from the execution of his plan, of suddenly falling on the conspirators in the night and crushing their insurrection in its very head — by representations of the dangers incurred by a night movement of this kind, and the necessity of calling a larger force to his aid — nothing would satisfy the bold and enterprising young king but an immediate onslaught upon the desperate conspirators.

Having first taken the precaution to order the gates of London closed and guarded, and egress refused to all but well-known friends of the king, Henry sallied out with his forces about midnight; and among the thickets just back of St. Giles, in a place known as Ficket's Field, or Ficket-field,* he suddenly encountered — not twenty thousand Lollards! nor a twentieth of that number! but something less than *one hundred* persons! most of

* *Elmham* calls the place where the Lollards were discovered by the king's troops — "*Fykettefelde* not far from Westminster." — *Vita Hen. Quint.* Chap. XVI., p. 30.

whom were unresistingly captured or killed. But, among them all was not Lord Cobham, the reported *campiductor;* nor were there any signs of a military rendezvous. Of the captured and killed, we have the names of just *four* persons: one, a minister, the Rev. John Beverley; another, Sir Roger Acton; a third, John Brown, a brewer of London; and the fourth, William Murle, also a rich brewer of the town of Dunstable.* Besides these, a considerable number of persons, including some women and several clergymen, were arrested, either at the time or afterwards, and thrown into prison. Of the seventy or eighty who were seized in the field, that night, between thirty and forty were hurried, with savage haste and without proof of guilt, or formal trial, to the gallows and the flames, amidst "the exultation of the persecuting party, and with processions and litanies." † And

* So Collier calls him. *Walsingham* describes him as *negocio braciator.*

† *Turner's Hist. Middle Ages,* III., 142.

Elham glories in this exploit of Henry, which he calls *ejus victoria gloriosa;* and describes with graphic exultation the joy of the people, the clergy, and the king, in witnessing these scenes of slaughter: "Quod fiunt processiones cum litaniis, et clero, et populo, ad regis mandatum." — *Vita Hen. Quint.* Chap. XVI.

And in his Latin poetry he describes in jubilant strains these *joyful* scenes: —

"Cum clerus procedit, rege jubente,
Et populus sequitur, ordine quisque suo,
Regia mens gaudet; præ plebs letatur et omnes."

In *Rymer* there is a royal proclamation: "De Processionibus faciendis pro suppressione Johannis Oldcastell et complicium." — 5 Hen. V., 1417.

all for what? For the crime of being found among the shrubbery in Ficket's Field, at midnight, in dead winter! This is the whole story! This is all that was ever proved against these men.

They had arms, it is said. It is quite likely that some of them had, for in that age, having arms and carrying them was a matter of every day occurrence. The law even required that every man, from fifteen to sixty years old, should have arms.* But there is no pretence that these men made any resistance to the king's soldiers—used their arms, if they had them. They, however, were Lollards: and the clergy had been denouncing the Lollards for thirty years, as "an execrable

* By a statute (13 Edward I., A.D. 1285) "repeated and expanded on many occasions in the after reigns," it was enacted "that every man have in his house harness, to keep the peace after the antient assize;—that is to say, every man between fifteen years of age and sixty years shall be assessed and sworn to armor, according to the quantity of their lands and goods—that is, to wit, [from] fifteen pounds lands, and goods forty marks, a hauberke, [coat of mail] a helmet [or breastplate] of iron, a sword, a knife [or dagger] and a horse; and from ten pounds of lands, and twenty marks goods, a hauberke, a helmet, a sword, and a knife [or dagger]; from five pounds lands, a doublet, a helmet of iron, a sword, and a knife [or dagger]. For forty shillings lands, and for more unto one hundred shillings of land, a sword, a bow and arrow, and a knife [or dagger.] And he that hath less than forty shillings yearly, shall be sworn to keep bows and [ges-armes] knives and other less weapons, &c., &c. Review of armor shall be made every year two times, by two constables for every hundred, and franchise thereunto appointed; and the constables shall present, to justices assigned for that purpose, such defaults as they do find."—*Froude's Hist. Eng.*, vol. I., pp. 52, 53; *Statutes of the Realm*, Record Commission, vol. I., p. 98

sect of heretics, sowers of cockle" in the Lord's field, and as worthy of fire.*

The men taken at St. Giles were charged, it is true, with having conspired to dethrone the king and overturn Church and State; but one particle of proof that they had any such design is nowhere to be found. The charge rests on the naked assertions of their deadly enemies—Walsingham, Elmham, and Livy; who, though contemporaries, were all ecclesiastics, and hated the Lollards with all their hearts, and mentioned them only to abuse them. Of these writers, Walsingham alone is circumstantial in his account of this affair. But even his account, which is the most unfavorable to the Lollards, clearly implies that there was no positive proof against them. His words are: "Many of Oldcastle's associates were taken, who *were said* (*qui dicebantur*) to have conspired generally for the destruction of the king and the nobles, prelates, possessioned clergy, mendicant brothers, and the citizens; who being convicted of these things, were condemned, not only to be drawn and hanged, but after this miserable end, to be burned." † "Who were said!" So it was said—"reported,

* "Hæreticorum secta execrabilis, satores lolii."—*Elmham, Hen. Quint.*, p. 31.

† "Capti sunt tamen de suis asseclis plurimi, qui dicebantur conspirasse generaliter in destructionem regis et procerum, prelatorum, religiosorum possessionatorum, fratrum mendicantium atque civium, qui superhiis convicti, non solum tractioni et furcarum suspensioni sunt addicti, sed post infelicia fata cremati."—*Hist. Angl.* p. 386, l. 33.

among the heathen," in Nehemiah's time, "and Gashmer saith it, that the Jews thought to rebel" against Artaxerxes their king. If to accuse of crimes were sufficient proof of criminality, and of gross criminality too, sad indeed would be the record of the church from the days when Nehemiah and his faithful servants labored to build up Jerusalem, amidst the taunts and threats and lies of heathendom, to the days when Oldcastle and the Lollards of England laid down their lives for the truths of the gospel.

But, we are told that some of the men taken in St. Giles confessed the conspiracy. Should this be admitted, it would prove nothing; for there were, doubtless, spies among the Lollards in St. Giles — the bishops kept such creatures, to track out heretics and watch their assemblies — and these creatures, taken in the field among the disciples, and pretending to be of them, might make this confession, or any other which best suited their interests or their convictions, and their stories would be accepted as Lollard confessions. There is, however, nothing on record which deserves the name of a confession of the existence of a conspiracy for the purposes named. Suppose we take Walsingham's account of this affair, as colored by Lingard — and it is the most unfavorable to the Lollards that can be given — and what does it prove? It reads thus: "The roads were covered with insurgents repairing from all quarters towards St. Giles. The first comers, who, to the question

—'For whom are you?' replied by the preconcerted watchword—'For Sir John Oldcastle!' were disarmed and secured. By degrees a few made their escape; they spread the alarm, and the parties on their march precipitately dispersed." *

Does this story furnish any proof that there was any conspiracy? and that Lord Cobham was actually in St. Giles that night? or if he was there, that he had any unlawful design in being there? Not one of these things is proved; and least of all is it proved that Cobham, if there, was there by pre-arrangement, to head an army to march against the king and the State, the prelates and the Church.

Walsingham's own words are less unfavorable to our supposition than Lingard's. He tells us, that "the king's forces took possession of the field; where it happened that many, coming to the enemy's camp from remote parts, first entered by mistake the royal camp; where, it being asked them—What they sought (*quid quæverent*) they answered—'Our Lord of Cobham'—*responderunt Dominum suum de Cobham.*" It could never have entered the old Benedictine's head, that he was here furnishing the Lollard's watchword, as Lingard assumes.

Admitting that every word of Walsingham's story is true—which is by no means probable—and that this question was answered by real Lol-

---

* *History of England*, vol. v., chap. I.

lards, and not by the bishops' hireling spies, it must require a lively imagination indeed to work this answer into a confession of a conspiracy. There might have been men in St. Giles that night who hoped and expected to see Lord Cobham there. But to suppose that this was the watchword of a band of conspirators, by which they were to know each other in the dark, is simply absurd. It is possible that there were men in that assembly who expected to see Cobham; and if so, I suppose that it had been whispered round — first, perhaps, by the spies themselves — that Lord Cobham was to be in St. Giles on the night of January 10th; and some persons might have gone thither — yea, many — for the express purpose of seeing a man who had suffered so much for his principles, and who deservedly stood so high among the Lollards. But this would prove nothing whatever against Cobham, or the men who went to see him. It would not prove that Cobham was there at all, or had any thought of being there; much less, that he was there with any evil intent.

We are told, indeed, of his leaving Wales and lurking about London, and of his various plans and purposes; but never a particle of proof is there given that he ever came near London, from the time that he escaped from the Tower until he was brought, a wounded prisoner, in a horse-litter, to be burned to death, four years after this affair.

Much stress is laid by some writers on the fact that the king and parliament, in official documents, charge the Lollards with a conspiracy. But he who reads carefully any of the official documents of those days in which the Lollards are mentioned, will understand that it was the uniform practice of the ruling powers in Church and State, to denounce these poor Christians as the worst of malefactors: as robbers, traitors, execrable, malicious and damnable creatures; and yet, when these same "wretches" are brought to trial, nothing worse is proved against them than a denial of transubstantiation and the lordly power of the prelates, and a general preference for the Bible over the decrees of the pope and "holy mother church." Let any one compare the edicts — statutes, constitutions, bulls and briefs — noticed in a preceding chapter of this work, with the charges actually made on trial against these same Lollards, and for which they were doomed to suffer the loss of all their worldly goods, their liberty and their lives; and he will see at once, that neither treason, nor robbery, nor crime nor immorality of any kind was ever proved against them. Submission to the lordly will of the archbishop of Canterbury and his "fellow-brethren" would have covered the sins of the very worst of them. Even he whom Walsingham calls the "campiductor" of the Lollards, Cobham himself, might have escaped the flames on these terms. The fact that these men in St. Giles were called conspirators, is not, therefore, any proof of their guilt; even though the King of England and his parliament may have thus called them.

But if these Lollards were not conspirators, what were they doing at midnight, in January, among the thickets back of St. Giles? The answer given at the time is probably the true one: They were assembling in the night, as the primitive Christians did, and as Christians in all ages have done in times of persecution, to worship God, and to hear the gospel preached, and to commune with one another; none of which things could they do openly, except at the sacrifice of their lives.

This, in my judgment, is the simple and true version of the story of the formidable Lollard insurrection, of which the church writers in those days, and in our own, have made so much account; and which occasioned the imprisonment of great numbers of innocent persons, and the shameful death of many.* It may be satisfactory

* There is some discrepancy in respect to the number taken, imprisoned and executed for their complicity with the St. Giles affair. *Fox* says: that Sir Roger Acton, John Brown and John Beverley were put to death in January, "with others to the number of *thirty-six*, if the story be true." — Vol. I., pp. 668–669. — *Fabyan* says *thirty-six* were taken besides Acton, Beverly and Brown. *Chron.* p. 578.

Bishop Kennet's Complete History of England, contains a more circumstantial statement. We there read, that thirty were hanged, and seven were hanged and burned, in St. Giles' Field, January 12th, 1413–14; that four more were hanged, January 19th; and

to the reader to compare this version of the St. Giles insurrection, with the statements and opinions of some of the old English chroniclers of the sixteenth century, and of a few standard historical writers.

Fabyan is quite brief in his account of this affair. Under the head of A.D. 1413 he says: "In this year and month of January, certain adherents of Sir John Oldcastle, intending the destruction of this land and subversion of the same, assembled them in a field near unto Saint Giles in great number; whereof the king being informed, took the field before them, and so took a certain of them; among the which was Sir Roger Acton, knight, Sir John Beverley, priest, and a squire, called Sir John Browne; the which, with thirty-six more in number, were after convict of heresy and treason,

---

that Sir Roger Acton was drawn and hanged, February 10th.— *Vol.* I., p. 311.

Walsingham is very indefinite in respect to numbers. Indeed, his whole account seems rather to be a summary of common rumors than an exact historical detail of facts. He says *many (plurimi)* were captured on the field and thrust into prison; and those who sought safety by flight, were pursued by the royal forces, and *some (quosdem)* taken and *some* destroyed — "quosdem cepere, quosdem peremere." In another place he says, that *many* priests and laymen were taken, convicted, and condemned. And still further on he informs us, that if the king had not taken the precaution to have the gates of London closed and guarded, there would have gone out against the king that night, *as it was said (prout fertur)* fifty thousand servants, apprentices, together with certain citizens, and even some magistrates.— *Walsingham, Hist. Angl.*, 385–386. *Ypod. Neust.*, 577–578.

and for the same hanged and burnt within the said field of Saint Giles." *

Hall says: — "After this time, in a certain unlawful assembly, was taken Sir Robert [Roger] Acton, knight, a man of great wit and possessions; John Brown, Esqr.; John Beverley, clerk; and a great number of other, which were brought to the king's presence, and to him declared the cause of their commotion and rising; and accused a great number of their sort and society. Which confession, because I have not seen, I leave at large. After this foolish act, so many persons were apprehended, that all the prisons in and about London were replenished with people." After giving an account of the execution of "*twenty-nine*" persons, who were "adjudged for treason to be drawn and hanged, and for heresy, to be consumed with fire, gallows and all," he adds: — "Some say, that the occasion of their death was the conveyance of the Lord Cobham out of prison. Others write, that it was both for treason and heresy, as the record declareth. Certain affirm, that it was for feigned causes, surmised by the spirituality [bishops, etc.,] more of displeasure than truth: the judgment whereof I leave to men indifferent. For surely all conjectures be not true, nor all writings the gospel." †

Holinshed, after reporting the matter as told by

* *The New Chronicles*, or Concordance of Histories, p. 578, quarto, 1811.

† *Chronicle*, pp. 48–49, quarto.

Walsingham, Titus Livius, and Hall, says, that by the excessive number of Londoners (50,000,) which the historian reports to have been prepared to join in the St. Giles affray, had not the gates been closed and guarded — "it may appear, that Walsingham reporteth this matter according to the common fame, and not as one that searcheth out an exquisite truth." *

He also says, that "certain affirm, that they [the people assembled in St. Giles on the night of January 10th, 1413–14] were assembled to hear their preacher (the aforesaid Beverley) in that place there, out of the way from resort of people; since they might not come together openly about any such matter, without danger to be apprehended; as the manner is, and hath been ever of the persecuted flock, when they are prohibited publicly the exercise of their religion." †

Bishop Kennet's History of England says of this assembly of Lollards in St. Giles: — "The meeting seems to have been nothing else but a religious assembly, for the worship of God; which, because the Lollards could nowhere enjoy for fear of their adversaries, who had grown very watchful and insulting by reason of the king's favor, they were forced, like the first Christians in times of persecution, to celebrate in the night, in woods and thickets: but the clergy having got information of their intendment, improved it into a plot;" which, it is

* *Chronicles*, III., 63. † *Ib.* p. 64.

further said, was easily made credible, because the party was numerous about London, and met in great numbers, and that many times armed, not to create any disturbance, but to defend themselves against the injuries of the papists.*

Turner, in view of the representations of Walsingham himself, says of this pretended insurrection, etc.: — "It is a series of supposition, rumor, private information, apprehension, and anticipation. That the king was acted on by some secret agents, is clear; that the plots asserted were really formed, there is no evidence. The probability is, that Henry's generous and lofty mind was found to start at the violences which the bigotry of the papal clergy had resolved upon; and that artful measures were taken to alarm it into anger and cruelty, by charges of treason, rebellion, and meditated assassination! This effect took place." †

Turner, nevertheless, expresses the opinion in a subsequent volume (III., 152) that it is probable that the Lollards assembled in St. Giles, "meant to pursue some violent measures against the possessioned church."

Echart regards this meeting in St. Giles as a religious assembly; and gives no credit to the reports of their enemies — that these Lollards were met for insurrectionary purposes. ‡

Rapin takes substantially the same view of the

---

* *A Complete Hist. Eng.* vol. I., p. 311, folio ed.

† *Middle Ages*, II., 473. ‡ *Hist. Eng.* vol. I., pp. 436–437.

matter.* So does Speed, who calls the place of meeting—"*Thicket*-fields;" which, he says, was "then overgrowne with bushes, and unfit for battell." "If we will believe," he says, "their professed enemies, four-score of the faction [Lollards] were apprehended. Those few were, in likelihood, assembled unto John Beverley, a godly man, their preacher, without any intent of Treason." †

It would be easy to increase the number of authors of standard authority on historical subjects, who take essentially the same view of the inoffensive character of the meeting in St. Giles. ‡

That the version now given of the St. Giles af-

---

* *Hist. Eng.* vol. I., bk. 2, p. 509, folio.

† *Hist. Eng.* p. 626, folio.

‡ It is but fair to apprise the reader, that all Protestant historians do not agree in this view of the St. Giles affair. Collier, as might be anticipated from his high-church prejudice against the Wickliffites, is disposed to regard this as an insurrectionary affair. He follows Walsingham blindly.—*Ecc. Hist. G.B.* vol. III., pp. 297–298

Carte, also adopts Walsingham, Elmham and Livy's account, manifest errors and all, and adds to these some errors of his own. —*Hist. Eng.* II., 674, folio.

Hume, who was ever ready to believe evil of good men, and much more ready to slur over any matter in which religious principle was involved, than to investigate it thoroughly—takes for granted the guilt of the Lollards.—*Hist. Eng.* vol. II., ch. 19.

And so does Guthrie, who appears disposed to be impartial.—Vol. II., p. 451, folio. And so do others, whose honesty we have no reason to question.

What chiefly influences honest, impartial men to believe in this pretended Lollard insurrection, is not so much Walsingham's hearsay, prejudiced account of it, as the public documents, which seem to imply its existence. Of these documents I have already spoken, and shall have occasion to speak again at the close of this chapter.

fair is the true one, may be argued, not only from a reasonable construction of all the facts alluded to, but from the proceedings of the king himself, after the first excitement of the affray had passed off. If there had been any foundation for the story, that a wide-spread and desperate conspiracy had been arranged among the Lollards, having in view the destruction of the king and his brothers, the murder of the prelates and clergy, and the overthrow of Church and State; and that 20,000, or, as some will have it, 50,000 men were under orders to rendezvous about St. Giles' Fields on the night of January 10th, 1413–14, very many persons must of necessity have been privy to the plot; and betrayals and discoveries of complicity in the affair, and prosecutions and executions for the conspiracy, would inevitably have been exceedingly numerous, and the butchery of the Lollards without color of law, perhaps even greater than the legal executions. If one would understand how great conspiracies and insurrections were dealt with in that period of English history, let him read the details of the suppression of the Wat Tyler insurrection, about thirty years previous to this date; more than fifteen hundred poor creatures were destroyed before the government was satiated with blood. And Henry V. was not a prince who stopped with half-measures, or who greatly hesitated to shed human blood.

The fact however is, that *not one person perished* for this bold and desperate insurrection — which, according to report, contemplated nothing less than the utter subversion of the government, civil and ecclesiastical, the murder of the king, his brothers and friends, the destruction of the prelates, monks, and others—not a person lost his life, or suffered severely, except those who were killed in the field, or were taken and executed before the king's alarm and anger had time to abate and his sober reason to act in the premises.

The king charged these men with being in St. Giles for the purpose of carrying out a conspiracy against himself, his brothers, and the Church and State of England. He had been told that such was the purpose of the Lollards; that they were to meet in St. Giles on the night of January 10th, to commence this work of destruction; he found these men there, on that very night;—and what more natural, than to jump to the conclusion, that they were there for the very purpose for which their enemies had said they would be there. The king, therefore, immediately issues out his commission—on the very night of their arrest, or the day following—authorizing an inquiry concerning all insurrections by those vulgarly called Lollards and other persons. And in compliance with this command, we find on record an indictment, or indictments, said to have been found by twelve jurors, under oath, against Sir John Oldcastle, Sir Roger Acton, John Beverley, John Brown and others; but dated, on the "Wednesday next after the feast of Epiphany," which was the *eleventh* *day of January*, 1413–14! so that it is utterly impossible that any investigation could have been made of the guilt or innocence of these six-and-thirty or more doomed and condemned Lollards.*

The king was evidently alarmed and exasperated by the frightful stories told about the Lollards; the truth of which seemed for the moment to be confirmed by his own discoveries in St. Giles; and without due consideration, he doomed the poor men on whom he first laid his hands, to the halter and the flames. But, when he had had time to reflect, he saw the improbability and absurdity of this hierarchal story, and conformed his after-course of treatment to his wiser and better second thoughts. Instead therefore of commissions and indictments, as there would have been had he believed in this insurrection, we find successive proc-

---

* The official papers referred to above, and others, may be found in the appendix to Bale's Chronicle of Sir John Oldcastle, as published originally, London, 1729. 8vo, 157 pages. There is a copy of this work in the Boston City Library. See also, *Fox*, I., 668–669; and *Complete State Trials*, vol. I., Cobham's Trial.

The king's commission is addressed to W. Roos de Hamelak; H. le Scrop; W. Crowmere, mayor of London; H. Huls, and associated justices of the king; and is dated January *tenth*, 1413–14. But, as the St. Giles assembly was on the night of the 10th, and the arrests were not made until midnight or after, the commission must have been made out before the alleged crime was committed, or antedated, by design or accident. "Epiphany" occurs on January the *sixth;* and January 1413 commenced on *Sunday;* Epiphany, accordingly, must have fallen on *Friday* of that year; and "the Wednesday next after Epiphany," of course was the *eleventh day* of January.

lamations of pardon for suspected and accused and condemned Lollards, for any supposed complicity with the affair of St. Giles.

As early as March 23d, 1413–14, a general pardon is proclaimed to all the accused and suspected Lollards throughout the kingdom, *except* John Oldcastle, and eleven others who are named; those who had fled to privileged places; those who were actually under arrest and in various prisons; and those who had broken prison. On May the 20th, 1414, less than two months after the first, another proclamation is made, pardoning Philip Turnour, and twenty-seven other persons who are named, including several clergymen and one woman, charged with conspiring against the king, the Church and the State of England, and of being concerned in the St. Giles affair. On November 6th, 1414, one John Wykham — who, with others, we are told, had been indicted before William Roos de Hamelak and his associate justices, and doomed to death for this same conspiracy — was pardoned by public proclamation. And on the 16th of December of the same year, pardons were proclaimed for John Longacre, indicted and condemned as above, and eleven others whose names are given. Of these men, it is said expressly, that they were indicted by justice Roos and his associate judges, and denied their guilt, but were nevertheless condemned to be drawn and hanged. Yet were they all pardoned by public proclamation, without any reason assigned other than the good pleasure of the king.*

Now, these numerous acts of pardon, coupled with the fact that there was certainly but one execution or trial (that of William Murle, of Dunstable) † so far as appears from history or public documents, for this crime of conspiracy in St. Giles' Field, among all the suspected, accused, and imprisoned Lollards, after the first ebullition of vengeance, which was poured out on Acton, Beverley, Brown and their thirty-three associates, who were hung and burned immediately;—these things I say, all go to show, that the king himself, after he had recovered from the first paroxysms of fear and anger, took a very different view of the whole affair from what he did at first, and became convinced that there was no good ground for the insurrectionary charges against the Lollards.

The St. Giles affair is historically important, as illustrating the bitter enmity of "the church" against the Lollards, and showing how the lives of the poor christians in those dark days were wantonly sacrificed to the fear and the suspicion of the rulers of Church and State. It is also im-

---

* See *Rymer's Fœdera,* vol. IV., part 2, pp. 72, 76, 92, 100, 101. Hague, edition of 1749.

† Walsingham's account would lead us to believe that even Murle was taken immediately after the affray in St. Giles, and perished with the others named, by the halter and the flames. — *Hist. Angl.*, 386.

portant, because it induced the king to make proclamation, and offer a reward for the arrest of Lord Cobham, whom the clergy had artfully implicated in this affair, though not a particle of evidence is furnished that he had any part or lot in the affair, whatever may have been its character. And if that assembly cannot be proved to have been insurrectionary, then, of course, the whole superstructure of abuse against Cobham, as a traitor,* falls in ruins to the ground.

---

* *Fox* argues at great length, the innocency of Cobham, and of the Lollards generally, in respect to this St. Giles affair. He treats the indictment which was brought into parliament in 1417–18, and on which Cobham is said to have been executed, as a forgery.— See *Acts and Mons.*, vol. I., pp. 647–668.

Hargrave speaks of "the *forged indictment and outlawry of Sir John Oldcastle, Lord Cobham,* for high treason," * * "the indictment itself appears," he says, "*by many marks, to be a forgery.*"— *Complete State Trials*, vol. I., columns 254 and 265, Cobbet's ed., 8vo., 1809.

The indictment is on the *Rolls of Parliament* —5 Henry V., Dec. 1417; but forged parliamentary documents were the subjects of repeated complaints, even by the Commons of England themselves, down to near the close of the reign of Henry VI.—The reader will find this matter discussed in *Reeve's Hist. Eng. Law*, vol. III., pp. 235–237 and 253 and on; also, in *Dwarris' Treatise on Statutes*, pp. 29–33, Lond. 8vo., 1830; and in *Hallam's Middle Ages*, part 3. chap. 8.

44

CHAPTER XIV.

THE MARTYRDOM OF JOHN CLAYDON.—EXTENSIVE AND VIOLENT PERSECUTIONS OF THE LOLLARDS.

The holocaust gathered in St. Giles' Field on the night of January 10th, 1413–14, seems to have satisfied the church, or at least the king, for some time; and we hear of no further Lollard martyrdoms until 1415.

In the mean time Arundel, after being archbishop of Canterbury seventeen years, had passed to his dread account, and Henry Chicheley, a worse man if possible than his immediate predecessor, had been enthroned at Canterbury.

On the 17th of August, 1415, the second year of Chicheley's reign and the third of Henry V., there was gathered in London an imposing company of spiritual and lay dignitaries, to inaugurate the new archbishop's reign of terror. There were Henry of Canterbury, Richard of London, John of Coventry and Litchfield; Fauconer, the mayor of London; together with men skilled in theology; others learned in canon law; doctors of civil law; numerous clergymen and notaries; and other learned men, and laymen in great numbers; and all for what? To try a humble mechanic of London, John Claydon, a leather-dresser, for "heretical pravity" — for being a Lollard!

This poor man had already spent five years in prison, for his Lollardy: two in Conway castle, and three in the Fleet prison, London. He was now arraigned before these inquisitors to be tried for his life. He was charged with being, and having for a long time been, "notoriously defamed on account of heretical pravity, and for heresy, and for opinions and errors contrary to the Catholic faith and the determinations of the church; in that, for twenty years back and onward, he had held the sentiments commonly known as Lollardy and heretical pravity;" and he was still further charged with having twice abjured these opinions and errors.

These charges having been made, he was first asked, if, since his abjuration, he had not had in his possession, or in his keeping, sundry books written in English? — Theological books written in English, which the common people could read, or understand when read to them, were the terror of the hierarchy.

Claydon admitted that he had in his house many books written in English. One of these books was then produced in court, by the mayor of London, who had searched the prisoner's house, and finding some English books, had seized them and arrested Claydon for having these dangerous things in his possession. His Honor the Mayor pronounced these books "the worst and most perverse books that he ever read or saw." The one selected for exhibition was handsomely written on parchment, and beautifully bound in red morocco, and had cost Claydon a very considerable sum of money, he having had it copied and bound at his own expense.

This book appears to have been what was commonly known among the Lollards as "The Lantern of Light;" and was greatly valued by them, and proportionately detested by the Papists.

Being asked who wrote this book; Claydon replied, John Greime, or Greene. Being asked where he was: he answered that he did not know. He was next asked, if he had ever read in that book, or heard any one else read it. In reply, he said that he did not know how to read; but that he had heard about a quarter-part of the book read by one John Fuller.

He was asked, if he commended the contents of that book as catholic, and useful, and good, and true. He answered, that much of what he had heard of the contents of that book, was very useful for the safety of his soul, and good; and that he particularly valued the book on account of a sermon which it contained, preached at Horfaldowne.

He was next asked, whether, since his abjuration, he had communicated with a certain Richard Baker, a citizen of London.

He replied that he had; for the said Richard often came to his house for the purpose of having communications with him.

Did he know that said Richard was suspected and defamed of heretical pravity?

He did.

Here the examination of the prisoner rested. The archbishop then submitted the books found in Claydon's possession, to certain learned churchmen and others, to be examined; and adjourned the court of inquest for two days.

Agreeably to adjournment, the inquisition assembled on Monday, August 19th. Two witnesses, apprentices to Claydon and members of his family, were then introduced, to prove his familiarity with this hated "Lantern of Light."—There was nothing so much hated and feared by the hierarchy of those days as light.

David Berde (or Beard) was a member of the prisoner's family, and remembered the book, the "Lantern of Light;" and that it contained, among other things, the Ten Commandments in English, and an Exposition of the Commandments, also in English. He had repeatedly heard J. Fuller read in that book at his master's house, in St. Martin's Lane; and his master greatly delighted in hearing the contents of that book read, and commended them much; and it seemed to the witness, that Claydon approved of every thing in the book, and condemned nothing.

Another apprentice swore that Fuller, Baker, and Montfort, all Lollards, were repeatedly at Claydon's house.

The committee to whom was referred the examination of "The Lantern of Light," reported, that it contained *fifteen* heresies and errors.

The admissions of the prisoner, and the testimony of his apprentices, together with the "heretical" character of the books found in his possession, were deemed sufficient proof against him; and the court proceeded, first, to sentence all Claydon's books to the flames; and next, to declare that he was a relapsed heretic, and as such, to condemn him, and to give him up to the secular arm to be burned.

This sentence was speedily executed, and the ashes of another poor Lollard enriched the soil of Smithfield.

According to Fabyan, Richard Turming, a baker, another Lollard, was burned at the same time.*

"The Lantern of Light"—the possession of which contributed so materially to the condemnation of John Claydon—like many of the manuscript books of the Lollards, contained several distinct tracts. Among them were the Ten Commandments in English, with an Exposition and

* The official account of Claydon's trial, which I have chiefly followed, is in *Wilkins' Concilia*, III., 371–375. See also *Fox's Acts and Mons.*, I., 727–728; *Clarke*, p. 51; *Fabyan's Chronicles*, p. 578.

Commentary, also in English; and a Sermon, preached at Horfaldowne, probably by some Lollard minister. According to the report of the inquisitors to whose examinations this book was submitted by the archbishop, the book contained, among other "iniquitous" sentiments, the following: — On the text (Matt. 13: 25,) "And while men slept, his enemy came and sowed tares among the wheat, and went his way," the comment says: 'The worst antichrist (or enemy of Christ,) to wit the Pope, over-sows the laws of Christ with putrid and corrupt papal laws, which have no authority, strength or power.' — That when archbishops and bishops are spoken of indifferently, they are the seats of the "beast," mentioned in Revelations, who sits and reigns upon them. — That the authority claimed by the bishops to give episcopal letters, authorizing men to preach the gospel, is a characteristic of the beast, i. e., of antichrist. — That the Roman Court is the principal head of antichrist; bishops the body; and the new sects of monks, canons &c., introduced not by Christ, but by the pope, are the poisonous and pestiferous tail of antichrist. — That the church consists of those only who are to be saved; since the church is none other than the congregation of faithful souls, who keep, and shall continue to be kept to the end, in faith and charity, in both word and deed. — That Christ never planted any private religions (i. e., orders of monks, friars, and nuns); that they are all useless branches in the church, and fit only to be destroyed. — That the frequent singing in the churches has no foundation in Scripture; and therefore that it was unlawful for priests to spend their time in singing, when they should be engaged in studying the laws of Christ, and in preaching his word. — That indulgences were unwarranted. — That prelates were not to be obeyed, unless they were faithful in watching for souls that they might give account to the Lord. — That there should be no pilgrimages to shrines and images; and that all worship and veneration of images were unlawful. — That ecclesiastical things should not be adorned with gold and silver and precious stones; nor should the ministers of Christ be other than his humble imitators, worshipping him in simple mansions.

The above are, for substance, the heresies and errors said to have been found in this pestiferous book, which John Claydon so loved to have read to him, and which did his soul so much good. If these were the *worst* things in the "Lantern of Light," the reader can guess at the general character of the book.*

In July 1416 were published abroad archbishop Chicheley's inquisitorial "Constitutions," already repeatedly referred to.† These opened a new persecuting campaign; and from this date, to about the year 1431, the official registers of the archbish-

---

* See *Wilkins' Concilia*, III., 374; *Turner's Hist. of Eng.*, III., 133.

† See *Ante*, pp. 370–372.

ops' and the bishops' courts prove that the work of persecution went rapidly forward. A great number of persons were arrested, imprisoned, ironed, and tormented. Some of these recanted, and did penance, as they went half-naked around the cathedrals and the market-places, day after day, receiving repeated flagellations at the hands of the bishops' officers; or were made to fast on bread and water for successive years. And besides these who fell into the bishops' cruel hands, whole households, both men and women, were compelled to flee and hide themselves from the ecclesiastical spies. Fox has preserved the names of some thirty persons, who suffered in these ways during the year 1416 alone; and refers to great numbers, whose names are not given, particularly in the county of Kent, in the towns of Romney, Tenterden, Woodchurch, Cranbrook, Staplehurst, Benenden, Halden, and Rolvenden.*

About this time many persons were also arrested and arraigned before Chicheley, for having suspected books. Benedict Ulleman of London, was hanged, drawn and beheaded for scattering papers against popery.† Thomas Grantner was condemned to seven years' imprisonment. Ralph Mungin for keeping company with a suspected person, and for having and dispersing certain books of John Wickliffe and Peter Clark, and for speaking against indulgences etc., was condemned to

* *Fox*, I., 731.

† *Clarke*, 52.

perpetual imprisonment. William Tailour, a presbyter and Master of Arts, after repeated trials, was condemned, degraded *in forma*, given up to the secular court, and burned in Smithfield. Henry Webb, for preaching without license, was condemned to be whipped, stark-naked, in the processions in St. Paul's Cathedral, London, and at Worcester, and at Bath. And John Florence of Shelton, in Norwich, a turner by trade, was sentenced to be whipped three successive Sundays in the cathedral church at Norwich, and three more Sundays in his parish church.*

Fox, after giving the names of three persons — all that could be made out, by reason of "the antiquity of the monument" from which he copied — who were seized in the town of Bungay, in the diocese of Norwich, and committed to "the custody of the Duke of Norfolk, at his castle of Fremingham," adds:— "Besides these, we also find in the said old monuments, within the diocese of Norfolk and Suffolk, especially in the towns of Beckles, Ersham, and Ludney, a great number, both of men and women, to have been vexed and cast into prison; and after their abjuration, brought to open shame, in churches and markets, by the bishop of the said diocese, called William, and his chancellor, William Burnham; John Exeter being then Register therein: so that, within the space of three or four years — that is, from the

* *Wilkins*, III., 404–413; *Fox*, I., 748–750.

year 1428 unto the year 1431 — about the number of *one hundred and twenty* men and women were examined, and sustained great vexation, for the profession of the christian faith; of whom some were only taken upon suspicion, for eating of meats upon vigil-days; who upon their purgation made, escaped more easily away, and with less punishment." * * * "The others, were more cruelly handled, and some of them were put to death and burned." *

The doctrines generally charged against these "heretics," by their persecutors in Norfolk and Suffolk, show conclusively that these people were Lollards: — They were accused of rejecting auricular confession, and priestly absolution — Denying the power of the priest to turn the sacramental bread and wine into the very body and blood of Christ — Asserting that every true christian man was a priest unto God — Saying that no man was bound under pain of damnation, to observe Lent or any other fast-day enjoined by the church of Rome — Calling the pope, antichrist, and his prelates, the disciples of antichrist; and denying that the pope had power to bind and loose on earth — Holding that a christian man might do any bodily work (sin only excepted) on "holy-days" — That it is lawful for priests to marry — That the excommunications and other ecclesiastical censures of the prelates ought not to

---

* *Acts and Mons.*, I., 751.

be regarded — That it is not lawful to swear in private cases — That men ought not to go on pilgrimages — That no honor should be given to crucifixes and images — That "holy water" (or water hallowed in churches,) is no holier than any running or well water; for the Lord blessed all water at the creation — That Thomas à Becket's death was neither holy nor meritorious — That relics (as dead men's bones, etc.) ought not to be removed from graves, or put in shrines, or worshipped — That prayers made in all places are acceptable to God — That men ought not to pray to any saint; but to God only — That the bells and the ringing in the churches, were ordained for no other purpose than to fill the priests' purses — That it is no sin to withstand the ecclesiastical precepts — And that the [true] catholic church is only the congregation of the elect.

They seem also to have denied the Romish doctrine, that an unbaptized infant must, of course, be lost; holding that the blood of Christ might save a soul, even if water was not applied in baptism: and to have denied that marriage was a sacrament.

Among the martyrs of Norfolk and Suffolk, were Father Abraham, so called, of Colchester; William White, a priest; and John Wadden, also a priest. White was a follower of Wickliffe, and the pastor and teacher of a Lollard church, and suffered martyrdom in Norwich, by order of William, the bishop of Norwich, "to the great dolor and grief of all the good men of Norfolk;" when at the stake, it is reported concerning him, that beginning to exhort the people and confirm them in the truth, "one of the bishop's servants struck him on the mouth, thereby to force him to keep silence!" Many of his congregation, also, were "severely handled" by the bishop of Norwich. Some were imprisoned, some banished from the diocese, some beaten, while half-naked, around the markets on market-days, and in the churches on Sundays.*

Robert Hoke, rector of the parish church of Braybroke, in the diocese of Lincoln, "vehemently suspected of the crime of heretical pravity and Lollardy," was repeatedly arrested and examined on suspicion; and finally was imprisoned, his house searched for heretical books, some of which were found, containing "great and abominable errors and heresies." Among other things, it was charged against him, that, for two years he had not, after the manner of the faithful, worshipped the cross; and that he had encouraged his parishioners in similar neglect. He was ordered into "safe-keeping" — which, it may be presumed, meant into the bishop's dungeon of "Little Ease" — until he was ready to recant, or death eased him of his sorrows.†

The Convocation of the clergy which met in

---

* *Clarke*, p. 53; *Fox*, I., 751–754.

† *Wilkins*, III., 433–435.

London, July 5, 1428, and continued its sessions by adjournments until Dec. 7, was largely occupied with measures for suppressing Lollardism. Several of the hated reformers were also arraigned before the convocation: — as Ralph Mungyn; William Harvey, of Tenderden; Richard Monk, a presbyter; Peter Clark; John Jourdelay; Katharine Dertford; William Wawe; Bartholomew Cornmonger; N. Hoper; Master Robert, brought from the Tower of London, Rector of Higgeley, and doomed to perpetual imprisonment; Thomas Garenter; N. Shadworth, a citizen of London; and John Calle, for having a New Testament in English.

Mungyn is charged with having been a Lollard preacher from twelve to twenty years; Hoper had been a servant of Sir John Oldcastle; and that was enough to render him a suspicious character. Garenter was a priest.

The minutes of this convocation fill ten of the ample folio pages of Wilkins' Concilia, and are almost entirely devoted to Lollardy in some form.* Before the final adjournment of the convocation, archbishop Chicheley exhorted and commanded his prelates and clergy, to make special inquisition in their respective dioceses and parishes against the Lollards. He also proposed a committee of prelates and learned men, to devise some *effectual measures* to stop the growth of Lollardism; for,

---

* *Wilkins*, III., 493–503.

he admitted, that, notwithstanding all his laborious diligence in persecuting these heretics, even unto death; and the exertions of his predecessor in office, they grew in numbers daily; and he thought they would continue to grow until some *fit remedy* was provided.* What that remedy should be, the archbishop does not tell us, and it is not easy to conceive; for the rulers of the hierarchy had now for more than a quarter of a century, been doing their pleasure with the poor dissenting Lollards;—hunting them by night and day; watching them, by means of spies, in all the private acts and words of life; dragging them into ecclesiastical courts, and there compelling them to become their own accusers; then beating them about the streets; inflicting fasts and grievous penances on them; imprisoning them in filthy dungeons; loading them with manacles; killing them by slow tortures, or bringing them out to be burned to death before all the people:—these were some of the chief *remedies* which Chicheley and Arundel had been diligently employing for six and twenty years at least, to suppress Lollardism! And what more *fit remedies* could antichrist devise? Yet, these labors of blood were, confessedly, powerless to suppress the truth!

The poor Lollards in the diocese of Norwich, seem to have been hunted up with very special diligence, and punished with most relentless cru-

---

* *Wilkins*, III., 495.

elty. We find on record such illustrations as the following:—John Beverly, alias Battild, a laborer, being suspected of Lollardy, was arrested by the vicar of Southcreke and others, and sent up to the bishop's commissary, who sent him to the castle of Norwich, to be imprisoned in irons until he could be examined. And though, on examination, his accusers failed to prove any thing against him, except that he had eaten meat on Easter day, had not confessed to a priest during Lent, nor received the sacrament on Easter day, he was nevertheless sentenced to undergo severe fasting on bread and water, for successive days, to be beaten along the road from the castle, and banished forever from the diocese.* John Skilley, of Faxon, a miller, being convicted by his own confession of being a Lollard, of entertaining the Rev. William White, and John Wadden, a priest, "famous, and notorious, and damnable heretics;" though he abjured his errors, was yet sentenced to seven years' imprisonment in the monastery of Langly, in the diocese of Norwich; and, as he had allowed himself to eat meat on Fridays, he was doomed to bread and water on every Friday for seven years! and for two years after the expiration of the seven years' penance, he was required to appear twice during Lent before the bishop or his commissary, in the cathedral church in Norwich, to do open penance among the penitents there to be found.†

* *Fox*, I., 754.

† *Fox*, I., 754.

These are merely a sample of what was done to numbers of poor men in that diocese, who had not the courage or grace to endure the perpetual imprisonments, or the terrible deaths which were inflicted on others. But the very severity of these penances illustrates the merciless cruelty of the persecuting prelates, and gives one a lively conception of the dreadful tortures which were inflicted on the men who resisted to the end: "For if they do these things in a green tree, what shall be done in the dry?" — If the recanting and abjuring Lollards were thus dealt with, what tortures must have been inflicted on the persistent and persevering Lollards?

If one would understand the system of espionage which was encouraged by the hierarchy in the different towns and parishes of England, he should read the bishops' records. Thus, for illustration, the Register of the bishop of Norwich, in the year 1429, contains the minute reports of informers against sundry men and women; showing that their words and actions were watched, and reported, and represented in the worst light, to the ecclesiastical inquisitors: One William Wright informs the bishop, "that William Tailor told John Pery, of Ludney, that William White was a good and holy doctor. — That William Tailor, of Ludney, was one of the sect, and went to London with Sir Hugh Pie, and had conversations often with William White on the Lollards' doctrine. — That Alice, the wife of Thomas Moon, is of the same sect, and favored and received them often; and also, that the daughter of Thomas Moon is partly of the same sect, and can read English.— That Richard Fletcher, of Beckles, is a most perfect doctor in that sect, and can very well and perfectly expound the Scriptures, and has a book of the New Law (the New Testament) in English, which was Sir Hugh Pie's, first.— That Richard Belward, son of John Belward, of Southelem parish, is one of the same sect, and has a New Testament, which he bought in London for four marks and forty pence; and taught the said William Wright, and Margery his wife, and wrought with them diligently by the space of one year, and studied diligently upon the New Testament." *

Fox gives entire columns of such details, extracted from the bishops' registers; which, though passed over by many readers as useless gossip, are yet most deeply interesting and instructive, as illustrating the state of society in England at the time, and the abominable system of espionage which was set up and urged forward by the archbishops of Canterbury, in order to destroy the protestant christians of those days.†

* 'Four marks and forty pence' were equal to about *thirteen dollars and sixty cents,* Federal money! So that, this poor christian was willing to pay about as many *dollars,* as we do *cents* for a New Testament. And when we consider that gold and silver in those days was of nearly *twelve times* the value which it now is — we cannot but admire the high estimate which these good men placed on the Word of God.

† See *Fox's Acts and Mons.*, I., 755–756.

But, notwithstanding this inquisitorial persecution of the Lollards, they persevered in their meetings and communings together, and their search after truth in their dearly-bought New Testaments, the very possession of which exposed them to suspicion, persecution and severe punishment. These meetings they held in private houses, in barns, and probably in the fields and woods. It is charged against one Thomas Moon, in the diocese of Norwich, that he received the Lollards to his house, where they "assembled oft times together, and there conferred upon their doctrine."* And we find another company charged with assembling in a barn, to hear the New Testament read.

Besides the persecutions carried on by the bishops in their respective dioceses, the Convocation of Canterbury kept itself in practice, from time to time sending a Lollard preacher to Smithfield, to be a burning and shining witness to the sincerity of his profession and the strength of his faith. Thus, in 1428, the Convocation of the prelates and clergy of Canterbury had before it several persons who were suspected of heresy; and condemned, excommunicated, degraded, and sent first to prison and afterwards to the stake, Thomas Bagley, a priest, vicar of Maunden, or Monendon, near Malden, in Essex county. The crimes charged on Bagley were — that he denied the real, corporal presence in the sacramental bread and wine —

---

* *Fox*, I., 756.

adhered to the doctrines of Wickliffe, and refused to recant.*

In 1430, we read that Richard Hovenden, a wool-comber, or winder, of London, received the crown of martyrdom, because "he could, by no persuasions, be withdrawn or plucked back from the opinions of Wickliffe." He was burned "hard by the tower of London." †

Scotland, as well as England, furnished Lollard martyrs about this time. James Presby, a priest, was burned at St. Andrews, in 1421, for his Lollardy; and Paul Crew, a Bohemian, was burned to death in the same place, in 1431, for maintaining the opinions of the Lollards. ‡

We have now reached the end of the great and fiery persecution of the Lollards, which commenced in the second year of Henry IV., A.D. 1400, and continued for more than thirty years.

Henry V. died in France, August, 1422, in the tenth year of his reign, at the age of thirty-four years. His reign is reckoned among the glorious ones of England. But the most memorable events of it were the persecution of the Christian dissenters of his own kingdom, and the empty triumph of his arms in the conquest of France.

---

* *Wilkins,* III., 515; *Fox,* I., 758. Fox places this martyrdom under the year 1431. Wilkins gives an account of Bagley's examination, under date of 1428; but not of his condemnation. He was first committed to prison in the care of the Bishop of London; and, as we learn from Fox, afterwards burned.

† *Fox,* I., 756. ‡ *Fox,* I., 758; *Knox's Chh. Scot.,* lib. I., 1–4.

The sin and misery involved in the persecution and the conquest are both attributable mainly to the archbishops of Canterbury, Arundel and Chicheley, and the hierarchal clergy of England.*

By the untimely death of Henry V. the crown passed to his only son, an infant nine months old; and the kingdom was placed under a protectorate. To the usual troubles connected with the government of England in the middle ages during the minority of a king, were added in this instance the necessity of maintaining an almost incessant struggle in France, to retain the costly, but yet worthless conquests of the late king. Step by step, nevertheless, the English were driven from their French possessions; until, in 1451 — or less than thirty years from the conqueror's death — noth-

---

* To divert the king from a proposed reform in the hierarchy, Chicheley advised Henry to attempt the conquest of France, and offered the assistance of the clergy in defraying the expenses. See *Hall's Chronicle. Parl. Hist.* I., cols. 324–329 & *Collier's, Ecc. Hist.* vol. III., pp. 303–309, contain the archbishop's crafty and warlike speech, and a general account of this matter.

Those who are familiar with Shakspeare, will remember his treatment of this subject, in the first act of King Henry the Fifth. It is historically very truthful. Chicheley's words to the bishop of Ely are: —

> "I have made an offer to his majesty —
> Upon our spiritual convocation,
> In regard of causes now in hand,
> Which I have opened to his grace at large,
> As touching France — to give a greater sum
> Than ever at one time the clergy yet
> Did to his predecessors part withal."

ing remained of all his dearly-bought conquests; and of all her French possessions, there remained to England only her ancient domain of Calais.

The distracted state of the kingdom; the public discontent; the plots and insurrections; and the bloody contests between the houses of Lancaster and York; together with the declining years and final death of Chicheley,* prevented the persecution of the Lollards to any considerable extent for a number of years during the sixth Henry's feeble reign, which terminated in 1461. And for some twenty years after this, during the turbulent reign of the profligate, but courageous and indomitable Edward IV., and while the house of York, in the person of Edward V. and of Richard III., continued the struggle to maintain itself on the throne of England, there was enough to occupy Church and State without persecuting the Lollards to any great extent. These, and probably other causes combined, secured a comparative respite for these dissenting Christians of the kingdom, of some fifty

---

* *Fuller* says of Archbishop Chicheley: "He was thorough-paced in all spiritual popery, which concerned religion (which made him so cruel against the Wickliffites); but in secular popery (as I may term it, touching the interests of princes) he did not so much as rack; and was a zealous asserter of the English liberties against Romish usurpation. He continued in his archbishopric (longer than any of his predecessors for 500 years) full twenty-nine years; and died April 12th, 1443." — *Worthies of England*, vol. II., p. 519.

Collier praises Chicheley much for his patronage of learning. He founded two colleges at Oxford, All Souls and Bernards. His bounty to indigent scholars also is said to have been considerable. — *Ecc. Hist.* III., 373.

years: not an absolute freedom from persecution — for, as Fox says, "from the time of Richard II. there is no reign of any king, in which some good man or other has not suffered the pains of fire, for the religion and true testimony of Christ Jesus."

In 1485 the struggle between the houses of York and Lancaster was finally terminated, by the success of Henry, Earl of Richmond, and the death of Richard III., on the field of Bosworth; where the Lancastrian, or Tudor conqueror was proclaimed and crowned king of England, under the title of Henry VII. The next year he made more sure his title to the crown, by marrying the Lady Elizabeth, of York, the eldest daughter of Edward IV.; thus uniting on his throne the two rival houses of York and Lancaster.

This first Tudor soon began to exhibit the intolerant, persecuting spirit which characterized his ancestors, the fifth and the fourth Henries; or perhaps it should rather be said — to show the same subserviency to the clergy, and disposition to court their favor, by persecuting the friends of the gospel, who still abounded in England.

During the very first year of Henry VII., a severe persecution of protestant dissenters was commenced in the diocese of Coventry and Litchfield. Under date of March 9th, 1485, Fox gives the names, and some particulars of the persecution, of nine, who, "amongst divers and sundry other good men in Coventry," were arraigned before the bishop of Coventry and Litchfield, in St. Michael's church, for their antipapistical opinions touching the sacrament, prayers and alms for the dead, confessions to priests, worship of images, going on pilgrimages, reading the gospels and the epistles in English, etc., etc. In all these particulars these persecuted people appear to have agreed substantially with the Lollards of earlier date, and were probably the fruits of the seed scattered in all that neighborhood, a long time before, by such men as Swinderby, or "William the Hermit." *

The first public execution under this new king, appears to have been on the 28th of April, 1494, when an aged and respectable widow, of three score and twenty years, was burned to death in Smithfield, for holding "eight of Wickliffe's opinions, so firmly that all the doctors in London could not turn her from one of them." She was a brave old Christian; for, "when it was told her that she should be burnt for her obstinacy and false belief, she set nothing by their menacing words, but defied them; for she said, she was so beloved of God and his holy angels, that she cared not for the fire; and in the midst thereof she cried unto God, to take her soul into his holy hands." Her name was Joane Boughton, mother of Lady Young. During the night following her martyrdom, Fox informs us that "most of her ashes were had away, of such as had love unto the doctrine that she died for." †

* See *ante* pp. 402–411. *Acts and Mons.*, I., 882–883.

† *Acts and Mons.*, I., 829.

We begin now again to hear of numbers being required to do public penance for their heretical opinions, and of the burning of heretical books, and of heretical men too. In 1498 several persons were burned. In May, of that year, a priest was burned at Canterbury, who was "so strong in his opinions, that all the clerks and doctors there being, could not remove him from his faith." In July "a certain godly man and a constant martyr of Christ, named Babram," was burned in Norfolk; and probably in the same month, an old man was burned at Smithfield.*

In 1506 began a severe persecution of the Protestants in the diocese of Lincoln, a section of country long noted for Lollardism.† Among these, mention is made of the burning in Amersham, of William Tylsworth. And to aggravate the sufferings of the victim and his family, an only daughter of Tylsworth, herself a "faithful woman," was compelled to set fire to the faggots which consumed her own father! At the same time sixty or more persons were compelled to do penance, bearing faggots around the burning martyr; and afterwards to go around the neighboring towns, wearing badges and doing penance. Several of these men were branded on the cheek, and probably bore these marks of "the beast" to the day of their death. Some of them were doomed to do the penance enjoined, for seven years. One of the

* *Fox*, I., 829, 830, 877.

† See back, p. 402.

number, Robert Bartlett, being a rich man, was deprived of his property, and imprisoned in the monastery of Ashryge for seven years, wearing on his sleeve a badge of his penance.*

---

* Amersham was one of the most noted resorts for "heretics" in all England, out of London. It was an ancient borough market town, about thirty miles from London, in Bucks county, "situated in a valley among the beautifully-wooded chalk hills which cover this part of the country. Here Fox informs us among other Lollards, was burned William Tillsworth, in the time of Henry VII., by order of Dr. Smyth, bishop of Lincoln, for talking against pilgrimages and the worship of images, and for reading the Scriptures in English. His murder was made memorable by one of the most refined acts of cruelty ever perpetrated even by the intolerant papists of that day. They caused the daughter to carry the torch and set fire to the pile which was to be the horrible means of putting him to death." — *British Gazetteer*, art. Amersham.

James Mordon and Thomas Bernard were also burned here. The memory of these martyrs was preserved in the town and neighborhood, by a curious phenomenon, said to mark a particular spot of ground, where according to tradition the martyrs were burned — one or more of them. The matter is thus related by a writer in the *Gentlemen's Magazine* for October, 1811 : — "Some public papers having noticed the grave of a martyr at Amersham, * * I have been led to make inquiry respecting the truth of the statement; and find from concurrent and indisputable testimony, that there is a spot of ground deemed sacred, from being the place where a martyr was burnt. — It is about twenty-four yards in circumference. And when the field is fallow or when in corn, that particular spot cannot be discovered ; but when the rest of the field begins to flourish and become green, the blades of grass or corn on this mysterious spot, begin to look unhealthy and dwindle. As the harvest approaches, it looks more and more unfruitful; and though particular pains have been taken by extra manuring, removing the earth, &c., it has remained barren in spite of man's efforts to fertilize it. This year the field is sown with wheat, and discovers the place of martyrdom." — See *Lipscomb's Hist. and Antiquities of the County of Buckingham*, vol. III., p. 147.

"About the same time of the burning of William Tylsworth," says Fox, "was one Father Roberts burned at Buckingham. He was a miller, and dwelt at Missenden. At his burning there were about twenty persons that were compelled to carry faggots, and do such penance as the wicked pharisees compelled them to."

In the course of two or three years after this, there were two men burned at Amersham, in the same fire: Thomas Bernard, a husbandman; and James Mordon, a laborer. A large number of persons were at the same time branded in the cheek and compelled to carry faggots. Two of these, "Father Rogers and Father Reive," were afterwards themselves burned. This Father Rogers had been fourteen weeks in the bishop's prison, night and day; where "he was so cruelly handled with cold, hunger and irons" — and probably doubled up in that Episcopal hole, "Little Ease" — that to the day of his death he was unable to walk upright. The cause of all this persecution was, says Fox, that these men "would talk against superstition and idolatry, and were desirous to hear and read the Holy Scriptures"! *

In this same persecution at Amersham and vicinity, occurred a case of peculiar violence and malignity. There was a man of Amersham by the name of Thomas Chase, whose virtuous life,

---

* *Acts and Mons.*, I., 878.

and "godly, sober and honest behavior," were well remembered by those who knew him, even in Fox's day. He could not, however, abide the idolatry and superstition of the papal church; nor could he hold his peace in regard to such matters. The wicked, of course, hated him, and reported him to the bishop of the diocese. He was forthwith seized by the bishop's officers, and thrust into the dungeon of the bishop's palace at Woburn, near by. This was the Episcopal taming-place. Here poor Chase was kept chained and half starved, and otherwise tormented, until the bishop found it useless any longer to try the fortitude of this christian man. There being no hope of making him recant, he was secretly made way with — strangled and pressed to death in prison. The body was carried out and buried in the woods; and word given out, that Chase had hanged himself. The falsity of this charge, Fox sets forth in the fact, that the poor prisoner was so ironed and chained that he could not have hanged himself had he been disposed; and further, that the dungeon in which he lay, was so low that he could not have hanged himself had he been without irons; and so contrived, for the punishment of heretics, that a man could not stretch himself in any direction; and still further, that the woman who kept this prison, testified after Chase's death, to hearing him, in his last moments, when his murderers were making way with him, commend himself fervently to

God; and that after his death, she saw his body covered with manacles, so that he could not when alive have moved hand or foot.*

Such were the tender mercies of the prelates of a hierarchy claiming to be the only true, apostolical church, out of whose pale there could be no salvation. One is tempted to exclaim:—"Gather not my soul with [such] sinners!"—"Any thing but the everlasting society of such men!"

Not far from this same time perished Thomas Harding, one of the Amersham protestants; Thomas Morris, at Norwich (March 31, 1507); and soon after, Laurence Ghest, or Guest, at Salisbury, who, after being confined in prison two years, was led to the stake. When just ready to be offered up, his wife and seven children were brought to him, in order to shake his purpose of dying rather than denying his Lord. When his wife besought him to save his life; he begged her "not to be a stumbling block to him, for he was in a good course, running toward the mark of his salvation. And so fire being put to him, he finished his life, renouncing not only wife and children, but also himself, to follow Christ."

"A godly woman" whose name is not given, was condemned to the flames by Dr. Whittington, the bishop's chancellor, and suffered martyrdom at Chipping Sodbury, in the county of Gloucester, with great fortitude, about the year 1507.†

---

* *Acts and Mons.*, I., 878–879. † *Acts and Mons.*, I., 879–880.

These examples of suffering for the truth's-sake, during the reign of Henry VII., who died April 22d 1509, will sufficiently illustrate the truth of Fuller's remark:—that "to the Lollards he was more cruel than his predecessors"; and correct Collier, where he says:—"It is observed, there were few prosecutions [against the Lollards] in Henry VII.'s reign, and those that were, went seldom any further than penance, and carrying faggots."* Fox's estimate of the reign of Henry VII. appears much more accurate, where he says:—"It is to be noted in the days and reign of this king Henry the Seventh, how mightily the working of God's gospel hath multiplied and increased, and what great numbers of men and women have suffered for the same with us in England." †

The accession of Henry VIII. to the throne of England—though hailed by the people with a measure of joy, equalled only by their intense satisfaction at the removal of his tyrannical and miserly father—was followed by no alleviation of the sufferings of the Lollards. Indeed, for some years after this very able, but arbitrary prince began his reign, the sufferings of the protestant Christians in England were rather increased than diminished.

Between the years 1510 and 1527, there were very many sufferers for the truth in London. Fox

---

* *Ecc. Hist. Eng.* vol. III., pp. 447–448.

† *Acts and Mons.*, I., 880.

gives the names of eighty-seven men and women, who, among others, were arraigned, at different times, before bishop Fitz James, and after him, before bishop Tonstall, of London, for Lollardy in some form. Many were accused of speaking against pilgrimages and the worship of the cross and of images, and praying to saints; of being opposed to the doctrine of the carnal presence of Christ in the sacrament; of having read and used certain English books, impugning the faith of the Romish church: such as the Four Gospels! Wickliffe's Wicket, a Book of the Ten Commandments of Almighty God, the Revelation of St. John, the Epistles of Paul and James, "with other like;" of despising the authority of the pope of Rome and his clergy; of saying, "that God commanded no holy days to be kept, but only the Sabbath day;" of keeping company with persons suspected of heresy; sitting up all night to read, or hear read heretical books; and of not having, according to the laws of the church, accused and presented their teachers to the bishop or his ordinary; with saying that the church was too rich; and with refusing to have holy water sprinkled around them: — with some one, or with several of these heresies and errors the poor people were charged; and for their heretical opinions and criminal conduct in these particulars, they were imprisoned, excommunicated, compelled to do penance, and burned at the stake.*

* *Fox*, vol. II., pp. 4–22. Folio, 1684.

Among the martyrs of those days were William Sweating and John Brewster, who were burned together at Smithfield, October 18, 1511. And about the same time William Carder suffered like punishment, at the hands of the archbishop of Canterbury. And also Agnes Grebyll, John Grebyll her husband, and Robert Harrison, who were burned together May 2, 1511. Agnes was convicted by the forced testimony of her husband and two sons; and Harrison, by the same testimony; and John by the testimony of his own sons. And near this time a Mr. Stile was condemned to be burned at Smithfield, with a volume of the Revelation in English.

In 1514 one Richard Hunne, a merchant tailor of London, unfortunately got into a dispute with a priest about his mortuary dues. The priests claimed, as their due, the last dress worn by a deceased person whom they were called on to bury. Hunne had taken an infant child of five weeks old, to be buried by his parish priest. He claimed the "bearing sheet," used on the occasion. Hunne replied, that the child had no property in the sheet, and the claim was therefore not just. This was a mortal offence; and the common resort of the priests for keeping the people quiet under exactions, and punishing refractory ones, was appealed to: charges of heresy were immediately trumped up, and Hunne was committed to the Lollard's Tower. Among other heinous crimes laid to his account was this: "That the said Richard Hunne has in his keeping divers English books, prohibited and condemned by the law: as the Apocalypse in English, Epistles and Gospels in English, Wickliffe's damnable works, and other books containing infinite errors, in which he has been for a long time accustomed to read, teach, and study daily." Soon after his committal Hunne was secretly murdered in his cell, by "the procurment of Master William Horsey, chancellor to my lord [bishop] of London," as was found by the inquest of a jury called to investigate the matter. The bishop, Fitz James, and his clergy tried to prevent this investigation, but failed; and the bishop's chancellor and his aiders were found guilty of murder. Cardinal Wolsey, however, interfered, screened the chancellor at the solicitation of the bishop, and he was allowed to escape with his life.*

As a further illustration of those days of darkness and cruelty when popery reigned triumphantly in England, take the following story:—Some time in the year 1517 a man by the name of John Browne, of Ashford, took his seat in a Gravesend barge, by the side of a stranger, who immediately complained that Browne sat too near him, and asked him if he knew who he was. Browne replied that he did not know.

"Well," said the stranger, "I am a priest."

"What, sir, are you a parson, or vicar, or a lady's chaplain?"

---

* *Fox*, II., 8–17; *Clarke*, pp. 60–61.

"No," quoth he, "I am a soul-priest. I sing for a soul."

"Do you so," saith Browne, "that is well done. I pray you, sir, where find you the soul when you go to mass?"

"I cannot tell thee," said the priest.

"I pray you," continued Browne, "where do you leave it sir, when the mass is done?"

"I cannot tell thee," said the priest.

"Neither can you tell," remarked Browne, "where you find it when you go to mass, nor where you leave it when mass is done: how can you then save the soul?"

"Go thy way," said the priest, "thou art an heretic, and I will be even with thee."

Immediately on landing, the priest rode directly to archbishop Warham, and laid information against Browne. Three days after, Browne was arrested, put upon a horse, his feet bound under the horse's belly, and he taken away, he knew not whither, nor did any of his family. This was on "Low-sunday." He was taken to Canterbury and kept in prison until Friday, (May 29). His feet were burned to the bone on live coals, and he was then placed in the stocks. All this failing to make him recant, he was finally sent to the stake, at Ashford; because, as he told his wife, he would not deny his Lord: "which I will never do," said he; "for if I should deny my Lord in this world, he would hereafter deny me." The night before his martyrdom, his wife went to him, and sat by him the whole night. She then received from his own lips the story of his cruel sufferings, as he lay with his crippled feet fast in the stocks. His parting exhortation to his faithful companion was: "I pray thee, good Elizabeth, continue as thou hast begun, and bring up my children virtuously in the fear of God." The next day, being Whitsunday-even, this godly martyr finished his course at the stake. His last words were: "Into thy hands I commend my spirit. Thou hast redeemed me, O Lord of Truth." * Warham, and Fisher, bishop of Rochester, were partners in this murder.

"Good Elizabeth," we have reason to believe, faithfully kept her husband's dying charge; for we find one of her sons, Richard Browne, in prison, waiting to be "offered up," when that miserable woman Queen Mary died. Had she lived one day longer, the son would have followed the father through the fire.

Among those who suffered death in the London persecutions, were John Stilman and Thomas Man; both of whom were burned at Smithfield in 1518.

The charges made against one of these martyrs, and his admissions, on his trial before the bishop of London, forcibly illustrate the wide diffusion of Lollard sentiments at this time.

It was deposed against Man — or *Dr.* Man, as he was called by the brethren, though he appears to have been only a plain, intelligent layman —

---

* *Fox,* II., 7–8.

that "he had been in divers places and countries in England, and had instructed very many: as at Amersham, at London, at Billerica, at Chelmsford, at Stratford-Langthorn, at Uxbridge, at Burnham, at Henly upon Thames, in Suffolk and Norfolk, at Newbury, and divers places more."

These charges he did not deny. And furthermore, thanked God that he had been made the instrument of turning *seven hundred* persons from the errors of popery! He also confessed that he had found large companies of men and women of like mind with himself, in the neighborhood of Newbury, and at the forest of Windsor. One of these companies, he said, had lived in peace and "sweet society for fifteen years; when they were betrayed by a certain lewd person, whom they trusted and made of their counsel," and were persecuted, some unto death. The other, "a godly and great company," which he found in his travels, "continued in that doctrine and teaching twenty-three years"; when the bishop of Lincoln raised a great persecution against them. Their meeting-place seems to have been in or near the forest of Windsor. They had four principal readers or instructors; all of whom were finally murdered by the bishops. Their names were — Tylsworth, Chase, Cosin, and Man. These men and women were Lollards.

Against Man, one of their teachers, it was charged, that he opposed auricular confession — Denied the corporal presence of Christ in "the sacrament of the altar," believing that material bread and wine were the memorial of Christ — That he taught that all holy men of his sect were only priests — Believed contrary to church doctrine in regard to extreme unction — Taught that images ought not to be worshipped, nor the crucifix — And that the popish church was not the church of God, but a synagogue; and that holy men of his sect were the true church of God.*

It was charged against John Stilman, first: — That he had once, eleven years before, recanted and abjured his opinions, which now he declared he was sorry he had ever done, and had not then suffered manfully for them; for they were good and true, and he would now abide by them and die for them. He was, therefore, "a relapsed heretic." He was also accused of having said — That going on pilgrimages and worshipping images were not to be used — That the carnal, corporal presence of the Lord was not in the sacrament — Of having spoken against "our holy father, the pope, and his authority, damnably; saying, that he is Antichrist, and not the true successor of Peter, or Christ's vicar on earth; and that his pardons and indulgences which he granteth in the sacrament of penance are naught, and that he, [Stilman] will have none of them." — "Likewise, that the college of cardinals be limbs of the said Antichrist; and that all other inferior prelates and priests are the synagogue of Satan" — "That the

* *Fox*, II., 18–21; *Clarke*, 66.

doctors of the church have subverted the truth of holy Scripture, expounding it after their own minds; and therefore their works be naught, and they in hell" — "but that Wickliffe is a saint in heaven; and that the book called his 'Wicket' is good; for therein he showeth the truth". — And that he, Stilman, had "divers times read the said book, called Wickliffe's Wicket, and one other book of the Ten Commandments, which, on his first apprehension, he hid in an oak tree, and did not reveal them to the bishop of Salisbury, before whom he was abjured of heresy about eleven years before."

These, for substance, were the charges laid against Stilman, by the bishop of London, Fitz James; and on which the poor man was committed to the flames in Smithfield, October 25, 1518.*

During this same year, Robert Cosin was burned to death at Buckingham, by the bishop of Lincoln, for persuading Joane Norman, of Amersham, not to pray to saints, nor go on pilgrimages, nor make confession to a priest.† Christopher Shoomaker, of the parish of Great Missenden, was also burned at Newbury, for reading the gospel to John Say, and teaching him that bread remained after consecration, and that pilgrimages, the worshipping and setting up of candles to saints, were unprofitable, and ought not to be practised.*

In 1519 there was a bitter persecution carried

---

* *Fox*, II., 18. † *Ib.*, 21.

on in Coventry. Seven persons were burned at the stake, after enduring severe imprisonment in underground dungeons. The particular crimes charged against these men and women were — that they taught their children and servants the Lord's Prayer, the Ten Commandments and the Creed in English! †

About the years 1520–1521 persecution raged with increased violence in different parts of the kingdom; especially in Buckinghampshire, in the towns of Amersham, Uxbridge, Henly and Newbury: it was also quite violent in the diocese of London, in Essex, Colchester, Suffolk and Norfolk, and other places: and "this was before the name of Luther was heard of in these counties among the people." These counties seem to have swarmed with dissenters from popery, who were, so far as I can discover, essentially Lollards; some going further than others, but all seeming to agree in regarding the Word of God as the only sufficient rule of faith and practice — in rejecting the pope, and the English hierarchy — denying transubstantiation — confession to a priest — pilgrimages — praying to saints, and like doctrines.

No open preaching of the gospel was allowed in those days; but the good work of converting men from the errors of popery was carried on, chiefly, by one person speaking to another privately on the great subject; by neighbors and friends

---

* *Fox*, II., 23. † *Ib.*, 181–182.

sitting up all night together and reading portions of God's Word; and by the use of religious tracts and books, such as Wickliffe's Wicket, The Lantern of Light, and books of like character.*

The value which these poor men attached to these books — for most of those of whom I am now writing were actually *poor* mechanics, farmers and laborers — is illustrated by the sacrifices which they cheerfully made to get possession of books, particularly of portions of the Bible in English; and the hazards which they ran in reading these dear-bought volumes.

Fox tells us that some of these persecuted christians paid *five marks* (or about sixteen dollars, Federal money!) "some more, some less," for an English book; and that a load of hay was given for a few chapters in English of James' Epistle, or of one of Paul's! The martyrologist adds: that though they were thus destitute of books, and much more so of teachers, yet, in reading the bishops' registers, which give an account of the trials for heresy of these poor people, "he did greatly marvel, to note and consider how, notwithstanding, the word of truth multiplied so exceedingly among them. Wherein is to be seen, no doubt, the marvellous working of God's mighty power; for I find and observe, in considering the registers, how one neighbor, resorting and conferring with another, soon, with a few words, did win

---

* *Fox,* II., 23.

and turn their minds to the truth of God's Word and his sacraments."

He also expresses the belief, that the "secret multitude of true professors" in England, at that time, was not much less than after the Reformation, in his own day; "while their labors, their earnest seeking, their burning zeal, their readings, their watchings, their secret assemblies, their love and concord, their godly living, their faithful marrying with the faithful — may make us now, in these our days of free profession, to blush for shame."

These humble, faithful believers, who were known to each other as persons rooted and grounded in the truth, as just and established men, called each other — "Known Men" — "Just Fast Men."* They were essentially the same sort of believers as were Wickliffe's disciples, called by the papists Lollards; and as those who a little later were called Puritans — Independents.

These were the kind of men and women of whom John Longland, bishop of Lincoln, made terrible havoc about the years 1520–21. By his spies he made himself acquainted with their secret assemblies and marked some of the chief of the flock for destruction.

He first seized several persons who had previously abjured, and compelled them, by threats and promises, upon oath, to betray others. He seized

---

* *Acts and Mons.*, II., 23.

wives and made them betray their husbands; and husbands, their wives; parents their children, and children their parents;—thus making a man's bitterest foes literally those of his own household. By these means, according to Fox, "an incredible multitude of men, women and maidens, were brought to examination, and strictly handled." Several hundreds in that diocese alone were thus speedily "detected as heretics." Some of these poor people were burned to death; others were so tormented and worn down by afflictions, and by distress of mind, that they died broken hearted; others were branded on the cheek and compelled to do shameful and painful penance; confined in monasteries, and otherwise punished, for believing the truth, and striving to live in obedience to it.

The bishop at length became alarmed at the multitude of these people; and either did not know what to do, or did not dare to go forward without some special authority from the king. For this, he applied, and immediately received the king's letter, commanding "all mayors, sheriffs, bailiffs, and constables, and all other officers, and subjects," to aid, help, and assist, "the right reverend father in God, the bishop of Lincoln, who hath now within his diocese no small number of heretics, as it is thought, to his no little discomfort and heaviness."

Armed with this extraordinary authority and power, bishop Longland, gave full vent to his raving, persecuting spirit. He called before him all known or suspected dissenters in his diocese, and by subtlety and by threats, made them detect and condemn themselves and their friends, as being anti-papists; and then poured out upon them the vials of ecclesiastical wrath, in the form of penance, painful and shameful; imprisonments, hard and long continued; and death at the stake. In the case of one of these martyrs, John Scrivenes — as in another case already mentioned — the children of the martyr were compelled to set fire to the faggots which consumed their own father!

The crimes, heresies and errors of which these poor christians in Longland's diocese were "detected," are given at length by Fox; together with the names of several hundred persons who were troubled thus by the bishop of Lincoln; and the parishes, towns, and counties in which they belonged. It is a striking commentary on the extent of Lollard, or Protestant heresies in England, at that time, that there were men and women found in this single diocese from thirty-nine different counties, towns and parishes of England, who were thought worthy to suffer persecution for the truth's sake.

Among the enormities charged against these sufferers, were the following: — Reading or hearing read portions of the Bible in English, (the Epistles of James and Peter being favorite portions, probably from the special appropriateness of these epistles to their circumstances,) — Reading or hearing read expositions of Scripture and other English books; particularly Wickliffe's Wicket, and the Shepherd's Kalender. A book of William Thorpe's, who was one of Wickliffe's most learned and excellent "poor priests," is also mentioned.— Opposing the worship of images as idolatry, and calling images "dead things," "carpenter's chips," "stocks and stones"; and saying that nothing graven with man's hand was to be worshipped— Opposing pilgrimages and the worship of saints— Denying the doctrine of purgatory; saying that they who die pass straight, either to heaven or hell — Rejecting the doctrine of transubstantiation, or the real, bodily presence of Christ in the sacrament of the Lord's supper — Denying the power of the pope to forgive sin — Saying that matrimony was not a sacrament — Learning the Ten Commandments in English, and teaching them to others; "namely, that [a man] should have but one God, and should worship nothing but God alone; and that to worship saints and go on pilgrimage, was idolatry"— Working on holy-days, as well as work-days — Speaking against the singing service used in the churches — Saying that God never made priests, for in Christ's time there were no priests— That "true pilgrimage was, barefoot, to go and visit the poor, weak and sick; for they are the true images of God" — Denying the necessity of confession to a priest.

Eleven persons in this persecution were "accused, because, at the marriage of Durdant's daughter, they assembled together in a barn and heard a certain epistle of St. Paul read; which reading they well liked, but especially Durdant, and commended the same."

Some of these poor Christians — for they were generally simple husbandmen, mechanics or laborers — had taken pains to commit large portions of the Bible to memory, that they might always have the Scriptures with them, and yet not be exposed to detection by having books about them. And it was charged against one John Burret, a goldsmith, that "he was heard in his own house, before his wife and maid there present, to recite the epistle of St. James, which epistle, with many other things, he had perfectly without book." And one Alice Colins is said to have been "a famous woman among them, and had a good memory, and could recite much of the Scriptures and other good books. And therefore, when any conventicle of these men did meet at Burford, commonly she was sent for, to recite unto them the declaration of the Ten Commandments and the epistles of Peter and James."

It was for crimes like these, which I have recited from the bishop's own register, that this popish successor of the apostles made havoc of the poor Chsistians in his diocese.*

In other parts of England, persecutions continued to rage, from year to year, up to the very commencement of the English Reformation. Good men and learned men were arrested, imprisoned

---

* See *Fox's Acts and Monuments*, vol. II., pp. 23–46.

in chains, tormented in various ways, and numbers of them burned, for their hatred of popery and love of the gospel, as any one will see who will take the trouble to look into Fox or Clarke, or in fact, into any of the ample histories of those eventful times.

But "The Beast" was soon to receive a check and a deadly wound. "Under the altar, the souls of them that were slain for the word of God, and for the testimony which they held," against Popery in all its hateful forms, had long been accumulating, and their loud cry was about to be heard:—"How long O, Lord, holy and true, dost thou not judge and avenge our blood on them that dwell on the earth!"

END OF VOL. I.

www.ingramcontent.com/pod-product-compliance
Lightning Source LLC
LaVergne TN
LVHW021314110826
845150LV00003B/570

* 9 7 8 1 4 2 5 5 6 3 1 1 0 *